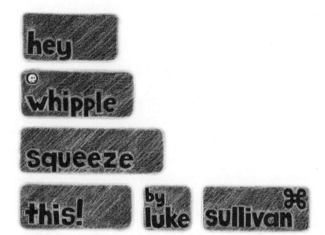

hey whipple squeeze this! by luke sullivan

The Classic Guide to Creating
Great Ads

Fourth Edition

WITH
SAM BENNETT

WILEY

John Wiley & Sons, Inc.

Published by John Wiley & Sons, Inc., Hoboken, New Jersey.
Published simultaneously in Canada.

For general information on our other products and services or for technical support, please contact our Customer Care Department within the United States at (800) 762-2974, outside the United States at (317) 572-3993 or fax (317) 572-4002.

Wiley publishes in a variety of print and electronic formats and by print-on-demand. Some material included with standard print versions of this book may not be included in e-books or in print-on-demand. If this book refers to media such as a CD or DVD that is not included in the version you purchased, you may download this material at http://booksupport.wiley.com. For more information about Wiley products, visit www.wiley.com.

Library of Congress Cataloging-in-Publication Data:

Sullivan, Luke.
  Hey, Whipple, squeeze this : the classic guide to creating great ads / Luke Sullivan. — 4th ed.
    p.   cm.
  Includes index.
    ISBN 978-1-118-10133-9 (pbk); ISBN 978-1-118-22383-3 (ebk); ISBN 978-1-118-237182 (ebk); ISBN 978-1-118-243763 (ebk)
      1. Advertising copy.   I. Title.
  HF5825.S88   2012
  659.13'2—dc23   2011039737

Printed in the United States of America

10 9 8 7 6 5 4 3 2 1

TO MY DEAR WIFE,
CURLIN,
AND OUR KNUCKLEHEADS,
REED AND PRESTON

CONTENTS

FOREWORD

COMING UP WITH A GOOD IDEA is hard, but it's not that hard. What's harder is coming up with ideas on demand and on time. What's really hard is bringing your ideas to smart, elegant life in the real world.

My guess is Mr. Edison wasn't the first genius to look into the darkness and see the need for light, but creating a working light bulb—that was a world-changing achievement. It's said that he and his team developed and studied more than 3,000 approaches before landing on one that worked. That's 3,000 failures on the way to one success.

Advertising isn't quite that brutal, but sometimes we talk about it as if it is. Like other businesses that aren't nearly as macho as they pretend to be (Wall Street!), the ad business talks of war rooms, concepts that are killed, and bloody battles between creatives and suits.

It's silly, especially when you consider that there are actually two different and engaging ways to find joy in this business of advertising.

The first is to be part of a team that produces strategies and creative work that are, to borrow a phrase from Steve Jobs, "insanely great." Like entertainment, the arts, product design, cooking, and surgery, advertising is one of those businesses that gives its practitioners an occasional opportunity to do something marvelous. That marvelous something might inspire laughs or smiles or thoughts or even action. It probably won't change the world, but it could make at least a little dent. It could make the world a little more interesting. A little better. Do something like that occasionally and your peers will give you awards and your clients will give you money. Unfortunately, this is very difficult and it doesn't happen very often.

The second path to bliss in this business is to find joy in the work itself. You would think this would be easy. In advertising, you're surrounded by intelligent, witty people. There's no heavy lifting. You occasionally go to Santa Monica and stay at Shutters while producing videos that will appear on screens large and small. You rub shoulders with filmmakers and every once in a while with stars. You can play video games under the guise of "keeping up with technology" or "keeping up with the kids."

Life is short and we spend much of it—much more than 40 hours a week of it—doing our jobs. It's possible that the only secular salvation in this not-necessarily-evil circumstance lies in turning our jobs into art—and then creating exceptional art. This is true of writing music, painting canvases, sculpting, plumbing, delivering the mail, and preparing tax forms. And making ads.

A confession. We work very hard at making ads, but not only because it's what's best for our clients. We do it because it's what's best for us. What's best for us as human beings is to work at the craft of our chosen arts. And these are, we repeat, "arts": persuasion is one, design is another. Writing, photography, filmmaking—all arts. (Marketing research, often mistaken for a science, is another.)

Great films come from the minds of great filmmakers. Great meals come from the talents of great chefs. Great art comes from the vision of great artists. And great ads from the ideas and intuitions of great advertising people.

The world rewards us for our passion. It has long been proven that the best-crafted positions—selling arguments and ads—aren't just the most delightful, they're the most effective. They are, when all is said and done, true hard-sell advertising.

The only worthwhile test of an ad or a movie or a book is how it does in the real world with real people. (The movie executives who turned down *E.T.* because of its test scores deserved their fate.)

There are no rules in our business, but there are a few things we believe. We believe the right side of the consumer's brain buys faster and with more conviction than the left side. We believe in the discipline of focus. We believe in and welcome and live for and fear competition. We hate to lose. We believe that what's brilliant in this business is also what's smart in this business.

We believe in consumers. We believe in magic.

I envy the young and would-be advertising people who are reading Luke's book for the first time. In these pages they'll discover both the possibilities for moments of genius and the joy of the work itself. They'll marvel as I do at Luke's ability to find fresh and funny ways to tell us truths. They'll go back to their studies, their work, or their job hunt with fresh enthusiasm. They'll be eager to tackle new challenges.

I also suspect that those of us who still have dog-eared copies of the first editions of *Whipple* will be eager to see what Luke has to say about the new media in this new and improved version. Once again he's been able to nail the fears we all have about change: once again he shows us how to cope and maybe even how to excel. (I bet a lot of us will find ourselves reading the whole thing all over again.)

So whether you're a *Whipple* newbie or a returning past master, you're in for a real education and an awfully joyful ride.

Enjoy.

—Mike

PREFACE

THIS IS MY FANTASY.
We open on a tidy suburban kitchen. Actually, it's a room off to the side off the kitchen, one with a washer and dryer. On the floor is a basket full of laundry. The camera closes in.

Out of the laundry pops the cutest little stuffed bear you've ever seen. He's pink and fluffy, he has a happy little face, and there's one sock stuck adorably to his left ear.

"Hi, I'm Snuggles, the fabric-softening bear. And I . . ."

The first bullet rips into Snuggles's stomach, blows out of his back in a blizzard of cotton entrails, and punches a fist-sized hole in the dryer behind. Snuggles grabs the side of the Rubbermaid laundry basket and sinks down, his plastic eyes rolling as he looks for the source of the gunfire.

Taking cover behind $\frac{1}{16}$th-inch of flexible acrylic rubber, Snuggles looks out of the basket's plastic mesh and into the living room. He sees nothing. The dining room. Nothing.

Snuggles is easing over the backside of the basket when the second shot takes his head off at the neck. His body lands on top of the laundry, which is remarkably soft and fluffy. Fade to black.

We open on a woman in a bathroom, clad in an apron and wielding a brush, poised to clean her toilet bowl. She opens the lid.

But wait. What's this? It's a little man in a boat, floating above the sparkling waters of Lake Porcelain. Everything looks clean already!

With a tip of his teeny hat, he introduces himself. "I'm the Ty-D-Bowl Man, and I . . ."

Both hat and hand disappear in a red mist as the first bullet screams through and blows a hole in curved toilet wall behind the Ty-D-Bowl Man. Water begins to pour out on the floor as the woman screams and dives for cover in the tub.

Ty-D-Bowl Man scrambles out of the bowl, but when he climbs onto the big silver lever, it gives way, dropping him back into the swirling waters of the flushing toilet. We get two more glimpses of his face as he orbits around, once, twice, and then down to his final reward.

We open on a grocery store, where we see the owner scolding a group of ladies for squeezing some toilet paper. The first shot is high and wide, shattering a jar of mayonnaise.

*Figure 1.1   Hey, Mr. Whipple, better put that Charmin
down right now.*

1

Salesmen Don't Have to Wear Plaid

Selling without selling out

I GREW UP POINTING A FINGER GUN at Mr. Whipple. He kept interrupting my favorite shows. The morning lineup was my favorite, with its back-to-back *Dick Van Dyke* and *Andy Griffith* shows. But Whipple kept butting in on Rob and Laura Petrie.

He'd appear uninvited on my TV, looking over the top of his glasses and pursing his lips at the ladies in his grocery store. Two middle-aged women, presumably with high school or college degrees, would be standing in the aisle squeezing rolls of toilet paper. Whipple would wag his finger and scold, "Please don't squeeze the Charmin." After the ladies scurried away, he'd give the rolls a few furtive squeezes himself.

Oh, they were such bad commercials.

The thing is, I'll wager if Whipple were to air today, there would be a hundred different parodies on YouTube tomorrow. But back then? All we had was a volume knob. Then VCRs came along and later DVRs, and the fast-forward button became our defense. And now today we have the nuclear warhead of buttons, the dreaded OFF button. We can just tell Whipple to shut the hell up, turn him off, and go get our entertainment from any number of other platforms and devices.

To be fair, Procter & Gamble's Charmin commercials weren't the worst thing that ever aired on television. They had a concept, although contrived, and a brand image, although irritating—irritating even to a ninth grader.

If it were just me who didn't like Whipple's commercials, well, I might write it off. But the more I read about the campaign, the more consensus I discovered. In Martin Mayer's book *Whatever Happened to Madison Avenue?* I found this:

> [Charmin's Whipple was] one of the most disliked . . . television commercials of the 1970s. [E]verybody thought "Please don't squeeze the Charmin" was stupid and it ranked last in believability in all the commercials studied for a period of years . . .[1]

In a book called *The New How to Advertise,* I found:

> When asked which campaigns they most disliked, consumers convicted Mr. Whipple. . . . Charmin may have not been popular advertising, but it was number one in sales.[2]

And there is the crux of the problem. The mystery: How did Whipple's commercials sell so much toilet paper?

These shrill little interruptions that irritated nearly everyone, that were used as fodder for Johnny Carson on late-night TV, sold toilet paper by the ton. How? Even if you figure that part out, the question then becomes, why? Why would you irritate your buying public with a twittering, pursed-lipped grocer when cold, hard research told you everybody hated him? I don't get it.

Apparently, even the agency that created him didn't get it. John Lyons, author of *Guts: Advertising from the Inside Out,* worked at Charmin's agency when they were trying to figure out what to do with Whipple.

> I was assigned to assassinate Mr. Whipple. Some of New York's best hit teams before me had tried and failed. "Killing Whipple" was an ongoing mission at Benton & Bowles. The agency that created him was determined to kill him. But the question was how to knock off a man with 15 lives, one for every year that the . . . campaign had been running at the time.[3]

No idea he came up with ever replaced Whipple, Lyons noted.

Next up to assassinate Whipple was a young writer: Atlanta's Joey Reiman. In a phone conversation, Reiman told me he tried to sell Procter & Gamble a concept called "Squeeze-Enders"—an Alcoholics Anonymous kind of group where troubled souls struggled to end their visits to Mr. Whipple's grocery store—and thereby perhaps end the Whipple dynasty. No sale. Procter & Gamble wasn't about to let go of a winner. Whipple remained for years as one of advertising's most bulletproof personalities.

As well he should have. He was selling literally billions of rolls of toilet paper. *Billions.* In 1975, a survey listed Whipple's as the second-most-recognized face in

America, right behind that of Richard Nixon. When Benton & Bowles's creative director, Al Hampel, took Whipple (actor Dick Wilson) to dinner one night in New York City, he said, "It was as if Robert Redford walked into the place. Even the waiters asked for autographs."

So on one hand, you had research telling you customers hated these repetitive, schmaltzy, cornball commercials. And on the other hand, you had Whipple signing autographs at the Four Seasons.

It was as if the whole scenario had come out of the 1940s. In Frederick Wakeman's 1946 novel *The Hucksters,* this was how advertising worked. In the middle of a meeting, the client spat on the conference room table and said: "You have just seen me do a disgusting thing. Ugly word, spit. But you'll always remember what I just did."[4]

The account executive in the novel took the lesson, later musing: "It was working like magic. The more you irritated them with repetitious commercials, the more soap they bought."[5]

With 504 different Charmin toilet tissue commercials airing from 1964 through 1990, Procter & Gamble certainly "irritated them with repetitious commercials." And it indeed "worked like magic." Procter & Gamble knew what it was doing.

Yet I lie awake some nights staring at the ceiling, troubled by Whipple. What vexes me so about this old grocer? This is the question that led me to write this book.

What troubles me about Whipple is that he isn't *good.* As an idea, Whipple isn't good.

He may have been an effective salesman. (Billions of rolls sold.) He may have been a strong brand image. (He knocked Scott tissues out of the number one spot.) But it all comes down to this: if I had created Mr. Whipple, I don't think I could tell my son with a straight face what I did at the office. "Well, son, you see, Whipple tells the lady shoppers not to squeeze the Charmin, but then, then he squeezes it *himself.* . . . Hey, wait, come back."

As an idea, Whipple isn't good.

To those who defend the campaign based on sales, I ask, would you also spit on the table to get my attention? It would work, but would you? An eloquent gentleman named Norman Berry, once a British creative director at Ogilvy & Mather, put it this way:

> I'm appalled by those who [judge] advertising exclusively on the basis of sales. That isn't enough. Of course, advertising must sell. By any definition it is lousy advertising if it doesn't. But if sales are achieved with work which is in bad taste or is intellectual garbage, it shouldn't be applauded no matter how much it sells. Offensive, dull, abrasive, stupid advertising is bad for the entire industry and bad for business as a whole. It is why the public perception of advertising is going down in this country.[6]

Berry may well have been thinking of Mr. Whipple when he made that comment in the early 1980s. With every year that's passed since, newer and more virulent strains of vapidity have been created: I'm Digger the Dermatophyte Nail Fungus—Ring Around the Collar—Snuggles, the fabric-softening bear—Dude, you're getting a Dell!—He loves my mind *and* he drinks Johnnie Walker Red—Don't hate me because I'm beautiful—I'm not a doctor, but I play one on TV—Head on! Apply directly to forehead!—I've fallen and I can't get up!—Hail to the V.

Writer Fran Lebowitz may well have been watching TV when she observed: "No matter how cynical I get, it's impossible to keep up."

Certainly, the viewing public is cynical about our business, due almost entirely to this parade of idiots we've sent into their televisions and desktop screens. Every year, as long as I've been in advertising, Gallup publishes their poll of most and least trusted professions. And every year, advertising practitioners trade last or second-to-last place with used car salesmen and members of Congress.

It reminds me of a paragraph I plucked from our office bulletin board, one of those e-mailed curiosities that makes its way around corporate America:

Dear Ann: I have a problem. I have two brothers. One brother is in advertising. The other was put to death in the electric chair for first-degree murder. My mother died from insanity when I was three. My two sisters are prostitutes and my father sells crack to handicapped elementary school students. Recently, I met a girl who was just released from a reformatory where she served time for killing her puppy with a ball-peen hammer, and I want to marry her. My problem is, should I tell her about my brother who is in advertising? Signed, Anonymous

---

THE 1950s: WHEN EVEN X-ACTO BLADES WERE DULL.

My problem with Whipple (effective sales, grating execution) isn't a new one. Years ago, it occurred to a gentleman named William Bernbach that a commercial needn't sacrifice wit, grace, or intelligence in order to increase sales. And when he set out to prove it, something wonderful happened.

But we'll get to Mr. Bernbach in a minute. Before he showed up, a lot had already happened.

In the 1950s, the national audience was in the palm of the ad industry's hand. Anything that advertising said, people heard. TV was brand new, "clutter" didn't exist, and pretty much anything that showed up in the strange, foggy little window was kinda cool.

Author Ted Bell wrote: "There was a time in the not too distant past when the whole country sat down and watched *The Ed Sullivan Show* all the way through. To sell something, you could go on *The Ed Sullivan Show* and count on everybody seeing your message."[7]

World War II was over, people had money, and America's manufacturers had retooled to market the luxuries of life in Levittown. But as the economy boomed, so too did the country's business landscape. Soon there was more than one big brand of aspirin, more than two soft drinks, more than three brands of cars to choose from. And advertising agencies had more work to do than just get film in the can and cab it over to Rockefeller Center before Milton Berle went on live.

They had to convince the audience their product was the best in its category. And modern advertising as we know it was born.

On its heels came the concept of the *unique selling proposition,* a term coined by writer Rosser Reeves in the 1950s, and one that still has some merit. It was a simple, if ham-handed, notion: "Buy this product, and you will get this specific benefit." The benefit had to be one that the competition either could not or did not offer, hence the unique part.

This notion was perhaps best exemplified by Reeves's aspirin commercials, in which a headful of pounding hammers could be relieved "fast, fast, fast" only by Anacin. Reeves also let us know that because of the unique candy coating, M&M's were the candy that "melt in your mouth, not in your hand."

Had the TV and business landscape remained the same, perhaps simply delineating the differences between one brand and another would suffice today. But then came the "clutter." A brand explosion that lined the nation's grocery shelves with tens of thousands of logos and packed every episode of *I Dream of Jeanie* wall to wall with commercials for me-too products.

Then, in response to The Clutter, came The Wall. The Wall was the perceptual filter that consumers put up to protect themselves from this tsunami of product information. Many products were at parity. Try as agencies might to find some unique angle, in the end, most soap was soap and most beer was beer.

Enter the Creative Revolution—and a guy named Bill Bernbach, who said: "It's not just what you say that stirs people. It's the way you say it."

"WHAT?! WE DON'T *HAVE* TO SUCK?!"

Bernbach founded his New York agency, Doyle Dane Bernbach (DDB), on the then-radical notion that customers aren't nitwits who need to be fooled or lectured or hammered into listening to a client's sales message. This is Bill Bernbach:

> The truth isn't the truth until people believe you, and they can't believe you if they don't know what you're saying, and they can't know what you're saying if they don't listen to you, and they won't listen to you if you're not interesting, and you won't be interesting unless you say things imaginatively, originally, freshly.[8]

This was the classic Bernbach paradigm.

From all the advertising texts, articles, speeches, and awards annuals I've read over my years in advertising, everything that's any good about this business seems to trace its heritage back to this man, William Bernbach. And when his

Lemon.

This Volkswagen missed the boat.
The chrome strip on the glove compartment is blemished and must be replaced. Chances are you wouldn't have noticed it; Inspector Kurt Kroner did.
There are 3,389 men at our Wolfsburg factory with only one job: to inspect Volkswagens at each stage of production. (3000 Volkswagens are produced daily; there are more inspectors than cars.)
Every shock absorber is tested (spot checking won't do), every windshield is scanned. VWs have been rejected for surface scratches barely visible to the eye.
Final inspection is really something! VW inspectors run each car off the line onto the Funktionsprüfstand (car test stand), tote up 189 check points, gun ahead to the automatic brake stand, and say "no" to one VW out of fifty.
This preoccupation with detail means the VW lasts longer and requires less maintenance, by and large, than other cars. (It also means a used VW depreciates less than any other car.)
We pluck the lemons; you get the plums.

Figure 1.2   In the beginning, there was the word. And it was Lemon.

agency landed a couple of highly visible national accounts, including Volkswagen and Alka-Seltzer, he brought advertising into a new era.

Smart agencies and clients everywhere saw for themselves that advertising didn't have to embarrass itself in order to make a cash register ring. The national TV audience was eating it up. Viewers couldn't wait for the next airing of VW's "Funeral" or Alka-Seltzer's "Spicy meatball." The first shots of the Creative Revolution of the 1960s had been fired.*

How marvelous to have actually been there when DDB art director Helmut Krone laid out one of the very first Volkswagen ads (Figure 1.2): a

---

*You can study these two seminal commercials and many other great ads from this era in Larry Dubrow's fine book *Creative Revolution, When Advertising Tried Harder* (New York: Friendly Press, 1984).

black-and-white picture of that simple car, no women draped over the fender, no mansion in the background, and a one-word headline: "Lemon." This was paired with the simple, self-effacing copy that began: "This Volkswagen missed the boat. The chrome strip on the glove compartment is blemished and must be replaced. Chances are you wouldn't have noticed it; Inspector Kurt Kroner did."

Maybe this ad doesn't seem earth-shattering now; we've all seen our share of great advertising since then. But remember, DDB first did this when other car companies were running headlines such as "Blue ribbon beauty that's stealing the thunder from the high-priced cars!" and "Chevrolet's 3 new engines put new fun under your foot and a great big grin on your face!" Volkswagen's was a totally new voice.

As the 1960s progressed, the revolution seemed to be successful and everything was just hunky-stinkin'-dory for a while. Then came the 1970s. The tightening economy had middle managers everywhere scared.

And the party ended as quickly as it had begun.

THE EMPIRE STRIKES BACK.

The new gods wore suits and came bearing calculators. They seemed to say, "Enough of this Kreativity Krap-ola, my little scribblers. We're here to meet the client's numbers. Put 'new' in that headline. Drop that concept and pick up an adjective: Crunch-a-licious, Flavor-iffic, I don't care. The client's coming up the elevator. Chop, chop."

In *Corporate Report,* columnist William Souder wrote:

> Creative departments were reined in. New ads were pre-tested in focus groups, and subsequent audience-penetration and consumer-awareness quotients were numbingly monitored. It seemed that with enough repetition, even the most strident ad campaigns could bore through to the public consciousness. Advertising turned shrill. People hated Mr. Whipple, but bought Charmin anyway. It was Wisk for Ring-Around-the-Collar and Sanka for your jangled nerves.[9]

And so after a decade full of brilliant, successful examples such as Volkswagen, Avis, Polaroid, and Chivas Regal, the pendulum swung back to the dictums of research. The industry returned to the blaring jingles and crass gimmickry of decades previous. The wolf was at the door again—wearing a suit. It was as if all the agencies were run by purse-lipped nuns from some Catholic school. But instead of whacking students with rulers, these Madison Avenue schoolmarms whacked creatives with rolled-up research reports like "Burke scores," "Starch readership numbers," and a whole bunch of other useless left-brain crap.

Creativity was gleefully declared dead, at least by the big fat agencies that had never been able to come up with an original thought in the first place. And in came the next new thing—*positioning.*

"Advertising is entering an era where strategy is king," wrote the originators of the term *positioning,* Al Ries and Jack Trout. "Just as the me-too products killed the product era, the me-too companies killed the image advertising era."[10]

Part of the positioning paradigm was the notion that the consumer's head has a finite amount of space to categorize products. There's room for maybe three. If your product isn't in one of those slots, you must de-position a competitor in order for a different product to take its place. The Seven-Up Company's classic campaign from the 1960s remains a good example. Instead of positioning it as a clear soft drink with a lemon-lime flavor, 7UP took on the big three brown colas by positioning itself as "The Uncola."

Ted Morgan explained positioning this way: "Essentially, it's like finding a seat on a crowded bus. You look at the marketplace. You see what vacancy there is. You build your campaign to position your product in that vacancy. If you do it right, the straphangers won't be able to grab your seat."[11] As you might agree, Ries and Trout's concept of positioning is valid and useful.

Not surprisingly, advertisers fairly tipped over the positioning bandwagon climbing on. But a funny thing happened.

As skillfully as Madison Avenue's big agencies applied its principles, positioning by itself didn't magically move products, at least not as consistently as advertisers had hoped. Someone could have a marvelous idea for positioning a product, but if the commercials sucked, sales records were rarely broken.

Good advertising, it has been said, builds sales. But great advertising builds factories. And in this writer's opinion, the "great" that was missing from the positioning paradigm was the original alchemy brewed by Bernbach.

"You can say the right thing about a product and nobody will listen," said Bernbach (long before the advent of positioning). "But you've got to say it in such a way that people will feel it in their gut. Because if they don't feel it, nothing will happen." He went on to say, "The more intellectual you grow, the more you lose the great intuitive skills that really touch and move people."[12]

Such was the state of the business when I joined its ranks in 1979. The battle between these opposing forces of hot creativity and cold research rages to this hour. And it makes for an interesting day at the office.

As John Ward of England's B&B Dorland noted, "Advertising is a craft executed by people who aspire to be artists, but is assessed by those who aspire to be scientists. I cannot imagine any human relationship more perfectly designed to produce total mayhem."[13]

PORTRAIT OF THE ARTIST AS A YOUNG HACK.

When I was in seventh grade, I noticed something about the ads for cereal on TV. (Remember, this was before the Federal Trade Commission forced manufacturers to call these sugary puffs of crunchy air "part of a complete breakfast.") I noticed the cereals were looking more and more like candy. There were flocks of leprechauns or birds or bees flying around the bowl, dusting sparkles of sugar over the cereal or ladling on gooey rivers of chocolate-flavored coating.

The food value of the product kept getting less important until it was finally stuffed into the trunk of the car and sugar moved into the driver's seat. It was all about sugar.

One morning in study hall, I drew this little progression (Figure 1.3), calling it "History of a Cereal Box."

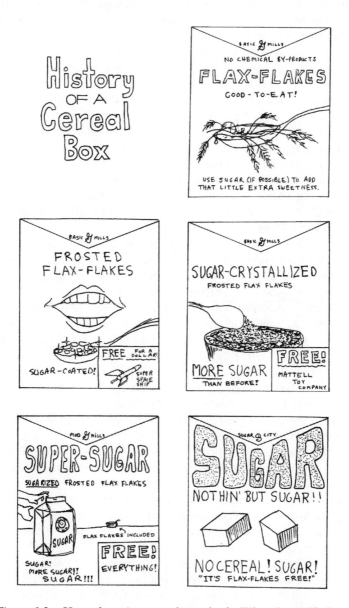

Figure 1.3   Hype doesn't persuade anybody. When I was 12, I was appalled by the stupidity of all the cereal commercials selling sugar, so I drew this progression of cereal box designs.

I was interested in the advertising I saw on TV but never thought I'd take it up as a career. I liked to draw, to make comic books, and to doodle with words and pictures. But when I was a poor college student, all I was sure of was that I wanted to be rich. I went into the premed program. The first grade on my college transcript, for chemistry, was a big, fat, radioactive F. I reconsidered.

I majored in psychology. But after college I couldn't find any businesses on Lake Street in Minneapolis that were hiring skinny chain-smokers who could explain the relative virtues of scheduled versus random reinforcement in behaviorist theory. I joined a construction crew.

When the opportunity to be an editor/typesetter/ad salesperson for a small neighborhood newspaper came along, I took it, at a salary of $80 every two weeks. (Thinking back, I believe I deserved $85.) But the opportunity to sit at a desk and use words to make a living was enough. Of all my duties, I found that selling ads and putting them together were the most interesting.

For the next year and a half, I hovered around the edges of the advertising industry. I did pasteup for another small newsweekly and then put in a long and dreary stint as a typesetter in the ad department of a large department store. It was there, during a break from setting type about "thick and thirsty cotton bath towels: $9.99," that I first came upon a book featuring the winners of a local advertising awards show.

I was bowled over by the work I saw there—mostly campaigns from Tom McElligott and Ron Anderson from Bozell & Jacobs's Minneapolis office. Their ads didn't say "thick and thirsty cotton bath towels: $9.99." They were funny or they were serious—startling sometimes—but they were always intelligent.

Reading one of their ads felt like I'd just met a very likable person at a bus stop. *He's smart, he's funny, he doesn't talk about himself. Turns out he's a salesman. And he's selling? . . . Well, wouldn't you know it, I've been thinking about buying one of those. Maybe I'll give you a call. Bye. Walking away you think, nice enough fella. And the way he said things: so funny.*

Through a contact, I managed to get a foot in the door at Bozell. What finally got me hired wasn't my awful little portfolio. What did it was an interview with McElligott—a sweaty little interrogation I attended wearing my shiny, wide 1978 tie and where I said "I see" about a hundred times. Tom later told me it was my enthusiasm that convinced him to take a chance on me. That and my promise to put in 60-hour weeks writing the brochures and other scraps that fell off his plate.

Tom hired me as a copywriter in January 1979. He didn't have much work for me during that first month, so he parked me in a conference room with a 3-foot-tall stack of books full of the best advertising in the world: the One Show and *Communication Arts* awards annuals. He told me to read them. "Read them all."

He called them "the graduate school of advertising." I think he was right, and I say the same thing to students trying to get into the business today. Get yourself a 3-foot-tall stack of your own and read, learn, and memorize. Yes, this is a business where we try to break rules, but as T. S. Eliot said, "It's not wise to violate the rules until you know how to observe them."

As hard as I studied those awards annuals, most of the work I did that first year wasn't very good. In fact, it stunk. If the truth be known, those early ads of mine were so bad I have to reach for my volume of Edgar Allan Poe to describe them with any accuracy: ". . . a nearly liquid mass of loathsome, detestable putridity."

But don't take my word for it. Here's my very first ad. Just look at Figure 1.4 (for as long as you're able): a dull little ad that doesn't so much revolve around an overused play on the word *interest,* as it limps.

Figure 1.4   My first ad. (I know . . . I know.)

Rumor has it they're still using my first ad at poison control centers to induce vomiting. *("Come on now, Jimmy. We know you ate all of your sister's antidepressant pills and that's why you have to look at Luke's bank ad.")*

The point is, if you're like me, you might have a slow beginning. Even my friend Bob Barrie's first ad was terrible. Bob is arguably one of the best art directors in the history of advertising. But his first ad? The boring, flat-footed little headline read: "Win A Boat." We used to give Bob all kinds of grief about that. It became his hallway nickname: "Hey, Win-A-Boat, we're goin' to lunch. You comin'?"

There will come a time when you'll just start to get it. When you'll no longer waste time traipsing down dead ends or rattling the knobs of doors best left locked. You'll just start to get it. And suddenly, the ads coming out of your office will bear the mark of somebody who knows what the hell he's doing.

Along the way, though, it helps to study how more experienced people have tackled the same problems you'll soon face. On the subject of mentors, Helmut Krone said:

> I asked one of our young writers recently, which was more important: Doing your own thing or making the ad as good as it can be? The answer was "Doing my own thing." I disagree violently with that. I'd like to pose a new idea for our age: "Until you've got a better answer, you copy." I copied [famous Doyle Dane art director] Bob Gage for five years.[14]

The question is, Who are you going to copy while you learn the craft? Whipple? For all the wincing his commercials caused, they worked. A lot of people at Procter & Gamble sent kids through college on Whipple's nickel. And these people can prove it; they have charts and everything.

Bill Bernbach, quoted here, wasn't big on charts.

> However much we would like advertising to be a science—because life would be simpler that way—the fact is that it is not. It is a subtle, ever-changing art, defying formularization, flowering on freshness and withering on imitation; what was effective one day, for that very reason, will not be effective the next, because it has lost the maximum impact of originality.[15]

There is a fork in the road here. Mr. Bernbach's path is the one I invite you to come down. It leads to the same place—enduring brands and market leadership—but it gets there without costing anybody their dignity. You won't have to apologize to the neighbors for creating that irritating interruption of their sitcom last night. You won't have to explain anything. In fact, all most people will want to know is: "That was so cool. How'd you come up with it?"

This other road has its own rules, if we can call them that—rules that were first articulated years ago by Mr. Bernbach and his team of pioneers, including Bob Levenson, John Noble, Phyllis Robinson, Julian Koenig, and Helmut Krone.

Some may say my allegiance to the famous DDB School will date everything I have to say in this book. Perhaps. Yet a quick glance through their classic Volkswagen ads from the 1960s convinces me that the soul of a great idea hasn't changed in these years.* Those ads are still great. Intelligent. Clean. Witty. Beautiful. And human.

So with a tip of my hat to those pioneers of brilliant advertising, I offer the ideas in this book. They are the opinions of one writer, the gathered wisdom of smart people I met along the way during a career of writing, selling, and producing ideas for a wide variety of clients. God knows, they aren't rules. As Hall of Fame copywriter Ed McCabe once said, "I have no use for rules. They only rule out the brilliant exception."

---

*Perhaps the best collection of VW advertisements is a small book edited by the famous copywriter David Abbott: *Remember Those Great Volkswagen Ads?* (Holland: European Illustration, 1982).

Figure 2.1   This early ad for my friend Alex Bogusky's agency in Miami makes a good point. A smart strategy can take the same message and make it work better.

2

A Sharp Pencil Works Best
Some thoughts on getting started

IS THIS A GREAT JOB OR WHAT?

As an employee in an agency creative department, you will spend most of your time with your feet up on a desk working on an idea. Across the desk, also with his feet up, will be your partner—in my case, an art director. And he will want to talk about movies.

In fact, if the truth be known, you will spend a large part of your career with your feet up talking about movies.

The brief is approved, the work is due in two days, the pressure's building, and your muse is sleeping off a drunk behind a Dumpster or twitching in a ditch somewhere. Your pen lies useless. So you talk movies.

That's when the project manager comes by. Project managers stay on top of a job as it moves through the agency. This means they also stay on top of *you*. They'll come by to remind you of the horrid things that happen to snail-assed creative people who don't come through with the goods on time.

So you try to get your pen moving. And you begin to work. And working, in this business, means staring at your partner's shoes.

That's what I've been doing from 9:00 to 5:00 for more than 20 years—staring at the bottom of the disgusting tennis shoes on the feet of my partner, parked on the desk across from *my* disgusting tennis shoes. This is the sum and substance of life at an agency.

In movies, they almost never capture this simple, dull, workday reality of life as a creative person. Don't get me wrong; it's not an easy job. In fact, some days it's almost painful coming up with good ideas. As author Red Smith said, "There's nothing to writing. All you do is sit down at a typewriter and open a vein."[1] But the way it looks on *Mad Men*, creative people solve complicated marketing problems between wisecracks, cocktails, and office affairs.

Since the 1970s, the movie and TV agencies have always been kooky sorts of places where odd things are nailed to the walls, where weirdly dressed creative people lurch through the hallways metabolizing last night's chemicals, and the occasional goat wanders through in the background.

But that isn't what agencies are like—at least not the four or five agencies where I've worked. Again, don't get me wrong. An ad agency is not a bank. It's not an insurance company. There is a certain amount of joie de vivre in an agency's atmosphere.

This isn't surprising. Here you have a tight-knit group of young people, many of them making significant salaries just for sitting around with their feet up, solving marketing problems. And talking about movies.

It's a great job because you'll never get bored. One week you'll be knee-deep in the complexities of the financial business, selling market-indexed annuities. The next, you're touring a dog food factory asking about the difference between a "kibble" and a "bit." You'll learn about the business *of* business by studying the operations of hundreds of different kinds of enterprises.

The movies and television also portray advertising as a schlocky business—a parasitic lamprey that dangles from the belly of the business beast. A sort of side business that doesn't really manufacture anything in its own right, where it's all flash over substance, and where silver-tongued salespeople pitch snake oil to a bovine public, sandblast their wallets, and make the 5:20 for Long Island.

Ten minutes of work at a real agency should be enough to convince even the most cynical that an agency's involvement in a client's business is anything but superficial. Every cubicle on every floor at an agency is occupied by someone intensely involved in improving the client's day-to-day business, in shepherding its assets more wisely, sharpening its business focus, widening its market, improving the product, and creating new products.

Ten minutes of work at a real agency should be enough to convince a cynic that you can't sell a product to someone who has no need for it. That you can't sell a product to someone who can't afford it. And that good advertising is about the worst thing that can happen to a bad product.

In 10 minutes the cynic will also see there's no back room where snickering airbrush artists paint images of breasts into ice cubes, no slush fund to buy hookers for the clients' conventions, and no big table in the conference room where employees have sex during the office Christmas party. (Um, scratch that last one.)

Advertising isn't just some mutant offspring of capitalism. It isn't a bunch of caffeine junkies dreaming up clever ways to talk about existing products.

Advertising is one of the main gears in the machinery of a huge economy, responsible in great part for creating and selling products that contribute to one of the highest standards of living the world's ever seen. That three-mile run you just clocked on your Nike+ GPS watch was created in large part by an agency: R/GA. The Diet Coke you had when you cooled down at home was co-created with an agency: SSCB. These are just two of tens of thousands of stories out there where marketer and agency worked together to bring a product—and with it, jobs and industry—to life.

Like it or not, advertising's a key ingredient in a competitive economy and has created a stable place for itself in America's business landscape. It's now a mature industry, and for most companies, a business necessity.

Why most of it totally *blows chunks*, well, that remains a mystery.

Carl Ally, founder of one of the great agencies of the 1970s, had a theory about why most advertising stinks: "There's a tiny percentage of all the work that's great and a tiny percentage that's lousy. But most of the work—well, it's just there. That's no knock on advertising. How many great restaurants are there? Most aren't good or bad, they're just adequate. The fact is, excellence is tough to achieve in any field."[2]

———

WHY NOBODY EVER CHOOSES BRAND X.

There comes a point when you can't talk about movies anymore and you actually have to get some work done.

You are faced with a blank slate, and you must, in a fixed amount of time, fill it with something interesting enough to be remembered by a customer who, in the course of a day, will see thousands of other ad messages.

You are not writing a novel somebody pays money for. You are not writing a sitcom somebody enjoys watching. You're writing something most people try to avoid. This is the sad, indisputable truth at the bottom of our business. Nobody wants to see what you are about to put down on paper. People not only dislike advertising, they're becoming immune to most of it—like insects building up resistance to DDT.

The way Eric Silver put it was this: "Advertising is what happens on TV when people go to the bathroom."

When people aren't indifferent to advertising, they're angry at it. If you don't believe me, go to the opening night of a big Hollywood movie. When the third commercial comes up on the screen and it's not the movie, those moans you hear won't be audience ecstasy. People don't *want* to see your stinkin' commercial. Your spot is the comedian who comes on stage before a Rolling Stones concert. The audience is drunk and they're angry, and they came to see the Stones. And now a *comedian* has the microphone? You had better be great.

So you try to come up with some advertising concepts that can defeat these barriers of indifference and anger. Maybe it's an ad. Maybe it's an online experience. Or even street theater. *Whatever* the ideas may be, they aren't conjured in a vacuum. Because you're working off a strategy—a sentence or two describing the key competitive message your ad must communicate.

In addition to a strategy, you are working with a brand. Unless it's a new one, that brand brings with it all kinds of baggage, some good and some bad. Ad people call it a brand's *equity*.

A brand isn't just the name on the box. It isn't the thing in the box, either. A brand is the sum total of all the emotions, thoughts, images, history, possibilities, and gossip that exist in the marketplace about a certain company.

What's remarkable about brands is that in categories where products are essentially all alike, the best-known and most well-liked brand has the winning card. In *The Want Makers,* Mike Destiny, former group director for England's Allied Breweries, was quoted: "The many competitive brands [of beer] are virtually identical in terms of taste, color and alcohol delivery, and after two or three pints even an expert couldn't tell them apart. So the consumer is literally drinking the advertising, and the advertising is the brand."[3]

A brand isn't just a semantic construct, either. The relationship between the brand and its customers has monetary value; it can amount to literally billions of dollars. Brands are assets, and companies rightfully include them on their financial balance sheets. In Barry's *The Advertising Concept Book,* he quotes a smart fellow named Nick Shore on the power of brands: "If you systematically dismantled the entire operation of the Coca-Cola Company and left them with only their brand name, management could rebuild the company within five years. Remove the brand *name* and the enterprise would die within five years."[4]

When you're writing for a brand, you're working with a fragile, extraordinarily valuable thing. Not a lightweight job. Its implications are marvelous. The work you're about to do may not make the next million for the brand's marketer or bring them to Chapter 11. Maybe it's just an online banner that runs for a week. Yet it's an opportunity to sharpen that brand's image, even if just a little bit. It's a little like being handed the Olympic torch. You won't bear this important symbol all the way from Athens. Your job is just to move it a few miles down the road—without dropping it in the dirt along the way.

■■■■■■■

STARING AT YOUR PARTNER'S SHOES.

For me, writing any piece of advertising is unnerving.

You sit down with your partner and put your feet up. You read the strategist's brief, draw a square on a pad of paper, and you both stare at the damned thing. You stare at each other's shoes. You look at the square. You give up and go to lunch.

You come back. The empty square is still there. Is the square gonna be a poster? Will it be a branded sitcom, a radio spot, a website? You don't know. All you know is the square's still empty.

So you both go through the stories you find online, on the client's website and other places. You go through the reams of material the account team left in your office. You read that the bourbon you're working on is manufactured in a little town with a funny name. You point this out to your partner.

Your partner keeps staring out the window at some speck in the distance. (Or is that a speck on the glass? Can't be sure.) He says, "Oh." Down the hallway, a phone rings.

Paging through an industry magazine, your partner points out that distillers sometimes rotate the aging barrels a quarter turn every few months. You go, "Hmm."

On some site, you read how moss on trees happens to grow faster on the sides that face a distillery's aging house.

Now *that's* interesting.

You feel the shapeless form of an idea begin to bubble up from the depths. You poise your pencil over the page . . . and it all comes out in a flash of creativity. *(Whoa. Someone call 9-1-1. Report a fire on my drawing pad 'cause I am SMOKIN' hot.)* You put your pencil down, smile, and read what you've written. It's complete rubbish. You call it a day and slink out to see a movie.

This process continues for several days, even weeks, and then one day without warning, an idea just shows up at your door, all nattied up like a Jehovah's Witness. You don't know where it comes from. It just shows up.

That's how you come up with ideas. Sorry, there's no big secret. That's basically the drill.

A guy named James Webb Young, a copywriter from the 1940s, laid out a five-step process of idea generation that holds water today.

1. You gather as much information on the problem as you can. You read, you underline stuff, you ask questions, you visit the factory.

2. You sit down and actively attack the problem.

3. You drop the whole thing and go do something else while your subconscious mind works on the problem.

4. "Eureka!"

5. You figure out how to implement your idea.[5]

Step two is what this book is about: attacking the problem.

This process of creativity isn't just an aimless sort of blue-skying—a mental version of bad modern dance. Rather, it's what author Joseph Heller (a former copywriter) called "a controlled daydream, a directed reverie." It's imagination disciplined by a single-minded business purpose. It is this clash of free-flowing imagination and focused business purpose that makes the creative process such a big mess.

———

WHY THE CREATIVE PROCESS IS EXACTLY LIKE WASHING A PIG.

I'm serious. Creativity is exactly like washing a pig. It's messy. It has no rules. No clear beginning, middle, or end. It's kind of a pain in the ass, and when you're done, you're not sure if the pig is really clean or why you were washing a pig in the first place.

The creative process is chaotic to its core and, for me at least, the washing-a-pig metaphor works on several levels.

The account person walks in and says, "Dude, the client's coming here at 3:00 PM, and I need you to wash that pig over there."

So you go online to see if there's any advice or inspiration, kinda hoping you'll find titles like "So You Want to Wash a Pig" or "Pig Washing: The McGuire 4-Step Method."

But you don't. So you find your partner, grab a hose, maybe a bucket, and some soap. And you just sorta start. You've never done anything like this before, so you feel kind of stupid at first. All your first attempts fail messily. The pig keeps getting away from you and for awhile you think you won't be able to do this.

Around 2:00 your partner tries distracting the pig with some vanilla wafers he found, and suddenly between the two of you, you think maybe the pig is starting to get clean. As the client pulls into the parking lot, you're both drying off the pig and second-guessing your work: "Is the pig really clean?"

Usually what happens here is that the client walks in and says, "Hey, I was thinkin'. Could you guys maybe wash a *warthog* instead?"

You go home wondering many things, mostly why you spent the day washing a pig.

I'm not the only one who thinks washing a pig is a decent metaphor for the creative process. A professor in the Advertising Department at Florida State University, a fellow named Tom Laughon, agreed that washing a pig might make for a good "lab experience" in chaos and creativity. You can see his class in the middle of the creative process in Figure 2.2 and the entire series of photos is online.

In the videos you can sorta see where they figured out the part about vanilla wafers, which is basically their moment of inspiration that moved the creative job into the completion phase.

Without that little moment of inspiration, your pig's gonna stay dirty. The problem with inspiration is it visits whenever the hell it wants. It's random. With a handful of creative jobs, inspiration may come quickly but most days it feels like our muse is sleeping off a crack binge somewhere in the stairwell of an abandoned federal building. It's because inspiration is random that it's so hard for a creative person to say exactly when a job will be done.

In his book *Hegarty on Advertising*, Hegarty puts it this way: "Creativity isn't a process. *Advertising* is a process. Creativity is a manic construction of absurd,

Figure 2.2   I'm serious. The entire creative process is exactly *like washing a pig.*

unlikely irreverent thoughts and feelings that somehow, when put together, change the way we see things. That's why it's magic. If you want to be ordinary, then, yes, use a process."[6]

It is from this uncertainty that all the pressure and insanity of the agency business is born. In fact, any enterprise where someone pays someone else to perform a creative act has this tension built into it, whether it's a client paying an agency or a studio paying a screenwriter.

This simple observation about the role of inspiration in the creative process, although obvious to most creative people, is lost on many. The fact is, most normal people have jobs where they can survey the amount of work needed, make an estimate, and then complete the work in the allotted time. We, on the other hand, have to wash a pig. It's really hard to say when the pig's gonna be clean. By three o'clock? Maybe. Maybe not.

My old friend Mike Lescarbeau wrote this about the creative process: "Coming up with ideas is not so much a step-by-step process as it is a lonely vigil interrupted infrequently by great thoughts, whose origins are almost always a mystery."

———

So you start to write. Or doodle. (It doesn't matter which. Good copywriters can think visually; good art directors can write; good technical people can concept.) You just pick up a pencil and begin. All beginnings are humble, but after several days, you begin to translate that flat-footed strategy into something interesting.

The final idea may be a visual. It may be a headline. It may be both. It may arrive whole, like Athena arising out of Zeus's head. Or in pieces—a scribble made by the art director last Friday fits beautifully with a headline the writer comes up with over the weekend. Eventually you get to an idea that dramatizes the benefit of your client's product or service. *Dramatizes* is the key word. You must dramatize it in a unique, provocative, compelling, and memorable way.

And at the center of this thing you come up with must be a promise. The reader must get something out of the deal. Steve Hayden, most famous for penning Apple Computer's "1984" commercial, said, "If you want to be a well-paid copywriter, please your client. If you want to be an award-winning copywriter, please yourself. If you want to be a great copywriter, please your reader."[7]

Here's the hard part. You have to please your reader, and you have to do it in a few seconds.

Paul Keye, a well-known West Coast creative, had a good way of putting this: "How to write an interesting ad? Try this: 'Hello. I want to tell you something important or interesting or useful or funny. It's about you. I won't take very long and there's a prize if you stay till the very end.'"[8]

The way I picture it is this: It's as if you're riding down an elevator with your customer. You're going down only 15 floors. So you have only a few seconds to tell him one thing about your product. One thing. And you have to tell it to him in such an interesting way that he thinks about the promise you've made as he leaves the building, waits for the light, and crosses the street. You have to come up with some little *thing* that sticks in the customer's mind.

By "thing," I don't mean gimmick. Anybody can come up with an unrelated gimmick. Used car dealers are the national experts with their contrived sales events. *("The boss went on vacation, and our accountant went crazy!")* You might capture somebody's attention for a few seconds with a gimmick. But once the ruse is over and the salesman comes out of the closet in his plaid coat, the customer will only resent you.

Bill Bernbach: "I've got a great gimmick. Let's tell the truth."

The best answers always arise out of the problem itself. Out of the product. Out of the realities of the buying situation. Those are the only paints you have to make your picture, but they are all you need. Any shtick you drag into the situation that is not organically part of the product or customer reality will not be authentic and will ring false.

You have more than enough to work with, even in the simplest advertising problem. You have your client's product with its brand equities and its benefits. You have the competition's product and its weaknesses. You have the price-quality-value math of the two products. And then you have what the customer brings to the situation—pride, greed, vanity, envy, insecurity, and a hundred other human emotions, wants, and needs, one of which your product satisfies.

THE SUDDEN CESSATION OF STUPIDITY.

"You've got to play this game with fear and arrogance."

That's one of Kevin Costner's better lines from the baseball movie *Bull Durham*. I've always thought it had an analog in the advertising business.

There has never been a time in my career I have faced the empty page and not been scared. I was scared as a junior-coassistant-copy-cub-intern. And I'm scared today. Who am I to think I can write something that will interest millions of people?

Then, a day after winning a medal in the One Show (just about the toughest national advertising awards show there is), I feel bulletproof. For one measly afternoon, I'm an Ad God. The next day I'm back with my feet up on the table, sweating bullets again.

Somewhere between these two places, however, is where you want to be—a balance between a healthy skepticism of your reason for living and a solar confidence in your ability to come up with a fantastic idea every time you sit down to work. Living at either end of the spectrum will debilitate you. In fact, it's probably best to err on the side of fear.

A small, steady pilot light of fear burning in your stomach is part and parcel of the creative process. If you're doing something that's truly new, you're in an area where there are no signposts yet—no up and down, no good or bad. It seems to me, then, that fear is the constant traveling companion of advertising people who fancy themselves on the cutting edge.

You have to believe that you'll finally get a great idea. You will. You'll probably fail a few times along the way, but like director Woody Allen says, "If you're not failing every now and again, it's a sign you're not doing anything very innovative."

And there is nothing quite like the feeling of cracking a difficult advertising problem. What seemed impossible when you sat down to face the empty white square now seems so obvious. It is this very *obviousness* of a great idea that prompted Polaroid camera inventor, E. H. Land, to define creativity as "the sudden cessation of stupidity." You look at the idea you've just come up with, slap your forehead, and go, "Of course, it has to be this."

IT'S ALL ABOUT THE BENJAMINS.

Solving a difficult advertising problem is a great feeling. Even better is the day, weeks, or months later when an account executive pops his head in your door and says sales are up. It never ceases to amaze me when that happens. Not that I doubt the power of advertising, but sometimes it's just hard to follow the thread from the scratchings on my pad all the way to a ringing cash register in, say, Akron, Ohio. Yet it works.

Figure 2.3   Two screen shots of the Nike+ app.

People generally deny advertising has any effect on them. They'll insist they're immune to it. And perhaps, taken on a person-by-person basis, the effect of your ad is indeed modest. But over time, the results are undeniable. It's like wind on desert sands. The changes occurring at any given hour on any particular dune are small: a grain here, a handful there. But over time, the whole landscape changes. At other times, an idea can change a brand's fortune very quickly.

The Nike+ campaign from R/GA is an incredible example of creative and monetary success. In 2006, Nike collaborated with Apple to create a device that recorded the distance and speed of a runner's workout. What made it a monstrous idea is that these statistics could then be instantly uploaded to the runner's app (Figure 2.3) or personal page on the Nike+ website, where it's shared with runners all over the world. That the device did other cool stuff like play particular songs at specific parts of a run, that was just icing on the cake. Cooler was the international online community the site created. And as for sales, it helped move Nike's share of the running category from 48 percent to 61 percent in just three years.[9]

More anecdotal, but equally impressive, were the results of the trade campaign created to attract advertisers to the pages of *Rolling Stone* magazine. After Fallon McElligott's Hall of Fame print campaign, "Perception/Reality," was up and running, publisher Jann Wenner was reported as saying, "It was like someone came in with a wheelbarrow of money and dumped it on the floor."

This is a great business; make no mistake. I see what copywriter Tom Monahan meant when he said, "Advertising is the rock 'n' roll of the business world."

BRAND = ADJECTIVE.

Each brand has its own core value. Dan Wieden says it another way: brands are verbs. "Nike exhorts, IBM solves, and Sony dreams." Even Mr. Whipple, as bad as he was, helped Charmin equal soft.

This is an important point, and before we talk about strategy, it bears some discussion.

People don't have time to figure out what your brand stands for. It is up to you to make your brand stand for something. The way to do it is to make your brand stand for one thing. Brand = adjective. Everything you do with regard to advertising and design—whether it's creating the product or designing the website—should adhere to absolutely draconian standards of simplicity.

I was on the phone with a client who works for a nationwide chain of grocery stores. This director of marketing mentioned in passing that the number of brands on the shelves in his stores had just passed 50,000.

That's 50,000 brands competing for a customer's attention—50,000.

And that was five years ago. There has to be many more by now.

This number alone should take the spring from the step of any advertising person whose job it is to make the silhouette of a brand show up on a customer's radar. Until recently, it's been reasonable to assume that the way to make customers remember a brand is to differentiate it from its competitors: "The model of car we're selling has incredible styling, and the other guy's brand doesn't."

But your competition isn't just the other guy's car.

When you sit down to create something for a client, you are competing with *every* brand out there. You're competing with every marketing message that's running on every platform on every device on the face of the planet. You're competing with the 50,000+ packaged-good brands on the shelves at the grocery store, as well as every other product and service and logo in the country. You're competing for attention with every TV commercial that has ever aired, with every text message ever sent, with each billboard on every mile of highway, with the entire bandwidth across the radio, and with every 1 of the 100 trillion pixels on the Web. *All those other advertisers want a piece of your customer's attention.* And they're going to get it at your client's expense.

Seen from this perspective, through the teeming forest of brands vying for customers' attention, cutting through the clutter may require more than giving a sharp knife-edge to your brand. It calls for a big, noisy, smoking chain saw. But a kick-ass Super Bowl commercial isn't what I mean by a chain saw.

The chain saw you need is simplicity.

SIMPLE = GOOD.

When you think about it, what other antidote to clutter can there possibly be *except* simplicity?

Perhaps we should try cutting through the clutter with clutter that's extremely entertaining? Should we air clutter that tests well? Or clutter that wins awards, or clutter with a big 800 number?

I propose that the only possible antidote to clutter is draconian simplicity.

Draconian simplicity involves stripping your brand's value proposition down to the bone and then again to the marrow, carving away until you get down to brand = adjective. Make your brand stand for one thing. Pair it with one adjective.

But which adjective?

If you ask consumers in focus groups to talk about buying a car, with sufficient amounts of Dr. Pepper and M&M's, they will amaze you with their complex analysis of the auto-buying process. I'm not kidding. These groups go on for hours, days. But if you ask a guy in a bar, "Hey, talk to me about cars," he'll break it down to a word—usually an adjective.

"Yeah, gonna get me a Jeep. They're rugged."

Porsches, they're fast. BMWs perform. And Volvos, they're . . . what?

If you said "safe," you've given the same answer I've received from literally every person I've ever asked. *Ever.*

In every speech I've ever given, anywhere around the world, when I ask audiences, "What does Volvo stand for?" I hear the same answer every time: "Safety." Audiences in Berlin, Los Angeles, Helsinki, Copenhagen, and New York City all give the same answer. The money Volvo has spent on branding has paid off handsomely. Volvo has successfully spot welded that one adjective to their marque. And here's the interesting bit: in the past couple of years, Volvo hasn't even made it onto the top 10 list of safest cars on the market. So here's a brand that, having successfully paired its logo to one adjective, rides the benefit of this simple position in customers' minds long after its products no longer even *merit* the distinction. Such is the power of simplicity.

The adjective you choose is key. Once it's married to a brand, divorce can be ugly. On the good side, once it's paired with the brand, that one square foot of category space is taken and nobody else can claim it.

If you find yourself in a position where all the good adjectives are taken, don't settle for the second best. *("Refreshing" is taken? Oh well . . . can we have "quenching?")* Second best won't be different enough. Try a polar opposite. Or consider a flanking move. In ketchup, the adjective everyone fought over for a long time was to be the "tomato-iest." Then one day Heinz came along claiming it was the "slowest," and sales went up—and stayed up. You can also try creating a whole new adjective that alters the playing field in your favor. (Axe cologne's "Bom Chicka Wah Wah" comes to mind.) The right adjective, the answer, will come out of the product—or from your customers. Ask them. They know the answer.

Find an adjective and stick to it. But it's the sticking to it that so many brands seem to have trouble with. The problem may be that, from a client's perspective, there are so many things to admire about its product.

"How can we narrow down our brand's value proposition to a word? Our product lasts longer, it's less expensive, it works better. All that stuff's important." Yes, those secondary benefits are important, and, yes, they have a place: in the brochures, on the packaging, or two clicks into the website. All those other benefits will serve to shore up the aggregate value proposition of a brand once customers try it. But what they're going to remember a brand for, the way they're going to label it in their mental filing system, is with a word.

Find that word.

As you think, don't let the word *adjective* get you thinking too small. A company's position could also be its purpose, its reason for existing, its social mission. The authors of *The Cluetrain Manifesto* remind us that "companies attempting to 'position' themselves [should instead] *take* a position. Optimally, it should relate to something their market actually cares about."[10]

You may argue that I have oversimplified here. And I have; I'll accept the criticism. Because I'm arguing for purism in an area where it's often impossible to think that way. Many brands do not lend themselves to such clean theoretical distinctions. All I'm saying is that you should at least try; try to find that one word. You're trying to own some real estate for your brand in a very crowded neighborhood. I like how John Hegarty defines it: "A brand is the most valuable piece of real estate in the world: a corner of someone's mind."[11]

Find that word. You're going to thank me when it comes time to sit down and come up with a big idea.

BEFORE YOU PUT PEN TO PAPER.

Before you do any new thinking, there's some background work to do. You won't be doing it alone, though. You'll have help from the people in account service.

The account folks are the people in charge of an account at an agency. They work with the clients to define opportunities, they set budgets and timelines, and they do a whole bunch of other stuff, some of it boring. They also help you present the work (they *sell* it, too, if you're working with good ones) to the client. Overall, they're the liaison between the client and the agency, explaining one to the other, running interference, and acting as the marriage counselor when the times call for it.

Some account people are great, some so-so, and some bad. It will pay to hitch up with the smart ones as soon as you can. The good ones have the soul of a creative person and will share your excitement over a great idea. They're articulate, honest, and inspiring, and like I said, the good ones have a better batting average at selling your work.

Here are some things I've learned from the great account people I've worked with.

Start by examining the current positioning of your product.

There's a book called *Positioning: The Battle for Your Mind,* one I recommend with many caveats. (Although the strategic thinking of the authors is sound, I have many differences with them on the subject of creativity, which they declare irrelevant.)

The authors, Ries and Trout, maintain that the customer's head has a finite amount of space in which to remember products. In each category, there's room for perhaps three brand names. If your product isn't in one of those slots, you must "de-position" a competitor to take its place.

Before you start, look at the current positioning of your product. What positions do the competitors occupy? What niches are undefended? Should you concentrate on defining your client's position, or do some de-positioning of the competition? Do they have an adjective? What's your adjective?

Get to know your client's business as well as you can.

Bill Bernbach said, "The magic is in the product. . . . You've got to live with your product. You've got to get steeped in it. You've got to get saturated with it."[12]

The moral for writers and art directors is: do the factory tour. I'm serious. Go if you get the chance. Ask a million questions. How is the product made? What ingredients does it have? What are their quality control criteria? Read every brochure. Read every memo you can get your hands on. You may find ideas waiting in the middle of a spec sheet ready to be transplanted kit-and-caboodle into an ad. Learn the company's business.

Your clients are going to trust you more if you can talk to them about their industry in *their* terms. They'll quickly find you boring or irrelevant if all you can speak about with authority is Century Italic. Your grasp of the client's marketing situation has to be as well versed as any account executive's. There are no shortcuts. Know the client. Know the product. Know the market. It will pay off.

Louis Pasteur said, "Chance favors the prepared mind."

On the other hand, there's value in staying stupid.

This dissenting opinion was brought to my attention by a great copywriter, Mark Fenske. Mark says, "Don't give into the temptation to take the factory tour. Resist. It makes you think like the client. You'll start to come up with the same answers the client does."

Mark believes, as many do, that keeping your tabula extremely rasa makes your thinking fresher. He may be right. There's also this to consider: When you're on the factory floor watching the caps get put on the beer bottles, you're a long way from the customer's backyard reality. All the customer cares about is, "What's in it for *me*?"

Get to know the client's customers as well as you can.

Once you get into the agency business, you'll meet another team member, called a *strategist*. Consider the strategist both a cultural anthropologist and a stand-in for the consumer of the brand. Strategists analyze the market, study the competition, and basically tell you what your brand's consumer audience is doing, how they're doing it, and what devices they're doing it on.

Read everything your strategists give you before putting pen to paper. Remember, most of the work you do will be targeted to people outside your small social circle, people with whom you have no more in common than being a carbon-based organism.

Take farming. I've written whole campaigns selling herbicides to soybean farmers, but what do I know about farming? As a kid, I couldn't even keep an *ant* farm alive for a week once it arrived in the mail. Getting into the mind-set of a soybean farmer took plenty of work—watching lots of recorded interviews and doing plenty of reading. Your strategists can give you piles of material to study.

But don't just read it. Feel it. Take a deep breath and sink slowly into the world of the person you're writing to. Go beyond the stinkin' demographics. Maybe you're selling a retirement community. You're talking to an older person. Someone living on a fixed income. Maybe that person is worried about becoming dependent on his kids. It hurts when he gets out of a chair. The idea of shoveling snow has dark-red cardiac overtones. How does it *feel* to be this person? Find the emotion.

Once you find the right emotion, you are miles ahead of someone who's just thinking about the brand.

Ask to see the entire file of the client's previous work.

The client or the account executives will have it somewhere. Study it. Maybe they tried something that was pretty cool, but they didn't do it right. How could you do it better? It will get your wheels turning. It'll also keep you from presenting ideas the client has already tried.

Make sure what you have to say matters.

It must be relevant. It must matter to somebody, somewhere. It has to offer something customers want or solve a problem they have, whether it's a car that won't start or a drip that won't stop.

If you don't have something relevant to say, tell your clients to put their wallets away. Because no matter how well you execute it, an unimportant message has no receiver. The tree falls in the forest. Crickets chirp.

Insist on a tight strategy.

Creative director Norman Berry wrote: "English strategies are very tight, very precise. Satisfy the strategy and the idea cannot be faulted even though it may appear outrageous. Many . . . strategies are often too vague, too open to interpretation. 'The strategy for this product is taste,' they'll say. But that is not a strategy. Vague strategies inhibit. Precise strategies liberate."[13]

Poet T. S. Eliot never worked at an ad agency, but his advice about strategy is right on the money: "When forced to work within a strict framework, the imagination is taxed to its utmost and will produce its richest ideas. Given total freedom, the work is likely to sprawl."

Dude nailed it. You need a tight strategy.

On the other hand, a strategy can become too tight. When there's no play in the wheel, an overly specific strategy demands a very narrow range of executions and becomes by proxy an execution itself. Good account people and strategists can fine-tune a strategy by moving it up and down a continuum that ranges between broad, meaningless statements and little purse-lipped creative dictums masquerading as strategies.

When you have it just right, the strategy should be evident in the campaign but the campaign should not be evident in the strategy. Jean-Marie Dru put it elegantly in his book *Disruption:*

There are two questions that need to be asked. The first is: Could the campaign I'm watching have been created without the brief? If the answer is yes, the odds are that the campaign is lacking in content. You have to be able to see the brief in the campaign. The second question is a mirror image of the first. . . . Is the campaign merely a transcription of the brief? If the answer is yes, then there has been no creative leap, and the campaign lacks executional force.[14]

Ultimately, a good strategy is inspiring. You can pull a hundred rabbits out of the same hat, creating wildly different executions all on strategy. Goodby, Silverstein & Partners' magnificent "milk deprivation" strategy called forth a long string of wonderful "Got milk?" executions.*

Insist on a tight strategy. Will you always get one? No. In fact, in this business tight strategies seem to be the exception, not the rule. But you must push for one as hard as you can.

"Small rooms discipline the mind; large rooms distract it."

— *Leonardo da Vinci*

---

*Go online to one of the ad archive sites and study the campaign. Or see *Communication Arts,* December 1995, for examples.

The final strategy should be simple.

Advertising isn't "rocket surgery."

People live and think in broad strokes. Like we said earlier, ask some guy in a mall about cars and he'll tell you Volvos are safe, Porsches are fast, and Jeeps are rugged. Boom. Where's the genius here? There isn't any.

You want people who feel X about your product to feel Y. That's about it. We're talking one adjective here. Most of the time, we're talking about going into a customer's brain and spot welding one adjective onto a client's brand. That's all. DeWalt tools = tough. Coke = happiness.

I'm reminded of how Steven Spielberg said he preferred movie ideas that could be summed up in a sentence. "Lost alien befriends lonely boy to get home."

The moral is: Keep it simple. Don't let the account executives or the client make you overthink it. Try not to slice too thin. Think in bright colors.

Question the brief.

The most important word a creative person can use is *why*, as noted by John Hegarty in his book. Not only does the word *why* demand that we constantly challenge everything, but it also helps the creative process. It's like that wonderful thing children do; they constantly ask, "Why? Why is it like that? Why do we do that? Why can't I go there? Why? Why? Why?"[15]

Obviously, asking questions of the client, account person, or strategist can help clarify your assignment. But often the questioning itself helps you begin to come up with ideas.

Testing strategy is better than testing executions.

This is the best of all possible worlds, and the day hell freezes over all clients will be testing this way. A few do this now. Here's how it works.

You sit down with the client, the strategists, and the account team. You explore all the possible strategies available to your brand. You settle on 5 or 6 to 10, if you want.

Then you make what are some places called "strategy boards." These are simple, flat-footed layout things that look and feel like ads but aren't, usually consisting of a picture with a headline that spells out with little fanfare exactly the strategy you'd like to test.

For example, say the client manufactures aspirin. The pictures could be anything really—a shot of a person nursing a headache or a close-up of two aspirins on a tabletop. Next to the picture on each board is a headline pitching a different angle on the product: "Faster-acting Throbinex." "Throbinex is easy on the stomach." "Smaller, easier-to-swallow pills." Just crank them out. These aren't ads. They're benefits.

Show 10 different boards like these to a focus group, and you'll come away with a good idea of which messages resonate with customers. It's a great place to start.

Listen to customers talk.

Every chance you get to hear what customers are saying, take it. If there's a website or chat room about a product or brand, go there. Eavesdropping is the best way to learn what customers think, and with all the tools now available on the Internet, monitoring public opinion has become too easy *not* to do it

Less useful (and usually more infuriating) is to hear what customers are saying about your work in focus groups. God, I hate focus groups. There are probably just two things in the world I hate *more* than listening to focus groups complain about an agency's ideas. (For the record, the two things are [1] sawing off my legs and walking into town on the stumps and [2] kissing the side of a passing train that's covered in sandpaper and then bobbing for cherry bombs in a vat of boiling ammonia.) Focus groups suck, and I'm not the only person who believes that showing rough ideas to people being paid $50 and a Diet Dr. Pepper is a bane on the industry. Not only does it hurt creativity, the horrible work that survives doesn't make the client nearly as much money as it might have and may actually lose the company money.

Fortunately, as advertising becomes less television- and print-based, it's gonna get harder and harder for any research company to tell a client with a straight face that they're adding any value. (More on this later, in Chapter 11.)

Scan the places where your work will appear.

Go online to the sites your work will likely appear. Check out what customers are responding to; see what videos they're watching. Go to the bookstore and look at the magazines you might appear in. Case the joint. Get a feel for the place your idea will be living.

Read the awards books; study the sites.

Take a little inspiration from the excellence you see there and then get ready to do something just as great. The best awards shows are the One Show and *Communication Arts,* as well as the British D&AD annuals. You should also study some of the newer sites and awards venues, such as thefwa.com, the Webby's, and the SxSW interactive awards.

Look at the competitors' advertising.

Each category quickly manages to establish its own brand of boring. Learn the visual clichés everybody else is using. Visit their websites and watch their commercials. Listen to them on Twitter and on Facebook. Creep through the woods, part the branches, and study the ground your competitors occupy. What seems to be their strategy? What's their look? Those schmucks. They don't know what's coming.

Now comes the fun part. Sharpening your pencil and sitting down to come up with some cool ideas.

Figure 3.1   A short, five-word course in advertising.

3

A Clean Sheet of Paper

*Coming up with an idea—
the broad strokes*

BEFORE WE BEGIN, A QUICK NOTE. The first edition of this book came out in 1998—last century, basically. At the time, the possibilities of advertising online were just starting to be realized, and since then the number of other media used to deliver advertising has gone kaleidoscopic.

That said, to begin our discussion of advertising ideas we still have to start somewhere. And for the purposes of this book, we'll make the humble print ad our starting point. No, it's not interactive, and it doesn't link to other print ads. You don't have to go to L.A. to make a print ad, and it usually ends life under a puppy or a bird. But in its simple two dimensions and blank white space, it contains all the challenges we need to discuss the creative process. In the little white square we draw on our pads, we'll learn design and art direction. We'll hone our writing. We'll learn how to be information architects—how to move a reader's attention from A to B to C—and these basic skills will stay with us and prove critical as we move from print ads to tweets. As Pete Barry says, "Print is to [all of] advertising what figure drawing is to fine art; it provides a creative foundation."[1]

We'll be talking mostly about the crafts of copywriting and art direction, two disciplines that are infinitely portable. Everything you learn about writing and art direction here applies to pretty much any surface you're working on, from bus sides to computer screens. Yes, there are some nuances when it comes to online, writing for search optimization, for example. But overall, these are the disciplines *someone's* gonna need to have when it comes time to make an ad, shoot a Web video, or record a radio spot.

Let's begin this part of our discussion with a quotation from Helmut Krone, the man who did VW's "Think Small," my vote for the industry's first great ad: "I start with a blank piece of paper and try to fill it with something interesting."

So if I'm working on a print ad, I generally do the same thing. I get a clean sheet of paper and draw a small rectangle.

And then I start.

SAYING THE RIGHT THING THE RIGHT WAY.

Remember, you have two problems to solve: the client's and yours.

Imagine the circle in Figure 3.2 is the target's bull's-eye of what the brand stands for. Any ad you create that lands inside this area is perfect. The client will love it. If it's outside the circle, they won't. Nor should they.

Okay, now imagine you have two circles, overlapping (Figure 3.3).

The one on the left is the client's bull's-eye, and on the right is the bull's-eye for what you think is a great ad. The trick is to hit that sweet spot where the two circles overlap.

You solve the account team's and the client's problem by saying exactly the right thing. That's relatively easy; it's the strategy. But you aren't finished until both problems are solved—until you've nailed the sweet spot. Bernbach said, "Dullness won't sell your product, but neither will irrelevant brilliance." Here, dullness is represented on the far left side of the left circle, and irrelevant

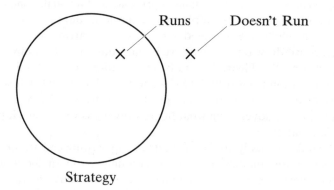

Figure 3.2   If your idea lands inside the client's brand space, the client will love it. If not, buh-bye.

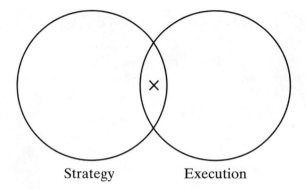

Strategy   Execution

*Figure 3.3   If your idea is only in the left circle, it
might be boring. Only on the right, it might be stupid.
Hit the sweet spot to win cash and prizes.*

brilliance, on the far right side of the right. In his excellent book *Advertising: Concept and Copy,* George Felton describes the circles this way:

> As you'll discover when you work on advertising problems, you often lose the selling idea in the act of trying to express it creatively. There is a continual push-pull between being on-strategy and being clever. Each wants to wrestle you away from the other. Your job as a thinker and problem solver is to keep both in mind, to spin the strategy without losing hold of it. As though to indicate this truth, the two most common rejections of your ideas will be "I don't get it" and "I've seen that before." In other words, either it's too weird or too obvious. That's why the great ones don't come easy.[2]

The moral? Do both perfectly. Hit the overlap.

Find the central human truth about your product.

Veteran copywriter Mark Fenske says your first order of business working on a project is to *write down the truest thing you can say* about the brand or the product. You need to find the central truth about your brand or about the whole product category. The central human truth. Hair coloring isn't about looking younger. It's about self-esteem. Cameras aren't about pictures. They're about stopping time and holding on to life as the sands run out.

There are ads to be written all around the edges of any product. But get to the ones written right from the essence of the thing. In *Hoopla,* Alex Bogusky is talking about this essence when he says, "We try to find that long-neglected truth in a product and give it a hug."[3] Notice he says they "find" this truth, not invent it. The best ideas are old truths brought to light in fresh, new ways. As an example, check out this ad shown in Figure 3.4, created by my friend Dean

*Figure 3.4   The headline could have been something boring like:
"We're proud of our wide variety of beautiful flower
arrangements. One's just right for your budget."*

Buckhorn for the American Floral Marketing Council. He could have done
something about how "purdy" flowers are. He didn't, and instead focused on
one of the central human truths about this category—the use of flowers as a
ticket out of the Casa di Canine.

"Tell the truth and run."

This old Yugoslavian proverb is a reminder of the power of truth. Even if you
have an unpleasant truth, say it.

"We're Avis. We're only number two. So we try harder." Totally believable.
More important, I like a company that would say this about themselves. America
loves an underdog.

Perhaps the biggest underdog of all time was Volkswagen. VW was the king
of self-deprecation. The honest voice Doyle Dane Bernbach created for this
odd-looking little car turned its weaknesses into strengths. The ad shown in
Figure 3.5 is a perfect example.

Identify and leverage the central conflicts within your client's company or category.

Typically you'll have plenty of help from your agency's strategists when it comes
to getting a deep understanding of the company and category you're working for.
As you help the team dig, what you should be looking for is energy and conflict.

In my experience, the best strategies and the best work usually come from
a place of conflict. Sadly, many agencies create "strategies" that look more like
their client's company mission statement. *"We believe fresh foods mean better
health."* Better, I think strategies are built on top of—and *powered* by—either

thematic or cultural tensions. When a strategy can be built on top of one of these tensions—like a volcano along the edge of two tectonic plates—great work is built *into* the strategy and fairly bursts out of it. There's a natural energy at these points of cultural stress, a conflict of ideas or themes that can be a fertile place for ideas of force and substance.

It makes your house look bigger.

Cars are getting to be bigger, so houses are getting to look smaller.

But one little Volkswagen can put everything back in its proper perspective.

A VW parked in front does big things for your house. And your garage. To say nothing of small parking spots and narrow roads.

On the other hand, a VW does make some things smaller.

Gas bills, for instance. (At 32 mpg, they'll probably be half what you pay now.)

You'll probably never add oil between changes. You'll certainly never need antifreeze. Tires go 40,000 miles. And even insurance costs less.

One thing you'd think might be smaller in a Volkswagen is the inside.

But there's as much legroom in front of a VW as there is in the biggest cars.

When you think about it, you really have only two choices:

You can buy a bigger house. Or a Volkswagen for $1,595.*

Figure 3.5 Many other clients would have urged the agency to avoid, hide, or deny the small size of their car. Not VW.

In *The On-Demand Brand,* the redoubtable Alex Bogusky discussed how his agency capitalized on these tensions:

> There are themes that are going through pop culture. And they're unsettling themes, questions. We find a little piece of that, and we try to hook our creative into that, so that when the work comes out, it's part of a larger conversation. And that it's going to stir a little bit of talk. . . . [W]ith something like "Subservient Chicken,"* a lot of that technology came out of [the] X-rated websites. That tension created, I think, a lot of what made that viral.[4]

For example, a thematic cultural tension might be "man versus machine." (Apple has been exploiting this tension since "1984.") Another thematic tension might be simply "depravation"; having something taken away from you is a platform leveraged for years by Goodby, Silverstein & Partners in their iconic "Got Milk?" campaign. Even the tagline has tension built into it; an unanswered question. Google "Got Milk?" and you'll find many entertaining commercials that *all* spring from that tense theme of deprivation.

Tension can also come from an actual conflict built into a category. Take a category such as banking. I happen to hate fat-cat bankers because they crashed the economy while tipping their golf caddies with my overdraft fees. My guess is other people feel the same way and that there's some emotion in this area, some conflict. With the right campaign these tensions could be leveraged in the right client's favor.

A great example of how tension sparks creativity is Fallon's famous "Cat Herders" Super Bowl spot for EDS. Their positioning statement had conflict built into it: "EDS thrives on defeating complexity"—a particularly powerful platform for a technical category.

Other category examples come to mind: there's tension in our love of cars, given they're how most of us get to work yet their exhaust hurts our planet. There's tension in simply being employed: we need the money, but we need to be ourselves, and we need time off.

Look for polarities. Where you find them you will also likely find tension. And where you find tension, you will find creative sparks.

A FEW WORDS ON AUTHENTICITY.

There was a time (the 1950s and early 1960s) when simply running an ad in a magazine made you an authority. *("See, honey, it's printed right here. In a magazine.")* A cigarette ad could actually claim there wasn't "a cough in a car load." Facts didn't count. Authority did. Pick up an old magazine sometime and see if you don't agree; almost every ad and every article feels like a pronouncement from an authority.

---

*The famous Subservient Chicken has been well reported on in many places. Google it.

Sometime in the mid-1950s, however, this omnipresent voice of authority started to lose its credibility. How this came to be is perhaps a story for another day, but it happened. Now, imagine if you were to run the 1950s Plymouth ad shown in Figure 3.6 in next week's *Time* magazine. I'll bet even if you updated the ad's look and feel, its presumptuous tone (*"Big is glamorous, dammit!"*) would still make today's readers snicker at its authoritarian cluelessness. You simply wouldn't get away with it today. Things are different now.

We've become a nation of eye-rollers and skeptics. We scarcely believe anything we hear in the media anymore, and marketers can't make things true simply by saying they're true. In *The Art of Immersion,* Frank Rose writes, "People today are experiencing an authenticity crisis, and with good reason. Value is a

Figure 3.6   *This car is great because the manufacturer*
says it's great, dammit.

function of scarcity, and in a time of scripted reality TV and Photoshop everywhere, authenticity is a scarce commodity."[5] And although real authority certainly continues to exist in places, what people look for today, and what they believe in and are persuaded by, is authenticity.

Merriam-Webster says something is authentic when it actually *is* what it's claimed to be. This makes authenticity in advertising an especially tricky proposition, given that advertising is at its heart self-promotion and driven by an agenda. And yet although Americans today are suspicious of anyone with an agenda, being authentic doesn't always require the absence of an agenda, only transparency about it.

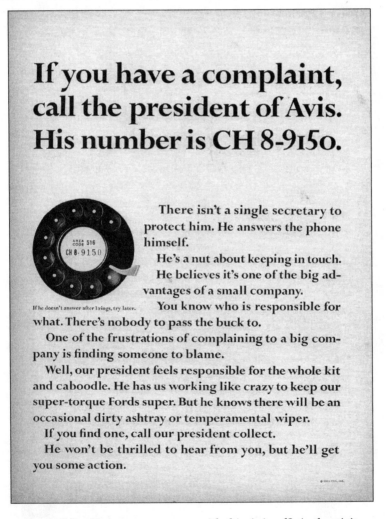

If you have a complaint, call the president of Avis. His number is CH 8-9150.

AREA CODE 516
CH 8-9150

If he doesn't answer after 3 rings, try later.

There isn't a single secretary to protect him. He answers the phone himself.

He's a nut about keeping in touch. He believes it's one of the big advantages of a small company.

You know who is responsible for what. There's nobody to pass the buck to.

One of the frustrations of complaining to a big company is finding someone to blame.

Well, our president feels responsible for the whole kit and caboodle. He has us working like crazy to keep our super-torque Fords super. But he knows there will be an occasional dirty ashtray or temperamental wiper.

If you find one, call our president collect.

He won't be thrilled to hear from you, but he'll get you some action.

Figure 3.7   How can you argue with this Avis ad? Authenticity isn't something you "claim." It's something you are.

Admitting that your commercial is a paid message with an agenda is one way to disarm distrust. Alex Bogusky says, "This generation knows you're trying to sell them something and you know they know, so let's just drop the pretense and make the whole exercise as much fun as possible."[6] Underpromising and overdelivering is perhaps another way to disarm distrust. Even self-deprecation can help establish authenticity; VW's "It's ugly but it gets you there" is perhaps the most memorable example. DDB's early Avis work was similarly authentic, whether it was admitting to shortcomings ("We're only number two.") or giving any customer with a complaint the actual phone number of the chief executive officer (Figure 3.7).

Canadian Club's masterful print series (Figure 3.8) is an excellent modern example of an advertiser leveraging reality, warts and all, to sell its wares. An

Figure 3.8   Compare this campaign to pretty much every other liquor campaign ever done. I actually believe this one. It's authentic.

unapologetic statement of "Damn right your dad drank it" coupled with images of 1970s dads (somehow still cool in their bad haircuts and paneled basements) leveraged authenticity instead of authority.

So too does a marvelous TV campaign for Miller High Life. In this, the second famous High Life campaign from Wieden + Kennedy, the beer truck delivery guy takes *back* cases of his beer from snooty people who aren't truly appreciating the Miller High Life. Grumbling on his way out the door of some hoity-toity joint *("$11.95 for a hamburger? Y'all must be crazy.")*, he is himself a spokesman for authenticity.

In *Hoopla,* Warren Berger puts it like this: "To effectively 'hype' something today, you must find a way to cut through 'the hype.' . . . This necessitates telling the truth." Bogusky points out, "There are truths to almost every product, and yet most advertisers shy away from those truths." As consumers get savvier, Bogusky continues, "the brands that are unwilling to have a real and truthful conversation with consumers will become completely irrelevant and therefore invisible."[7]

Try the competitor's product.

What's wrong with it? More important, what do you like about it? What's good about the advertising? As Winsor and Bogusky warn in *Baked In,* "Don't rationalize away what you [like about their product]. Find the truth they are exploiting that you are not."

Then try this trick. In *Marketing Warfare,* Ries and Trout suggested, "Find a weakness in the leader's *strength* and attack at that point."[8] A good example comes to mind, again from the pens of Bernbach's crew. Avis Rent A Car was only number two. So Avis suggested you come to them instead of Hertz because "The line at our counter is shorter."

Pose the problem as a question.

Creativity in advertising is problem solving. When you state the problem as a bald question, sometimes the answers suggest themselves. Take care not to simply restate the problem in the terms in which it was brought to you; you're not likely to discover any new angles. Pose the question again and again, from entirely different perspectives.

In his book *The Do-It-Yourself Lobotomy,* Tom Monahan puts it this way: "Ask a better question." By that he means a question to which you don't know the answer. He likens it to "placing the solution just out of your reach," and in answering it, you stretch yourself.[9]

As philosopher John Dewey put it: "A problem well-stated is a problem half-solved." It can work. Eric Clark reminds us just how it works in his book *The Want Makers.*

In the 1960s, a team wrestled for weeks for an idea to illustrate the reliability of the Volkswagen in winter. Eventually they agreed that a snowplow driver would make an excellent spokesperson. The breakthrough came a week later when one of the team wondered aloud, "How does the snowplow driver get to his snowplow?"[10]

If you've never seen it, the VW "Snowplow" commercial is vintage Doyle Dane. A man gets in his Volkswagen and drives off through deep snow into a blizzard. At the end, we see where he's driving: the garage where the county snowplows are parked. The voice-over then asks, "Have you ever wondered how the man who drives a snowplow . . . drives *to* the snowplow? This one drives a Volkswagen. So you can stop wondering."

Don't be afraid to ask dumb questions.

That blank slate we sometimes bring to a problem-solving session can work in our favor. We ask the obvious questions that people too close to the problem often forget. In the question's very naïveté, we sometimes find simple answers that have been overlooked.

Ask yourself what would make you want to buy the product.

This is a simple enough piece of advice and one I often forget about while I'm busy trying to write an ad. Sit across from yourself at your desk. Quiet your mind. Then ask, "What would make me want to buy this product?"

Then try the flip side: "What would I do if I were the one bankrolling the campaign?"

There was a writer at my agency who was also an investor in a new product, some kind of running gear. He was both the writer and the client. When he sat down to do ads for a company whose failure would cost him a significant amount of money, he saw how some of the things he hated hearing from clients had merit.

Copywriter John Matthews wrote, "You learn a lot more about poker when you play for money and not for chips."

Dramatize the benefit.

I don't mean the features of the product, but the benefit those features provide the user, or what some call "the benefit of the benefit." There is an old advertising maxim that expresses this wisdom in a way that's hard to improve upon: "People don't buy quarter-inch drill bits. They buy quarter-inch holes."

Avoid style; focus on substance.

Remember, styles change; typefaces and design and art direction, they all change. Fads come and go. But people are always people.

They want to look better, to make more money; they want to feel better, to be healthy. They want security, attention, and achievement. These things about people aren't likely to change. So focus your efforts on speaking to these basic needs, rather than tinkering with the current visual affectations. Focus first on the substance of what you want to say. Then worry about how to say it.

Find a villain.

Find a bad guy you can beat up in the stairwell. Every client has an enemy, particularly in mature categories, where growth has to come out of somebody else's hide.

Your enemy can be the other guy's scummy, overpriced product. It can also be some pain or inconvenience the client's product spares you. If the product's a toothpaste, the villain can be tooth decay, the dentist, the drill, or that little pointy thing Laurence Olivier used on Dustin Hoffman in *Marathon Man.* ("Is it safe?") A villain can come from another product category altogether, in the form of what's called an *indirect competitor.* Parker Pens, for example, could be said to have an indirect competitor in e-mail.

A gracefully raised knee to a villain's groin isn't just fun; it's profitable — because competitive positioning is implicit in every villain paradigm.

It's also an easy and fun place from which to write. Mom was always telling us about "constructive criticism." Yeah, well highly underrated and much more fun is the concept of "destructive criticism."

Make the claim in your ad something that is incontestable.

Since an advertising idea is basically an argument on behalf of a brand, it makes sense to present a case good enough to end any further argument — with facts; facts that can't be refuted. This approach is often referred to as the "Hey Schmuck" approach and is ascribed to Hall of Fame copywriter Ed McCabe. McCabe's work was often so compellingly put, it was as if you could tack the words ". . . you schmuck" at the end of his headlines; for example, this one for Volvo: "A car you swear by, not at." (You schmuck.)

Form your strongest argument, advises Pete Barry in *The Advertising Concept Book,* and then think of a counterargument you might hear from some loud guy at a bar. Okay, now create a comeback that sinks this guy's boat. "If you [can think of a comeback] that would shut him up, you should consider working on a campaign based on this argument."[11]

Of course, there are products to which this advice won't apply: products that are all image or products with no real difference worth hanging your hat on like, I don't know, paper clips. But when you have a fact at your command, use it. When you can say, "This product lasts 20 years," what's to argue with?

The lesson? State fact, not manufactured nonsense about, oh, say, how "We Put the 'Qua' in 'Quality.'"

Try some of these "strategy starters" and see if ideas start to form.

- Do a straight on us vs. them approach.
- Show life before and after the product.
- Instead of trying to change how consumers think, change what they *do*.
- Is there a compelling story about the heritage behind your brand?
- Can your brand dispense some smart advice about the whole category?
- Is there a story in the founders of the brand? Or in their original vision?
- Can you turn a perceived negative attribute of your product into a positive?
- Can you demonstrate on-camera or online your product's superiority?
- Can you move your product out of its current category and reposition it in another?
- Can your brand be insanely honest about itself, admitting to some short-comings while winning on the important thing?

———

GET SOMETHING, ANYTHING, ON PAPER.

The artist Nathan Oliveira wrote, "All art is a series of recoveries from the first line. The hardest thing to do is put down the first line. But you must." Here are some ideas to help you get started.

First, say it straight. Then say it great.

To get the words flowing, sometimes it helps to simply write out what you want to say. Make it memorable, different, or new later. First, just say it.

Try this. Begin your headline with: "This is an ad about . . . " And then keep writing. Who knows? You might find, by the time you get to the end of a sentence, you have something just by snipping off the "This is an ad about" part. Even if you don't, you've focused, a good first step.

Whatever you do, just start writing. Don't let the empty page (what Hemingway called "the white bull") intimidate you. Go for art later. Start with clarity.

Restate the strategy and put some spin on it.

Think of the strategy statement as a lump of clay. You've got to sculpt it into something interesting to look at. So begin by taking the strategy and saying it some other way, any way. Say it faster. Say it in English. Say it in slang. Shorten it. Punch it up. Try anything that will change the strategy statement from something you'd overhear in an elevator at a sales convention to a message you'd see spray painted on an alley wall.

Club Med's tagline could have been "A Great Way to Get Away." It could have been "More Than Just a Beach." Fortunately, Ammirati & Puris had the account, and it became: "Club Med. The Antidote for Civilization."

Be careful, too, not to let your strategy show. Many ads suffer from this transparency, and it happens when you fail to put enough creative spin on the strategy. Your ad remains flat and obvious; there's no magic to it, and reading it is a bit of a letdown. It's like Dorothy discovering that the Wizard of Oz is just some knucklehead behind a curtain.

In his book *Disruption,* Jean-Marie Dru described this kind of idea:

You can tell when ads are trying too hard. Their intentions are too obvious. They impose themselves without speaking to you. By contrast, there are some that grab your attention with their executional brio, but their lack of relevance is such that after you've seen them they leave you kind of empty. Great advertising combines density of content with the elegance of form.[12]

Density of content and elegance of form. Great advice.

Put the pill inside the baloney, not next to it.

Don't let your concept get in the way of the product. Bernbach said, "Our job is to sell our clients' merchandise . . . not ourselves. To kill the cleverness that makes us shine instead of the product." This can happen, and when clients kill work for this reason, they may be right.

From more than one client, I've heard this dreaded phrase: "Your concept is a 'visual vampire.'" What they mean is the concept's execution is so busy it sucks the life out of their commercial message. Be ready for this one. Sometimes clients use the phrase as a bludgeon to kill something unusual they don't like. But sometimes, a few of them are right.*

This usually happens when the product bores you. Which means you haven't dug deep enough to find the thing about it that's exciting or interesting. Or maybe you need to reinvent the brief. Or perhaps you need to reinvent the product. But instead, you settle for doing some sort of conceptual gymnastics up front and tacking your boring old product on the backside, hoping the interest from the opening will somehow bleed over to your sales message. But the interesting part of an ad shouldn't be a device that points to the sales message; it should *be* the sales message.

To understand what it means to make your whole ad or commercial *be* the sales message, consider the analogy of giving your dog a pill. Dogs hate pills, right? So what do you do? You wrap the pill in a piece of baloney.

---

*I'm reminded of a garage sale sign I saw tacked to a neighborhood phone pole. To attract attention to the sign, they'd decorated it with balloons. But the wind blew the balloons across the sign and obscured the information.

Well, same thing with your commercial's message. Customers hate sales pitches. So you wrap your pitch in an interesting bit, and they're more likely to bite.

Unfortunately, most students take this to mean, "Oh, I see. All I have to do is show something interesting and funny for the first 25 seconds and then cut to the product." The answer is no—because the customer will eat up the 25 seconds of interesting baloney and then walk away, leaving the pill in the dog dish. You gotta wrap that baby right into the middle of the baloney. The two have to be one. Your interesting device cannot just point to the sales message; it must *be* the sales message.

Remember Bernbach's advice: "The product, the product, the product. Stay with the product." Don't get seduced by unrelated ideas, however cool and funny they are.

David Ogilvy used a classical reference to make this same point: "When Aeschines spoke, they said, 'How well he speaks.' But when Demosthenes spoke, they said, 'Let us march against Philip.'"

What's the mood you want your reader or viewer to feel?

Emotional purchase drivers connect with customers more deeply than rational ones. In fact, emotion usually trumps rational thought when it comes to buying something. So get to the emotion your brand or product evokes. Finding that emotion is often all you need in order to get the ideas flowing.

The *one* thing I remember about the series *Mad Men* was a pitch Don Draper made to Kodak selling the campaign for their new slide Carousel (a round container for slides, an improvement over the ordinary trays available at the time). The emotion of the character's words seemed perfect for the product and I remember it to this day.

> DRAPER: My first job, I was in-house at a fur company, and this old pro copywriter, a Greek named Teddy, and Teddy told me the most important idea in advertising is new. It creates an itch. You simply put your product in there as a kind of calamine lotion. But he also talked about a deeper bond with the product: nostalgia. It's delicate but potent. Teddy told me that in Greek, *nostalgia* literally means "the pain from an old wound." It's a twinge in your heart far more powerful than memory alone. This device [gesturing to the Kodak Carousel] isn't a spaceship; it's a time machine. It goes backwards, forwards . . . takes us to a place where we ache to go again. It's not called the wheel. It's called the Carousel. It lets us travel the way a child travels . . . around and around . . . and back home again . . . to a place where we know we are loved.[13]

Deciding which emotion to leverage is something you'll do early in the process. And the answer is always a combination of what your product is and whom you are talking to. If you're working on a website for a hospital, well, pie-in-the-face humor probably shouldn't be on the list of likely solutions. Pick a mood.

A feeling. You can change your mind later, but sometimes making this decision can give you focus. "Okay, this campaign is gonna be . . . thoughtful." Or it's gonna be angry, or stark, or . . . well, *you* decide. What's right for your client? What's right for the customer?

Stare at a picture that has the emotion of the ad you want to do.

Once you've decided what the right emotion is, it may help to put up some pictures that put you in the mood. Think about it: have you ever tried to write an angry letter when you weren't angry? Oh, you might get a few cuss words on paper, but there's no fire to it. The same can be said for copywriting. You need to be in the mood.

I once had to do some ads for a new magazine called *Family Life*. The editors said this wasn't going to be just another "baby magazine," which are very much like diapers—soft, fluffy, and full of . . . . My point is, they wanted ads that captured the righteous emotion of the editorial. Raising a child is the most moving, most important thing you'll ever do.

To get in the mood, I did two things. First, I reread a wonderful book by Anna Quindlen on the joys and insanities of parenting called *Living Out Loud*. I'd soak up a couple of pages before I sat down to write. Then, when I was ready to put pen to paper, I propped up a number of different stock photos of children, including the picture shown in Figure 3.9 of a cute little kid in a raincoat sitting in a puddle.

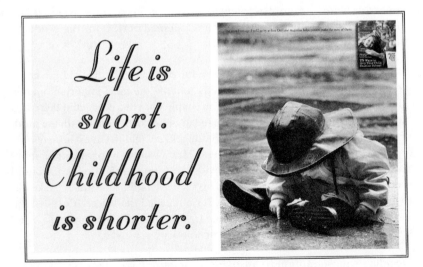

Figure 3.9   The headline was inspired by the photograph. The copy reads: "The years from age 3 to 12 go by so fast. Only one magazine makes the most of them."

As you can see in the ad reprinted here, the idea didn't come directly out of the photo, but in a way it did. It's worked for me. You may wanna try it.

Let your subconscious mind do it.

Where do ideas come from? I have no earthly idea. Around 1900, a writer named Charles Haanel said true creativity comes from "a benevolent stranger, working on our behalf." Novelist Isaac Singer said, "There are powers who take care of you, who send you patience and stories." And film director Joe Pytka said, "Good ideas come from God." I think they're probably all correct. It's not so much our coming up with great ideas as it is creating a canvas where a painting can appear.

So do what Marshall Cook suggests in his book *Freeing Your Creativity:* "Creativity means getting out of the way . . . If you can quiet the yammering of the conscious, controlling ego, you can begin to hear your deeper, truer voice in your writing, . . . [not the] noisy little you that sits out front at the receptionist's desk and tries to take credit for everything that happens in the building."[14]

Stop the chatter in your head. Go into Heller's "controlled daydream." Breathe from your stomach. If you're lucky, sometimes the ideas just begin to appear.

What does the *ad* want to say? Not you, the ad.

To hear what the ad wants to be, sometimes I picture the surface of my pad of paper as the bottom of one of those toy Magic 8 Balls. (You remember, the ones where the message slowly floated to the surface?) I try to coax the idea up from under the pad of paper, from under my conscious mind.

Try it. Just shut up. Listen.

In *The Creative Companion,* David Fowler says, "Maybe if you walked around the block you could hear it more clearly. Maybe if you went and fed the pigeons they'd whisper it to you. Maybe if you stopped telling it what it needed to be, it would tell you what it wanted to be. Maybe you should come in early, when it's quiet."[15]

Try writing down words from the product's category.

Most of the creative people I know have their own special system for scribbling down ideas. Figure out what works for you. For me—let's say we're selling outboard engines—I start a list on the side of the page: Fish. Water. Pelicans. Flotsam. Jetsam. Atlantic. Titanic. Ishmael.

What do these words make you think of? Pick up two of them and put them together like Legos. Sure, it sounds stupid. The whole creative *process* is stupid. Like I said, it's like washing a pig.

"Embrace the suck."

Once you get in the business, it's unlikely you receive assignments where the messaging is as simple, clear, and fun to tackle as, say, "It's the sourest candy you can buy" or "the biggest TV screen." Most of the time you'll be handed jobs where you have to talk about something that's maybe a little boring, or you may inherit some kind of dopey device or visual or slogan. It could be a client's geeky spokesperson, a long-running sale with a goofy name, or just some bad footage.

My advice here comes from Jason Elm, a creative director from Deutsch: If your assignment involves some must-have from the client that's geeky or boring, tackle it directly. Embrace the suck. Don't try to avoid it by doing something *you* think is cool and then burying the must-have in the corner or in the last 10 seconds of the commercial. Tackle it directly. When you embrace the suck, good ideas often spill out of the very thing your instincts tell you to avoid. It'll also likely result in executions where the pill is right inside the baloney because you've tackled it directly and not in some round-about way.

Allow yourself to come up with terrible ideas.

In *Bird by Bird,* her book on the art of writing fiction, Anne Lamott says:

> The only way I can get anything written at all is to write really, really crappy first drafts. That first draft is the child's draft, where you let it pour out and then let it romp all over the place, knowing that no one is going to see it and that you can shape it later. You just let this childlike part of you channel whatever voices and visions come through and onto the page. If one of the characters wants to say, "Well, so what, Mr. Poopy Pants?," you let her.[16]

Same thing in advertising. Start with "Free to qualified customers" and go from there. If it sounds like I'm asking you to write down the bad ideas, well, I am; there's something liberating about writing them down. It's as if you have to get them out of your system.

Also, remember this: notebook paper is not made only for recording your gems of transcendent perfection. A sheet of paper costs about one squin-tillionth of a cent. It isn't a museum frame. It's a workbench. Write. Keep writing. Don't stop.

Allow your partner to come up with terrible ideas.

The quickest way to shut down your partner's contribution to the creative process is to roll your eyes at a bad idea. Don't. Even if the idea truly and most sincerely blows, just say, "That's interesting," scribble it down, and move on. Remember, this is not a race. (Well, if it is, it's one of those nerdy three-legged races at the company picnic where you and your partner win or lose together.) You are not in competition with your partner. You are competing with your client's rival brands.

No matter what your partner says, see if you can take it and shape it and mold it. Then throw it back to him or her with your idea tacked on. In *Creative*

Advertising, author Mario Pricken likens this conceptual back-and-forth to a game: ". . . a kind of ping-pong ensues, in which you catapult each other into an emotional state resembling a creative trance."[17]

Share your ideas with your partner, even the kinda dumb half-formed ones.

Just because an idea doesn't work yet, doesn't mean it might not work eventually. I sometimes find I get something that looks like it might go somewhere, but I can't do anything with it. It just sits there. Some wall inside prevents me from taking it to the next level. That's when my partner scoops up my miserable little half-idea and runs with it over the goal line.

Remember, the point of teamwork isn't to impress your partner by sliding a fully finished idea across the conference room table. It's about how $1 + 1 = 3$.

That said, I feel the need to remind you not to say aloud every stinking thing that comes into your head. It's counterproductive. I worked with someone like this once and—in addition to trying to concept in a state of irritation—I ended up with a bad case of "idea-rrhea" that lasted the whole weekend.

Spend some time away from your partner, thinking on your own.

I know many teams who actually prefer to start that way. It gives you both a chance to look at the problem from your own perspective before you bring your ideas to the table.

Come up with a lot of ideas. Cover the wall.

It's tempting to think that the best advertising people just peel off great campaigns 10 minutes before they're due. But that is perception, not reality. My friend Jay Russell told me he remembers looking at more than 2,000 ideas—fairly polished, worked-out ideas—for the Microsoft phone campaign when he was at Crispin Porter + Bogusky. He said the pile of ideas he had stacked in the corner of his office came up to his waist. And this is without foam core, people.

As a creative person, you will discover your brain has a built-in tendency to want to reach closure, even rush to it. Evolution has left us with circuitry that doesn't like ambiguity or unsolved problems. Its pattern-recognition wiring evolved for keeping us out of the jaws of lions, tigers, and bears—not for making lateral jumps to discover unexpected solutions. But in order to get to a great idea, which is usually about the 500th one to come along, you'll need to resist the temptation to give in to the anxiety and sign off on the first passable idea that shows up.

In his fascinating essay "How to Have More Insights," neurologist Dr. David Rocks agrees, writing: "When we have a creative project we tend to get anxious and the uncertainty of not being able to find a logical solution creates anxiety in itself. The brain is primed to experience at least a mild threat from most forms of uncertainty. Learning to be okay with uncertainty is part of the process of having more insights, because the more anxious you are the less likely you are to notice any subtle insights."[18]

Learn to breathe through this anxiety and the ideas will start to come. Once they do, put as many of them up on the wall as possible. Linus Pauling says, "The best way to get a good idea is to get a *lot* of ideas. . . . At first, they'll seem as hard to find as crumbs on an oriental rug. Then they start coming in bunches. When they do, don't stop to analyze them; if you do you'll stop the flow, the rhythm, the magic. Write each idea down and go on to the next one."

Which leads to our next point.

Quick sketches of your ideas are all you need during the creative process.

Don't curb your creativity by stopping the car and getting out every time you have an idea you want to work out. Do details later. Just get the concept on paper and keep moving forward. You'll cover more ground this way.

Tack the best ideas on the wall.

Seeing them up there all in a bunch helps you determine whether there are campaigns forming and where there are holes that need to be filled. You keep working on the details on your pad. But up there on the wall the big picture begins to take shape.

Write. Don't talk. Write.

Don't talk about the concepts you're working on. Talking turns energy you could use to be creative into talking *about* being creative. It's also likely to send your poor listener looking for the nearest espresso machine because an idea talked about is never as exciting as the idea itself. If you don't believe me, call me up sometime and I'll describe the movie *Inception* to you.

There's an old saying: "A manuscript, like a fetus, is never improved by showing it to somebody before it is completed." Work. Just work. The time will come to unveil. For now, just work. The best ad people I know are the silent-but-deadly kind. You never hear them out in the hallways talking about their ideas. They're working.

Write hot. Edit cold.

Get it on paper, fast and furious. Be hot. Let it pour out. Don't edit anything when you're coming up with the ads. Then, later, be ruthless. Cut everything that is not A-plus work. Put all the A-minus and B-plus stuff off in another pile you'll revisit later. Everything that's B-minus on down, put on the shelf for emergencies.

"The wastepaper basket is the writer's best friend."
—Novelist Isaac Singer

Once you get on a streak, ride it.

When the words finally start coming, stay on it. Don't break for lunch. Don't put it off till Monday. You'd be surprised how cold some trails get once you leave them for a few minutes.

Athletes call this place (where everything is working, where all the pistons are firing) "the zone." Some artists call it "the white moment." I call it "that brief moment each week when I don't suck." The moral: Never walk away from a hot drawing pad.

Feed a baby idea lots of milk and burp it regularly.

Nurture a newly hatched idea. Until it grows up, you don't know what it's going to be. So don't look for what's wrong with a new idea; look for what's right. And no playing the devil's advocate just yet. Instead, do what writer Sydney Shore suggests: play the "angel's advocate." Ask what is good about the idea? Ask what do we like about the idea? Coax the thing along.

Does a medium lend itself to your message?

Some great ideas play off of the shape and size of the buy or are inspired by the very place they appear. You can arrive at these concepts by starting from a given medium and forming the idea, or coming up with an idea that requires a particular medium. To promote the German horror TV channel *13th Street*, Hamburg's Jung von Matt/Elbe turned bowling balls into creepy heads (branded on the "back" with the logo and tag: "Scream Your Head Off"). And for North Carolina tourism, the small size of a magazine ad is used to make their point (Figure 3.10).

Does the technology lend itself to your message?

Having a media person in the room with you off and on during the creative process can really help. These people know so much more than most creatives about the kind of venues out there, about what the consumer is reading, watching, and doing. Along with the creative technologists, they're often the first people in the agency to hear about new technologies. And as the line between idea and execution grows ever blurrier, it's likely the technology or the sites *themselves* will be what leads you to a cool idea.

The launch of the 1 Series on the BMW Graffiti Wall is a great example and one that began in the media department. For the launch of the 1 Series, BMW and GSD&M teamed up with the founder of the Graffiti application (very

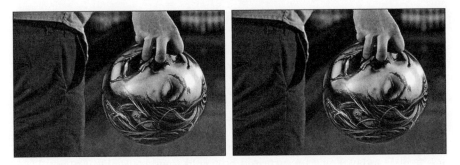

*Figure 3.10   Ideas that play off the medium where they
appear can be pretty cool.*

new at the time) to create the "Build Your Own" functionality on Facebook.
Knowing that the audience was young, interested in design, and highly aspira-
tional when it came to owning a BMW, giving people the opportunity to design
their own BMW with the application made perfect sense. Some customers spent
more than 5 hours interacting with the application, and *Forbes* called it one of
the best social media campaigns of the year.

If it makes you laugh out loud, make it work. Somehow.

You know those really funny ideas you get that make you laugh and say,
"Wouldn't it be great if we could really do that?" Those are usually the very best
ideas, and it's only your superego-parent-internalized client saying you can't do
it. You've stumbled on a mischievous idea. Something you shouldn't do. That's a
good sign you're on to something you should do. Revisit it. In fact, it often pays
to try to be naughty on purpose.

Try something naughty. Or provocative.

Sometimes the best way to bring the message home is to gallop into town and
splash mud all over decent citizens.

Naughty is good. It gets your client talked about, and with the capabilities of
today's social media, talk value is at an all-time high. So go over the line once
in a while and see what happens. And *please,* don't take this as permission to do
a "pee-pee" joke. If I see even *one* more ad with a sly nudge-nudge-wink-wink
reference to penises or to sex, I think I shall retire to my chambers, close the
door, and gently weep until dusk.

Remember, being provocative just because you *can* isn't the point. Like
Bernbach said, "Be sure your provocativeness stems from your product." The
ad shown in Figure 3.11 for the truth® youth-smoking prevention campaign
qualifies. Here's a client who wants to use the natural rebellious tendencies of

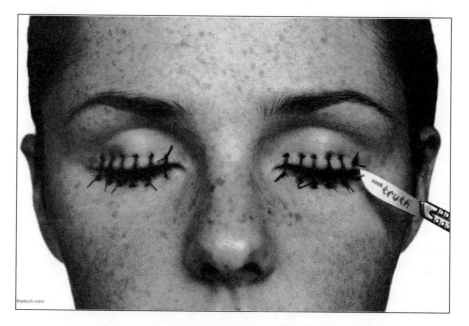

*Figure 3.11   Being provocative is good. Particularly when you
need to make people mad about something.*

teenagers and turn them on the lies of tobacco companies. It's exactly the right
time to pull out all the stops.

Maybe *naughty* isn't the right word. How about . . . *controversial? Provocative.*
My thesaurus also suggests: *devilish, sneaky, disobedient, mischievous, willful,
wayward, bad,* and *recalcitrant.* Do something you're not supposed to do. Break
a rule of some kind. Come up with an idea that makes you say, "We can't do
that, can we?" That's a sign it's a strong idea. The other question to ask is: "Will
somebody talk about this idea if we do it?"

Running a small-space ad with a headline "Fur Coat Storage Services" is
naughty. Well, it is when you know the rich ladies who called the number got a
recorded message from People for the Ethical Treatment of Animals about the
cruelty of the fur business and how they should "donate" their fur for proper
burial.

In Warren Berger's book *Hoopla,* Crispin Porter + Bogusky's Alex Bogusky
observes, "If you're about to spend advertising dollars on a campaign and you
can't imagine that anybody is going to write about it or talk about it, you might
want to rethink it. It means you probably missed injecting a truth or social tension into it."[19]

A truth. A social tension. Again, we come back to these themes of truth
and of tension. Think of truth, or social tension or naughtiness, as the bad guy
in a movie. Ever notice how the bad guy is usually a movie's most interesting
character? Kids wanna be Darth Vader, not Luke Skywalker. On Halloween,

I've never seen anybody wearing a Jamie Lee Curtis mask; it's always Michael Myers. Bad is good. The bad guy disrupts. He changes things, makes them interesting. Bad means gettin' some "Bom Chicka Wah Wah" from the Axe Effect or doing things in Vegas that have to stay there. Bad is why the "Subservient Chicken" was wearing a garter belt.

Do something devilish, disobedient, provocative, sneaky, mischievous, willful, wayward, bad, or recalcitrant. At every turn of the way, question authority.

Try doing something counterintuitive with a medium.

It's basically another form of naughtiness, using a medium "incorrectly." Why not write a 25-word outdoor board? Or put your poster in exactly the wrong place, like they did with this one for the *Economist* (Figure 3.12).

Why not use radio for something besides retail? What if you mailed your posters and posted your direct mail? What if you embedded a radio spot in your transit poster? What if you used the newspaper's classifieds to sell a thought instead of a car? What if you used a huge outdoor board to do the work of a classified ad?

Things get really interesting when you take this kind of thinking into the digital realm. Some folks call this *hacking*.

Burger King's Whopper Sacrifice was a form of hacking. BK asked Facebook members to delete 10 of their friends to get a free Whopper, which, if you think

Figure 3.12   The Economist's *signature red tells the reader whose poster this is from 100 yards away. And the pillars don't get in the way. They hold the concept up.*

about it, is precisely the "wrong way" to use that platform. But Facebookers loved the idea and soon the defriending started showing up on all kinds of activity feeds. Burger King and Crispin essentially hacked the Facebook system, turned the platform on its head and made it about disconnecting people.

Mullen hacked Twitter data to make their Brand Bowl app for the 2011 Super Bowl. The application simply monitored Twitter conversation around the Super Bowl television spots and ranked them based on the amount of conversation and preference. It was real-time feedback on a national scale and displayed in a simple easy-to-follow format.

To promote the release of the horror movie *The Last Exorcism,* Lionsgate used Chat Roulette, a notoriously pervy website where horny college-age males hoped their video feed would be randomly paired up with a pretty girl's. What viewers didn't realize was the pretty girl they had stumbled upon would stop in mid-strip and turn into a demon. Talk about creating an experience for a brand. The user reactions that Lionsgate captured later attracted more than five million views on YouTube (Figure 3.13).

As agencies get more adept at hacking the different emerging media, this sort of cross-platform creativity will become more common. These stunts tend to create a lot more talk value than what's traditionally been called advertising.

If you have to do an ad, does it have to be a flat page?

Try a pop-up, a gatefold, a scratch and sniff, a computer chip, something, anything.

Typically, liquor companies trot out these print extravaganzas during the holiday season, spicing their inserts with talking microchips and pop-up devices. But why wait for the holidays when other advertisers might be doing it? Also, there are less expensive tricks you can try. Sequential ads. Scratch-off concepts. Die cuts. Different paper stocks. Acetate film. There's even a magnetized paper now. What can you do with the ad itself to make it more than just an ad?

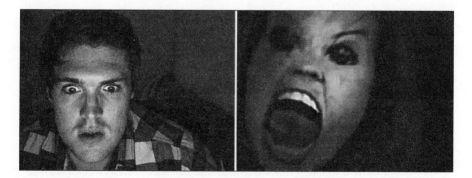

Figure 3.13   To promote The Last Exorcism, *Lionsgate Studios adds a demonic twist to the already-creepy Chat Roulette site.*

Crispin Porter + Bogusky's entire print buy for the MINI featured stunts like the one pictured in Figure 3.14. They had to; Detroit was outspending them in magazines 100 to 1. So their stunts weren't just a couple of one-offs for the holidays; almost every single MINI ad was a stunt, each one basically an event held into a magazine with staples. One ad had peel-off decals to put on your MINI. Another featured a car-deodorizing pine tree. My favorite was a flattened cardboard milk carton inserted into the magazine. The copy invited you to reassemble it to look like an empty milk carton, which was just the excuse you needed to get in your MINI and motor.

I've seen an ad for a beer that could be folded into a bottle opener. An ad for a green product that photo-reacted to sunlight. Another ad (for a suntan lotion and made of tinfoil) supplied its reader with one of those reflectors for under-the-neck beach tanning. Then there was the one where you put your iPhone on top of the face in the ad; when the mouth on screen moved it looked like the person in the ad was taking to you.

Remember, too, that a stunt doesn't always have to involve inserts. Check out the cool ad for the U.S. Air Force from GSD&M shown in Figure 3.15.

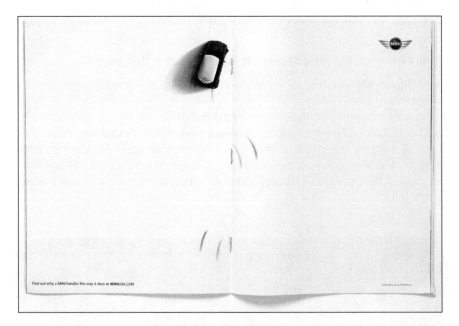

Figure 3.14   It's hard to see in this reprinting, but Crispin bought the center spread of Rolling Stone *magazine and had the MINI slaloming around orange-colored staples. The copy: "Find out why a MINI handles the way it does at MINIUSA.com."*

Dummy editorial copy on the left side is burnt to a crisp by the afterburners on the F-15.

Try not to look like, or act like, or sound like, or be like an ad.

People don't buy magazines to look at ads. They don't buy TV's to look at the stinkin' commercials. So why look like advertising? This doesn't mean you should make nonsense. But do we always have to look like an ad? An ad says, "Click to the next page" or "Turn off the TV" when it *should* say, "Pretty cool, huh? Where do you want to go next?"

Do you always need to stick a logo in the lower right-hand corner? Does it really need to be an ad? Can it be four 5-second TV spots? Can it be an inter-active display in Times Square? In Red Square? Can you turn a building into a QR code? Can your TV campaign be a soap opera? Or an opera opera? Can you make it a video game? An alternate reality game (ARG)? Try to make your message be *anything* but an ad. (We'll talk more about this stuff in Chapters 5 and 6.)

Remember: Do something devilish, disobedient, provocative, sneaky, mis-chievous, willful, wayward, bad, or recalcitrant. At every turn of the way, ques-tion authority.

―――――

"DO I HAVE TO DRAW YOU A PICTURE?"

"Do I want to write a letter or send a postcard?"

In his book *Cutting Edge Advertising,*[20] Aitchison offers up this early fork in the road. Do you want to write a letter or just drop a postcard? On a sliding scale, with all visual on one side and all verbal on the other, what's the right mix for your product and your message?

A postcard, says Aitchison, is an idea that's visually led. A single visual and a small bit of copy are all that are needed to make the point. For example, to demonstrate the cool technology in the new Mercedes (Figure 3.16), the cre-atives used mostly type but there's some art direction at work here too. But it's still very simple and is just a quick postcard from Mercedes making one quick point.

Another example of a more digital nature is the Kraft Macaroni & Cheese smile banner from Kraft and Crispin Porter + Bogusky (Figure 3.17). The simple challenge: show us you love it. The answer: a noodle that mimics the smile on your face via motion detection and the camera on your computer. A simple, entertaining, involving little postcard to get the point across.

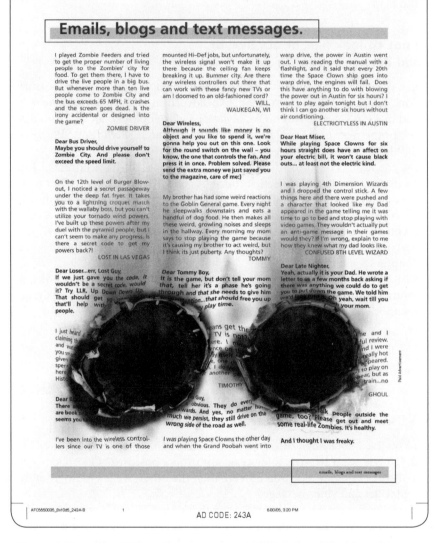

Figure 3.15a   The F-15 on the next page is torching the editorial on this page.

On the other hand, a letter is an ad that's predominantly copy-driven. It's probably better for ads that have to deliver a more complex message. Just the sheer weight of the body copy adds a sense of gravitas to the product regardless of whether the consumer reads a word of the copy. Check out the beautiful ad for Land Rover done by my friends at GSD&M (Figure 3.18).

You'll see both letter ads and postcard ads throughout this book. Take a look at how each visual or verbal format serves the different messages the brands are trying to convey.

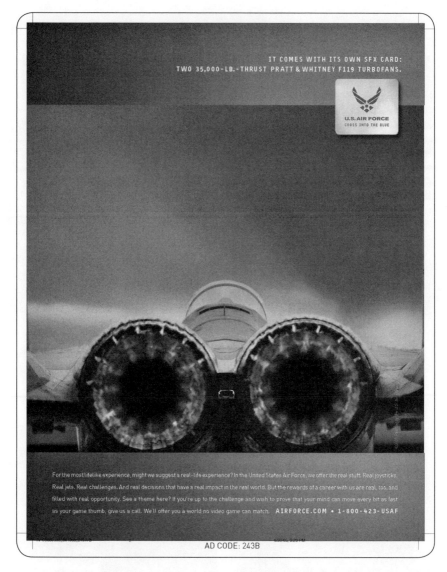

Figure 3.15b (continued)

See what it looks like to solve it entirely with the visual.

The screen saver on the computers at London's Bartle Bogle Hegarty reads, "Words are a barrier to communication." Creative director John Hegarty says, "I just don't think people read ads."

I don't think most people read ads, either—at least not the body copy. There's a reason they say a picture is worth a thousand words. When you first picked up this book, what did you look at? I'm betting it was the pictures.

Figure 3.16 "The first brake that reads the street."
An example of a postcard ad.

Figure 3.17 Postcards can be digital, too.
http://creativity-online.com/work/kraft-macaroni-cheese-show-your-love-banner/20363

Granted, if you interest readers with a good visual or headline, yes, they may go on to read your copy. But the point is, visuals work fast. As the larger brands become globally marketed, visual solutions will become even more important. They translate, not surprisingly, better than words.

Figure 3.18 "If we've learned one thing in 20 years of building Range Rovers, it is this. An ostrich egg will feed eight men." Followed by 630 words of Gold One Show body copy.

Figure 3.19   Long copy ads can be great. This is not one of them.

The ad for Mitsubishi's Space Wagon (Figure 3.19) from Singapore's Ball Partnership is one of my all-time favorites. The message is delivered entirely with one picture and a thimbleful of words. What could you possibly add to or take away from this concept?

Relying on one simple visual means it assumes added responsibilities and a bigger job description. You can't bury your main selling idea down in the copy. If readers don't get what you're trying to say from the visual, they won't get it. The page is turned.

Don't take my word for it. Watch people in the airport read a magazine. They whip through, usually backward, at about two seconds per page. They glance at the clock on the wall. They check their iPhone. They turn a page. They think about the desperate, pimpled loneliness of their high school years. They look at a page. They see your ad.

If you can reduce your idea to one simple thing that gets a customer to *lean in,* your ad is a resounding success. Break out the Champale. Call your parents. You are a genius.

Coax an interesting visual out of your product.

One day when he was a little boy, my son, Reed, and I were playing and we stumbled upon a pretty good mental exercise using his toy car. I held the car in its traditional four-wheels-to-the-ground position and asked him, "What's this?" "A car," he said. I tipped it on its side. Two wheels on the ground made the image a "motorcycle." I tipped the car on its curved top. He saw a hull and declared it a "boat." When I set it tailpipe to ground, pointing straight up, he saw propulsion headed moonward and told me, "It's a rocket!"

Look at your product and do the same thing.

Visualize it on its side. Upside down. Make its image rubber. Stretch your product visually six ways to Sunday, marrying it with other visuals, other icons, and see what you get—always keeping in mind you're trying to coax out of the product a dramatic image with a selling benefit.

What if it were bigger? Smaller? On fire? What if you gave it legs? Or a brain? What if you put a door in it? What is the perfectly wrong way to use it? How else could you use it? What other thing does it look like? What could you substitute for it? Take your product, change it visually, and by doing so dramatize a customer benefit.

Get the visual clichés out of your system right away.

Certain visuals are just old. Somewhere out there is a Home for Tired Old Visuals. Sitting there in rocking chairs on the porch are visuals like Uncle Sam, a talking baby, and a proud lion, just rocking back and forth waiting for someone to use them in an ad once again. And grousing, "When we were young, we were in all kinds of ads. People used to *love* us."

Remember: Every category has its own version of Tired Old Visuals. In insurance, it's grandfathers flying kites with grandchildren. In the tech industries, it's earnest people looking at computer screens. And in beer, it's boobs. Learn what iconography is overused in your category, and avoid it.

Check out the ad for Polaris watercraft in Figure 3.20. It's just a wild guess, but I'm thinkin' this is probably the first use of a hippo in the Jet Ski category.

Figure 3.20   In the watercraft category, a Tired Old Visual might be a happy, wet family having a grand time waterskiing. That is why this marvelous ad stands out.

Show, don't tell.

Telling readers why your product has merit is never as powerful as showing them. Figure 3.21 shows the classic ad by BMP in London for Fisher-Price's antislip roller skates; it is a good example of the benefits of showing your story over telling it. It's one of my all-time favorites.

Historically, Volkswagen has been successful just telling people about their cars. But for the launch of their 2010 GTI, they let people experience it by announcing the car exclusively through an iPhone app. (That the car had a very tech-savvy audience made this media strategy less risky than it sounds.) Partnering with a gaming developer that already had a cool app on the market called *Real Racing*, they released a free version of this $6.99 app, *Real Racing GTI* (Figure 3.22). The rollout was a success, and it didn't hurt that they gave away six limited-edition cars to people who took the virtual test drive.

Saying isn't the same as being.

This is a corollary to the previous point. If a client says, "I want people to think our company is cool," the answer isn't an ad saying, "We're cool." The answer is to *be* cool. Nike never once said, "Hey, we're cool." They just were cool. C'mon, think about it. The Beatles didn't meet in the third-floor conference room and go over a presentation about how they were going to become known as cool. They just were cool.

The folks at Crispin Porter + Bogusky think the same way, focusing often on what they call proof points. As an example, for the MINI Cooper they could

Figure 3.21 The mental image this ad paints of two kids landing on their duffs is more powerful than actually showing them that way.

Figure 3.22   This app for VW's GTI gave users a small
but real experience of the brand.

have run a TV commercial that said, "Hey, America, this is one unconventional car that puts the fun back in driving!" Instead, they mounted a MINI on *top* of an SUV (typically the space where you strap down the fun stuff like bikes and surfboards) and drove the hulking gas-guzzler around town with a message that said, "What are you doing this weekend?" The damn car *fit* up there. And when you saw this thing drive by you on the street, it was more than just a claim of unconventionality and fun. It was proof.

As Miss Manners politely points out, "It is far more impressive when others discover your good qualities without your help."

"THE REVERSE SIDE ALSO HAS A REVERSE SIDE."

When everybody else is zigging, you should zag.

There was this really dumb supervillain in the old Superman comics, Bizzaro-Man. He did everything . . . opposite. It was really stupid (and cool). Try being Bizzaro-Man.

If your product is white sheets, write the headlines in mud. If your product is beautiful, show something ugly. If your product is an insurance ad, design it like a poster for a rock concert. Try writing your copy backward. Encircle the logo for your bank client with hot dogs. I'm not saying all this Bizzaro crap makes your idea great. But you should at least search as far outside the boundaries of convention as you can. It's likely you'll end up pulling back a bit, but you won't know what's out there until you go.

Steve Dunn, a fabulous art director from London, put it this way: "One thing I recommend is at some point you should turn everything on its head. Logos usually go lower right, so put them top left. Product shots are usually small, make them big. Instead of headlines being more prominent than the body copy, do the opposite. It's perverse, but I'm constantly surprised how many times it works."[21]

Winsor and Bogusky hit on this same topic in *Baked In*. They encourage people to figure out how to do something "perfectly wrong."

The key here is the word *perfectly*. To design something wrong is easy. A little wrong is no good, and a lot wrong is even worse—whereas perfectly wrong can be perfect. The key? The wrongness must be in direct opposition to prevailing wisdom. The world is filled with perfectly wrong successes. A shoe with the toe higher than the heel? Earth shoes. A car shaped like a box? Scion.[22]

Don't be different just to be different.

You must have a reason to zag, one beyond just the desire to be different. Bill Bernbach said it best:

> Be provocative. But be sure your provocativeness stems from your product. You are not right if in your ad you stand a man on his head just to get attention. You are right if [it's done to] show how your product keeps things from falling out of his pockets. Merely to let your imagination run riot, to dream unrelated dreams, to indulge in graphic acrobatics is not being creative. The creative person has harnessed his imagination. He has disciplined it so that every thought, every idea, every word he puts down, every line he draws . . . makes more vivid, more believable, more persuasive the . . . product advantage.[23]

Consider the opposite of your product.

What doesn't the product do? Who doesn't need the product? When is the product a waste of money? Study the inverse problem and see where negative thinking leads.

I saw a great opposite idea in a student book. It was a small poster for a paint manufacturer that painters could put up after their job was finished. Above the company's logo, this warning: "Dry Paint."

Avoid the formula of saying one thing and showing another.

"Your kids deserve a licking this summer" . . . and then you have a picture of some kids with lollipops. Get it?

Again, this isn't a rule. But if you use this sort of setup, make sure the difference between word and picture is breathtaking. The polarity between the two should fairly crackle. A good example is the ad from Leagas Delaney shown in Figure 3.23.

*Figure 3.23   A good example of image playing off word,
done by some naughty British boys.*

Move back and forth between wide-open, blue-sky thinking and critical analysis.

It's like this: Up there in my brain, there's this poet guy. Smokes a lot. Wears black. He's so creative. And chicks dig 'im. He's got a million ideas. But 999,000 of them suck. He knows this because there's also a certified public accountant up there who tells him so.

"That won't work. You *suck.*"

The CPA is a no-nonsense guy who clips coupons and knows how to fix the car when the poet runs it into the ditch on his way to Beret World. Between the two of them, though, I manage to come up with a few ideas that actually work.

The trick is to give each one his say. Let the poet go first. Be loose. Be wild. Then let the CPA come in, take measurements, and see what actually works. I sense that I'm about to run this metaphor into the ground, so I'll just bow out here by saying, go back and forth between wild dorm-room creativity and critical dad's-basement analysis, always keeping your strategy statement in mind.

Make sure you don't get stuck always doing the ol' exaggeration thing.

Sometimes I think there's this tired old computer program inside every copywriter's and art director's head. I call this programming circuitry the *Exaggeration chip.*

Say you're doing an ad for, oh, a water heater. The Exaggeration chip's first 100 ideas will be knee-jerk scenarios about how cold the water will be if you don't buy this water heater: *"What if we had, like, ice cubes comin' out of the water faucet. See? 'Cause it's so cold, the water faucet will have like ice cubes, see? Ice cubes . . . 'cause . . . 'cause they're cold."*

Now, granted, there are plenty of great commercials out there that use exaggeration to great effect. I'll just warn you that the E-chip is typically the first mental program many creatives will apply to a problem.

> Buy a lottery ticket and you'll be so rich that _____ . (Fill in with I'm-really-rich jokes here.)

> Buy this car and you'll go so fast that _____ . (Insert cop-giving-ticket jokes here.)

It's just a little too easy. But here's the other thing. The E-chip will rarely lead you to a totally unexpected solution. You'll likely end up somewhere in the same neighborhood as you started, just a little further out on the whacky edge, but still nearby. A place you will likely share with everybody else who's working on the problem with an E-chip. In which case, it'll simply come down to who has the wackiest exaggeration.

I'm not sayin' it's off-limits. Just be *aware* when you're employing the Exaggeration chip. Pete Barry further cautions that if you're going to do an exaggeration scenario, make sure you base it on a truth; otherwise, you have an only silly contrivance—as in this cousin of the E-chip Teressa Iezzi identifies in her book *The Idea Writers:* the "I'm so distracted by the awesome nature of the product that I didn't notice (insert outrageous visual phenomenon here!!)."[24]

A tired old idea to which we say . . . *"Meh."*

Interpret the problem using different mental processes.

From a book called *Conceptual Blockbusting,* by James Adams, I excerpt this list[25]:

build up	dissect	transpose
eliminate	symbolize	unify
work forward	simulate	distort
work backward	manipulate	rotate
associate	transform	flatten
generalize	adapt	squeeze
compare	substitute	stretch
focus	combine	abstract
purge	separate	translate
verbalize	vary	expand
visualize	repeat	reduce
hypothesize	multiply	understate
define	invert	exaggerate

Put on different thinking caps.

How would the folks at today's top agencies solve your problem? R/GA, for instance. How would they solve it at Crispin Porter + Bogusky? At Goodby, Silverstein & Partners? How would they approach your problem at Pixar? At Google?

Shake the Etch A Sketch in your head, start over constantly, and come at the problem from wildly different angles. Don't keep sniffing all four sides of the same fire hydrant. Run like a crazed dog through entire neighborhoods.

Whenever you can, go for an absolute.

This will be hard because in today's market there are often very few differences between a product and that of its competitors. What usually happens here is that the client or agency ends up trying to leverage some rice-paper-thin difference that nobody gives a fig about. *("Legal won't let us say anything else.")* But try your hardest *not* to settle for an "-er." As in a product being *quieter.* Or *faster.* Or *cleaner.* Go for an absolute; go for an "-est." *Quietest, fastest, cleanest;* that's all people will remember anyway. All the rest of the claims in that middle ground are boring.

Metaphors must've been invented for advertising.

They aren't always right for the job, but when they are, they can be a quick and powerful way to communicate. Shakespeare did it: "Shall I compare thee to a summer's day?"

In my opinion (and the neo-Freudian Carl Jung's), the mind works and moves through and thinks in and dreams in symbols. Red means ANGER. A dog means LOYAL. A hand coming out of water means HELP. Ad people might say that each of these images has "equity," something they mean by dint of the associations people have ascribed to them over the years. You may be able to use this equity to your client's advantage, particularly when the product or service is intangible such as, say, insurance. A metaphor can help make it real.

What makes metaphors particularly useful to your craft is they're a sort of conceptual shorthand and say with one image what you might otherwise need 20 words to say. They get a lot of work done quickly and simply.

The trick is doing it well. Just picking up an image/symbol and plopping it down next to your client's logo won't work. But when you can take an established image, put some spin on it, and use it in some new and unexpected way that relates to your product advantage, things can get pretty cool.

As soon as I put those words on paper, I remembered an execution from the marvelous British campaign for the *Economist.* Reprinted here (Figure 3.24), an unadorned keyhole is simply plopped down next to the logo. One stroke is all it takes to give the impression that this business magazine has inside information on corporations. So much for rules.

Figure 3.24   Metaphor as ad. Keyhole = competitive business information.

Still, I stand by the advice. Symbols lifted right off the rack usually won't fit your communication needs and typically need some spin put on them.

Example: By overlaying the image of stairs descending into the ocean, the creative team is able to paint a very quick picture of what awaits you at the Sydney Aquarium (Figure 3.25).

Verbal metaphors can work equally well. I remember a great ad from Nike touting their athletic wear for baseball. Below the picture of a man at bat, the headline read, "Proper attire for a curveball's funeral." In Figure 3.26, another verbal metaphor is put to good use to describe the feeling of flooring it in a Porsche.

"Wit invites participation."

Part of what makes metaphors in ads so effective is that they involve the reader. They use images already in the reader's mind, twist them to the message's purpose, and ask the reader to close the loop for us. There are other ways you can leave some of the work to the reader, and when you do it correctly, you usually have a better ad.

Here's an example. Nikon cameras ran an ad with the headline: "If you can picture it in your head, it was probably taken with a Nikon." Above this headline were four solid black squares, and inside each square was a small headline in white type describing a famous photograph.

"A three-year-old boy saluting at his father's funeral."

"A lone student standing in front of four tanks."

"An American President lifting his pet beagle up by the ears."

"A woman crying over the body of a student shot by the National Guard."

*Figure 3.25   Metaphors use concepts you already understand
to help you see new concepts.*

Instead of showing these famous photos, the negatives are developed in the reader's head. The reader sees JFK Jr. He sees Tiananmen Square. He sees LBJ and Kent State. "Hey, I know all these photos." The reader connects the dots and, in doing so is rewarded for applying intelligence, rewarded for staying with the ad. The client is rewarded, too, with a reader actively closing the loop between the famous photos and the cameras that took them.

*Figure 3.26   Verbal metaphors work just as well as visual ones.**

In a great book called *A Smile in the Mind: Witty Thinking in Graphic Design*, authors McAlhone and Stuart say that "wit invites participation."

> When wit is involved, the designer never travels 100 percent of the way [towards the audience]. . . . The audience may need to travel only 5 percent or as much as 40 percent towards the designer in order to unlock the puzzle and get the idea . . . it asks the reader to take part in the communication of the idea. It is as if the designer throws a ball which then has to be caught. So the recipient is alert, with an active mind and a brain in gear.[26]

Their point about traveling "only 5 percent or as much as 40 percent" is an important one. If you leave too much out, you'll mystify your audience. If you put too much in, you'll bore them.

Testing the borders of this sublime area will be where you spend much of your time when you're coming up with ads. Somewhere between showing a picture of a flaming zebra on a unicycle and an ad that reads "Sale ends Saturday" is where you want to be.

Check out the marvelous VW ad shown in Figure 3.27. Isn't that a nice feeling? When the little >CLICK< happens inside and you get it?

*Figure 3.27   The reader leans in because something interesting is going on.
And then the reader gets it. Poof. A smile in the mind.*

The wisdom of knock-knock jokes.

Consider these one-liners from stand-up comedian Steven Wright: "If a cow laughed, would milk come out her nose? . . . When you open a new bag of cotton balls, are you supposed to throw the top one away? . . . When your pet bird sees you reading the newspaper, does he wonder why you're just sitting there staring at carpeting?"

Well, okay, *I* happen to think it's funny. In the last bit, for instance, the word *newspaper* begins as reading material and ends as cage-bottom covering. A shift has happened and suddenly everything is slightly off. I don't know why these shifts and the sudden introduction of incongruous data make our computers spasm; they just do.

You may find that jumping from one point of view to another to introduce a sudden new interpretation is an effective way to add tension and release to the architecture of an ad. That very tension involves the viewer more than a simple expository statement of the same facts.

Creative theorist Arthur Koestler noted that a person, on hearing a joke, is "compelled to repeat to some extent the process of inventing the joke, to recreate it in his imagination." Authors McAlhone and Stuart add, "An idea that happens in the mind, stays in the mind . . . it leaves a stronger trace. People can remember that flash moment, the click, and recreate the pleasure just by thinking about it."

A good example is the famous poster for VW from the United Kingdom, shown in Figure 3.28. As a viewer, you don't need it spelled out; in your head you quickly put together what happened, backward.

"And that, dear students," said the professor of Humor 101, "is why the chicken crossed the road." Suddenly, that's how this section on humor feels to

Figure 3.28   Does this ad rock, or what?

me. Pedantic. So I'll just close by saying that jokes make us laugh by introducing the unexpected. An ad can work the same way.

Don't set out to be funny. Set out to be interesting.

Funny is a subset of interesting. Funny isn't a language. Funny is an accent. And funny may not even be the right accent.

I find it interesting that the Clios, a highly overrated awards show with far too many categories, had a category called Best Use of Humor. And, curiously, no Best Use of Seriousness. Funny, serious, heartfelt—none of it matters if you aren't interesting first. Howard Gossage, a famous ad person from the 1950s, said, "People read what interests them, and sometimes it's an ad."

———

SIMPLE = GOOD, PART II.

If you take away one thing from this book, let it be this advice: simple is almost always better.

Maurice Saatchi, of London's M&C Saatchi, on simplicity: "Simplicity is all. Simple logic, simple arguments, simple visual images. If you can't reduce your argument to a few crisp words and phrases, there's something wrong with your argument."

"Simplicity, simplicity, simplicity!"

Henry David Thoreau, sitting in his shack by the famous pond, penned this oft-quoted line. Seems to me Hank needs a dose of his own medicine:

Simplicity, ~~simplicity, simplicity~~!

There. That's better. Do the same thing with your ads. That reminds me. There's an old axiom called *Occam's razor:* when you have two correct answers that both solve the problem, the more correct answer is the simplest one. Why? Because it solves the problem with fewer moving parts. It solves the problem more elegantly.

> "How difficult it is to be simple."
> —*Vincent van Gogh*

Simple is hard to miss.

I've always thought a stop sign is a perfect metaphor for a good ad. It makes me stop. It is relevant. It has one word. And most of all, it is simple. It says, "STOP."

There is no introduction to "stop." No asterisks are needed to understand "stop." You don't have to link to another site to understand it. And "stop" needs no snappy wrap-up. Google, Answers.com, and Wikipedia.com are good site examples of stop signs. You see their home pages and you know exactly what you're looking at and what you need to do.

So how is a stop sign different from a good ad in a magazine? I'm turning the pages and suddenly right in my face is a big, simple, relevant message. How can I ignore it? Check out the simple CNN piece shown in Figure 3.29. Every single extraneous thing has been shaved away.

Simple is bigger.

On May 7, 1915, a German U-boat sank a passenger ship, the *Lusitania,* killing some 1,190 civilians, many of them women and children. America was finally too angry to stay out of the Great War, and enlistment posters began to appear in shop windows, one of which is reprinted here (Figure 3.30).

Most other World War I posters were not as visual and instead used headlines such as "Irishmen, Avenge the Lusitania!" and "Take Up the Sword of Justice." Seems to me, all these decades later, they're not nearly as powerful as this one simple image, this one word.

Look at Google, one of the biggest brands in the world and the best search engine out there. Yet the simplicity of their home page could hardly be scrubbed down any further; in fact, it hasn't changed much since they first went online. It's

Figure 3.29   CNN cameraman as news source.

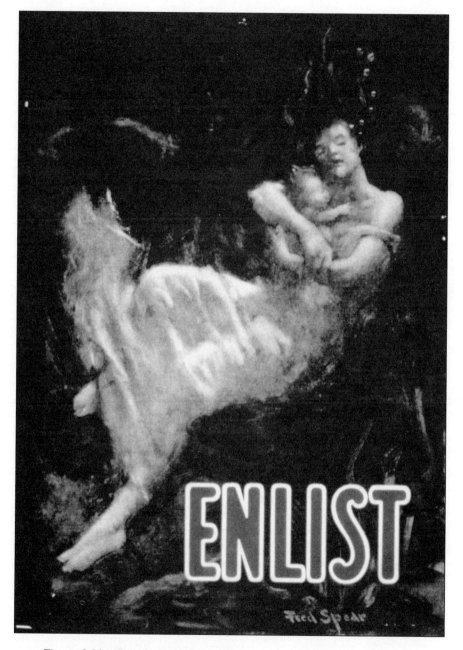

*Figure 3.30   Simple graphic images are powerful. Even decades later,
this World War I recruitment poster still works.*

very simplicity makes it easy to approach, easy to use. If they ever start adding stuff to the home page *("To see more links to YOUR favorite activities, click here!")*, I'll probably search somewhere else.

Remember, in a cluttered TV or print environment, and in a world where your customers are sometimes watching three screens at once, less is truly more. So have your radio spot be one guy saying 40 words. Have your print ad be all one color. Lock the camera down and do your entire TV spot on a tabletop. Show a scorpion walking up a baby's arm; I don't know. Just do something *simple.* Simple is big.

The artist Paul Cezanne said, "With an apple, I will astonish Paris."

Simple is easier to remember.

On a rainy November day in 1863, a U.S. senator named Edward Everett walked up to a podium and gave a two-and-one-half-hour speech consecrating a new cemetery. It was an impassioned speech, I'm sure, but I have been having trouble finding a transcript of this speech at the library.

The speaker who followed gave a 273-word speech, beginning with the words "Four score and seven years ago . . ."

Which of the two Gettysburg addresses given that day are you more familiar with?

Simple breaks through advertising clutter.

As we noted earlier, the only effective antidote to clutter is simplicity. How can anything else but simplicity break out of clutter?

Even the Super Bowl, with its annual collection of eye-popping TV commercials, has its own brand of clutter. Call it "pretty good clutter" if you will. But it's clutter just the same, and you have to find a way to improve what a scientist might call its signal-to-noise ratio. You have to break out. You can do that only with an idea of sparkling simplicity.

The commercial that introduced the ultrathin Mac Air computer was (as are most Apple spots) a study in simplicity. To the tune of a cool current song, viewers saw the open computer and got a look at its great screen. Then the machine was closed and slipped into one of those tan office routing envelopes, all against Apple's signature white background. That was it. I don't remember the copy but that hardly matters; they made their point visually. And did it so well I remember hearing a customer in my local Apple store ask to see "that envelope computer."

Keep paring away until you have the essence of your ad.

Let's start with three observations from three different men: one dead, one British, and one crazy.

Robert Louis Stevenson said, "The only art is to omit."

Tony Cox, a fabulous British writer: "Inside every fat ad there's a thinner and better one trying to get out."

And then there's Neil French, an absolutely stellar writer from Singapore. I had lunch with him one day and he walked me through this exercise in the art of omitting, of reductionism.

He started by drawing a thumbnail sketch of a typical ad (number one in Figure 3.31). You have your headline, your visual, some body copy, a tagline, and a logo.

Okay, he asked, can we make this ad work without the body copy? Maybe we could do that by making the headline work a little harder. We can? Good, let's take out the body copy. That leaves the slightly cleaner layout of number two.

What about that tagline? Is it bringing any new information to the ad? No? Then let's broom it. Look, the third layout's even better.

Now, about that headline. Is it doing something the visual can't do? And that logo—isn't there some way we can incorporate it into the visual?

Ultimately, Neil reduced his ad to one thing. He suggested I do the same with my next ad. Get it down to one thing. Sometimes it's just a headline. Sometimes a picture. Either way, he said, the math always works out the same. Every element you add to a layout reduces the importance of all the other elements. And conversely, every item you subtract raises the visibility and importance of what's left.

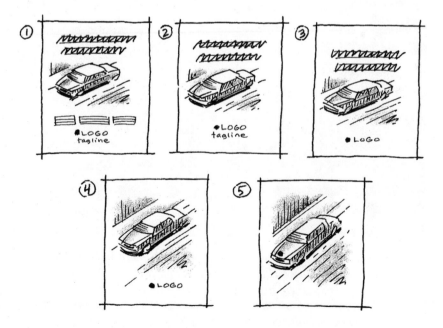

Figure 3.31　Neil's cool idea: reductionism. Ad number five is almost always going to be better than ad number one.

I admit, this kind of draconian reductionism is hard to pull off, especially when you have a client wanting to put more in an ad, not less. In my career I've done it only once. But to this day, that ad remains one of my favorites. It's the one you see here, reminding store buyers to stock Lee jeans (Figure 3.32). No logo. No headline.

The less you have to put in the ad, the better. The writer Saki said, "When baiting a trap with cheese, always leave room for the mouse."

When you have distilled a good idea into its simplest form, you're in the neighborhood of "great." This is where you wanna be. John Hegarty described great this way:

I always love the fact that, when you look back at a piece of really successful advertising, a great piece of work looks so simple. I suppose in many ways that's its hallmark—it looks bloody obvious. It's "obvious" because it is so right for the brand. And while it may all look simple, getting to that place takes sweat, perseverance, determination, intelligence and, of course, that thing that creativity provides: magic.[27]

Figure 3.32   It's hard to read as it's reprinted here, but the little warning sign says: "This changing booth is monitored by store personnel to prevent theft, particularly theft of Lee jeans, the #1 brand of women, something that would really cheese off our store buyers, especially now that Lee has lowered their wholesale prices and the store stands to rake in some serious profit."

A FEW WORDS ABOUT OUTDOOR.
(THREE WOULD BE IDEAL, ACTUALLY.)

Billboards, banner ads, posters, 15-second TV—they all force you to be simple.

These media may be some of the best places to practice the art of simplicity. Because there's no room to do much *else* other than get right to your idea. There's no drum roll here, folks, just cymbal crash.

It's been said that an outdoor board should have no more than seven words. Any more and a passing driver can't read it. But then you have to add the client's logo, which is one or two words. Now you're up to nine words. And if your visual is something that takes one or two beats to understand, well, in my opinion, you've already got too much on your plate.

When you think about it, is a banner ad any different? You're cruising along the Internet at about 90 clicks an hour and—zoom—what was that we just passed? *("Oooooo, was that a banner ad? Pull the car back around, honey.")* Given the speed of our passing audiences, I suggest draconian measures. Shoot for three words, tops. It doesn't mean you'll be able to keep it to three. But start with three as your goal. The board from the 1960s pictured in Figure 3.33 works with just one word.

Here's a great way to test whether your outdoor ad is simple enough and works fast. It's also a great way to present it to the client. Walk up to your client, holding the layout of your idea with its back to your audience. Say, "Okay, here's a board we were thinking about" and then flip it around and show them the idea for two seconds.

Just two seconds—one Mississippi, two Mississippi—then flip it back around again.

Check out the wonderful board in Figure 3.34 for a new flavor of Altoid's Curiously Strong Mints. It's marvelous. And it's fast. Two words and a product shot. You hardly have to count past one Mississippi to get it. Same thing for the

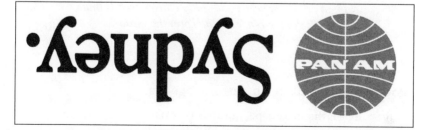

*Figure 3.33   This old 1960s billboard for Pan Am Airlines
does its job with one word.*

great board for the JFK Museum (Figure 3.35). One visual, three words. Elegant and very fast.

Your outdoor ideas will have to work just as quickly. Visualize precisely how your idea is going to be viewed by the customer. Car approaches, billboard whizzes by, and it's gone. Web surfer zooms by and is gone. If the ideas you're showing are as fast as the ones pictured here, this presentation technique can be persuasive. Remember, the rule is your idea has to go at least 65 miles an hour.

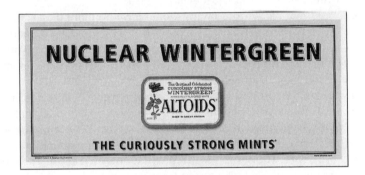

Figure 3.34   An example of a billboard so simple you could actually present it to a client in 2 seconds.
Reprinted with permission of Callard & Bowser-Suchard, Inc.

Figure 3.35   Three beautifully chosen words that make the reader reinterpret the visual.

Outdoor is a great place to get outrageous.

Big as they are on the landscape, outdoor boards are an event, not just an ad. In fact, what makes for a good print advertisement doesn't necessarily make for a good billboard. Whatever you do, don't create something just okay. The final size of a billboard out there in the world only magnifies how your okay idea is just

OKAY.

You don't wanna be just okay.

Check out the outdoor idea shown in Figure 3.36; it's way better than okay. Go Fast! is one of Amsterdam's more popular energy drinks. Y&R used Amsterdam's much-photographed canals as a place to launch water bikes with the Go Fast! logo on the side; water bikes driven by actors and powered by a fast, silent, and invisible motor. The cameras came out in droves and the idea ended up being viewed online by a global audience.

Outdoor begs for the ostentatious. Go for broke. Remember, you're in "made-you-look, made-you-look" territory here. Outdoor companies, prop makers, and tech firms can help bring just about any wild idea to life. And now with the confluence of the Web and mobile phones, people on the street can interact with boards. There are some good examples of this on the OBIE awards website.

Your outdoor must delight people.

Except for the handful of great ideas in the One Show every year, most of the outdoor I see really sucks. The thing is, when an idea sucks online, I click and it's gone. But if I live across the street from a bad outdoor concept, there's nothing I can do about it except close my curtains and drink myself to sleep.

Figure 3.36   An example of "outdoor as event."

Copywriter Howard Gossage didn't believe outdoor boards were a true advertising medium:

> An advertising medium is a medium that incidentally carries advertising but whose primary function is to provide something else: entertainment, news, etc. . . . Your exposure to television commercials is conditional on their being accompanied by entertainment that is not otherwise available. No such parity or tit-for-tat or fair exchange exists in outdoor advertising . . . I'm afraid the poor old billboard doesn't qualify as a medium at all; its medium, if any, is the scenery around it and that is not its to give away.[28]

The city of Sao Paulo, Brazil, has already outlawed billboards, and here in America, several states are weighing similar bans. (Yay.) So, until the day billboards are outlawed altogether (either as "corporate littering" or perhaps "retinal trespassing"), you owe the citizens of the town where your outdoor appears—you owe them your very best work. Let your work enrich their lives in some way. *Delight* them.

A FEW THINGS BEFORE WE BREAK FOR LUNCH.

Two questions to help you gauge the size of an idea.

"What is the press release of my idea?"

This first question is credited to the folks at Crispin, where creatives are often advised against presenting their campaigns by showing the TV, the website, the print, and the outdoor. Instead they're asked to answer the question: "What is the press release of your idea?" Is your idea cool as words on a clean sheet of paper? Do the words that describe something so interesting that the press would want to talk about it? A tall order, I know, but it gets easier when you quit trying to come up with "advertising ideas" and work instead on coming up with ideas worth advertising.

"Is my idea cool enough that people would seek it out and watch it on demand?"

This question comes from PJ Pereira of San Francisco's Pereira & O'Dell, who goes on to elaborate:

> When I started in advertising, I was taught to ask if my ideas were big. Today, I'd rather ask if they are interesting enough to be worth experiencing on-demand—not only as on-demand TV, but any form of user-initiated media consumption. . . . The good news is that contrary to what some people tried to make us believe, consumers don't mind being advertised to, as long as these ads are interesting enough for them. Otherwise, Nike's "Write the Future" wouldn't have reached seven million views on YouTube in less than five days.[29]

Learn to recognize big ideas when you have them.

There will come a time when you see a great idea in a One Show annual, a campaign that'll make you go, "Damn! I thought of that once!" It's a hard thing to see, "your" idea done—and done well. That's why you have to be smart enough to pursue a promising idea once you've stumbled onto it. I'm reminded of a line by Ralph Waldo Emerson: "In every work of genius we recognize our own rejected thoughts."

See that one idea you have up on the wall? The one that's so much better than the others? Investigate why. There may be oil under that small patch of land. A big idea is almost always incredibly simple. So simple, you wonder why nobody's thought of it before. It has "legs" and can work in a lot of different executions in all kinds of media. Coming up with a big idea is one skill. Recognizing a big idea is another skill. Develop both.

Big ideas transcend strategy.

When you finally come upon a big idea, you may look up from your pad to discover that you've wandered off strategy. Well, sometimes that's okay. Good account people understand this happens from time to time and will help you retool the strategy to get the client past this unexpected turn in the road.

My friend Mike Lescarbeau compares a big idea to a nuclear bomb and asks, "Does it really have to land *precisely* on target to work?"

Don't keep runnin' after you catch the bus.

After you've covered the walls with ideas and you've identified some concepts you really like, stop. And I mean covered the walls. This isn't permission to stop because you're tired or you have a few things that aren't half-bad. It's a reminder to keep one eye on the deadline.

Blue-skying is great. You have to do it. But there comes a time (and you'll get better at recognizing it) when you'll have to cut bait and start working on the really good ideas. You have a fixed amount of time, so you'll need to devote some of it to making what's good great.

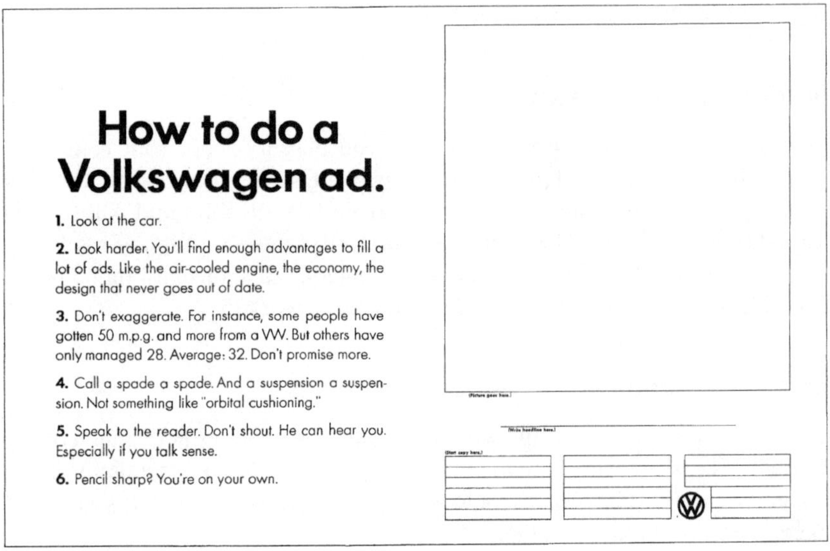

How to do a Volkswagen ad.

1. Look at the car.

2. Look harder. You'll find enough advantages to fill a lot of ads. Like the air-cooled engine, the economy, the design that never goes out of date.

3. Don't exaggerate. For instance, some people have gotten 50 m.p.g. and more from a VW. But others have only managed 28. Average: 32. Don't promise more.

4. Call a spade a spade. And a suspension a suspension. Not something like "orbital cushioning."

5. Speak to the reader. Don't shout. He can hear you. Especially if you talk sense.

6. Pencil sharp? You're on your own.

(Picture goes here.)

(Write headline here.)

(Start copy here.)

Figure 4.1   A short course in copywriting from one of the best teachers in the world: Volkswagen.

4

Write When You Get Work
Completing an idea—some finer touches

BEFORE WE START TALKING ABOUT DOING THE WORK, let's talk briefly about the spirit we bring to our craft.

WHATEVER YOU'RE MAKING, MAKE IT WAY BETTER THAN IT *HAS* TO BE MADE.

Remember how it felt the first time you held a new iPod or iPhone? Remember the delight you felt with every detail? The texture of the metal; the precious curve of the housing; the precise click of each button? I doubt I'm the only one who thought these angelic details made those little devices from Cupertino feel *perfect*—not just good, but *perfect*. At Apple, they call this design ethos making something "insanely great."

I call it making something way better than it has to be, and Apple isn't the only place you can enjoy the benefits of fanatical attention to detail. You can hear it in the slam of the door on a new Audi. Feel it in the delicious weight of a Waterford crystal glass. Or hear it in any Beatles song. (Sue me. I still love 'em.) All these things are made way better than they have to be.

As we begin to discuss the crafts of writing and art direction in more detail, I want to impress upon you here the importance of doing work that is insanely great, of employing these crafts to the very best of your ability. Because in the end they are all you have at your command to get a reader or viewer to *lean in.* And this leaning in is the ultimate goal for any artist, especially us advertising artists.

Let me describe leaning in this way: Over the years I've judged many advertising award shows, and for the print portion of these competitions, thousands of ads are laid out on a series of long tables. The advertising judges (usually slightly crispy from the carousing in the bars the night before) wander up and down the aisles looking for work they think worthy of recognizing and reprinting in the award annuals. During the many times I've watched the judges judge, I've always seen a magic little moment when the judge stops, bends at the waist, and leans in to more closely study a particular piece. What *is* it, I wondered, that made the judge lean in?

Over the years, I've come to believe the operative element is subliminal; not subliminal advertising the way Vance Packard complained about in his conspiracy book *The Hidden Persuaders.* No, the operative element we're talking about here is *subliminal quality.* The very word *sublime* helps explain my point. *Limen* is Latin for "threshold." *Subliminal,* then, is below the threshold of awareness. We're talking about baking quality so far into a thing that people who look at it perceive this quality subconsciously. They know they're looking at something of quality before they're even *conscious* of it because when a thing is made way better than it has to be, its quality comes off of it in waves.

In his marvelous book, *Paste-Up,* my old Fallon friend Bob Blewett agrees: "I believe the effort and struggle to create simplicity and grace live on in the work like a soul . . . and as the ad leaves the agency, your effort and care stand over the ad like a benediction."[1]

Blewett's benediction is the force I've been getting at here; the force that makes someone lean in to study whatever it is you've created. There's no shortcut around Blewett's requirement; it takes "effort and struggle to create simplicity and grace." It means sweating the details of whatever ad or script or site you're working on and going to any length to get it right—and then going beyond that. It means not letting even the smallest thing slide; if a thing bothers you even a teeny bit, you work on it till it doesn't bother you and then you keep working until it actually *pleases* you.

What you get for your trouble is described by Dave Wallace in his book on creative theory, *Break Out.* He likens the final approach toward a perfect idea to the sounds different kinds of glassware make. A so-so concept is like an ordinary jam jar. Hit it with your fingernail and you get an uninspiring tung sound. A tap on a nice wine glass might give you a tang. But a Waterford crystal idea, where you've done a thing perfectly, when all the molecules march in step and the stars align, there's that unmistakable ting.[2]

Tung. Tang. Ting. Don't stop until you get to ting.

Curiously, poet William Butler Yeats also used the metaphor of sound to convey perfection in an idea. He said the sound a good poem makes when it finishes is like "a lid clicking shut on a perfectly made box."

This extra effort is how *all* of life's pursuits are turned into art; yes, even advertising. An old man from Bali once patiently explained to an anthropologist studying his culture: "We have no 'art.' We do *everything* as well as possible." Not only will this unwavering attention to detail improve your craft and improve your client's fortunes, it will improve you.

Okay, . . . *now* we can talk about the crafts of copywriting and art direction.

---

95 PERCENT OF ALL ADVERTISING IS POORLY WRITTEN. DON'T ADD TO THE PILE.

A cursory glance at most award shows will give the incorrect impression that all the best advertising is visual. Actually it's all the best *award shows* that are visual, due chiefly to the globalization of the judging panels. It's simply easier for judges to agree on visual language. (Plus, visual solutions are, in fact, pretty cool.)

But for most new recruits to advertising, visual solutions may have to wait, because most of the jobs you'll get early on in your career will have no photography budget. You'll just be handed a couple of stock shots of a car or a smartphone and 24 hours to come up with a campaign. This means you're going to have to solve the problem with words. As cool as visuals are, most of the business on the planet is conducted with language.

Figure 4.2 is an example of an ad where we had no budget, no time, no stock photos—we didn't even have a logo. Art director Bob Brihn and I had pencils and paper and that was about it. Yet I think the headline and body copy do a respectable job giving Independent Television a competitive and an entertaining voice.

In *Breaking In,* Ty Montague, founder and partner of Co:, put it this way: "The idea swirling around that words are dead is, I think is pretty silly. What do you spend most of your time on the internet doing? Reading—texts, e-mails, blogs, whatever, and I predict that behavior will continue. So the ability to string together a coherent argument using words will get you a long way."[3]

Let's talk then about writing. Writing is hard. "Talking is the fire hydrant out front, gushing into the street," said Oscar-winning screenwriter Warren Beatty. "Writing is the drip of the faucet on the third floor."

Before you write anything, write the brand manifesto.

A *manifesto* is your brand's Magna Carta, Rosetta Stone, and Declaration of Independence all rolled into one; it's the halftime locker room speech given by the CEO; the words the founder heard on the mountaintop before bringing down the stone tablets. Reading a great brand manifesto should make you wanna run out and try the product. You should feel the brand fire in your bones.

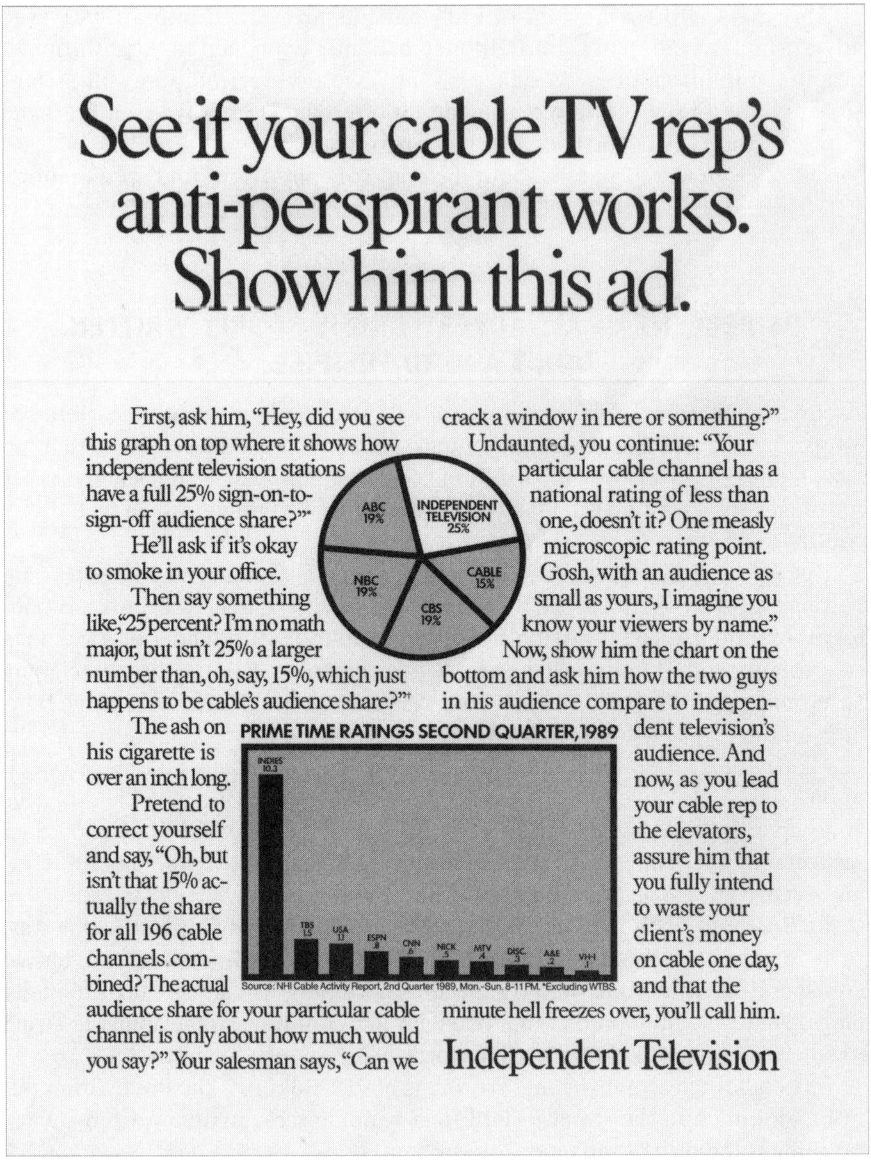

See if your cable TV rep's anti-perspirant works. Show him this ad.

First, ask him, "Hey, did you see this graph on top where it shows how independent television stations have a full 25% sign-on-to-sign-off audience share?"*

He'll ask if it's okay to smoke in your office.

Then say something like, "25 percent? I'm no math major, but isn't 25% a larger number than, oh, say, 15%, which just happens to be cable's audience share?"†

The ash on his cigarette is over an inch long.

Pretend to correct yourself and say, "Oh, but isn't that 15% actually the share for all 196 cable channels combined? The actual audience share for your particular cable channel is only about how much would you say?" Your salesman says, "Can we

crack a window in here or something?"

Undaunted, you continue: "Your particular cable channel has a national rating of less than one, doesn't it? One measly microscopic rating point. Gosh, with an audience as small as yours, I imagine you know your viewers by name."

Now, show him the chart on the bottom and ask him how the two guys in his audience compare to independent television's audience. And now, as you lead your cable rep to the elevators, assure him that you fully intend to waste your client's money on cable one day, and that the minute hell freezes over, you'll call him.

INDEPENDENT TELEVISION 25%
ABC 19%
CABLE 15%
NBC 19%
CBS 19%

PRIME TIME RATINGS SECOND QUARTER, 1989

INDIES 10.3 | TBS 1.5 | USA 1.1 | ESPN .8 | CNN .6 | NICK .5 | MTV .4 | DISC .2 | A&E .2 | VH-1 .1

Source: NHI Cable Activity Report, 2nd Quarter 1989, Mon.-Sun. 8-11 PM. *Excluding WTBS.

Independent Television

Figure 4.2   You won't always have the budget to take a photo or even buy a stock shot. Basically, words are all you have to solve the problem.

Typically these screeds are written only for new business pitches or brand overhauls. They can also serve as true north on a brand's compass and be used for all kinds of creative decisions. Figure 4.3 is an example of a good brand manifesto; it was written for the winning Miller High Life pitch by Jeff Kling when he was at Wieden + Kennedy.

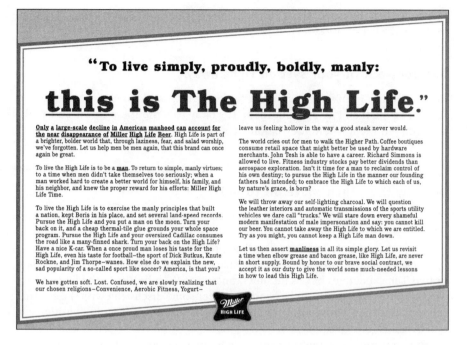

Figure 4.3 A brand manifesto is the blueprint of a brand, its DNA in words.

Read Jeff's manifesto and you'll see how it served well as a springboard for writing all those great High Life spots. I include here three of the scripts from that marvelous campaign.

- (VIDEO OF A MAN LOOKING AT HIS NEIGHBOR'S SUV:) Leather seats. Automatic transmission. Nowadays you'll hear people call this a "truck." Well, a man knows a station wagon when he sees one. *This* car will see off-road action only if the driver backs over a flower bed. If this vehicular masquerade represents the high life to which men are called . . . we should trade in our trousers for skirts right now.

- (VIDEO OF MAN SAWING WOOD IN BASEMENT SHOP:) When you enjoy your work and you're suited to it, the hours just fly by. Before you know it, you're in danger of logging some unintentional overtime. That won't do. Fortunately, every High Life man comes with a built-in timer that automatically alerts him to the end of the workday. Thank you, five o'clock shadow. Feels like it's Miller Time.

- (VIDEO OF MAN'S HANDS PREPARING POTATO SALAD:) It's hard to respect the French when you have to bail 'em out of two big ones in one century. But we have to hand it to 'em on mayonnaise. Nice job, Pierre.

For another example of writing that brings a brand roaring to life I recommend the video for Johnnie Walker called "The Man Who Walked Around the World."

It handily won the One Show's Best of Show award and is viewable online all over the place. Extraordinary.

Get puns out of your system right away.

Puns, in addition to being the lowest thing on the joke food chain, have no persuasive value. It's okay to think them. It's okay to write them down. Just make sure you put them where they belong and don't forget to flush.

Don't just start writing headlines willy-nilly. Break it down. Do willy first. Then move on to nilly.

Okay, when it comes time to write, don't just start spitting out headlines. Instead, methodically explore different attributes and benefits of your product as you write.

Here's an example from my files. The project is a bourbon.

The client can afford only a small-space newspaper campaign and a billboard or two. The executives have said they want to see their bottle, so the finished ads will likely be just a bottle and a headline. After some discussion with the account folks about tone ("thoughtful, intellectual"), the art director and I consider several avenues for exploration.

The bourbon's age might be one way to go. Bourbon, by law, is aged a minimum of two years, often up to eight, sometimes longer. So we start there to see what happens. We put our feet up and immediately begin discussing the first *Terminator* movie. Sometime after lunch we take a crack at the "aging" thing.

AGE IDEAS

Order a drink that takes nine years to get.

Like to hear how it's made? Do you have nine years?

(Note: On the pages from the actual file, there are about five false starts for each one of these headlines. Tons of scratch-outs and half-witted ideas that go nowhere.)

Nine years inside an oak barrel in an ugly warehouse. Our idea of quality time.

After nine years of trickle-down economics, it's ready just in time.

Nine long years in a barrel. One glorious hour in a glass.

Okay, nine years. What else happens in nine years? What about the feeling of the slow passage of time?

Continental drift happens faster than this bourbon.

Mother Nature made it whiskey. Father Time made it bourbon.

We can't make it slow enough.

What wind does to mountains, time does to this bourbon.

On May 15th, we'll be rotating Barrel #1394 one-quarter turn to the left. Just thought you'd like to know.

Tree rings multiply. Glaciers speed by. And still the bourbon waits.

Maybe one of these might work. There's another take on age we might try — namely, how long the label's been on the market. Not the age of the whiskey, but of the brand.

HISTORY OF BRAND IDEAS

First bottled when other bourbons were knee high to a swizzle stick.

First bottled back when American History was an easy course.

First bottled when American History was called Current Events.

First bottled when the Wild West meant Kentucky.

Smoother than those young whippersnapper bourbons.

Back in 1796, this bourbon was the best available form of central heating.

The recipe for this bourbon has survived since 1796. Please don't bury it in a mint julep.

Write us for free information on what you can do with wine coolers.

We've been making it continuously since 1796. (Not counting that brief unpleasantness in the 1920s.)

If you can't remember the name, just ask for the bourbon first bottled when Chester A. Arthur was president.

110 years old and still in the bars every night.

If we could get any further behind the times, we would.

Are we behind the tymes?

A blast from the past.

First bottled before billboards.

This premium bourbon was first marketed via ox.

Introduced 50 years before ice cubes.

Okay, maybe there's some stuff we could use from that list. Maybe not. So far we've played with aging and brand history. What about where it's made?

KENTUCKY IDEAS

Kind of like great Canadian whiskey. Only it's bourbon. And from Kentucky.

Kind of like an old Kentucky mule. Classic, stubborn, and plenty of kick.

From the third floor of an old warehouse in Kentucky, heaven.

Warming trend expected out of Kentucky.

Now available to city folk.

If this ad had a jingle, it'd be "Dueling Banjos."

What the Clampetts would serve the Trumps.

This bourbon is the real McCoy. Even the Hatfields agreed.

It's not just named after a creek in Kentucky. It's made from it.

This is a beautiful picture of a tiny creek that flows through the back hills of Kentucky. (Picture of bottle.)

Old as the hills it's from.

Smooth. Deep. Hard to find. Kind of like the creek we get the water from.

Hand-bottled straight from a barrel in Kentucky. Strap in.

Tastes like a Kentucky sunset looks.

Its Old Kentucky Home was a barrel.

Maybe those last two might also make for good outdoor, given how short they are. We make a note. Remember, the point here isn't, hey, let's see how many headlines can we write, but rather how many different doors can we go through? How many different ways can we look at the same problem?

Okay, now let's see what can be done with the way some people drink bourbon—straight. Or perhaps the time of day it's drunk. (Wait a minute. Bad word.)

HOW-YOU-DRINK-IT IDEAS

With a bourbon this good, you don't need to show breasts in the ice cubes. In fact, you don't need ice cubes.

Neither good bourbons nor bad arguments hold water.

Water ruins baseball games and bourbon.

For a quiet night, try it without all the noisy ice.

Great after the kids are in bed. Perfect after they're in college.

Mixes superbly with a rocking chair and a dog.

You don't need water to enjoy this premium bourbon.

A fire might be nice.

Perfect for those quiet times. Like between marriages.

As you can see, each one of these doors we went through—age, history, Kentucky—led to another hallway, full of other doors to try. Which is one of the marvelous things about writing. It's not simply a way of getting things down on paper. Writing is a way of thinking—thinking with your pencil, your wrist, and your spine and just seeing where a thing goes. Clearly, a few of the bourbon ideas presented here aren't very good. (Lord knows, you may think they all suck.) But like Pickett's Charge at Gettysburg, with 15,000 soldiers, one or two are going to make it over the wall.

The lesson here is this: disciplined writing is not willy-nilly; it's a process. In *Breaking In,* creative director Pat McKay reminds young creatives, "[I often see books] where I want to tell the writer, 'You've only got one line that feels like you went through a process.' I want to see that you have a writing process, because that's what writers do. We have a process."[4]

One more little case study, this one for one of the nation's largest airlines. The airline had just purchased a whole bunch of new 777s and A320s (read: "roomier wide-body jets"), and they wanted to promote the benefits to business travelers.

Well, if we break it down, perhaps some of the concepts could focus on more personal space and some on the comfort of the seat itself. We could further break it down into ideas that are headline-driven and ideas that are visually driven.

PERSONAL-SPACE IDEAS, HEADLINE-DRIVEN Maybe we could try some headlines that would work by themselves as an all-type ad (or perhaps with a "flat" visual like a shot of a wide aisle or a roomy seat).

Most passengers would give their right arm for more room for their right arm.

Everyone who'd like more personal space, raise your hand, if possible. (✔)

Getting incredibly close to people is fine for encounter groups, not planes.

Now even luggage has more elbow room.

You can use a camera lens to make your planes look big. Or you can buy big planes.

Wouldn't it be great if an airline advertised wider planes instead of wider smiles?

Choose one: Bigger bags of peanuts. Bigger smiles. Bigger planes. We thought so.

Airline math: The wider the plane, the shorter the flight feels.

PERSONAL-SPACE IDEAS, A LITTLE MORE VISUALLY DRIVEN

This, only higher.

(VISUAL: A well-worn La-Z-Boy recliner.)

There are two places you can stretch out and let someone solve your problems. With ours, you get miles.

(VISUAL: Shrink's office.)

Which one would you take on a long trip? Exactly. Now let's move on to planes.

(VISUAL: Small car versus big SUV.)

We put it in our planes.

(VISUAL: Man in his living room, football game on TV, quizzically looking at flattened area of shag rug where his La-Z-Boy recliner used to be.)

Traveling has always been easier when you have room to yourself.

(VISUAL: Old family photo of three kids fussing at each other in the backseat of a station wagon.)

Da Vinci never designed a plane that worked, but he had this cool idea about personal space.

(VISUAL: Da Vinci drawings of the body showing the arc of the arms, motion of legs.)

EMOTIONAL BENEFITS, A LITTLE MORE VISUALLY DRIVEN   What would happen if we concentrated more on the emotional benefits of a wider more comfortable seat?

If our new seat doesn't put you to sleep, try reading the whole ad.

    (VISUAL: Airline seat with long copy and lots of callouts.)

It doesn't matter how roomy a seat is if you don't like the service.

    (VISUAL: Little boy dwarfed in a big dentist's chair.)

Almost every passenger arrives feeling human.

    (VISUAL: Dog getting out of airline pet carrier.) (✔)

"Some settling may occur during shipment."

    (VISUAL: Seat shot with sleeping passenger.)

With our new seats, you won't have to count for long.

    (VISUAL: A single sheep with caption under it: "One.") (✔)

When you fly with us, never promise "I'll work on the plane."

    (VISUAL: Close-up shot of computer screen with menu button of "Sleep" backlit.) (✔)

Have you always done your best thinking way up high somewhere?

    (VISUAL: A kid's tree house seen from way at bottom of ladder, two sneakered feet sticking out of the door.)

After I've finished writing a list about this long, I'll go back over it and make a little mark (✔) next to my favorites. Then I transfer those few ideas over to a clean sheet of paper and start all over.

I mean, start *all* over. Pretend you have nothing so far. The fact is, there are only 22 airline ideas in the preceding list—22. We cannot seriously believe we'll have crafted a ticket-selling, brand-building, One Show–winning ad after 22 stinking tries. We'll need hundreds. If that sounds daunting, get ready for a long and hard career. This is the way it's done.

Remember, the wastepaper basket is the writer's best friend.

If the idea needs a headline, write 100.

Sorry, but there's no shortcut. Write 100 of them. And don't confuse this with Tom Monahan's exercise of 100-Mile-an-Hour Thinking.[5] (That's a pretty good exercise, too, but better for the very beginning of the creative process. In that exercise, Tom advises creative people to turn on the fire hydrant for 20 minutes and catch every single first thought that comes out. Each idea goes on a separate Post-it Note, with absolutely no editing.) Nope, what we're talking about here is sitting down and slowly and methodically cranking out 100 workable lines—100 lines that range from decent, to hey not bad, to whoa that rocks. The key is they *all* have to be pretty good.

To prove this very point, Sally Hogshead bravely posted all of the BMW motorcycle headlines she came up with to get to her final five ads featured in the

Figure 4.4   The headline reads: "It has 3,129 integrated parts. One of which is named Bill."

One Show and *Communication Arts* (Figure 4.4). Read the list and you'll see a copywriter really thinking it through, rattling different doorknobs up and down the conceptual hallway, sometimes writing about the union of rider and bike, sometimes about goose bumps. They're all pretty darn good. (She's good at other stuff, too—particularly career advice for creatives. Check out her website at sallyhogshead.com.)

Even atheists kneel on a BMW. • Some burn candles when praying. Others, rubber. • There are basilicas, cathedrals, mosques. And then there's Route 66. • Buy one before the Church bans such marriages. • People take vows of chastity to feel this way. • More Westminster Abbey than Cal Tech. • Runners get a high from jogging around a track at 8 miles per hour. Pathetic. • This is exactly the sort of intimacy that would frighten Jesse Helms. • Fits like a glove. A metallic silver, fuel-injected, 150-horsepower glove. • You don't get off a BMW so much as take it off. • Relationships this intimate are illegal in some states. • Usually, this kind of connection requires surgery. • Didn't George Orwell predict man and machine would eventually become one? • The Church has yet to comment on such a marriage of man and machine. • Somebody call Ray Bradbury. We've combined man and machine. • Do you become more machine, or does it become more human? • And then there were two. • "Oh look, honey. What a sweet looking couple." • If you ever connect like this with a person, marry them. • Fits tighter than OJ's glove. J • Why some men won't stop and ask directions. • "Darling, is that . . . a smudge of motor oil on your collar?" • The road is calling. Don't get its message by voice-mail. • The feeling is more permanent than any tattoo. • "Yippee! I'm off to my root canal!" • Your inner child is fluent in German. • The last day of school, any day of the year. • Your heart races, your senses tingle. Then you turn it on. • There is no known antidote once it gets into your blood. • There are no words to describe it. Unless "Wooohoo!" counts. • No amusement park ride can give this feeling. • If he had a mood ring on, it'd be bright green. • Never has a raccoon baking in the sun smelled sweeter. • How "joie de vivre" translates into German. • Put as much distance as possible between you and the strip mall. • Off, off, off, off-road. • If it had a rearview mirror, you'd see your troubles in it. • There's something worth racing towards at the end of this road: another 25 miles. • The best psychotherapy doesn't happen lying on a couch. • A remote control is a more dangerous machine. • A carnivore in the food chain of bikes. • If you're trying to find yourself, you sure as hell won't find it on the sofa. • If you had eight hours, alone, no radio, imagine what you could think about. • Where is it written the love for your motorcycle must be platonic? • Seems preoccupied. Comes home later than usual. Always wanting to get out of the house. • You possess a motorcycle. You're possessed by a BMW. • Let's see. You're either riding it, or wishing you were riding it, or thinking about the last time you rode it. • Men who own a BMW have something else to think about every 22 seconds. • What you're seeing is his soul. His body's in a meeting in Cincinnati right now. • Merge with traffic. Not every other motorcycle owner. • Your estimated time of arrival just got moved up. • Where do you drive when you daydream? • What walking on air actually looks like. • The invitation said to bring your significant other. • Lust fueled by gasoline. • The bike, the girlfriend. Guess which model he'll trade in first. • She wonders why she sometimes feels like a third wheel. • Room for luggage. None for baggage.

The point here is both quantity *and* quality. You don't get to great until you do a whole bunch of good. It's part of the process.

Save the operative part of the headline for the very end.

You know that single part of a headline where the concept comes to life? That key word or phrase where the idea is unveiled? Save that unveiling for the end of your headline.

Take, for example, this headline from the preceding list of airline ideas.

Almost every passenger arrives feeling human.

(VISUAL: Dog getting out of airline pet carrier.)

The line could have been constructed other ways:

You'll feel human when you arrive, thanks to our new seats.

When the seats let you sleep, almost everybody feels human on arrival.

Some of the punch is missing, isn't it? It feels better when you save your wrap-up punch for the end of your sentence. It has more surprise and power.

Never use fake names in a headline.
(Or copy. Or anywhere else for that matter.)

"Little Billy's friends at school call him different." Lines like this drive me nuts.

"Little Billy will never know his real father."

Hey, little Billy, c'mere. Go back and tell your copywriter that a strange man in the park said to tell him he's a *hack*. Anybody reading this kind of crap knows these ad names are fake—and an irritating kind of fake at that. Like those man-ufactured relatives they put inside of picture frames at stores.

Avoid fake people. Avoid fake names.

There are times, however, when using a person's name is the only way the con-cept *will* work. And in the hands of a seasoned team, as in the VitroRobertson ad for client Taylor guitars (Figure 4.5), it can be done beautifully. It comes down to style. To how gracefully and believably you pull it off.

Don't let the headline flex any muscles when the visual is doing the heavy lifting.

As it is in dancing, one should lead, one should follow. If your visual is a hard-working idea, let your headline quietly clean up the work left to it. And if the headline is brilliant, is well crafted, and covers all the bases, the visual (if one exists at all) should be merely icing on the cake.

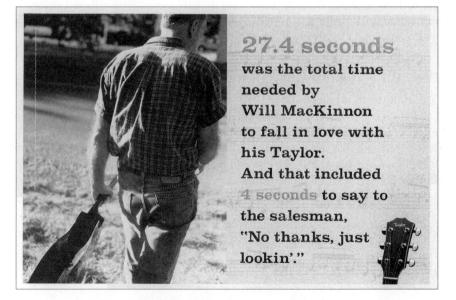

Figure 4.5   When you have a wild visual, the headline should be straight. When the headline's doing all the work, like this one, the visual shouldn't hog the stage. It should just "be there."

Figure 4.6   A perfect marriage of word and picture.

Remember, the rule of thumb is never show what you're saying and never say what you're showing. Figure 4.6, an ad for Harley-Davidson motorcycles, is a perfect example. By itself, the visual is fairly tame. By itself, the headline is dull and almost meaningless. But together, they make one of the best ads I've ever seen.

When it's just a headline, it'd better be a pretty good headline.

One of the best campaigns of all time (in this writer's opinion) is Abbott Meade Vickers's work for the *Economist* (Figure 4.7). This campaign was basically an outdoor campaign of brilliant headlines against a backdrop of the color red (lifted from the magazine's masthead). Several of the finished ads are pictured throughout this book, but the lines all by themselves are also great lessons in brilliant copywriting. I include my favorites here:

Think someone under the table.

If you're already a reader, ask your chauffeur to hoot as you pass this poster.

"Can I phone an Economist reader, please, Chris?"

Don't be a vacancy on the board.

If your assistant reads The Economist, don't play too much golf.

Look forward to school reunions.

It's lonely at the top, but at least there's something to read.

$E = iq^2$

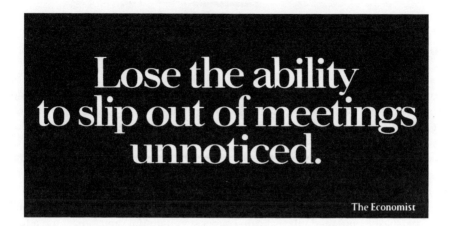

Figure 4.7   What an elegant way to say that reading the Economist *can help make your business thinking indispensable.*

If they did brain transplants, would you be a donor or a recipient?

In opinion polls, 100 percent of Economist readers had one.

If someone gave you a penny for your thoughts, would they get change?

Would you like to sit next to you at dinner?

Think outside the dodecahedron.

Ever go blank at the crucial . . . thingy?

Cures itchy scalps.

"Is it me, or is quantum physics easier these days?"

Certain headlines are currently checked out. You may use them when they are returned.

Lines such as "Contrary to popular belief . . ." or "Something is wrong when . . ." are pretty much used up. (Sorry, I used one or two of them myself.) But they're gone now. Get over it. Time for something new.

Remember, anything that you even think you've seen, forget about. The stuff you've never seen? You'll know that when you see it, too. It raises the hair on the back of your neck.

Don't use a model number in the headline.

Product numbers such as "TX-17" may seem familiar to you and to the client. But you're used to it; you work on the account. In a headline, they serve only as a speed bump. They're not words, they're numerals, so they force readers to switch gears in their heads to 17, x45, 13z42 to get through your sentence.

WRITING BODY COPY

Writing well, rule #1: write well.

I don't think people read body copy. I think we've entered a frenzied era of coffee-guzzling, text-sending channel surfers who spell "are you" as "r u" and have the attention span of a flashbulb. If the first 7 words of body copy aren't "OMG! It's beer and $$$$ for *everybody*!! . . . word 10 isn't read. Just my opinion, mind you.

Raymond McKinney at the Martin Agency had it right when he wrote a line for those condensed-book study aids: "Cliff Notes. When you don't have time to see the movie."

Yet when I write body copy, long or short, I work hard at making it as smart and persuasive and readable as I can. I suggest you do the same—because a few people are going to read it. And the ones who do, you want. They're interested. They're peering in your shop window. They are *leaning in.*

So as much as I hammer away on the importance of visual solutions, when you have to write, write smartly. Write with passion, intelligence, and honesty. And when you've said what you need to say, stop.

Write like you'd talk if you were the brand.

As we discussed when we were talking about brand manifestos, every brand has a personality. You could describe Apple Computer's personality perhaps as "benevolent intelligence." Read any piece of copy in any Apple ad from the past 10 years—doesn't matter if it's an old ad for an Apple Lisa or an iPhone or an iPad. No matter what Apple work you read, you'll feel like you're listening to the same smart big brother, one who wants to sit in the chair with you in front of the keyboard and show you how simple, smart, and beautifully designed technology can be. Successful brands discover their own distinct voices and then stick with them year after year.

If you're inheriting an established voice, you can learn its cadences by reading their previous advertising. But if you have a new brand or you're creating a new voice for an old brand, consider yourself lucky. It's one of the most creative and rewarding things you can do in this business—discovering "who" a brand is and giving it shape and form and voice.

This isn't done to create stylish writing. What you're doing is creating a brand personality, an important point in a marketplace where the physical differences between products are getting smaller and smaller.

Let's say, for example, you're working on a car account. Most of the time, it's likely you'll have to show the car. Your idea may feel half art-directed already and in a sense it is. So if it comes down to showing just a headline and a picture of a car, your headline ought to have a voice no one else does.

Here are two car headlines:

If you run out of gas, it's easy to push.

We'll never make it big.

Here are two more:

A luxury sedan based on the belief that all of the rich are not idle.

The people with money are still spending it, but with infinitely more wisdom.

And two more:

Let's burn the maps. Let's get lost. Let's turn right when we should turn left. Let's read fewer car ads and more travel ads. Let's not be back in ten minutes. Let's hold out until the next rest stop. Let's eat when hungry. Let's drink when thirsty. Let's break routines but not make a routine of it. Let's Motor.

Let's put away the middle finger. Let's lay off the horn. Let's volunteer jumper cables. Let's pay a stranger's toll. Let's be considerate of cyclists. Let's keep in mind automobiles were created to advance civilization. And for crying out loud, let's remember to turn off those blinkers. Let's Motor.

Can you tell which ones are from MINI? From VW? From BMW? It's pretty easy. Which is as it should be.

At the same time, remember to write like you talk.

Now that you know you need to write like that brand, I also have to encourage you to write like people talk; in the copy you write for ads, in e-mails to clients, and letters to the editor, write like regular people *talk*. For some reason, when handed a pen and asked to write something that will be seen by others, 9 out of 10 people decide an authoritarian tone is somehow more persuasive than clear English.

There's a cost to this which the authors of *The Cluetrain Manifesto* made clear in their famous 95 Theses: "In just a few more years, the current homogenized 'voice' of business—the sound of mission statements and brochures—will seem as contrived and artificial as the language of the 18th century French court . . . [C]ompanies that speak in the language of the pitch, the dog-and-pony show, are no longer speaking to anyone."[6]

This horrible boring voice is everywhere in this business. Consider this memo from my files, written by a man about whom, were you to meet him, you'd say, "Sharp guy, that Bob. I want him on my account." Yet Bob wrote the following memo. (What he was trying to say was the program was killed because it was too costly.)

Effective late last week the Flavor-iffic® project was shelved by the Flavor-Master Consumer Products Division Management. The reasoning had to do with funding generated covering cost of entry, not cost of entry as it would relate to test market in 2012, but as it would relate to expansion, if judged successful across major pieces of geography in 2013 and beyond. In sum, the way Flavor-Master new products division served up Flavor-iffic® to Consumer Products Division Management was that if Flavor-Master were to relax financial parameters for Flavor-iffic® in 2012, 2013 and 2014, in effect have Corporate fund the program, Consumer Products Division could recommend to Corporate to proceed with the program. The decision was made at the Consumer Products Division Management level that Corporate would most probably not accept that and the subject was taken no further.

Except for the name Flavor-iffic, I swear, every word of this memo is real.

The program was killed because it was too costly. That's nine words. Bob, in 143 words, was not only unable to get that nine-word message across, he effectively lobotomized his audience with a torrent of corporate nonsense that said nothing. It couldn't be decoded.

Bob proudly dictated this Rosetta stone, snapped his suspenders, and took the elevator down to the lobby, thinking he'd done his bit to turn the wheels of capitalism for the day. Yet when he got home, he probably didn't talk that way to his wife.

Honey, RE: supper. It has come to my attention, and the concurrent attention of the other family members (i.e., Janice, Bill, and Bob Jr.), that your gravy has inconsistencies of viscosity (popularly known as "lumps"), itself not a disturbing event were it not for the recent disappearance of the family dog.

Write like you talk.

Write with a smooth, easy rhythm that sounds natural. Obey the rules of grammar and go easy on the adjectives. Short sentences are best, especially online. One-word sentences? Fine. End with a preposition if you want to. And if it feels right, begin a sentence with "and." Just be *clear*.

Through it all, remember, you are selling something. Easy to forget when you start slinging words.

Pretend you're writing a letter.

Why write to the masses? It's one person reading the Web page you're working on, right? So write to one person.

Write a letter. It's a good voice to use when you're writing copy. It's intimate. It keeps you from lecturing. The best copy feels like a conversation, not a speech. One person talking to another. Not a corporate press release typed in the public relations department by some minion named "Higgs."

Visualize this person you're writing the letter to. She's not a "Female, 18 to 34, household income of blah-blah." She's a woman named Jill who's been thinking about getting a newer, smaller car. She's in an airport, bored, trying to get a Gummi Bear out of her back tooth, and reading *Time* magazine backward.

Before you start writing copy, have the basic structure of your argument in mind.

Know where you're going to go. "Okay, I've got to come off that headline, then hit A, B, and then end on C." If you neglect this preparation, you will buzz about in a meaningless pattern, like a fly on a summer screen.

Don't have what they call a pre-ramble in your body copy.

The first paragraph of copy in many ads is usually a waste of the reader's time, a repetition of what's already been said in the headline. Consider the analogy of a door-to-door salesman. Your headline is what he says through the crack in the door: his name, what he is selling, and why it's better than the other guy's stuff.

Okay, the reader has let you in. And now you're in the foyer. Don't waste time in your first paragraph being reintroductory. "Hi. Remember me? Same guy who was out in front of your door two seconds ago? Remember? Said my name, what I'm selling, and why it's better than that other guy's stuff?"

Get to the point. It's time for the details. Put your most interesting, surprising, or persuasive point in the first line if you can. You're lucky if people read your headline and luckier yet if they let you into the foyer by reading your copy.

Your body copy should reflect the overall concept of the idea.

When you start writing, borrow from your concept's imagery; lift colors from its palette. This advice isn't given for stylistic reasons. It helps keep your work clean and simple. One concept, one voice, one style.

Five rules for effective speechwriting from Winston Churchill.

1. Begin strongly.
2. Have one theme.
3. Use simple language.
4. Leave a picture in the listener's mind.
5. End dramatically.

"It's not fair to inflict your own style on a strategy."

This is from Ed McCabe, one of the great writers of the 1970s. Your job is to present the client's case as memorably as you can, not to come up with another great piece for your portfolio. You want to do both. But you aren't likely to do both if you're concentrating on style. Don't worry about style. It will be expressed no matter what you do. Style is part of the way your brain is wired. Just concentrate on solving the client's problem well. The rest will just happen.

Eschew obfuscation.

My point exactly. Those words say what I mean to say, but they aren't as clear as they could be. This doesn't mean your writing has to be flat-footed, just understandable.

E. B. White said, "Be obscure clearly."

Provide detail.

In headlines, in body copy, anywhere you can say something specific and concrete, do it. It will make your argument more persuasive and your ad more interesting.

Here's an old example from Goodby, Silverstein & Partners that shows the power of detail. The headline read: "It began 400 years before Christ. It is visible from Mars. You can touch it this spring." Punctuated by a small picture of the Great Wall of China, the details in this headline made me keep reading about Royal Viking's cruises to China.

Once you lay your sentences down, spackle between the joints.

Use transitions to flow seamlessly from one benefit to the next. Each sentence should come naturally out of the one that precedes it. To use Peter Barry's metaphor, an "invisible thread" should run through your entire argument, tying everything together. When you've done it well, you shouldn't be able to take out any sentence without disrupting the flow and structure of the entire piece. Novelist Wallace Stegner nailed it when he penned, "Hard writing makes for easy reading." (This fragile coherence of beautiful writing is lost on many people and is the main reason copywriters are often seen mumbling to themselves at bus stops.)

Break your copy into as many short paragraphs as you can.

Short paragraphs are less daunting. I've never read William Faulkner's classic *Intruder in the Dust* for this very reason. Those eight-page paragraphs look like work to me. Remember, nobody ever had to read *People* magazine with a bookmark. This isn't an argument for dumbing down your work. Be as smart as you can be. Just don't write paragraphs the size of shower curtains, okay?

When you're done writing the copy, read it aloud.

I discovered this one the hard way. I had to present some copy to a group of five clients. I read it to them aloud. It was only during the act of reading it this way that I discovered how wretched my copy was. Just hearing the words hanging out there in the air with their grade-school mistakes, seeing the flat reaction of the clients' faces, hearing my voice crack, feeling the flop sweat . . . it's all coming back to me.

When you're done writing, read it aloud. Not just your radio scripts, but copy for print, for online, for anything you wanna make sure sounds like speech. Awkward constructions and wire-thin segues have a way of revealing themselves when read aloud.

When you're done ~~writing your body copy~~, go back and cut it by a third.

Proofread your own work.

Don't depend on Spell-check. First of all, it won't notice mistakes like this in you're writing. Second, using Spell-check is just *lazy*. Seriously, if you have to use some stupid computer program on your writing, use Suck-check, whenever that one comes out.

If you have to have one, make your tagline an anthem.

Try to write about something bigger than just your client's product. Own some high ground. In my opinion, the best ever written was for Nike: "Just Do It." This exhortation is not about shoes. Nor is it about just sports. It's about life; it's about the competitive spirit; it's about kicking ass. And yet it sold a lot of shoes.

As you work, you might want to try getting to a cool tagline with both deductive and inductive reasoning. Working deductively means taking the work you've got up on the wall and boiling its essence into an evocative, provocative, or anthemic tagline. Working inductively, you take a line you like and see what executions you can pull *out* of it and put up on the wall.

A FEW NOTES ON DESIGN AND ONE ON THINNING THE HERD.

Something has to dominate the ad.

Whether it's a big headline, a large visual, or a single word floating in white space, somebody's got to be the boss.

It's easy to spot ads where the art director (or perhaps client) couldn't decide what was most important. The ads are usually in three big pieces. The visual takes up a third of the page. A headline takes up the next third. And a combination of body copy–logo–tagline brings up the rear. The whole thing has about as much cohesion as a cookie in the rain.

An ad needs a boss. So does a home page, or any screen for that matter. There needs to be an overall visual hierarchy. The late Roy Grace, one of the famous art directors from Doyle Dane Bernbach, spoke on this issue:

> There has to be a point on every page where the art director and the writer want you to start. Whether that is the center of the page, the top right-hand corner, or the left-hand corner, there has to be an understanding, an agreement, and a logical reason where you want people to look first.[7]

Avoid trends in execution.

Don't take your cues from design trends you see in the awards books. (For one thing, if they're in the books, they're already two years old. The One Show book arrives, literally, on a slow boat from China where it's printed.) But this is about more than being up to date. It's about concentrating on the soul of an ad instead of the width of its lapels. Do as you wish, by all means, but I'll warn you of two things. Riding the wave of every passing fad will make your work look trendy and derivative. Also, when you enter your piece in a show, the judges (who've seen just about every trend come and go) will likely deep-six it in a heartbeat.

Develop a look no one else has.

You've got to find something your client can call his or her own: a shape, a color, a design—something that is unique.

Helmut Krone: "I was working on Avis and looking for a page style. That's very important to me, a page style. I feel that you should be able to tell who's running that ad at a distance of twenty feet."[8]

What's interesting about Krone's statement is that he's not talking about billboards but print ads. And if you look at his two most famous campaigns, they stand up to the test. You could identify his Volkswagen and Avis ads from across a street (Figure 4.8).

The longer I'm in this business, the more I'm convinced art direction is where the major battle for brand building happens. Once you establish a look, once you stake out a design territory, no one else can use it without looking like your brand. The *Economist* practically *owns* the color red. IBM continues to letter-box its television with those iconic blue bars. And Apple Computer's signature color of a clean white screams "Apple" before the first word of copy is read.

Own something visual.

Be objective.

Once you've put some good ideas on paper and had time to polish them to your satisfaction, maybe it's time to cart them around the hallways a little bit, even before you take them to your creative director. You're not looking for consensus here, just a disaster check.

This may not be your style, and if you're not comfortable doing this, don't. But it can give you a quick reality check, identify holes that need filling, and point out directions that deserve further exploration. Be objective. Listen to what people have to say about your work. If a couple of people have a problem with something, chances are it's real. Keep in mind that when you're showing your work around the agency, you're showing it to people who *want* to like it. Once your work's out the door, it's quite the opposite. People will approach your stuff thinking it's going to be as bad as everything else they see.

Avis is only No. 2 in rent a cars. So why go with us?

We try harder.
(When you're not the biggest, you have to.)
We just can't afford dirty ash-trays. Or half-empty gas tanks. Or worn wipers. Or unwashed cars. Or low tires. Or anything less than seat–adjusters that adjust. Heaters that heat. Defrosters that defrost.

Obviously, the thing we try hardest for is just to be nice. To start you out right with a new car, like a lively, super-torque Ford, and a pleasant smile. To know, say, where you get a good pastrami sandwich in Duluth. Why?
Because we can't afford to take you for granted.
Go with us next time.
The line at our counter is shorter.

Figure 4.8   In an interview, art director Helmut Krone said that the Avis look came from a deliberate reversal of the VW look. VW had large pictures; Avis, small. VW had small body type; Avis, large. Note the absence of a logo.

So listen to them. There's the old maxim: "When 10 people say you have a tail, sooner or later you oughta turn around and look."

Kill off the weak sister.

If your campaign has even one slightly weaker piece in it, replace that piece with something that's as great as everything else. I have often talked myself into presenting campaigns that include weak sisters because time was running out. But readers don't care if *most* of your ideas are great. Out there in the world, they see your ideas one at a time, so they should *all* be great.

There's a saying the Japanese use regarding the strict quality control in their best companies: "How many times a year is it acceptable for the birthing nurse to drop a baby on its head?" Is even one time okay? There's another famous line. I don't know who wrote it. "Good is the enemy of great." It's true. Good is easy to like. Good throws its arm around you and says, "Hey, I'm not so bad, am I?" You talk yourself into it. Next thing you know you have a campaign that goes great—great—good. And that's bad.

Always, always show babies or puppies.

Oh, and another thing. Always—*always*—write every headline in the script of a child's handwriting. It's very cute, don't you think? And don't forget to have at least two of the letters be adorably backward. Backward Ǝ's are best. Backward O's don't work. Here's a regular O and here's a backward O. See? Not as adorable as a backward Ǝ. (Just checking to see if you're awake.)

———

WHAT TO DO IF YOU'RE STUCK.

First of all, being stuck is a good sign. Seriously.

Being stuck means you have moved through all the easy stuff. You've waded through all the crappy ideas and through the okay ideas, passed the low-hanging fruit, and are entering the outlying area of big, new thoughts. Being stuck is not only not unusual, it's what you want.

So don't be creeped out by those long silences that can happen during creative sessions. You can spend whole days, even weeks, trying very hard and coming up with diddly. But I've found it's only after you've suffered these excruciating days of meat loaf brain that the shiny and beautiful finally presents itself to you. The trick is to stay with it. Suffer through it. Remember, the only way out is through.

If you're stuck, relax.

Most of the books that I've read on creativity keep bringing up the subject of relaxation. You can't be creative and be tense. The two events are never in the same room together. Stay loose. Breathe from the stomach. If you're not relaxed, stop until you are. Just the simple act of physical relaxation will bring on new ideas. I promise. As John Hegarty reminds us: "There's a book on playing tennis . . . which has a very simple conclusion: relax, and let your true self perform."[9]

But remember, you do, in fact, need a certain amount of pressure to be creative. Creativity rarely happens when things are perfectly under control. To make the kettle boil, a little fire is necessary, and a deadline that's a month and a half away isn't always a good thing. I find that if I have too much time to complete a project, I'll put off working on it until two or three weeks before it's due just so I can dial up the pressure a little bit.

The trick is to control the pressure, not let it control you. Relax.

Leave the room and go work somewhere else.

A conference room maybe. Or leave the agency. Work in a public place. Some restaurants are close to empty between one and five in the afternoon. And as Sally Hogshead reminds us, "Domino's delivers to Starbucks."

There are other things you can do. If the in-store isn't coming, polish the online. If you can't write the headline, write the body copy. And if it's not happening during office hours, stop in the middle of dinner and write.

> "If you are in difficulties with a book, try the element of surprise: attack it at an hour when it isn't expecting it."
> —H. G. Wells

Get off the stinkin' computer.

If your keyboard freezes up, get a pen and paper. In fact, you may find handwriting brings an altogether different part of your brain into play. David Fowler agrees: "Try it. . . . It's just different. The connection between your hand and the page via a tiny strand of ink imparts something that's somehow closer to your heart."[10]

Ignore the little voice that says, "I'm just a hack on crack from Hackensack."

We all feel that way. Even the superstars in this business secretly believe they're hacks at least twice a day. The difference is they get better about ignoring the voice telling them this. In their book *Pick Me,* Vonk and Kestin give advice on making the evil little voice shut up.

> You have to learn to mute the voice. Or just use it to spur you on to do better. The painful truth is that all the awards in the world don't take away the tyranny of the blank page. The only thing that does is making a mark on it. Somehow, just getting those first few thoughts out is helpful, even if they genuinely do suck. The act of moving the pen across the paper is the antidote to the belief that you can't do it.[11]

Go to the store where they sell the stuff.

There is demographic data typed neatly on paper. And then there's the stark reality of a customer standing in front of a store shelf looking at your brand and at Brand X. I'm not saying you should start bothering strangers in store aisles with questions. Go ahead if you like. I find it inspiring just to soak in the vibes of the marketplace. Just watch. Think. I guarantee you'll come back with some ideas.

Author Jack London's advice: "You can't wait for inspiration. You have to go after it with a club."

Ask your creative director for help.

That's what they're there for. There is no dishonor in throwing up your hands and saying, "I'm in a dark and terrible place. Help me or I shall perish."

Your creative director may be able to see things you can't. She hasn't had her nose 2 inches away from the problem for the past two weeks like you have. She knows the client, knows the market, and can give you more than an educated guess on what's jamming up your creative process. Sometimes all it takes is a little push, 2 inches to the left, to get you back on track. (*You hack on crack from Hackensack.*) Oops, there's the evil voice again. Begone, self-loathing. I banish thee.

Get more product information.

You may not know enough about the problem yet, or you may not have enough information on the market. So ask your account folks or planners to go deeper into their files and bring you new stuff. It's likely they edited their pile of information and gleaned what they thought most important. Get to the original material if you can.

Go into it knowing—knowing—there's a chance you could fail.

This isn't heart surgery, folks. No one's gonna die. And as much as a client may hate to hear it, in this business failure *is* a possibility. In fact, if your ideas don't fall on their face every once in a while, dude, you're not tryin' very hard.

The story has it that Dan Wieden once told one of his top creative directors, "I have no use for you until you've made at least three *monumental* mistakes." Clearly, Wieden believes creative people don't develop unless they're willing to fail and fail and fail again. It's a credo so ingrained in the agency, they created a huge work of art for the hallway to remind them (Figure 4.9). Made entirely of more than 100,000 pushpins, it's a daily reminder that you aren't pushing it creatively if every one of your ideas turns out just hunky-stinkin'-dory.

Failing harder is good, and when it comes to digital, failing *faster* is even better. In Stefan Mumaw's *Chasing the Monster Idea,* managing director at Innosight, Scott Anthony, discusses failure: "Figuring out how to master this process of

Figure 4.9 At Wieden + Kennedy, failure is nothing to be ashamed of. Not swinging for the fences is.

failing fast and failing cheap and fumbling toward success is probably the most important thing companies have to get good at." Writer Jena McGregor agrees, calling it "getting good at failure."[12]

At an SXSW Interactive seminar I chaired, most folks in the audience agreed failure is the new black. You have to risk a belly flop. In the online space, a sense of play is important, and part of play is failure; the skinned knee, the black eye. Everyone, to a person, said to push past the pain and "fail forward, fail harder, fail gloriously." Whatever flavor of fail you get, our group said, walk it off and go for it again.

Read an old *Far Side* collection by Gary Larson.

The man is an absolute screaming genius. The cartoons are always funny. But look at the economy of his ideas. Look how simple they are. How few moving parts there are. At the very least, with a trip to Larson's sick little world you get a break from the tension. But you might get that small nudge you need. I know I have.

I also get that nudge by leafing through magazines from different categories. I'll be working on an insurance campaign, but if there's a snowboarding magazine on the conference room table, I'll pick it up and go through it.

One student told me when she's stuck she likes to go online, often to sites like StumbleUpon.com. Not a bad idea. Probably any site that's has cool stuff and is a little random may help fool your brain into coming up with something new.

Leafing through the awards annuals is okay, too. The shows are a good learning tool, early in the business; they're a good starting point, early in the ideation process. But at some point, they will begin to steer your thinking. I know plenty of absolutely stellar advertising people who don't own a single *CA* or One Show. They realize, sooner or later, they're going to have to unmoor and sail into the unknown.

Go to a bookstore and page through books on your subject.

Say you're working for an outboard engines client. Go to a bookstore and page through books on lakes, oceans, submarines, vacation spots, fish, pistons, hydraulics, whatever. Just let your brain soak up those molecular building blocks of future concepts.

You might get the ideas flowing right there in the store. And even if you don't, what's to risk, except maybe getting the hairy eyeball from the clerk who thinks you ought to be buying something? *("Hey, whaddaya think this is? A li-berry?")*

Sometimes it's good to work on three projects at once.

You may find that the ideas come faster if you move between projects every hour or so. Designer Milton Glaser said, "Working on one thing at a time is like facing a rhinoceros; working on ten things at a time is like playing badminton."

Don't burn up too much energy trying to make something work.

Follow the first rule of holes: if you are in one, stop digging. In the book *Lateral Thinking,* Edward DeBono uses this metaphor: don't dig one hole and keep digging down until you hit oil; dig lots of shallow holes first, all over the yard.

Even when you do manage to force a decent idea onto paper, after hours of wrestling with it, it usually bears the earmarks of a fight. You can count the dents where you pounded on the poor thing to force it into the shape you wanted. There's none of the spontaneous elegance of an idea born in a moment of illumination.

Be patient.

Tell yourself it will come. Don't keep swinging at the ball when your arms hurt. Maybe today's not the day. Give up. Go see a movie. Come back tomorrow. Pick up the bat and keep trying. Be patient.

Learn to enjoy the process. Not just the finished piece.

I used to hate the long process of writing an ad. I simply wanted the work to be done, the idea to be there on my desk. But thinking this way made my job way harder than it had to be. The fact is, most of your time in this business will be spent in some cluttered, just-slightly-too-warm room, thinking, not admiring your finished work. And nowadays with work that appears online, there isn't really "I'm finished now." You'll likely *never* be done. Customers will keep responding to your idea, new stuff will come to light, cool ideas will walk in the side door, and everything will keep changing.

So, remember to let the fun be in the *chase*. Even if you have an award-winning career, only 0.00000002 percent of it will be spent walking up to the podium to accept an award at the One Show. All the rest of the time you will likely spend in a small room somewhere, under fluorescent lights, trying to decide whether *crisp* or *flaky* is the right word to use.

Remember, you aren't saving lives.

When you get stressed and the walls are closing in and you're going nuts trying to crack a problem and you find yourself getting depressed, try to remember that you're just doing an ad. That is all. An ad. A stupid piece of paper. It's not even a whole piece of paper you're working on. It's just a half of a piece of paper in a magazine, and somebody else is buying the *other* side. Or it's a stupid landing page. Or a stupid radio spot. Remember, advertising is powerful and even a "pretty okay" idea can increase sales. (I know, I know. Don't tell my clients I said this. But we're talking times when it feels like your mental health is at stake.) Don't kill the goose trying to get a golden egg on demand.

Bertrand Russell said: "One of the symptoms of an approaching nervous breakdown is the belief that one's work is terribly important."

———

INSANITY, OFFICE POLITICS, AND AWARD SHOWS.

Identify your most productive working hours and use them for nothing but idea generation.

I happen to be a morning person. By three in the afternoon, my brain is meat loaf and a TV campaign featuring a grocer named Whipple doesn't seem like such a bad idea. But you might be sharper in the afternoon. Just strike while your iron is hot. And save those down hours for the busywork of advertising. What I call "phone calls and arguments."

Quit wasting time reading e-mails and Facebook, wandering around the office, or coming in late.

From the *New York Times,* I quote: "Employees in info-intensive companies waste 28 percent of their time on unnecessary e-mails and other interruptions."

Here's the thing, people. Every creative assignment you'll ever receive will have a deadline. You'll have only a certain amount of time to come up with something great. Yet I'll wager if any of us could watch a film of ourselves on a typical day at the office, we'd turn beet red seeing how much time we waste screwing around with coffee breaks, phone calls, texting, Facebooking, Twittering, and yuckin' it up out in the hallways.

In fact, we are so eager to be distracted that, left uninterrupted, we'll inter-rupt *ourselves,* and we do this because of what's called "resistance to writing." It's a sort of self-imposed writer's block that creative people practice when faced with a creative challenge. Oh, we'll sit down to work but we'll leave the TV on, or keep our e-mail open nearby as a sort of trapdoor we can sneak through when the ideas aren't coming and anxiety strikes. A smart woman named Linda Stone calls this frazzled state of mind *continuous partial attention.*

For today, all we need to do is acknowledge that this defense mechanism exists and, when we sit down to work, commit to it completely. Unplug your landline, turn off your smartphone, turn off the e-mail, find a pen and paper, put your feet up, and give it your whole mind.

"Be orderly in your normal life so you can be violent and original in your work."

I don't know much about novelist Gustave Flaubert, except he said the cool line you just read, and it seems to fit in right about here.

Many creative people find that a dash of ritual in their lives provides just the structure they need to let go creatively. I happen to prefer an extremely clean and empty room in which to write. That may sound weird, but I've heard of stranger things.

In *The Art and Science of Creativity,* George Kneller wrote: "Schiller [the German poet] filled his desk with rotten apples; Proust worked in a cork-lined room. . . . While [Kant was] writing *The Critique of Pure Reason,* he would con-centrate on a tower visible from his window. When some trees grew up to hide the tower, [he had] authorities cut down the trees so that he could continue his work."[13]

Your office manager may not like it, but if some trees are bugging you, hack those suckers down.

"Temper your Irish with German."

That's great advice for creative people. See, the thing is, this is a business. That whole chaos-is-good, whiskey-and-cigarettes, showing-up-late-for-work thing? That's fine for artists and rock stars, but advertising is only half art. It's also half business. The thing is, both halves are on the deadline.

So don't be sloppy. Don't be late. Meet your deadlines. Don't put off doing the radio because the mobile is more fun. Yes, the trains we dream up in this business are imaginary, but they all gotta run on time.

This also applies to expense reports and time sheets. Learn how to do them and do them impeccably. Be a grown-up. Sure, they're boring. But, like watching an old episode of *The Brady Bunch,* if you just sit down and *apply* yourself, the whole unpleasant thing will be over in a half hour.

Don't drink or do drugs.

You may think that drinking, smoking pot, or doing coke makes you more creative. I used to think so.

I was only fooling myself. I bought into that myth of the tortured creative person, struggling against uncaring clients and blind product managers. With a bottle next to his typewriter and his wastebasket filling ever higher with rejected brilliance, this poor, misunderstood soul constantly looks for that next fantastic idea to rocket him into happiness.

In a business where we all try to avoid clichés, a lot of people buy into this cliché-as-lifestyle. I can assure you it is illusion. As is all that crap about how writers need to "work from pain." Oh, puh-lease, it's a coupon ad for Jell-O.

> "A writer should be joyous, an optimist. Anything that implies rejection of life is wrong for a writer, and cynicism is rejection of life. I would say participate, participate, participate."
> —*George Gribbin*

Keep your eye on the ball, not on the players.

Don't get into office politics. Not all offices have them. If yours does, remember your priority—doing ads. Keep your eye on the ad on your desk.

You are a member of a team.

Don't ever forget that. Never get into that "I did the visual" or "I came up with the platform" thing. You work as a team; you suck as a team; you rock as a team.

You are not genetically superior to account executives.

During my first years in the business I was trained to look down on account executives. At the time, it seemed kind of cool to have a bad guy to make fun of. *("Oh, he couldn't sell a joint at Woodstock." "She couldn't sell a compass to Amelia Earhart.")* But I was an idiot. It's wrong to think that way. They are on my side. Make sure they are on yours.

Come to think of it, you're not genetically superior to anybody. Save the trash talk for basketball.

As we'll see in Chapter 14, advertising attracts all kinds of people, some of whom kinda suck. The ones I'm thinking of here are the trolls who hide under bridges like AgencySpy.com and anonymously post poisonous comments deriding other people's work and trashing other agencies. If you're not familiar with it, I encourage you to go online right now, read the comments posted there by these broken angry souls, and then ask yourself, "What kind of person do *I* want to be in this industry?"

If you can't put your name next to an opinion you're publishing, are you really different from the spineless boneweeds on YouTube calling some kid's video "gay"?

Stay in touch with the real world.

"Young creative people start out hungry. They're off the street; they know how people think. And their work is great. Then they get successful. They make more and more money, spend their time in restaurants they never dreamed of, fly back and forth between New York and Los Angeles. Pretty soon, the real world isn't people. It's just a bunch of lights off the right side of the plane. You have to stay in touch if you're going to write advertising that works."[14]

　　　　　　　　　　　　　　　　　　　—Jerry Della Femina

Stay in touch with the world. Read. Listen. Go places. One of my personal favorites is to watch TV all the time. (Is this a great business or what?)

"What are you doing, honey?"

"Oh, I'm in here analyzing the psyche of my culture—absorbing the zeitgeist, as it were. I can't be bothered."

Read books and magazines. Explore all the websites. Try all the new technology. Hang out for an hour at an Apple store. (They're used to it.) See all the cool new movies. What apps are being featured this week? Go to the weird new exhibits at the museums. Know what's out there, good and bad. It's called keeping your finger on the pulse of the culture, *all* of which has direct bearing on your craft.

On the value of awards shows.

I shouldn't talk. In my younger days, I was a pathetic awards hound.

But I won't be too hard on myself. Our work isn't signed. And when you're new in the business, there's no better way to make a name for yourself than getting into "the books." Awards shows allow tiny agencies to compete with the behemoths. They serve as great recruiting tools for agencies. And they expose us to all kinds of work we'd not see otherwise. So I recommend them—with some caveats.

Don't make the wrong name for yourself by entering too many campaigns for easy, microscopic, or public service clients. They might get *in*.

Don't talk about awards shows around clients or account executives. You'll devalue yourself in their eyes and make your work suspect. *("Is that last ad she did on strategy, or is it just another entry into Clever-Fest?")*

Don't enter every show. As of this writing, I count 39 different national awards shows in this industry. No kidding—39. It's pathetic how much this industry awards itself. (Remember, we aren't saving lives. Even Hollywood isn't this award-crazy.) Thirty-nine, and that's not even counting the local shows.

Here's the deal. Only three of them have any merit. In my opinion, the best are the One Show and *Communication Arts,* and, in England, D&AD. Cannes is a very big deal too, but in my opinion (and that of friends who've judged the festival) it's a little political.

One last thing: if awards are why you want to get into the business, don't get into the business.

Awards are candy. They're fun. But by nature of their exclusivity, they represent about 0.000002 percent of all the work being created every year. If you hang your self-esteem on such odds, you're likely to be disappointed.

Here's the other thing. If winning awards becomes true north on your compass, you'll warp your understanding of what this business is about: building brands and increasing sales.

Yes, I want you to win all kinds of awards by hitting that sweet spot we talked about in Chapter 3—coming up with ideas that are great for your book and great for the client's sales. But when you sit down to work on an idea, make sure you're trying to get into a customer's head and not into the award books.

I remember a long, interesting talk with my former boss, Mike Hughes, of the Martin Agency. Over lunch one day, we wondered what it would be like if there were no award shows. Or barring that, what if our respective agencies actually banned creatives from entering their work in them?

What would the creative teams come up with if we took away the gravitational pull of the shows? Where would creatives go if all constraints, all presuppositions, and every bit of influence were removed, *including* the influence of the design and advertising trends being lauded in the latest awards annuals? Our opinion was that the teams would probably start experimenting in some fresh and entirely unexplored areas.

As it turns out, neither of us had the guts to stop our agencies from entering work in the award shows. We understood that peer recognition is an important part of any endeavor. Still, we looked at each other and wondered, "What if?"

Figure 5.1   The QR in QR codes will soon stand for "quite retro." (This one happens to be for a book promotion.)

5

Concepting for the Hive Mind

Creativity in analog and digital

BECAUSE I AM FREQUENTLY ACCUSED OF BEING OLD, I feel the need to point out that I was not a winner in—nor even *in attendance at*—the 1902 award ceremonies for the One Show. However, since you brought it up, I believe it was a very short program actually. They announced winners in two media categories—best WANTED poster and best sandwich board—and pretty much called it a night.

Times have changed. The other day I found myself in a meeting where somebody managed to keep a straight face as she proposed making a blog-isode or maybe a content-mercial. She also wanted to organize a tweet-up and a webinar.

I can wrinkle my patrician Merriam-Webster nose all I want, but the fact is, we've *had* to start inventing words for all the new media platforms that have been created since the whole grid reached critical mass. A truncated list of what's called emerging media might includes banners, blogs, branded entertainment, microsites, buzz marketing, user-generated content, experiential marketing, gaming tie-ins, digital billboards and kiosks, intranets and extranets, SMS texting, Web apps, native apps, mobile video, PDA downloads, public relations and owned media, rich media, screen savers, video on demand, widgets, i-ads, keywords, and those gross viral videos you e-mail to friends even though their company firewalls block them.

Online is where the clients are spending more of their marketing dollars, and there's a dirt-simple reason for it: it's the first place we look, people. It's the first place *everybody* looks for everything. And since big advertisers are usually hoping to attract a younger, higher-income market, this is the place you'll likely find them. I recently read (online, of course) a description of this coveted consumer profile:

Noah has a blog, a couple Websites, a Facebook profile, a LinkedIn profile, a Flickr account for his photos, a YouTube channel for his videos, a SlideShare account of his biz presentations, a Last.fm profile for the music he's listening to, a Delicious account for the web pages he wants to bookmark, a Twitter account for the random observations and comments, and a Dopplr account so he and his friends can track one another's whereabouts and maybe meet up if they find themselves in the same city.[1]

(Okay, first I need to admit that I'd like to, well, I'd like to punch Noah . . . maybe just a little bit. I mean, dude, come on, just put the iPad down and go take a walk, see a movie, do *somethin'*, man. . . .) But I digress. The point here is this: digital is not so much a media channel as it is a way of life. People live digitally. Note also that this Noah character likely skips over the commercials on his DVR, plays online games with friends in Budapest, and probably hasn't held a magazine since that time at the dentist when he thumbed through a five-year-old issue of *Hunting & Fishing*.

In *The On-Demand Brand,* author Rick Mathieson describes the new marketing challenge very bluntly: "Today your audience is simply and relentlessly rejecting media—and brand marketers—that fail to fit into their increasingly interconnected, digital lifestyles."[2]

There is no "digital revolution" anymore. It's over and digital won. But so did people in general because consumers are almost entirely in charge now. They watch and read what they want and do it when they want on the devices they want. Part of this huge change was caused by what Seth Godin calls a "shift in scarcity and abundance." Media space and storage capacity, once scarce, have been made nearly infinite by the Internet and technology. On the other hand, our capacity for sustained attention threatens to disappear entirely. In *Engage,* Brian Solis nearly writes its obituary: "If you subscribe to the theory of attention economics, we're indeed living in an era of information overload that is pushing us to the edge of attention bankruptcy."[3]

Into this flux add the fact that brands and marketers are no longer in charge of mass media communication. A consumer's best selection of content was once 2 hours of prime-time TV. But in the last month alone, more content was uploaded to YouTube than was broadcast by the networks over the past *60 years.*[4] Yes, most of it sucks, but the fact remains that today anybody with a good idea and a YouTube channel can create content that could be seen by millions of people within a week—stuff people wanna watch way more than network TV. Watching Charlie Sheen on *Two and a Half Men* simply isn't as interesting as watching the online video of Charlie Sheen being insane.

And finally, to top all this off, consumers have learned to use this powerful new platform to their advantage. The mighty Dell Computer had its ass handed to it by one mistreated and unhappy customer. Then the mighty United Airlines publicly denied that its baggage crew had wrecked some guy's guitar; the guy writes a funny song that turns into a huge hit online, quickly gets to 10 million views, and suddenly United has real baggage to deal with.

It's unlikely United or Dell would make the same mistakes today. Marketers and agencies everywhere seem to be getting more savvy, and where once TV and print used to be the big boys, interactive is taking over as the hub. Online is often where a core brand lives, and the other media are used to drive customers to its digital hub.

A fellow named Joshua Baze said, "Everything you've done in digital the last seven years won't matter within a matter of months." Which may cause some to wonder, "Mr. Sullivan, why should we finish the rest of your stupid chapters on digital if it's all gonna be obsolete soon?" A fair question, and my answer is this: State-of-the-art technology will become obsolete. State-of-the-art thinking is another matter.

There *are,* in fact, some very smart ways for you to think about this stuff, some basic approaches that will help you think in a new way about digital marketing, instead of just trying to retrofit lessons learned in traditional media, something that still happens quite a lot. In a speech by David Gillespie, he described this "classic McLuhan-esque mistake of appropriating the *shape* of the previous technology as the *content* of the new technology." Many early efforts in digital did exactly this; direct mail became e-mail; billboards were resized as banners. My friend Stephen Land at GSD&M agrees, describing digital efforts that don't leverage the interactivity of the platform as mere "print-eractive." But this was understandable, says Gillespie, because at the time the alternative was standing still. Now it's time to push through.[5]

This pushing through will involve rethinking how we approach work in all media. In a little book called *Oh My God, What Happened and What Should I Do?* authors from Innovative Thunder put it this way:

> One day, one of our ex-bosses said while talking to traditional creatives: "If an idea doesn't work online, it's not a good idea." He was right, because when you realize that your idea only works in a print ad or as a TV spot, it becomes obvious this idea can't be that great. Of course, this quote also works the *other* way around. When an idea only works online or with a specific medium, it probably hasn't got enough relevance or potential to become an integrated campaign.[6]

So, as we work on pushing through, we're not going to worry about becoming experts in digital, because we never will. All we can do is try our hardest and keep our head in what they call a "permanent beta mentality." We just have to keep tryin' different stuff and, if something doesn't work, try something else. Then, even when it *does* work, we try something else.

If you're perhaps a little tired of hearing about digital-schmigital, keep in mind that all technological changes come with this kind of attention and chatter. It takes a while for anything new to go from being a novelty to becoming another common platform. It'll happen. Soon we won't be talking about digital advertising anymore. We'll all be talking mobile this and mobile that. And so it goes.

Traditional or digital, this is a fantastic time to be in this business. Creativity and the crafts matter now more than ever. We can't buy people's attention anymore. We can't keep interrupting all the stuff people are interested in; we have to *become* the stuff they're interested in. We have to become so stinkin' interesting that people actually put down what they're doing to come over, lean in, and see what we're all about.

———

BRAVE NEW MARKETING

I often think that in the old days, presenting an advertising/marketing plan sounded like a general planning the invasion of a country of really stupid people.

> *We've identified our target and we're going to carpet bomb these people with massive buys of TV using "roadblocks" across all the networks so there's no escape. We'll penetrate the market and fire off weekly mailings and if they don't march in to our stores, Wham! We'll hit 'em with radio. Wham! We'll hit 'em with print, pow, pow, pow.*

As we begin to talk about the new marketing, it'll pay to leave this old marketing-think behind. Where we once talked to customers, we'll talk with them; where there were once only audiences, there will be communities; where once we focused on messaging, we'll also create content and experiences. We'll actually be invited to places advertisers used to have to barge in, and through it all we'll start thinking less "us vs. them" and more "we."

Obviously there won't be much "we" goin' on if our marketing plans sound like Desert Storm. So what does this brave new marketing look like?

It's less about messaging and more about content.

Up till now we've talked about the crafts of copywriting and art direction and how they apply to "makin' ads." But these crafts can also help you create things a consumer might actually look forward to seeing. So as we move into the new world, we'll expand our definition of advertising to include anything that brings a brand to life for customers. This could take almost any form: a mobile app, a blog, a game, a movie or TV show, a retail experience, a book, a song, an online service, a new product—pretty much anything but advertising. The key difference is that your creation be interesting in its own right and have a reason to exist beyond just the brand's messaging.

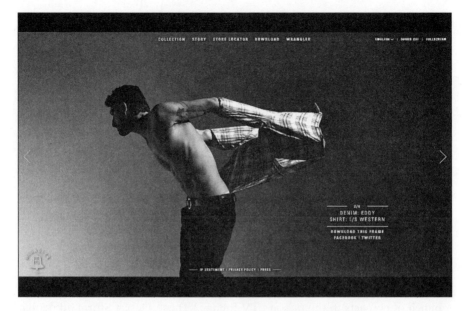

*Figure 5.2   Use your cursor to pull off the guy's clothes.
What a simple, graphic idea.*

This doesn't mean messaging goes out the window. No matter what we create, it'll have to report to some commercial purpose; otherwise it's just "art" . . . or something. But having a commercial purpose doesn't rule out being riveting. Wrangler created a commercial site clearly meant to show off their clothes, but they did it in a fashion so riveting you were happy to spend your time looking at it (Figure 5.2). When you arrived at the site, you were instructed to use your cursor to rip the clothes off the model. It sounds simple (great ideas always are), but the production values of the site made the interaction hypnotic.

It's less about ads and more about experiences.

Where the old Desert Storm model of advertising was about "targeting consumers with messages," think now about how you might also delight them with experiences. Ideas are things you tell someone; experiences you give.

For example, instead of running an ad with some claim about how Samsung phones stand up to punishment, From Stockholm With Love put up a live feed to 70 Samsung phones on a glass table over a concrete floor and a water tank. Customers could make phone calls to any of these phones, and if your call's vibrations rattled the phone off the table onto the concrete or into the tank, you won that phone. And you wanted the phone too, because your call told you it still worked.

One of my favorite recent examples of creating an experience is Droga5's "Decoded." To launch the memoir of rock star Jay-Z, Droga5 hid pages from his memoir in outdoor spots in 13 cities (mostly in the form of enlarged page-shots) (Figure 5.3). The cool part was they embedded these pages in or on spaces relevant to the content of the page. The first people who found the pages and logged onto a website got a chance at two lifetime tickets to Jay-Z's concerts. Cool customer experiences and the great public relations that concepts like this garner combined to put the book on the *New York Times*'s Best Sellers list. It won the Cannes Grand Prix for Outdoor to boot.

As much as we talk about experiences, brand ideas are still king. In fact, it's the brand idea from which all the experiences spring. But if all you create on behalf of a brand are ads that sit within the folds of a magazine, are you getting as close to the customer as possible? Brilliant advertising is important, too. We want people to lean in. But with a brand experience, we can make them fall in.

It's less about talking to and more about talking with.

Can we just all agree here that the only captive audience that exists anymore is a bunch of convicts in the prison's TV lounge? Those Desert Storm ad people may continue to think they can bark product benefits at captive audiences, but they're not there anymore.

Figure 5.3   When something is this cool, it doesn't feel like advertising.

The People Formerly Known as the Audience is a fun, if angry, little screed I found online in which the author seems to agree.

> Once they were *your* printing presses; now the blog, has given the press to us. . . . [S]hooting, editing and distributing video once belonged to you, Big Media. Now video is coming into the user's hands. . . . You were once (exclusively) the editors of the news. Now we can edit the news. . . . [Your] highly centralized media system had connected people "up" to big centers of power but not "across" to each other. Now the horizontal flow, citizen-to-citizen, is as real and consequential as the vertical one. . . . There's a new balance of power between you and us.[7]

Okay, he sounds kinda like a hippie with a megaphone at Berkeley in '68, but the dude has a point. He's essentially reprising the line from that old movie *Network: "We're mad as hell and we're not gonna take it anymore!"* Consumers aren't "eyeballs" anymore; they're voices, and they're talking with one another and sharing news, content, and strong opinions about brands out there in the communities. And if the mute button wasn't bad enough, now they can also hit the alarm button, as we saw with Dell Computer and United Airlines.

But, as we'll get to soon, if we make something of value for customers, they'll actually look at it and if they love it, they may create communities around our offering. And the community is a fantastic way for a brand to forge a relationship with its customers.

It's less about asking customers to listen and more about inviting them to talk.

If you were one of the account people on *Mad Men*, your job was to *control* the brand (in between cigarettes, highballs, and skullduggery). To this day, many marketers continue to believe they're the sole owners of their brands. But the two-way street created by digital technology has made it increasingly clear that the vitality of a brand is largely in the hands of customers.

The blogosphere has turned readers into writers, and YouTube has created millions of editors and directors. More and more we'll see how the new marketing allows these writers, directors, and editors to talk, even play, with a brand. John Hegarty suggests that doing this requires "inventiveness, daring, and creativity—all the attributes large companies are bad at deploying. And, if anything, those corporations are finding it difficult to deal with a medium where you have to let go and learn not to be in control."[8]

It's only when a brand doesn't try to *clinch* the reins that really marvelous things can happen, such as the YouTube version of Old Spice's campaign, "The Man Your Man Could Smell Like." The extraordinarily popular "I'm on a horse" TV spot attracted so many customer comments and Twitter requests

*Figure 5.4   From a Twitter request, the Old Spice spokesman delivered
some guy's marriage proposal to his girlfriend online.*

that Wieden + Kennedy decided to start responding in near real time. Working
together on the set, writers fed ideas to the client who gave near-instant approval
and the videos were filmed and posted, one after another (Figure 5.4). The
agency and client's quick and fluid response leveraged the current popularity of
the TV spot and moved the campaign into even higher orbit.

It's less about trying to make people want stuff and more about making stuff people want.

An ad may be the best way to tell customers about a sale or a new product.
But to get people to really engage with a brand, it's likely we'll need to create
something bigger, more important, more valuable than an ad. At R/GA they
have a house rule: when you're reviewing your ideas, ask yourself, "Is what
I'm creating adding something to someone's life? Is it useful, entertaining, or
beautiful?"

Remember that line. We'll be returning to it time and again.

None of us really wants an ad. I know *I* don't, and I work in this industry.
But if something is useful, entertaining, or beautiful, that's a different story.
Those three words perfectly describe Intel's marvelous Facebook application,
The Museum of Me. Although admittedly more entertaining and beautiful than
useful, the point here is that nearly 1 million people who didn't wake up thinking about Intel ended up spending an average of five minutes engaged with the
brand because of this wonderful site (Figure 5.5).

*Figure 5.5   The Museum of Me used images from your own social
sites to show off Intel's expertise.*

None of these principles of the new marketing sit well with Mr. *Mad Men/
Desert Storm* guy. He still wants to carpet bomb all God-fearing citizens with
TV commercials. But these basic principles about creating content and experiences, about building communities, inviting participation, and making things
people can actually use, this is where the renaissance of creativity is happening.
Ads and TV spots will still play a part, but a lot of people think the really fun
stuff is happening out here on the edge.

THE NEW CREATIVE PERSON IS T-SHAPED.

Despite all this change, the two crafts we discussed in the first chapters—
copywriting and art direction—are still the basic tools you'll need to create work
in this new world of analog and digital media. Even if we wake up tomorrow in
a Philip K. Dick novel, when it comes to creating advertising or content of any
kind, someone's gonna have to sit down and actually *make something* and that'll
still probably require the crafts of a writer and an art director.

The crafts are portable. They still matter in the new world, as do the disciplines of branding and positioning. As does being creative. In fact, given the
kaleidoscope of stuff competing for attention now, creativity is more important than ever. Our job hasn't changed in this respect. We still have to make
things that are so interesting people lean in to see what's goin' on. None of
what goes into creating a great idea changes; but as we've seen, the output is,
in fact, different.

Today, a creative person is expected to be able to come up with everything from an ad to a website, a mobile application to a TV show, and a tweet to a radio spot. Where once Bernbach's original team of two could tackle all the traditional media, creating for a world that includes digital requires more skill sets than just copywriting and art direction.

For big cool projects that involve online creative or digital content of any kind, you'll need to have at your side: interactive producers, digital designers and developers, as well as information architects (IAs) and user experience (UXs) people. In fact, the contributions of UX people are becoming so vital, more and more agencies are simply calling them "creatives" and not boxing them into basic production jobs like drawing wireframes (the rough plans for a digital product).

So now, where briefings once happened in a quiet room with four or five people, today you might find groups of 15 or more. At some agencies, it's possible you'll still find small groups but it's likely here the members are each capable of working in several disciplines, the "T-shaped" people. And to be an effective member of these new teams, you'll need to adapt and become more T-shaped yourself.

T-shaped is just a funny name used to describe a person who has very deep skills in one area (the deep vertical stroke of the T) as well as the ability to collaborate across disciplines he or she is not an expert in (that would be the horizontal stoke). Today's most successful creatives are a sort of hybrid, capable of expert contributions in their chosen fields of art direction or copywriting but fluent enough in other digital disciplines to collaborate effectively, occasionally even executing things on their own. The new creatives have both depth and breadth, and today their job description isn't "writing or art directing cool ads and TV spots." It's bigger. The job today is to create entertaining or useful experiences for your clients' brands. It might involve an ad; it might not. It's the main reason why over the past year, we've seen more agency titles change from creative director to creative director and strategist.

"I'm not even sure that the future is a writer-and-art-director team anymore," says Wieden + Kennedy creative director Tony Davidson in Spencer's *Breaking In*. "I get a sense that the kids coming through want to do a lot more. They want to be an animator, they want to be a director, they want to be a writer. I love the idea of a hybrid-ideas-person who can move between disciplines."[9]

Alex Bogusky discussed the importance of knowing how to make stuff in Eliza Williams's *This Is Advertising*:

> [At Crispin] we've talked about when there will be no specialization on the creative floor, but the technology moves so fast it's pretty difficult to keep up with it unless you specialize in it. . . . [So] you want the creative people sitting really close to the programmers and the information architects. Because

although they may not be charged with creative, they're going to have ideas and influences that the creative aren't going to get unless they're sitting adjacent to those folks. . . . It's a little weird to *not* know how to do that stuff, because the knowing really influences the execution of it.[10]

The thing is, when you can become at least conversant in these other more technical disciplines, you'll be a better creative and a better team member. But when you become *fluent* in them—and can even execute on occasion—you'll become the sort of go-to "creative alchemist" every agency on the planet is trying to hire.

In *Breaking In,* Google's Valdean Klump describes just how valuable this wider skill set is:

> What impresses me most is the ability to make things. More and more these days, young people are coming into the business able to shoot their own commercials, create websites, program games, take photos, make animations, build Facebook apps, and generally act as one-person ad agencies. This makes CDs salivate because getting ideas *off* of the page is at least as hard as getting them on paper in the first place . . . If you can make things and make them well, you will never be unemployed.[11]

Having been a creative director at an agency that was hiring, I remember wanting to recruit only the most techno-geeked-out, mobile-ready, code-slinging Web brats I could find. On the other hand, I wanted writers or art directors who knew how to take a blank sheet of paper and make something interesting and beautiful happen. The place where these two skills overlapped was the sweet spot. The ones who can do both of these things? They're the creatives of the future.

Now if you're already in the business, as either a "traditional" or "digital creative" (a distinction that's almost obsolete already), there are many things you can do to align yourself with the future.

For now, I find myself pushing both traditionals and digitals toward the middle. Pushing traditional creatives to use, study, and learn the emerging technologies. And pushing digital creatives to learn how to create things that are delightful and conceptual on paper; things that are cool even before any coding happens.

I'll use myself as an example.

Having come up in this business during the 1980s and 1990s, I think I'm probably pretty good at looking at a brand brief, figuring out the single most important thing to say, and then making something interesting happen: in print, on TV, outdoor, or radio. I kinda know what I'm doing there.

But I won't kid myself. I'm not what they call a digital native, someone who grew up with technology. I'm a digital immigrant, with a heavy enough old-world accent even the guys at the corner deli can't understand me. Yet I am not content to sit on Ellis Island wondering what delights await discovery on the new digital shores. I'm swimmin' across, people. Meaning, I stay very busy learning everything I can.

I am busy actually using the new media. I have an online presence, and I'm busy blogging about this stuff, tweeting about it, and watching webinars (I still can't say that word with a straight face): online seminars broadcast from cool places like Boulder Digital Works. I'm on lynda.com (where you can teach yourself Flash or Dreamweaver) and a whole bunch of other cool websites for inspiration and education. All of this so I can learn the new media, experience the new technologies, and help take my clients' brands out into the world to meet their customers. I do all this hoping my self-guided education will push me toward that sweet spot in the middle.

Now, if I were a digital native, someone whose deep part of the T shape is expertise in, say, HTML5, CSS, and Javascript? I'd get me a couple of the latest One Show annuals (insist on the kind made out of paper) as well as all the December issues of *Communication Arts' Advertising Annuals* that I could find. Then I'd turn off my cell phone, put my feet up, and read 'em cover to cover. I'd *inhale* them. And then I'd go find some more.

I'd probably start by studying the print of the 1980s Fallon McElligott, I'd watch the TV of the 1990s Goodby, Silverstein & Partners, and I'd understand how they tell an integrated story at today's Crispin Porter + Bogusky. I'd learn how to write headlines as good as the work Abbott Meade Vickers did for the *Economist* (Chapter 4). I'd learn how to say something provocative in a 10-word sentence. I'd learn how to tell an interesting story in 30 seconds.

I'd push myself toward the middle.

Ultimately, for any open job position in its creative department, an agency's gonna hire someone who is—drum roll—creative. But the tie's gonna go to the person who can express creativity over the widest variety of media and actually make stuff.

Before we move on to talk about advertising as content, there's one more job position now available in many agencies, one that's neither art director or copywriter—a profession called creative technology.

The creative tech is trained to be skilled in using new media technologies in the service of branding, advertising, and marketing. This person introduces emerging technologies into the concepting process and is involved from briefing through development to final delivery. Whether it's bringing a technical understanding of location-based platforms, designing communities, or executing Facebook applications, the creative tech helps turn the main campaign idea into cool online consumer experiences. In addition to blue-skying concepts along with the art director–copywriter team, she may build quick prototypes to test ideas, do some coding, or be a liaison to the client's information technology stakeholders.

A creative tech is even more helpful when she also has some polished skills of copywriting or art direction. So if you have any tech-geek in you, creative tech may be the way you want to go. Not a bad idea considering the whole world is *Matrix*-ing into 1s and 0s. We're going to need people who specialize in applying all the digital media technologies that come online every week.

CONTENT IS KING.

"Dudes! Come in here! Look at my computer screen!"

That's me in the year 1990, and the amazing "Flying Toasters" (Figure 5.6a) are making their first appearance on my 128k MacIntosh computer and its butt-kicking 8 MHz microprocessor. At the time, this soon-to-be-ubiquitous screen saver was pretty much all it took to amaze knuckleheads such as myself.

Hey, no laughing. Beyond a few Word document retrieval sites, in 1990 the Flying Toasters were "content." At least they were better than that grainy-ass picture of Felix the Cat, which comprised the first "show" on television (Figure 5.6b). You're not missing anything with this still photograph either; that's all it was—a shot of a stupid cat.

It has been interesting, my career, straddling as it has the years before and after the Web. Interesting too has been the evolution of all the content available in the media.

In 1994, TBWA\Chiat\Day's Lee Clow was our speaker guest at Fallon's creative retreat. We met at an old hunting lodge on a lake in northern Wisconsin, and to this day, I remember Lee leaning against the fireplace as he talked about Apple, examining the changes wrought by this amazing company and what it all meant for traditional creatives like us.

"Throughout history, the technology always comes first. It's just technology for a while," said Lee, "until the day we artists inherit it."

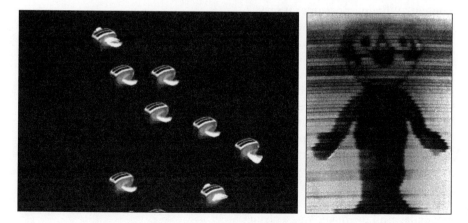

Figure 5.6   "Content" circa 1990 and 1928.

Lee was right. When television first came along, pretty much all the content and commercials sucked—*("I'm head over heels in Dove!")*—but people loved it because it was cool new technology. *("Honey, look. It's Felix!")* No one knew what we were missing until artists began to inherit the medium in the 1960s and realize its larger potential. Same thing happened in years previous with radio. Today we find ourselves in a digital era when the artists are just beginning to fully inherit the technology first wrought by Tim Berners-Lee.

Consumers are *also* inheriting technology, and theirs is giving them more control over all the same media. What started with a TV's on-off button changed to a mute button and then to time-shifting devices like VCRs, then DVRs, and now that consumers have complete control over everything they view online and offline, it's fair to ask, "How can a brand get any attention at all?"

The answer: Have better content than everyone else.

Quit interrupting the interesting things people want to look at and start *being* the interesting thing to look at.

Quality content trumps all.

This content can be anything; well, anything that's useful, entertaining, or beautiful, to borrow R/GA's terms again. Content can be a how-to video, a Q&A chat room, blogs, apps, or downloadable video games. Content can be a white paper, a non-PG video, or a ringtone. It can be almost anything as long as it has either entertainment value or is something a customer will find useful.

We're entering an era when all brands, big and small, will have to be in the content business. This means agencies will have to be in the content business, too. Interbrand's CEO Andy Bateman agrees: "Content and functionality are the new creativity."[12]

As with any commercial creativity, there's a discipline here and as you sit down to think content, you must have an objective. Why are you making this content? What purpose does it serve?

When ABC Entertainment created content for their show *Lost,* there was a clear objective: keep the fans involved in the show off-season. In *The On-Demand Brand,* ABC's Mike Beson described how they "actually started to bury web addresses in the final episodes of *Lost* after Season One, that took people to [fake websites like] Oceanic-Airlines.com. It was . . . content as marketing."[13]

Even insane content like the Skittles "Touch the Rainbow" YouTube series needed to report to a strategy. TBWA\Chiat\Day's Gerry Graf told me that Skittles's 1990s-era TV campaigns had helped Skittles "own" magic, but it was a PG-rated Disneyesque magic that needed some modernizing. "To bring it up to date we referenced things like Spike Jonze videos with Christopher Walken flying . . . our *own* version of magic. A big difference was that, in our world, the magic wasn't *amazing.* It was just part of life. Rabbits sing, beards are an appendage, all the magic was a given."

"Switch Singing Bunny" and "Beard" were, in fact, two of their most talked-about television spots, and these only whet their customers' online appetites for

Figure 5.7   Skittles: About as far as it gets from Felix the Cat.

more magical weirdness. What's even cooler is that in bringing the campaign to YouTube, BBDO Toronto took advantage of the laptop medium by inviting viewers to place a finger on the screen. A voice-over said: *"Touch the rainbow! No, seriously, put your index finger on the screen where the Skittle is. A video is going to start and your finger is going to be soooo delicious."* The videos were built to interact with the presence of a finger "in the scene" and in the most disturbing execution, a cat appears to be licking the viewer's finger and is pushed aside by a creepy man-cat who does the same thing (Figure 5.7).

As of this writing, there are a couple thousand delighted responses posted under this Skittles video; from "oohhhhhmyyyygod that was so weird" and "had to wash my finger!" to "favorite video ever!!!"

This particular execution hits on almost all the guidelines out there for creating good content. It should meet a brand's customers where they are, it should talk to them in their language, it should be extremely useful or entertaining, and if it can require participation from the viewer, all the better. (Check, check, check, and check.)

There are thousands of great examples of content online for you to study, content best seen *in situ* than the pages of a book. You might start with a quick look at Fallon's BMW Films. This work is credited as being the very first online-only content-driven brand campaign—a series of cool mini-movies called "The Hire," shot by A-list directors, starring A-list celebs and the latest BMWs. The breakthrough Fallon made with this idea wasn't so much the action or plot of the movies but the whole notion that a brand could come up with something so interesting that their marketing ceased to be an interruption and become a *destination,* a place customers actually wanted to go.

New and better examples of incredible content appear online almost daily now and anything I commit to paper here will date. Yet for the purposes of a short intro course in "content studies," I'll direct your attention to these early efforts which are — at this writing — still viewable online:

- Arcade Fire's music video "The Wilderness Downtown": Viewers participated by providing their address. This allowed images from the viewers' own streets and neighborhoods (pulled from Google Map's Street View) into the story of the music video.

- The launch of the game Halo 3: Instead of the typical commercial showing the clips of actual game-play, McCann San Francisco and AKQA posted a long video titled "Museum," where viewers could see the game's epic battles told as backstory and meticulously executed in the style of a museum diorama.

- For the JFK Museum, the Martin Agency created a site called We Choose the Moon, which "rebroadcast" the entire flight of Apollo 11 in real time from takeoff to splash down.

From these few examples, I see a few house rules to keep in mind as we begin our own work.

The first comes from Skittles's creepy man-cat. One of his YouTube viewers posted a note saying, "Doesn't work very well with a touch screen. It pauses the video." I'm guessing the creative team was aware these videos wouldn't work as well on touch-screens, didn't care, and went ahead anyway. (I would have.) Still, it's a good reminder that as you come up with ideas there'll be technical realities to keep in mind, such as making sure your idea is viewable from all the devices your customers use. The fancy-pants term for this is being *vendor agnostic.*

In addition to paying attention to technical differences like Apple vs. Android and Flash vs. HTML, you'll also need to design your content for the type of screen it'll likely be viewed on. Generally, people watch lengthier pieces on the big living room TV screen and "snack" on media elsewhere. For instance, I'm not likely to watch epic movies on my iPhone or to use a Foursquare app on my living room TV. Given these viewing habits, the rule of thumb is to concept for one overall screen, design for the big screen, and then optimize for the smaller ones.

Technical realities aside, having incredible content is what it's all about. We conclude here with Doc Searles simple message from *The Cluetrain Manifesto:* "There is no market for messages."[14]

WHAT THE NEW IDEAS LOOK LIKE, BESIDES COOL.

In the book *The Art of Immersion,* Nick Law, R/GA's CEO, frames up our opening problem nicely: "What should we be making? Twenty years ago, I'd be thinking, how do I turn this idea into a 30-second spot? [But] now I make a decision: Should we be doing something to encourage a community? Should we be giving information? Should we be nesting entertainment in there?"[15]

Nick's questions take us to our first point. When you get your assignment, remember what John Hegarty suggested in Chapter 2: "Question the brief." Since most briefs ask for an ad, question this first.

In fact, I recommend questioning everything: the media buy, the research, the whole reason the client is advertising—all of it. It's likely you won't be able to change anything one bit. *("The client has signed off on it and is vacationing in Bora Bora.")* But in the asking, in the challenging, whole new approaches may reveal themselves. Remember, the most important word a creative person can use is *why*. Look long and hard at your client's business problem and decide whether an ad is the solution. It might be. It might not.

The new ideas might not be "ads as we know them."

A planner at Fallon was overheard saying, "I am so *over* messages."

There are many in the business today who agree, who question the format itself—that of paid messaging. It worked fine in the 1950s, when TV was new and citizens were happy to listen to the boring man tell them Anacin worked fast-fast-fast.

But things are different today. As social media guru Ed Boches ("Bo-Chess") points out, "In an age when the manufacturer, publisher, broadcaster and programmer have lost power to the consumer, reader, viewer and user, the power of controlled messages has lost its impact."[16]

It may be getting to the point now where marketers can't make anything happen by employing messaging alone, no matter how authentic. Doc Searles, coauthor of *The Cluetrain Manifesto,* agrees, stating that a brand isn't what a brand says but what it *does*. What all this suggests is that perhaps the best way to influence behavior and opinion these days is to *do* things in addition to just saying things.

Where it once served our clients to make claims about their products, it may now be better to do things that are less claim-based and more action-based, or reality-based, or experiential—to *demonstrate in the execution itself* a brand's promise or a product's benefit. Boches could be right when he says, "Applications, utility, and platforms will trump messages as an agency's most important creative output."[17]

A good example is Coke's "Give It Back" initiative. Rather than *talk* about how much the company cares about sustainability, Coke proved it by putting up display racks made of corrugated cardboard, things people could see for themselves right in the store. To those who might say this sounds a little so-what *("Dude, you're talking about a cardboard display rack at the Hi-Lo. Seriously, this is 'cool'?"),* I'd say, consider the alternative: an ad. An ad with only Coke's claim that they're environmentally conscious and no proof of it. I'm reminded here also of Denny's Super Bowl offer to America: a free breakfast, and during a recession no less. This was an event as much as it was paid messaging, and America took them up on it. Also from Goodby, Silverstein & Partners came the Hyundai Assurance Program, the one that allowed customers who bought a new Hyundai to return it if they lost their job within the year. These aren't ads so much as they're events. They are not claims; they're actions.

In the end, it's clear that no matter how many ads we run, a brand cannot become X by saying they are X. They must actually *be* X. So after you've figured out what your brand needs to say, figure out what it needs to do. Same thing with customers: after you figure out what you want customers to think, what is it you want them to do?

The bottom line: Brand actions speak louder than words. Brand experiences speak louder than ads. Walk beats talk.

The new ideas come from culture, not commerce.

One way to do this stuff is to sit down, pore over a product's sheet of benefits, and then build a bridge out to your customers. But now that customers have so many ways to build bridges back to us, it often pays to begin our thinking out where *they* are. Instead of having our thinking driven entirely by the product manager's PowerPoint presentation, let's go out and immerse ourselves in the cultural milieu of the customer.

In *The Art of Immersion,* Billie Howard of Weber Shandwick says, "A brand becomes relevant by infusing itself directly into the culture. Advertising used to interrupt life's programming. Now advertising is the programming. And if you're being marketed to successfully, you'll have no idea (or you'll be enjoying yourself)."

What we're doing here is learning to ride the cultural currents and use them to our brand's advantage, doing what the Miami Ad School calls "pop culture engineering." Or as Alex Bogusky describes it, mixing just the right "cultural cocktail."

The first step in doing this to study the culture, and we do this the same way any anthropologist does: by immersing ourselves in it; by listening; by learning the language, both visual and verbal. What's popular out there right now? What news stories are customers talking about? What are the themes of our zeitgeist? What are the catch phrases and the images that keep popping up? These popular images and phrases are often referred to as *memes.* Originally a biological term, Merriam-Webster says the word now refers to "an idea, behavior or style . . . that spreads from person to person within a culture." Wikipedia calls it "a unit for carrying cultural ideas, symbols or practices."

The famous red and blue Obama poster was a meme. So's the YouTube video "Charlie bit my finger." These popular bits of condensed cultural material are often great jumping-off points to get to bigger culturally relevant ideas. In fact, a lucky few in our industry end up writing phrases so popular they *become* verbal memes: "Where's the beef?" "I'm on a horse," and my current favorite, Playstation's "Clean up, Aisle You."

The new ideas improve people's lives.

Brand generosity is a term you may hear bandied about. It's the idea that a brand should be out there adding good things to people's lives and to the culture. That's pretty cool, and if you have a client who believes this, lucky you. In practice, this

*Figure 5.8   The cool part was when the crane moved the sign to
point in the direction you asked for.*

brand generosity is a bigger version of R/GA's house rule: "Is what I'm creating
adding something to someone's life? Is it useful, entertaining, or beautiful?"

- *Inspire—Give them something beautiful or emotive:* IKEA's famous
"Dream Kitchens" site by Forsman & Bodenfors used beautiful photographs of people in IKEA kitchens frozen in *Matrix* "bullet time."
Hypnotizing panoramic 3D shots of people frozen in mid-story against
backdrops of IKEA kitchens inspired viewers to think about their own
kitchen's possibilities.

- *Provoke—Give them something that makes them think:* To drive interest
in Nokia's navigation products, agency Farfar looked for the oldest navigation tool around—"the pointy sign"—and resized it into "The World's
Biggest Signpost" (Figure 5.8). *So* way beyond cool, this huge digital
screen in the shape of arrow was lifted by crane six stories above London.
Nokia then asked Brits to point out the nation's "good things" by sending
live text messages directly to the sign. Delighted citizens watched as the
crane heaved the giant arrow around to point to their suggested locations
while its digital readout provided the exact distance.

- *Entertain—Give them something that's fun to do:* To promote its mobile
apps in San Francisco, Yahoo! put up 20 interactive bus shelters. The Bus
Stop Derby screens allowed people waiting for their bus to play games
against folks waiting at the other 19 bus stops throughout the city. Social
bragging rights were part of it, and the winning neighborhood also got an
OK Go! concert hosted in their neighborhood on Yahoo!'s nickel.

- *Status—Give something that confers kudos among their community:*
No one does this better than applications like Gowalla and Foursquare.

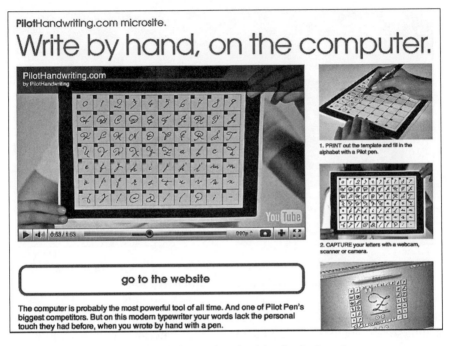

PilotHandwriting.com microsite.

Write by hand, on the computer.

Figure 5.9   Pilot Pens celebrates handwriting by letting viewers create a working computer font of their own script.

These platforms let people interact with friends to show both where they are and whom they're with. While they're out there checking in, they earn badges and the bragging rights that come with them. Badges started out with simple things such as being named mayor and explorer, but they have become monetized and can now involve discounts and other promotions. In an interesting cross-platform twist, the network Bravo began offering Foursquare players badges and prizes when their viewers checked in at locations featured in their most popular series.

- *Utility—Give them something that makes their life easier:* Every New Year's Eve, millions pack into Time Square and the most precious real estate in the city becomes a bathroom. To make their lives easier our old friend Charmin put up a 20-stall luxury bathroom there, probably to the cheers and relief of millions. (Somewhere Mr. Whipple is smiling down on an idea that doesn't suck.)

- *Access—Give them something they couldn't otherwise get:* For Pilot Pens, Grey España in Barcelona, let viewers turn their own handwriting into a type-able font (Figure 5.9). (Another thing that's cool about stuff like this? Once a client makes something like this, it exists. It's an asset. It's not an ad that runs one time. It's what they call "always on.")

Figure 5.10 The Forever 21 woman plucked real-time onlookers out of the crowd at Times Square.

The new ideas are shareable and participatory.

Everything is social now, *including* TV, print, radio, and outdoor. Everything can be liquid and linked and tied together, and a brand can now be a fascinating singularity no matter which medium a customer discovers it. If it's cool enough, a TV spot can be "Liked" on Facebook and sent to a hundred other friends. Radio can direct listeners to cool places online, and print ads can be the start of global treasure hunt. Given that all media is rolling into one giant SkyNet *(fist pumps to my sci-fi geeks who get the reference)*, it makes sense to create content that's so fun to engage with that people want to share it with friends.

I know that when *I* first saw Forever 21's augmented reality billboard I just had to put it on my Facebook Wall. In this cool installation (Figure 5.10) beautiful women in Forever 21 designs took real-time "Polaroids" of the Times Square crowds assembled below. Thanks to a good high-definition camera, and a big-ass computer somewhere, the models plucked individuals from the crowd and dropped them into a shopping bag or tucked them under their hats.

The new ideas don't fill a media space; they create one.

Perhaps the biggest change wrought by the Internet is the creation of a nearly infinite amount of media space. While the used-car dealers continue to squabble over who gets the last 30 seconds of air time left on the local news, there's room for everyone online; and if your content's good, you can become a broadcaster or a publisher and create new audiences and new communities for your brand ad infinitum.

Gary Vaynerchuk didn't buy space in the local newspaper to sell his wines. He started a podcast. (Sometimes also referred to as a "vlog," an ugly-sounding neologism better employed, in my opinion, as a description of what a platypus sounds like when it throws up.) These podcasts were media Gary created himself and filled with his own content, most of it filmed at his office desk. The content was interesting, his viewership grew, and next thing you know the dude's got a million-dollar 10-book deal with Harper.

The lesson: Why buy a medium when you can own it?

STORYTELLING.

Rick Boyko, long-time creative and President of VCU's Brandcenter, explains the ad biz very simply: "We are storytellers in service of brands."

Seven words, but they sum it up nicely. Our job is to get our brands' stories into the national conversation and ultimately into the firmament of popular culture. "To make them famous" as they say at Crispin. The thing is, we don't get people talking about our brands by feeding them product benefits out of the sales guy's spec sheets. People talk in stories and so must we.

There's a great book I recommend to ad students. It's not about advertising but screenwriting: Robert McKee's *Story: Substance, Structure, Style and the Principles of Screenwriting*. McKee makes a convincing case that the human brain is wired to hunger for story—that a structure of three acts, taking us from problem to unexpected solution, is something our brains crave. Story just sucks us in. Even when we *know* how the story is going to end on some late-night TV movie, we stay up later than we ought to just to watch the dang thing. Theorists suggest that story is actually a cognitive structure our brains use to encode information. So in addition to its drawing power, story has lasting power—it helps us remember things. *("Did you see that spot last night? The one where the . . .")*

Our job is to discover the stories behind our brands and tell them in a way that will get people's attention. "Told well," Bogusky and Winsor write, "they stick in our minds forever."[18]

What's interesting is that even though the ascendancy of digital and online looks to be a permanent change, the classic construct of a story not only continues to work in the new medium, but its narrative power is amplified. I'm reminded of a recent interview of *Avatar* director, James Cameron. Asked what permanent changes digital technology has made in filmmaking, Cameron replied, "Filmmaking is not going to ever fundamentally change. It's about storytelling." (Cameron's comment also explains why some of the *Star Wars* prequels kinda sucked—it was special effects over storytelling.)

Apple has been telling the same great story ever since they aired their famous "1984" Super Bowl spot, a story summed up in a line of copy from one of their early print ads: "Instead of teaching people more about computers, we taught computers more about people." Macs are designed around the way *we* work, not how the manufactures of PCs work. Macs are the "computer for the rest of us." Remember that huge image of 1984's Minister of Truth in Ridley Scott's dystopian Apple commercial? He's still saying the same things *("We'll make computers our way, maggots.")* but simply evolved into the tubby "I'm a PC" guy in the Mac vs. PC campaign.

The thing is, when a brand discovers its true story and sticks with it, others begin telling the story, too. At first, it's only within the company and its sales meetings. It spreads to its stores, then the commercials. After a while, if it's an interesting story, a credible one, customers will start telling the story.

The construct of a story serves us at this brand level, but we'll also need structure to write a TV commercial or online video, a radio spot, or—as we'll see—entire multimedia campaigns. TV remains my favorite medium for discussing the structure of story.

I think of television as a 30-second play with three acts. The curtain goes up on an interesting scene where some conflict is already evident. Also evident at a glance is a backstory (hints about who these people are or how things got this way). Things get tense or weird or complicated, usually because of some challenge to the characters. Finally, it's all resolved in an unexpected way, and the characters are changed because of it.

The end.

Of course, there are many great movies, spots, and novels outside this Hollywood sort of story arc, but for our purposes this is classic story structure. There are writers more qualified than I to teach story, and most of them will refer to Aristotle's original definition ("A whole is what has a beginning and middle and end"). Some will recommend anything by Chekov, but for those of you here in the middle-of-the-road with me, I say read any short story by Stephen King or Ray Bradbury.

"C'MON DAD, TELL US JUST ONE MORE INTERACTIVE OR TRANSMEDIA NARRATIVE, PLEEEASE?"

When it comes to brand storytelling there are a few significant differences from classic story structure. In classic story structure there's usually an ending, whereas the stories we tell on behalf of brands are a little more open-ended. The three-act format is more applicable to a self-contained story, where the story of a brand has is a longer tale told over time. But it's still a story, so it has many of the same things, among them, beginnings, bad guys, and lore.

Classic story structure also involves a passive audience sitting out in the theater soaking it all in. That was before people started talking back to the screen. *("Don't go down in the basement, girl!! That's where the murderer is!!")* Today's viewers, at least in the brand-customer universe, aren't passive. Not only do people want to interrupt the story, they want to change it, make comments, or tell their own stories, and there's no better place for them to do this than online. In traditional media, the story's all there and we just take it in. But on digital platforms it's a little more like those *Choose Your Own Adventure* children's books, with a quality often referred to as *interactive narrative.*

Nike (always a leading-edge marketer) had an early success with this model, ending a TV commercial with a website address where viewers could then go and choose different endings to the commercial. It gave customers an active role in telling the brand story. Today we're seeing entire mini-series online, such as Unilever's *In the Motherhood,* where viewers can own the content by voting on plot lines and influencing the direction of the story. Like *Choose Your Own Adventure,* the viewer gets a personalized experience.

As the Web matured and digital platforms multiplied, a new kind of narrative appeared. Stories no longer were limited to online but could be told over a variety of platforms simultaneously, like the early Nike idea but encompassing every type of medium. Called *transmedia narrative,* this structure allows multiple points of contact with a customer: TV, radio, print, direct, outdoor, mobile, Web, gaming, blogging, virtual or augmented reality, user-generated video, texting—and not just one of them, but all of them. Stories presented this way give an immersive experience you can't get using one medium alone and begin to complement one another, forming one overarching narrative. And when *social* media are included, viewers can invite friends into the story and build communities, and the brand's story can go into orbit.

More and more consumers now have a multiscreen lifestyle, and they pay special attention to this trend at Crispin Porter + Bogusky. Crispin's executive creative technology director, Scott Prindle, told me the traditional sitting in front of a PC with keyboard and mouse is fast becoming the smaller part of our digital lives.

As computers have become faster, cheaper, and smaller, computer processing has spread to every aspect of our environment, from smartphones, to automobiles, to appliances, to urban infrastructures, and every place imaginable. "When designing experiences for our brands, it's no longer enough to simply focus on the traditional PC experience. From the outset of the project and the earliest phases of concepting, we consider brand stories and ideas that work across the full range of consumer touch points in the rapidly expanding digital ecosystem. As our Matt Walsh says (Crispin's director of UX), There can be no 'dead ends.'"

Not every product or campaign requires the use of several media. Transmedia approaches are generally best for stories that involve a large universe, have a lot of backstory, or just tons of cool content that can't be realized in one medium. (This may be why TV shows with multiple story lines and characters were early adopters of this approach.)

When you have a multimedia stage on which to tell a brand story, it can become "participatory and often gamelike," says Frank Rose in *The Art of Immersion.* It's this deep media that allows stories to be "not just entertaining, but immersive, taking you deeper than an hour-long drama or a 30-second spot will permit."[19] It's here where advertising can move into long-form branded content like *In the Motherhood* just mentioned or into *alternate reality gaming* (ARG, in some circles).

In ARG, the viewer is immersed in an interactive narrative that takes place in real time. As with most games, there is a challenge—a puzzle to solve or a treasure to find—and the viewer makes choices while interacting with characters or situations in the game. Depending on the information players provide when they register, they can even get phone calls from the game. The game designers can also hide hints online, in the blogosphere, or on social platforms such as Facebook. As players share this new information with friends they're essentially marketing the brand. As we'll see in a minute when we discuss social media, it's not the stories we tell; it's the stories we get others to tell for us.

ABC's *Lost* hosted several games during its run (notably "FIND815"), but one of the earliest ARG's was Wieden + Kennedy's launch of Sega's ESPN NFL Football. It was centered around a website called Beta-7.com that seemed to be blowing the lid off a conspiracy to cover up the fact that the new game caused terrible side effects. (Subjects who'd agreed to test a beta of the game had blackouts and other symptoms.) Elements of backstory were embedded all over the Web, and what made this ARG particularly interesting, said creative director Ty Montague, was that "the game would never admit it's a game." In addition, because the creatives were adding to the story in real time, Montague likened it to "interactive theatre . . . or improv marketing—like doing SNL seven days a week."[20] It is this marriage of storytelling, entertainment, content, and marketing that makes it hard to call this advertising. But that's what it is and it's pretty cool.

Remember, though, it's all about story. No amount of multiple-platform razzle dazzle will save a boring story. As you investigate the feasibility of this kind of storytelling on behalf of your brand, also keep in mind both your product and your customers. An alternate reality game, for instance, is probably not the right way to introduce a new heart medication. *Chasing the Monster Idea* author Stefan Mumaw had some good advice in this regard:

> The hardest part of using stories effectively is making sure they're simple—that they reflect your core message. It's not enough to tell a great story, the story has to reflect your brand. Without this relevance, the story teaches nothing and we, as humans, are constantly looking for order and lessons from the stories we consume.[21]

THIS IS NOT "THE SECTION" ON SOCIAL MEDIA.

Let it be known from this day forward, in every hamlet and village across the land, that everything in our industry—nay, in every industry—will have some social aspect to it: print, mobile, TV, outdoor—all of it. It's all going to be social.

Social media is not a box you need to check. You don't put up your social media campaign on the wall along with your TV campaign. Social should run through all of it like a thread.

The Wikipedia community defines *social media* as "media designed to be disseminated through social interaction, created using highly accessible and scalable publishing techniques . . . [all] created to be shared freely."

In his popular blog, *Creativity Unbound,* Boches tenders this definition:

> Social media isn't a program, a campaign, a platform or an execution. Not an objective in and of itself, but a means, a tool to create deeper, more valuable relationships with customers. . . . Traditional marketers identify audiences, craft messages, fire those messages at their target, put money into a media plan and hope to penetrate the market. Social media marketers build community, craft experiences, fire off invitations, put resources into developing an interest plan, and look for ways to collaborate with customers.[22]

By way of antonym, one could argue this book is about as far from social media as you can get. For starters, there isn't going to be any new content here when you wake up tomorrow (well, maybe, if you're reading the eBook version). Also, if you want to share anything in this book, you've gotta get up and hand it to the person across from you on the subway (which I assume you know won't end well). Like any book, this a private experience; you can't comment on it in real time (again, the subway issue). And if it sucks, you're just gonna have to find out for yourself, when you could've been warned away by a friend. (Actually, books were the very first widespread socially linked product, given Amazon's Ratings & Reviews, and that was before anyone called such networking "social.")

Social media is our global virtual coffee shop and, like any coffee shop, there's a new one opening every 8 minutes. Among the many platforms out there (as of this writing) are Facebook, Google+, YouTube, Twitter, Flickr, Foursquare, SCVNGR, LinkedIn, Digg, Reddit, Tumblr, StumbleUpon, and the 200 million or so blogs (the best of which, according to some—me—is HeyWhipple.com).

Keeping in mind that people join social networks to keep in touch with people and not large corporations, any presence your brand has on a social platform needs to be useful, entertaining, or beautiful (those words, again). Also, as we noted earlier, it's not about the stories we tell through social media but the stories we get others to tell for us.

To make that happen, we'll have to present our brands in such an interesting and interactive way that people lean in, like what they see, and then share with friends. Think of social media as the ripple effect that happens after you lob something really cool into the grid. Coming up with the cool thing is one part of it; the other is planning for what recipients might do with your content, or say about it, once it's out there. Remember, here in the social space the metrics for success will be less about old-school stuff like the number of consumer impressions and more about customer involvement. How long do customers stay on your website? How many comments are showing up on the Facebook Fan page?

As you begin your thinking, sooner or later someone in a meeting is gonna say, "What should our social strategy be?" Resist the urge to hurl your coffee cup in their direction, even if the cup is empty. This is like asking, "What should our brochure strategy be?" Or our TV strategy. In *The On-Demand Brand,* author Mathieson says, "Ask *why* it should be, and why should consumers care?"[23] There's a good reason for this, which my friend Sam Bennett puts this way: "Social media is where ideas, which become experiences, go to become immortal. It's also where bad, selfish, or boring ideas go for public condemnation and death by stoning."

Before you begin, ask yourself. "Why am I doing this?" What do you want to achieve? What can the client get from a community, by listening and engaging with these people who are likely the company's best customers? Do we want feedback? Awareness, word-of-mouth, sales?

If the stated objective is sales, you'll need to be especially careful because social platforms are essentially gatherings. I liken Facebook to a backyard neighborhood barbecue, LinkedIn is work buddies at the bar, and Twitter, that's a big noisy cocktail party. A salesperson won't be welcome at any of these gatherings. Instead, go in thinking, "What does this brand stand for? What can we *do* for these people?" This is a social platform after all, and it's often best if a brand leads with its social mission, its purpose, and not with a sales pitch.

So here we arrive at a discussion of community and of conversation. In the real world (or as some say more colorfully, "here in meat space"), we'll do what any polite person does when walking into room of people. First, we listen.

IF CONTENT IS KING, CONVERSATION IS QUEEN.

I'm always amazed to see how the author bio on pretty much every other blog describes the author as a "social media expert." To me that's a little like being an expert in time travel. Social media's existed for—what?—20 minutes so far? And we're already surrounded by hundreds of "experts" dispensing years of hard-earned wisdom. (Whatev.)

My curmudgeonry aside, there are a few bona fide leaders in this field, one of them being Mullen's Edward Boches. (Scott Prindle, Brian Solis, Guy Kawasaki, and Eric Harr are also pretty smart.) Boches makes it clear that before there's any talk of content or technology, you have to listen. You need to understand who this community is you're trying to attract or gain entry to. How does your community want to engage?

Establish what kind of community your brand's best suited for.

In *Groundswell,* authors Li and Bernoff suggest there are five types of social media users: *joiners, spectators, creators, critics,* and *collectors.* They're all online for different reasons, looking for different things.

The biggest group is the *spectators,* and they're just what it sounds like: people who like to read the blogs and watch the videos. *Critics* are people who tend to react to all this content and post comments (some of them being, of course, spineless trolls). *Collectors* are geeks like me who like to study things and stay on top of trends. *Creators* are your user-generated-content people who love posting their own stuff. And finally there are the *conversationalists* and *joiners* out there in the communities updating their statuses and talking, talking, talking. Go online and listen to your brand's customers talk about the category. Read the tweets they hashtag with your brand (#yourbrandname). Log onto Technorati .com and key word search the brand. See what both the brand's advocates and detractors are saying.

Knowing the makeup of the online communities will make a difference in the content you put up, as well as how you plan on engaging with and inspiring these folks. If they're *creators,* make sure there's a way for them to add content, to embed videos, or post a joke. *Joiners,* they like special membership privileges, and as for *spectators*, all that matters is content that rocks. Answering these questions is critical to knowing both who's out there and the sites you'll find them gathering. You can also create a place for them to gather, and services such as Ning.com are a good place to start. Ning has all kinds of ready-made templates that can help you get a decent-looking social network up and running.

Map out a conversation strategy.

Planning how your brand's going to engage with customers will help you define what its content's going to be, how often and where you'll post it, and the mechanisms customers will likely use to share it all. Your plan can't come out of the blue. It has come from who your brand is, its DNA—from the brand's purpose, why it's here on the planet. So before you walk into the party, have a conversation strategy. Not one set in stone, mind you. After all, we're talking about dealing with people in real time, and who *knows* which way the conversation will go. Boches recommends brand teams gather regularly to make a plan.

> Gather your marketing team and map out product, advertising and promotion plans for the month. Set priorities and determine a compatible conversation strategy that avoids excess promotion and instead creates a not-too-intrusive balance of the following: questions that will stimulate reaction; content (video, images, entertainment) that will be both useful and welcome; and finally offers or incentives that can be tracked.[24]

Many agencies now have social media conversation managers on staff. They generally work with a copywriter (skilled in the brand voice), and together they tell engaging stories, create buzz, promote events, build a long-term relationship with customers, and stoke the conversation.

The first step in a conversation is starting one. That means having something to say, so it's the part many brands get wrong because "Sale Ends Saturday" is not having something to say, nor is pounding away on your brand's positioning statement. Remember, the social platform isn't so much a place to position a brand as it is to *take* a position.

Audi took a position and made a statement about its design ethos—"Design means conceptualizing the future and visualizing it in images"—when it launched the Audi Design Project, a large-scale initiative to take their design and innovation and apply it to the world beyond their cars. Taking inspiration from their new A7, Audi redesigned San Francisco's Powell Street Promenade, making it completely pedestrian-friendly, with bike racks, benches, landscaping, and solar lighting, and all of it had an Audi vibe.

Toyota started a big conversation about its tech DNA by asking how people, "How would you make the world a better place using Toyota's technology?" Thousands of people responded to the challenge of repurposing five distinct Toyota technologies to create new, nonautomotive applications that would benefit society.

Beginning a conversation can also start small with, say, a printable coupon. That's what coupons are for—trial—and that's what early conversations between strangers are anyway. *("Can I buy you a cup of coffee?")* But to keep a conversation going, you'll need to show up with some useful or entertaining content or there's no second date. *("Oh, my god, he was so boring. All he did was talk about himself.")* Boches's recipe is this: "One-third questions and conversation; one-third useful content; one-third a little bit of selling."[25] His last point, "One-third a little bit of selling," is worth some more conversation.

Wearing a plaid used-car-salesman jacket to a party is so not cool.

Imagine showing up at a party and saying, "Okay, everyone, quiet down please. I'm going to read this story about myself and then show some videos of all my stuff."

Consider what most of us actually do at a party. We show up bearing a small gift, perhaps flowers or wine. We mingle, maybe try to make someone laugh. We introduce one friend to another. We tell someone about this cool song we heard the other day, show a photo from a trip we took, tell the person about some great new restaurant. If things get a little dull, we might even say, "Let's play a game or go to a movie."

But trying to sell something the minute you get in the door? That isn't going to go well. However, the point here isn't that selling is bad, because people like buying stuff. The point is, this isn't the mall. Eric Harr reminds us that "social platforms were created as a *refuge* from corporate marketing. . . . Social media is a more elegant, nuanced two-way dialog."[26] So step lightly here. Take Boches's advice: "One-third a little bit of selling."

It's likely your product manager won't like this "one-third nonsense" very much, so the challenge becomes convincing our good clients that a full-time retail mentality simply won't fly here. Yes, promotions can work like gang-busters. A free giveaway can attract a big crowd, but without a relationship, the traffic will come and then go. Focusing exclusively on a fan count may attract a crowd, but it will be at the expense of building a community. And there's a big difference.

Thomas Knoll, Community Architect at Zappos, spelled out the difference between crowd and community at Austin's 2011 SXSW Interactive. "Crowds don't have a purpose," he said, "Communities do." Crowds show up to get stuff; communities like giving. Where crowds want benefits, community people want to belong. Where crowds are powered by inspiration, communities are powered by influence. And finally, crowds are sustained by service, where communities are sustained by story.

Purpose. Giving. Belonging. Influence. And story.

Wow. We're talking about a space where we ad geeks can effect positive social change, improve the world, bring people together, and leverage communities for good. We have travelled a looong way from "Ladies, please don't squeeze the Charmin."

Establish what kind of relationship your brand will have with its community.

This is Boches's next rule of thumb and the one he says is most important. Will your brand be a partner to this community? A jester? A coach? A friend?

Don't start with a concept, a campaign, or any technology, however cool any of it is. Start with the relationship. Understand what people are interested in talking about, how they'd like to engage, and then work *backward* from there toward your idea. In a speech at Boulder Digital Works, Boches said:

> Know your objectives and have a definition of success. What kind of value can I get from my community if I listen, engage and inspire? Ten well-connected fans who become evangelists or ambassadors might be more valuable than 5,000 semi-committed ones. Focus instead on what you want to accomplish—awareness, feedback, product trial, loyalty, positive buzz, sales—and concentrate on making that happen. If what you have to offer and share is valuable, guess what? The fans and followers will show up.[27]

"Ten well-connected fans. Evangelists. Ambassadors." These are the key words, because these are your brand loyalists and they're out there actually talking, taking the time to make product recommendations to friends. Most of them are those influential "mavens" Malcolm Gladwell wrote about in *The Tipping Point*. These people serve as an all-volunteer marketing department, making them the only people working for brands paid less than the interns.

> "Pampers were the only company I could find preemie diapers in," wrote one fan. "I figured if they use them in the NICU they were good enough for me."

That's a little word-of-mouth from a brand ambassador on Pampers's website. But few would have ever seen this product rating if products were all Pampers had to talk about on its website. Instead, Pampers decided early on that its relationship with customers wasn't going to be based around the diaper pail but around the idea of parenthood. In fact, its product ratings are at the bottom of the pull-down menus, and most of the site's real estate is given to the things moms really talk about: "Glad to know that picking him up all the time when he cries is the right thing to do," wrote one new mother responding to advice from a community member, "Glad I am not spoiling him. :-)"

Clearly establish what the user/viewer is getting out of it. What is the payoff?

A viewer's relationship with a traditional medium like television is passive and one way. When we create work for TV we ask, "What's the message we want viewers to get?" But when we're working in digital/interactive, we ask a different question: "What is the *payoff* for the end user?"

We ask this because in some of the interactive engagements we create, we're requiring consumers to devote some time and effort: uploading a photo, reading some instructions, going to another screen, allowing a Facebook Connect. In return, we have to come through with some type of payoff, something beautiful, entertaining, or useful. "This payoff," says Crispin's Scott Prindle, "needs to be equal to or greater in value than the time the user has contributed. If it's not, we'll see very low usage rates and have a very unhappy client."

It's almost as if we need to start looking at our advertising the way we look at products: what is the *benefit* of this website or this app or this interaction? When a product has a great benefit, we recommend it to others. So think the same way about your digital executions. What is the benefit, the payoff, and why would someone feel compelled to share it with others?

Creatively involve a community and they may tell the brand story for you.

What was the last thing you forwarded to someone? I'll go out on a (concrete) limb here and guess it was either wildly entertaining or something really useful your friend would want to know.

So again we're back to R/GA's question: "Is what I'm creating adding something to someone's life? Is it useful, entertaining, or beautiful?" Let's raise the bar here and suggest we *also* ask Crispin's question at the same time: "What is the 'press release' of this idea?"

When we have a good answer to both questions, we're entering some seriously cool territory. Useful, entertaining, and beautiful were the price of admission, and now we've raised the stakes by adding incredible.

"Is what I'm creating *incredible?*"

Finally, let's throw in two more words: "Is what I'm creating participatory and interactive?"

As you work, keep all six adjectives in your head and interrogate each idea with the question, "Is it useful, beautiful, entertaining, incredible, participatory, and interactive?" Yeah, it's *hard* to create an idea that hits on all these cylinders, but when you do hit all six it's like people can't move fast enough to start producing content for you.

So give people a podium to rant from, a game to play, or a camera to shoot. Let them imprint themselves into the clay of your brand in ways that are so beautiful or interesting that when they're done, they just have to show it off to friends.

"Hey, look at this cool photo I took of the dog with my Lego camera app."

"Check out the frames I just uploaded to the Johnny Cash Project."

"Did you get a phone call from Alec Baldwin? That was me."

"Check it. My new superhero, 'Over-Art-Directed Man.'"

All these examples were cool things that people could create and share while giving both them *and* their receiver a bit of a brand experience. It's like we're creating "a window users can talk to each other through," says Glue's Dominick O'Brien in *The On-Demand Brand*. "But it's from your friend, as opposed to 'from the brand.'"[28]

Games are another way a brand can create communities, as we've seen with alternate reality games like ESPN's Beta-7.com. Exploding in popularity as I write, Zynga cracked the code early on in the integration of social and gaming by launching games like Farmville and Mafia Wars on Facebook. They built social interaction into every one, and in so doing created a monster of a community. As of today, Mashable.com (a smart blog I recommend you follow) says Zynga has 232 million active monthly users.[29]

Share everything you know.

To continue the party metaphor, have you ever walked out of a get-together thinking, "Wow, I never knew she was so funny"? Maybe someone had his or her guard down a little bit, and you got to see a new side of the person and you left liking that person more than you did before. In the social space, this kind of transparency is good for brands, too.

Think about it. Haven't most of us seen how a stick-in-the-mud corporate yuck behaves at the office Christmas party? Never loosens his tie or goes "off script" and leaves at 7:15 when he's worried his hair isn't perfect. Transparency's a big part of being authentic and approachable. The thing is, in the social spaces brands are welcome to behave in ways that perhaps they can't in, say, their big TV commercials. See if you can get your clients to let their hair down. Maybe show the outtakes of a commercial that wasn't going well. If a product is buggy, talk about how you're working it.

Transparency can be about sharing cool and impressive stuff, too. In 1999's *The Cluetrain Manifesto,* the authors presciently spoke on behalf of customers: "We want access to your corporate information, to your plans and strategies, your best thinking, your genuine knowledge. We won't settle for a 4-color brochure, for websites [full of] eye candy but lacking substance."[30]

Sharing everything you know is a strategy executed brilliantly by Crispin Porter + Bogusky for Best Buy in its Cannes gold-winning initiative called the Twelpforce. This Twitter platform (more on Twitter in a minute) encouraged hundreds of the retailer's employees to freely handle online customer questions, using their own Twitter accounts or the company's. According to John Bernier, social and emerging media manager for Best Buy,

> The overriding principle was tied to one of our brand promises, which was to help the customer know what we know as fast as we know it. We . . . had observed that the Twitter platform didn't lend itself well to direct selling or one too many messaging. So we looked at our pool of assets and said, "Our employees know stuff, we can share stuff and we can do it quickly." The more we share about the products, the more we can demonstrate our actual knowledge and the value we can bring to the equation.[31]

Eric Harr summed all this up very nicely with "Social media puts the 'public' back into public relations."[32]

Experiment constantly and polish what works.

We'll end this part with a reminder that as cool as all of this stuff is, none of it's gonna end up in the British Museum. Once you've built something, move on.

Obviously, this doesn't mean abandoning things that are working. Keep an eye on the analytics and optimize the platforms that are working. Google Analytics is probably the best place to start, but there are many ways to find out what gets people talking about and interacting with a brand.

The trick, however, is not to stay in development until you're confident you've got the next Subservient Chicken. Light a hundred little fires and see what catches. Keep that constant beta mentality and experiment constantly. Building change and renewal into your conversation strategy will help keep your brand on John Q's radar.

FACEBOOK IS, 👍 Like , YOU KNOW, A BIG DEAL, OKAY?

We've all heard the stories about how big Facebook would be if it were a nation and the "almost bigger than China" syndrome is in fact eye-opening. More illustrative for my money was the story of the two Austrian girls who, trapped in a storm drain, got out their cellular phones and quickly did not call 9-1-1 but updated their Facebook statuses instead. (Friends online sent help.)

As of this writing in 2011, every person on Facebook has an average of 130 friends, and every time one of these members "Likes" something, posts a comment, and shares something, it's amplified across their network. The big news here for advertisers anyway (and why Zuckerberg was *Time*'s Person of the Year in 2010) is that brands finally had a way to connect with people in a place that wasn't about selling stuff. Brands can get as much or more attention on Facebook and other social platforms than they can with traditional paid media . . . for free. This pass-along, have-you-seen-this attention is called *earned media* (fancy-pants word for word-of-mouth), and its numbers go nuclear very quickly. Harnessing this force has been the focus of the entire industry for the last several years running.

It's only a matter of time before every single customer in every age group and level of digital savvy is on Facebook. This means if you're a student of this business, it hardly matters if you think you're a Facebook person or not. Sooner or later you're gonna need to drink the Kool-Aid, register, and log on. As with most of this digital stuff, you gotta use it to get it.

In *Engage,* author Brian Solis flatly describes Facebook as "the next chapter in business. A chapter in which commonplace terms such as Share, Like, Comment, and Add become the pillars for triggering a social tsunami."[33] Jim Hanna of Starbucks was quoted in *Fast Company* saying, "Facebook has become our de facto advertising platform."[34] Although Starbucks might be leading the way for brands and Facebook strategies, they're not alone. There's been a shift from building microsites and pouring money into corporate sites as brands figure out they can provide a lot of this same content and interaction on Facebook. Plus, they don't have to pay to drive people there. People are already there, in the hundreds of millions.

Interestingly, in the same issue of *Fast Company,* the editor noted a poll of 500 executives who said the most overrated trend in business is social media (likely due to the fact that so far no one's figured out how to track sales to social media). But as Facebook commerce emerges (F-commerce), it will allow people to buy and sell things without leaving the site and will likely shift the focus of the platform in coming years. But this book is about the creative side of the marketing business, so we'll leave the analytics and return on investment of social media to the number crunchers and limit our discussion to some of the cool, non-sales-guy-in-plaid-coat things one can do here.

Before you put it on Facebook, know your brand's face.

Before doing anything, we need to figure out who we *are* on Facebook. Pretty much everything we've talked about so far for other media also applies here: be authentic, be simple, produce content, stay on brand, stay on strategy—all that stuff. But with Facebook, you have more opportunity to make your brand human than probably anywhere else. Think about where Facebook came from. People are there to engage with *people,* so it's important your brand be human and have a personality.

There are three main reasons people follow brands. The brand offers them something exclusive, such as a discount or some deal. Or the person's *already* a happy customer of the brand and is inclined to press the "Like" button and pass on a good word. And finally, people follow brands that are always posting interesting content.

The first two are obvious; people like a deal; people who love brands like telling others about it. But the third point is what's often overlooked by brands. And it's the same reason we engage with people IRL (*in real life*—hip up, people). We hang with people we think are fun, interesting, smart, or entertaining. We're far more likely to engage with a brand if we can see the brand's human side.

Staying on brand and strategy is important. So is being human. But Facebook offers a new challenge because up till now, all we've talked about is what brands should say. In this medium, where brands can *do* and *be* things, there's a new twist.

The first thing many brands do on Facebook is to seed their market by dishing out the deals and coupons. That's fine, especially when you can treat the fan base as an exclusive community privy to members-only discounts. These deals will grow a fan base, but remind your client that counting fans is like sending out a million direct mail pieces and thinking you've accomplished something. What counts is how many write back. Boches says, "I'd rather have half as many 'Likes' and twice as many 'Comments.'" (Seriously, how hard is it to click a "Like" button?) But to talk, to leave actual comments, *that* is engagement. "A 'Like' is a first date," says my friend Sam Bennett. "What you do and say is what gets a second date."

There are a few unwritten rules of engagement regarding conversation on Facebook. Although your brand can, and should, occasionally talk about itself, it's better if it's busy asking questions, starting conversations, and doing things. Don't be like that dude at the party who traps you by the kitchen sink and talks about himself. Brands build active communities with good conversation and good ongoing content. You can study what a Facebook-savvy brand does by looking at Skittles's current feed. Or Starbucks's. Or Target's.

Target has nailed their personality and have put effort into creating good conversation and content on their pages. For instance, in summer 2011 Target had something new to say every day, through a "Make Summer Funner" theme. They announced new charities that fans could vote on, a new line of clothing tie-in with a rock star, a video showing the assembly of their outdoor event/ ad "the world's largest sprinkler," a poll about favorite summer activities, a Beyoncé video, behind the scenes at a Beyoncé concert, cooking demos, their very first print ad from way back, a Summer Fun Finder app, . . . and every third or fourth thing was a straight-up sales pitch for summer stuff like their squirt guns or sunglasses.

And as for conversation and comments? They started one huge conversation with the simple observation, "Summer is way too short. Your swimtrunks shouldn't be." Just that one statement, and they received *thousands* of comments.

> "Agree. I saw an old guy in the food court in Hawaii with speedos on, it totally ruined my appetite."
> "Just say no to man-kinis!!"
> "But guys trunks shouldn't look like a friggin' skirt either! Whatever happened to just above the knee?"

Thousands of comments about Speedos and then evvvvvery once in awhile, buried in the middle of all the talk, a store employee dropped a suggestion about Target's knee-length trunks for men.

Conversation strategy is important in all things social, and Facebook is no different. Before you start talking, think through what your brand has to say.

Provide content worth sharing.

If a simple comment about Speedo-size bathing suits can get people talking, imagine what can happen when you provide some cool content people just *have* to share, content that has value in and of itself without being a sale or a coupon. Again, we define cool content here as something that's beautiful, entertaining, or useful.

For example, it was entertaining when an orangutan named Nonja created a Facebook profile in 2007. Samsung wanted to prove how easy-to-use their new camera was and gave one to Ms. Nonja. She made lots of pictures, along with about 80,000 fans who loved sharing her story.

It was useful when Levi's made the Levi's Friends Store, where people could see what kinds of jeans their friends liked and could ask each other for advice on which jeans to buy.

It was useful when IKEA used the Facebook tag function to give away their products. An IKEA store manager created a profile page and then posted photos of rooms from IKEA's catalog—with a challenge. If you were the first to tag a product with your name, you won it. Anytime someone won an item, an announcement went up on that person's wall and then into all their friends'

News Feeds. That meant for every item tagged, an average of 130 friends got an eyeful of the digital looting going on over at IKEA and the whole thing went nuclear.

Entertaining happens to be the first approach most creatives take, but remember, posting whacky videos may attract a temporary crowd but what you want is community. Give people authentic reasons to engage in conversation by posting content worth sharing, and you'll be using "the Facebook" (as moms call it) for what it's best at—building a community.

Create ideas that let people create their own ideas.

It's one thing to provide content people can view and share, but it's another to create an opportunity for people to generate their *own* content. This is the sort of thing more and more people are going bonkers over.

A good example of this kind of idea was the Facebook page for the TV show *Glee*. Yes, they had the expected interviews from characters and on-set and off-set videos from the episode. But they took it one step further by letting fans feel like they're a part of the experience. If you were a "Gleek," you could update your Facebook profile picture with the *Glee* sign (Figure 5.11). You could also tag your friends with certain roles from the show. You could even create your own pop-up videos, all of it right on the Glee Facebook page.

When you have platforms where customers can create their own content, you have something close to a self-funded marketing campaign with an all-volunteer creative department. The content the fans create goes on to become a draw in and of itself, beyond your original platform idea, and if buzz and conversation help it go nuclear, a brand's idea can reach millions of people within a few weeks—all at a minimal cost.

Ah, but this is where the "famous for 15 minutes" kicks in.

*Figure 5.11   This is true
engagement of customer
and brand.*

On this or any other digital platform, even stuff that goes nuclear will very quickly become so five minutes ago. That's how it is with online marketing. Some ideas may have longer shelf lives than others (I'm thinking of 2010's Old Spice multimedia campaign), but sooner or later John Q's gonna roll his eyes and say, "What else you got?" The thing is, few people come online looking to visit a brand's fan page. *("I wonder what those maniacs at Buick are up to?")* You have to get into people's News Feeds by posting interesting content, and that's a good thing for us creatives. Someone's gotta keep the pipelines full.

Use Facebook's info and photos to personalize your message.

One of the most popular applications on Facebook is the Facebook Connect feature. By clicking it, a customer is saying, "Go ahead. If you've got some really cool customized thing to show me, have at it. Use all the info and photos I've put on my page."

Arcade Fire's music video "The Wilderness Downtown" is a good example (Figure 5.12). This video borrowed images from a user's Facebook page and

Figure 5.12   Milk & Koblin's breakthrough music video used imagery from Google Map's Street View.

Google Map's Street View and poured it all into a cool mash-up video. Intel's The Museum of Me application (see Figure 5.5) is another good example of the possibilities of letting a viewer customize your idea using their stuff.

Facebook can be a spoke or a hub.

Pretend you're a brand manager or an account manager at some agency. You want customers to interact with your brand, to use a new application, watch a video, or just give feedback. And you wanna do this in a cost-effective way. Well, you could spend $100k (at minimum) on a cool custom-made microsite and then buy media to drive people there (another $25k, again on the low end). Or you could build a Facebook application for say $15,000 to $50,000 (depending) and then press the "Share" button.

Consider this wonderful example done by students at the Miami Ad School Europe. They proposed that 1-800-Flowers.com create a Facebook app. Posted on the day of someone's birthday, the ad for the app reads "Make your birthday wish special. Send ONE flower and be part of Sam Bennett's Facebook Bouquet." Friends choose a flower, write a greeting, and soon enough there's a big bouquet of virtual flowers and notes from friends. At the end of the day, 1-800-Flowers delivers a *real* bouquet and all the notes right to Sam's door.

It's brill. The students combined digital with physical, utilized the power of community and the social network to build a collective gift, and created a Facebook-centric campaign that enabled people to interact with a brand and make a purchase they probably wouldn't have otherwise. Damn.

Facebook is also being used as a hub for product launches. Mainstream brands such as Ford, Vitamin Water, Oscar De La Renta, and Snickers have all launched major products here. Snickers launched their new Peanut Butter Snickers bar predominantly on television (the marvelous "shark focus group" spot—YouTube it), but they added a cool twist when they advertised it on Facebook (Figure 5.13). Since customers weren't just gonna *like* their new candy bar but *love* it, they suggested replacing Facebook's "Like" button with their own "Love" button. They took it a step further by creating functionality that allowed you to "Love" other stuff on Facebook and then regularly receive on your News Feed a current list of "Most Loved Stuff."

That Facebook is big enough now to launch products is evidenced by the number of TV commercials we see signed off with a Facebook logo in the corner. People see the logo and know they can find out more on Facebook next time they're there, which is likely soon.

For brands that already have robust e-commerce sites, it's likely most of its Facebook offerings will serve just as fun ways to engage customers. But the ascendancy of F-commerce and HTML5 will likely result in more commerce happening right on the pages of Facebook. For now, though, why spend a lot of time and money updating your brand's main corporate site for every new marketing initiative when the Facebook page could be headquarters for most of it.

Figure 5.13   Mars Candy has consistently been doing some
of the best social/digital work.

Making Twitter part of a brand's social footprint.

Twitter debuted at Austin's 2007 SXSW Interactive when the geeks discovered it was a great way to keep 40 balls in the air at once and keep tabs on everything everywhere on the planet simultaneously. As mentioned earlier, if Facebook is a backyard barbecue with friends, Twitter is that noisy cocktail party with tons of people where, after you get home, your head's buzzing with the sound bites of all the funny stuff and cool ideas you heard.

Brevity is the medium's strength. It's one headline of 140 characters.

Jack Dorsey, one of Twitter's founders, said the name represents a burst of birdsong, "a short burst of inconsequential information." There are those who are helping *keep* this information inconsequential with hourly updates of their workout's progress, but as Lee Clow said, the technology comes first and then we find smart ways to use it. Twitter has since become an incredible listening tool, research platform, service center, lead generator, promotion device, and as a community builder its power was never more evident than in the 2011 protests in the Middle East.

Personally? I use Twitter half the time as a listening post and half the time as a signpost, one that points the way to my latest blog entry (*always* fascinating). Many businesses found out about Twitter in a hurry when it became clear people were cramming less-than-complimentary messages into this public suggestion box. Comcast created its @comcastcares Twitter page only after discovering there was a howling blizzard of tweets all with hashtags like #hatecomcast and #comcastblows.

Hashtags, incidentally, are key words assigned to a piece of information, a bit of metadata that describes what another piece of data is about. Hashtags are great for making a tweet searchable and for making groups (or making history as a young Twitter user in Egypt did with her hashtag of #jan25, the first day of the 2011 protests). Although not exactly a hashtag, Kraft Foods used something similar in a promotion with the phrase "mac and cheese." Anytime anyone out in the Twitterverse happened to use those words in a tweet, they each got a link from "Mac & Jinx," and the first to give Kraft his or her address got five free boxes of Macaroni and Cheese.

Conversation strategy is just as important here as it is on Facebook, and I read again and again of either the 80/20 rule (promote others 80 percent of the time and your own agenda 20 percent) or the thirds rule (one-third industry-related stuff, one-third about your field or company, and one-third about your fine self).

All the other advice we've talked about in social applies equally to Twitter, among them being honest, authentic, transparent, and human. Southwest Airlines's social media officer says her rule of thumb is, "Be honest, be real, be fun, be quick"—the quick part being particularly important because tweets are perishable and have a briefer life span than a suicidal mayfly.

Depending on the number of people a person is following, a Twitter feed can move very swiftly, so when it comes to, say, creating a contest for a brand, the rule is "frequent $100 prizes beat one big $500 prize." It doesn't hurt either to build a unique phrase into your tweets as it can help them turn up on Twitter's Trending list, further boosting the audience. Since tweets are passed along by retweeting (an RT), it's also smart to keep your message 20 or so characters short of the allowed 140; the extra room makes it easier for the follower to add his or her RT information.

Make everything else as easy as you can, too. Visibly post the blue "Follow Us/Find Us" Twitter and Facebook buttons in the right places along with whatever other social platforms are right for your brand—LinkedIn, Foursquare, StumbleUpon, and so on—and then be sure to link them all so that your brand's whole spiderweb shakes no matter which thread a catch lands upon.

There are many creative possibilities with the Twitter platform beyond the obvious ones. Pay With A Tweet was an early example. If you Tweeted about a particular product, you got a discount on it. A cooler example happened when Volkswagen Brazil used a mash-up of Twitter and Google Maps to give away tickets to the huge music festival Planeta Terra in Sao Paulo. They hid tickets around the huge city in locations that were shown on a huge Google map of

Sao Paulo—a map shown from thousands of feet up. To get a tighter read on the locations, people had to start tweeting the hashtag #FoxAtPlanetaTerra. With every tweet, the zoom on the Google map got closer and closer until the specific hiding locations were revealed. In less than 2 hours, the campaign hashtag became the number one trending topic in Brazil, where it stayed for the length of the campaign.

In an interesting mix of Twitter and outdoor, Crispin used Twitter to gauge the world's mood and determine exactly how much we all were in need of a dose of Jell-O pudding. The installation in Times Square monitored the number of smile or frown emoticons on the global Twitter feed and adjusted the billboard's giant face to frown or smile depending on our collective digital mojo.

THE USUAL SUSPECTS: BANNERS AND RICH MEDIA.

As the Internet has matured, banners have begun to take a bad rap, some of it deserved. Customers aren't crazy about them and loathe in particular the kind that flash off and on with that seizure-producing strobe. Clients love 'em because they can "measure their effectiveness in real time." (But since 98 percent of them aren't very effective, why knowing in real time that something sucks remains a mystery to me.) Still, not all banners suck, but we'll get to that.

The two formats that irritate customers the most are interstitials and page takeovers. *Interstitials* (also called *transitionals*) are those ads that sometimes appear when you're moving from one website to another. And *page takeovers* are what they sound like. To understand a page takeover, imagine someone suddenly sticking his head between your face and this book and talking about acne medicine. Both interstitials and page takeovers are old-school interruptive-model advertising that's having its death throes online, and although I'm sure there are brilliant exceptions out there, I haven't seen many yet.

It is the banner, however, that's become the most common media buy online, and its effectiveness is measured by its *click-through rate,* the percentage of times people click on it and go on to the client's website (almost all banners run around 1 to 2 percent). The *conversion rate* is a higher bar, measuring as it does the number of people who click-through and then actually buy something.

A glance at any commercial website will show you there are a few standard sizes, all of which are expressed in *interactive marketing units,* or *IMUs.* The most forgiving shape is the rectangles of 350x200 and 180x50 IMU. The thin strip of the 728x90 *leader board,* however, and the tall 120x600 *skyscraper* pose challenges to the creative to make them look decent.

As much as some creatives might roll their eyes at the mention of its name, the lowly banner is actually an excellent place to start concepting for a multimedia campaign. On the surface, the little banner has the constraints of a

Figure 5.14   Another good example of using a medium "incorrectly."

small-space print ad, but as we have seen in other media, constrictions basi-cally force us to be creative. But a couple of square inches online is also very "deep" and can be connected to everything everywhere on the Web. Like a small print ad, it can play off of the editorial environment it appears in and (depending on the bandwidth the site allows) it can also be a bit like a quick, two-frame TV spot.

Even richer in creative possibilities is the appropriately named *rich media.* This format allows viewers to interact with the creative; can feature sound, video, or Flash; and for my money is the most fun you can have with paid media online. You can see some of the creative possibilities online at sites like the Webby Awards site (WebbyAwards.com).

As usual, cool clients like IKEA are at the leading edge with Cannes-winning little creations like their "Assemble-it-yourself" unit that allowed you to see in three clicks how easy it is to open a box and put together its products.

That weirdly shaped *leader board* unit I was just complaining about? The cre-atives on IKEA embraced the suck and brilliantly used its unforgiving shape to their concept's advantage (Figure 5.14). The headline read: "Smart solutions for any space. Click and drag to resize this banner." When you clicked and dragged you could see various IKEA pieces nicely fill all the different shaped rooms your interaction created.

One of the cooler things about rich media is that you can incorporate data from other places online dynamically, meaning the data is live. Selling a Patagonia raincoat is a little more compelling when the ad itself is reminding you of the 90 percent chance of rain today. The whole online media *buy* can also be triggered by dynamic data; no one in Chicago sees the ad for a cruise line's Caribbean itineraries until it's below freezing.

Rich media units can also allow a viewer to interact with them, see more details about an offer, and do it without taking the viewer off the site he or she is visiting. It's kinda like being able to look in a store window without having to go inside. It's noninvasive, and depending on the content you build into the unit, it can be pretty cool.

BBH did a cool rich media for Johnnie Walker Black (Figure 5.15). Called the "Gift Translator," the teeny ad was put on gift sites during the holidays. Type in whatever piece-of-•••• gift you were thinking of getting your guy friend and the man in the wreath would give you 1 of 70 different responses describing what your gift *really* says. (It was never good.)

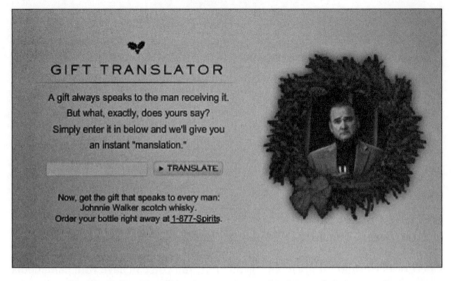

Figure 5.15   Type in what you were thinking of giving, and "Dr. Anderson" gives a customized description of what your gift says: "This gift says you should keep your receipt."

Figure 5.16   Using the small size of a banner as a launching point for a creative solution.

Before you start noodling with these ideas, it'll pay to keep in mind the realities of the client's budget as well as the vendor's technical limits. A little 40k banner can't support a lot of animation, and even when you're working in rich, too much animation in the creative may challenge the processing power of the viewer's computer and make for a long loading time (translation: *Buh-bye.* >CLICK<).

Because banners are both small and deep, they're interesting places to begin concepting for a bigger campaign. I'm not sure the creatives who did the Cannes-winning Banner Concerts for Belgium's Axion bank started concepting with banners, but they ended up with a cool campaign that creatively leveraged a banner's small space. To make the bank a little more visible to young people, they decided to have Axion sponsor mini-concerts of up-and-coming rock bands, emphasis on the mini. White boxes in the exact ratio of various banner sizes were built (Figure 5.16). Well-known Belgian acts were invited to perform live in these teeny spaces, and once they were filmed and edited, the agency had some cool ready-to-place banners. The banners all led to a site where young rockers could enter to win a chance to be featured in a Banner Concert, land a recording contract, and book a gig at a big venue.

To experience AXE's Virtual Hair Action rich media banner, viewers were asked to don headsets. When they did, they got to choose which of three beautiful women would whisper in their ears. Each told a different story, and of course all of the stories are about how hair by AXE is impossible to resist.

MOBILE IS THE NEW BLACK.

There's going to come a day when every single person on the planet will have a cell phone—including babies. In fact, even dead people will have cell phones (seriously), probably with brand names like iDead or Stiff-Berry. What I'm getting at is that mobile is where *EVERYTHING* is ultimately headed—the entire Web, the combined knowledge of all history, the ability to purchase any product from every brand and every store, on demand, everywhere, all the time, will be in everybody's pocket.

There are so many possibilities with this platform that this small book can't hope to cover them all. Technology is improving on the hour and "phone-wallets" are about to change everything all over again. NFC, or near-field communication, will let phones replace credit cards, rewards cards, coupons, and commuter tickets, and so we'll limit our discussion here to how mobile can fit into a brand's overall media mix. Google Wallet is the first one out there.

One of the simplest ways mobile fits a full media portfolio is as connective tissue. Put a smart code (QR) in a concert poster, and a fan can get a free song or buy tickets. Text a short code number from a print ad, and a reader gets a free sample in the mail. Scan the bar code in the store, and a shopper can see how much the product costs across the street.

As you can see from even these simple examples, what makes mobile one of the cooler media is that it's the place where brands can start *doing* things instead of just saying them. A place where brands can prove things, not just make claims.

As we said earlier, the new ideas are more about changing what customers *do* than what they think. So as you begin to work in mobile for your clients, encourage them to see the medium as more than just a teeny screen to surf the Web for their products. Yes, the extremely bored guy at the airport waiting for a flight may well be browsing, but research shows most people doing mobile searches are looking for a particular thing for a particular reason. "Instead of thinking of mobile as a new advertising distribution platform," writes Mathieson in *The On-Demand Brand*, "it's far more powerful as a response or 'activation mechanism' to commercial messages we experience in other media."[35]

In fact, outdoor and mobile seem to be made for each other. Dove posted a billboard asking passersby to vote on their idea of beauty (choosing between pictures) by using their cell phones. They then posted the results of the poll on the board, in real time.

NYC's Pathways to Housing projected an image of a homeless person sleeping at the foot of a building along with a super that read, "To get him off the street, text HOME to 5651." Once a donation was texted in, a virtual door appeared on the building's wall and the homeless person rose and walked into a home.

You can make an iFart app, or you can make something that will improve people's lives.

As of this writing the top 100 paid iPhone apps include silly crap like *Texts From Last Night* and *I Am T-Pain*. (It makes your voice sound stupid. I think I'll dub these things "*cr*apps®"). Aaanyway, there are also cool things like the hugely addictive Angry Birds, Craig's List Pro, and 10 pretty cool camera applications from Hipstamatic to the Lego camera mentioned earlier.

These are all kind of fun, but the stuff that excites most of the serious ad people is the possibility of creating seriously utilitarian ideas that tie directly into a brand's main offering. In fact, some experts believe that mobile apps may become the primary interface customers use to interact with a brand, and I refer again to Interbrand's CEO Andy Bateman statement: "Content and functionality are the new creativity."

Benjamin Moore's Color Capture app (Figure 5.17 on the left) is extremely functional. It lets customers take pictures of anything that has a cool color (a sunset, an aquarium) and then shows them the closest matching premixed colors ready and waiting on the store shelves.

The IKEA Mobile Catalogue (Figure 5.17 on the right) uses a phone's camera to allow customers to clearly picture what different IKEA furniture designs will look like in their own homes.

Most of us in the business have been in meetings where someone says, "We need an app by Friday!" This knee-jerk response to new technology may have abated somewhat by the time this book reaches your hands. But if one day you're asked this question, it'll pay to sit down and give some real thought to how you can bake your app idea into the firmament of your brand's true value proposition. There are two main kinds: one's called a *native app,* specifically made to be downloaded to a particular operating system (iPhone, Android, etc.), and the other is a *Web app.* Whereas native apps reside in your device, Web apps live on the servers and are accessible across different platforms.

Pizza Hut's ordering app is a good example of an idea that brings to life the main benefit of the brand; in fact, it nearly replaces the company's website,

Figure 5.17   Two cool and useful apps. On the left, Benjamin Moore helps you match colors; on the right, IKEA lets you see how its furniture will look in your house.

stores, and call centers. This native app lets customers order pizza almost instantly, repeat a previous order, order sides, and in its first three months it brought in $1 million in sales, a perfect example of how mobile can disrupt a category as well as improve people's lives.

With always-on ideas like this, a brand can earn a permanent place in users' mobile devices and stay present in their lives during the entire purchase cycle and life of a product.

Location-aware apps use mobile to its fullest.

Launched originally as a sort of mash-up of Google Maps and a social network, Foursquare is a location-based social network that allows users with GPS-enabled phones to "check in" at different venues, updating friends on their whereabouts. (I always thought it would also be a great app for burglars. *"Hey, I'm not at home right now. In fact, I'm waaaay across town at Jay's Bar & Grill."*) In the beginning, checking in was good just for bragging rights, but as Mr. Clow said, the technology comes first and now location-aware apps are being adopted by businesses everywhere, predominantly as digital rewards programs and virtual loyalty cards.

There are quite a few location-slash-social apps now: Loopt, Gowalla, and Facebook Places among them. They all marry the real and virtual worlds and bring with them possibilities for brand experiences that include gaming and community. Foursquare's tie-in with LivingSocial and Groupon also allows for possibilities of geomarketing promotions and discounts that go way beyond just "Free drinks for the Mayor!" In fact, checking in isn't even limited to actual *places* anymore. You can check in at TV shows, and gamers can check in at key points inside a game, letting friends know their virtual location within the game space.

Location-aware apps are particularly right for those alternate reality games mentioned earlier. There are smaller geocaching concepts like Coca-Cola's Foursquare "Coke Machine Fairy" promotion that alerted users to special prizes hidden in nearby vending machines. Or you can go huge like Mini Stockholm did with their extremely energetic alternate reality game to promote the MINI Countryman. They "parked" a virtual MINI in the streets of Stockholm, marking its location on a map in their Getaway Stockholm app. Once you were within 50 meters of the location, you were prompted to "Take the MINI now!" Once you had it, you had to get away as fast as you could because anyone else playing the game could swipe it for themselves once they got within 50 meters of you. The first player to have the car in his or her possession for a full week won a real MINI Countryman.

Augmented reality is another cool use of mobile. The term describes looking at a real-world environment whose elements are augmented by computer-generated sensory input such as sound, video, graphics, or GPS data. The Museum of London did an extremely cool augmented-reality app called StreetMuseum. Hold your phone up to various street scenes in London and the app overlaid old photos of the same street taken from the same angle (along with giving you tons of interesting historical information).

Less erudite but certainly more practical was an app from our friend Charmin. Charmin's app showed its desperate users the location and relative comfort of the nearest public bathroom. But Charmin, did you *have* to call it "Sit or Squat?" *Really?* Did you *have* to?

Everything is media.

It's not likely you're going to get a job order at work that asks you to announce the big sale on Saturday with an app, a print ad, some banners, a blog, a TV spot, a microsite, user-generated content, some outdoor, a gaming tie-in, a digital billboard and kiosk, a couple of radio spots, some texting and tweets, some mobile video, a little street theater, a rich media buy, a flash mob in Times Square, some video on demand, a widget, an i-ad, plus a video that goes viral.

You may just need an ad.

Then again, you may not. This sitting-down-to-make-an-ad thing is simply a much bigger deal than it once was. But that's where it's all going.

Today everything is interconnected. And when Google TV gets up some serious steam, humanity may become like the Borg. *(High fives to my sci-fi bros.)* Hive mind will become a reality, and those who can connect to it and concept in its space will have the edge.

Chris Kyle, vice president of Global Brand Communications at Adidas (aka, "the client") summed all this up very clearly: "Simply put, we don't need an advertising-focused agency anymore. We need a marketing agency that can think strategically and creatively, and deliver ideas that work across all channels. That's a much bigger challenge than making an ad campaign."[36]

Figure 6.1   The MINI was introduced to America with one of the smallest TV budgets ever—fortunately.

6

Big Honkin' Ideas
Putting it all together

IT'S TRUE. EVERYTHING IS MEDIA, LADIES AND GENTS. Everything is branding, and it's all for sale. Today you can print your client's good name on the stripes between car spaces in parking lots, and citizens are selling space on their cars, their homes, even their foreheads. It's crazy. It reminds me of one of my favorite *Onion* headlines: "Area 14-Year-Old Collapses Under Weight of Corporate Logos."

We can either bemoan how we've become the dystopia once imagined in the opening scene of *Blade Runner,* or we can decide to fill all these new analog and digital spaces with stuff that's interesting and cool. (Come to think of it, that *Blade Runner* scene was actually pretty cool.) One of Wikipedia's contributors nicely summed up the draw of new media: "Within the advertising business there is a blurring of the distinction between creative (content) and the media (the delivery of this content). New media itself is considered to be creative and the medium has indeed become the message."[1]

One last note here, before we talk about using all this cool media and technology. As explosive as digital is, it's not likely it's going to replace everything. Radio didn't replace magazines. TV didn't replace radio. And digital and social aren't gonna replace TV. With each technological breakthrough, what we've seen is everything rearrange and find new natural places in our lives. It keeps changing, but what *is* clear is that brands are going to have to create more complex forms of advertising, with more platforms, and a lot more integration. Logos may get smaller and "FIND OUT MORE" buttons bigger. Print ads may have hashtags, and outdoor may all become paired with mobile. This is where it's going.

But before we rush off and film a webi-sitcom, write tweets for a blimp's interactive billboard, or compose messages for every urban surface we can see from our office windows, it'll pay to first sit down and figure out a few things.

Imagine a day in the life of your customer.

Let's put our ad-writing pencils down for a minute and think way upstream about our client and the client's customer.

How does our client's typical customer spend a day? What does he do in the morning? Is Pandora playing music while he fixes breakfast, or does he grab something on the go? Does he drive to work? Does he have a tablet; if so, what kind? Does he recycle? What blogs does he read when he's supposed to be working? Does he run at a gym or on the streets, or does he run like me . . . into the kitchen for another Krispy Kreme?

This thinking doesn't have to be guesswork. It's likely that your agency colleagues have gathered all kinds of good research about the customer. So before you start work on a campaign, it's time to sit down with the account, strategy, and media team and map out a day in the life.

If your campaign has a digital component, it's also time to sit down with the UX person (stands for "user experience"). Your UX person will be a major part of mapping out this day in the life of a consumer's use of media. And when it comes to creating work for online, your UX person will help your team figure out the architecture of the online experience from start to finish. Similar to an architect building a house, a UX person goes through the entire place to make sure things like the correct outlets are on the right walls, that doors are where they should be, and so on; all very important functions but ones that have nothing to do with the idea or the aesthetics of the house, which is the creatives' job. Your UX person will start with the same objectives and strategy that you do, but his job is to use all that information to frame up the end experience and make it one that's as user-friendly and efficient as possible.

As your team begins to explore a consumer's typical day, you may see that newspapers play a part in this person's life, as well as other common media, such as television and radio. But those are the easy ones. And we're not making a media checklist here anyway. What we're doing is looking for *insight*. It's kinda like we're trying to see the aquarium from the inside out, to move through our customers' world exactly the way they do. We're looking for contact points with them that are unexplored. We're looking for places where customers might even *welcome* a cool message from our brand. Places where the right message could be less of an ad and more like information or entertainment.

A day in the life of a real estate agent is gonna be different than a corporate executive's day. A real estate agent practically lives online, and his cell phone rings constantly. The executive probably has people to answer her phone and gets information by listening to podcasts at the gym or reading business pubs on the plane.

Although all this different-strokes-for-different-folks stuff may seem a little obvious, it's surprising how many agencies buy the media before finding the insight, or simply use the same media plan to reach every audience. *("We'll buy TV for reach, magazines for frequency, and throw in a little radio for promotions.")*

During this exercise is also a good time to ask yourself, "What would a *generous brand* do to get out and meet its customers?" *Generous* is a term you may hear more and more. Fallon's John King says generous brands are empathetic and tend to make gestures that are not just commercially motivated; they pay less attention to their own marketing schedules and more to the consumers' calendars, "taking the time to know and understand what's going on in the audience's lives. Brands today should take cues from Google's ever-changing home page, asking how they can participate on St. Patrick's Day or Election Day instead of brainstorming ideas to 'Drive sales in Q3!'—a concept that has no relevance on the consumer calendar."[2]

Okay, now before we start writing, there's one other mental exercise that may be helpful.

Imagine the buying process.

After you've mapped a day in the life with your customer, switch gears. Now think through how a customer decides to buy your client's product. Here again, agency research and insights from your colleagues can help you see the entire buying process through a buyer's eyes.

Some folks call this the *purchase funnel,* although that's a little creepy for my money. I guess any number of visual metaphors might be helpful in visualizing the buying process. Whatever image you settle on, scribble it on a big pad and start visualizing what happens to your customer as he or she moves toward actually buying your client's product. Think it through. How is it that a normal person can move from a state of being perfectly happy without, say, your client's fabulous flat-screen TV, to noticing the flat screen in the sports bar, to thinking, "Geez, my old TV does kinda suck," to swooning in front of all the brands on display at the mall, to checking prices online, to triumphantly swiping his or her VISA card through the machine at Best Buy (or swallowing hard and hitting "Buy now with one click")? As you go through the process, think about the contact points that pop up—those times a customer might have occasion to think about a flat-screen TV or about the whole home entertainment category in general.

As you might imagine, the consideration process is different for a flat-screen TV than, say, buying a pack of gum, or a car, or insurance. Depending on the product the process can be long or short; the longer ones typically consist of phases. I'm sort of making up some phases here for a nonexistent product, but a customer could move from general awareness to short-listing to comparison to store contact to store visit to trial. Phases such as these may be useful to keep in

mind as you work on your overall idea. Different media will be in play at different parts of the purchase cycle, and each of them has its strengths.

Here's the thing to remember about this whole exercise: your main idea may
come out of one of these contact points—an idea you can then spread sideways
and backward to fill in the whole campaign. Find a cool contact point that leads
to an idea, then fan that flame into a big idea, and then take the big idea and turn
it into a multimedia experience.

What is the "press release" of your idea?

We're ready to sit down and start coming up with big honkin' ideas. Again, we'll
ask the same question we've mentioned before: "What is the 'press release' of
my idea?" Is the idea cool enough that the press would write a story about it?
And I don't mean a story in *Ad Age* but on the *News at 6*.

If your idea has heft, if it's truly amazing, you should be able to describe it
as news that's worthy of a press release. Yes, we're setting the bar high here, but
what else is going to move our clients' brand names into the national conversation? An ad? It goes back to Bogusky's observation: "If you're about to spend
advertising dollars on a campaign and you can't imagine that anybody is going
to write about it or talk about it, you might want to rethink it. It means you probably missed injecting a truth or social tension into it."[3]

Remember, instead of generating advertising ideas, generate *ideas worth
advertising.*

Pick a small customer contact point and then think big.

Okay, *now* we're ready to sit down and come up with big honkin' ideas. Oh, one
last thing. You can't do any TV or print.

That's right. When you sit down to begin work, start by imagining there are
no such things as TV commercials and print ads. They're all gone.

Here's where it gets interesting. You still have to get your client's product or
service into the social conversation, but you have to find entirely new ways of
doing it.

What are you going to do?

Don't get me wrong here. I'm not saying TV and print are passé. What I'm saying is that when you *start* with TV (and its usual side orders of print and radio),
you're solving problems in a prepackaged way. You may very well end up airing
a TV spot and that's fine, but you don't have to start there. We've used print as a
great starting point to talk about the craft, yes. But what we've really been talking about is thinking creatively. And now it's time to apply that creative thinking
free of form.

Start with a blank piece of paper. In fact, let's not even think paper. How would
you tell your brand's story around a campfire? How would you tell the story if
Motorola Zooms were your only medium? Or vending machines? What if all you
had to work with was the way the store operators answered the phone? What if

you made your whole campaign a free download from iTunes? How would you start bloggers talking about your product? What about getting customers to send a tweet for a free trial? As you can see, I'm exhorting you to start somewhere. You have to, obviously, but I urge you to pick one of the more intriguing consumer contact points and begin from there. It's sort of like that bumper sticker: "Act Locally, Think Globally." Go over the two lists you've just made: the a-day-in-the-life list and the one about the purchase process. What opportunities jump out?

In Laurence Minsky's book, *How to Succeed in Advertising When All You Have Is Talent,* Wieden + Kennedy's Susan Hoffman put it this way:

> Think holistically. . . . [What] would you do in the store? How can you pull the iconography of the campaign right into the clothing hang tag? A coupon? Online? The best work has legs to go everywhere and puts a strong, consistent, visual imprint on every consumer touch point. It's important to bring this kind of thinking to your work. . . . Take this inventiveness and apply it to the business. But do more than just ads. Produce an album, experiment with graffiti, invent a new product, shoot a film, or write a book.[4]

Think creatively about different media where your message can appear. Play out that day in the life of your customer, see where it matches up with the world of your product, and then just start screwing around with it.

For instance, the inside bottom of a paper coffee cup might be a good place to put a message about sweeteners. Maybe a dingy subway car is just the place to tell a glassy-eyed commuter she needs a cruise to St. Thomas. If your client is an organization for some social issue, why not paint your idea all over the building across from city hall? (A British agency actually projected a provocative ad directly *onto* Parliament.) Just go for it; maybe you can do it, maybe you can't, but until someone makes a phone call you don't know.

To reach the higher-ups, Abbott Mead Vickers put a message about the business magazine the *Economist* on top of a bus that rolled through London's financial district, the Square Mile (Figure 6.2.).

As for finding a startlingly effective place to put a client's message, the most brilliant I've ever seen was a spot that ran on the porn channel in hotels. (I know, I know, I said no pee-pee jokes, and here is the brilliant exception to the rule.) Virgin Atlantic wanted to tell business travelers about the nice new seats in their transatlantic flights. The team figured—cynically and correctly—that a day in the life of a traveling businessman might include a quick visit to the in-room adult channel. So that's where they placed their commercial, smartly labeling it "Free Movie." When you pressed "PLAY" you saw a 12-minute video that looked and sounded like porn but was really just a long, raunchy infomercial full of double entendres about the pleasures of flying across the Atlantic in a seat that goes all the way back. The idea was so naughty, its very existence drew tons of free media coverage.

The Virgin idea appeared only on in-room TV, but to fully realize the possibilities of a multimedia campaign, you're going to need to drag your main idea

Figure 6.2   Your ad doesn't have to appear in a magazine. Some of the best ones don't.

through each medium and start from scratch once you get there. What works in outdoor may suck as print. The challenge is to make your product look totally cool in each medium and then, at the end of the day, have your overall campaign and the overall experience hang together with one consistent look, one consistent message.

Bring your idea to life in one medium and then go on to the next.

Okay, we've talked about taking in the big picture before you write, thinking through a day in the life, considering a product's purchase cycle, and putting a typical media buy into the blender and hitting purée. Any one of these mental exercises should help free up your thinking and take you to some new places.

Now it's time to put it all together and use them to create a fully integrated multimedia campaign. As an example, let's look at some work done for the American Legacy Foundation's truth® youth smoking-prevention campaign. (Strategically, the campaign was brilliant, and although I won't go into it here, you should study the strategy behind this work. For our purposes today, we're talkin' tactics.)

Truth® wanted to point out to teenagers that Big Tobacco puts all kinds of horrible things in their cigarettes. One of the chemicals in cigarettes is ammonia. It's from here the creative team made their first creative leap. Their creative process looked a little like a technique some call "Fact Plus." Fact Plus takes an indisputable fact and then adds a creative twist on the end, a little something to give it more meaning, humor, or power. In this case, they arrived at this: "Cigarettes contain ammonia. So does dog poop."

Perfect. It's an unpleasant idea and a grotesque image. Next, after thinking for a while, they made their second creative leap (and it wasn't to a TV spot or a print ad).

"Hey, what if we stuck small signs directly into actual dog poop in city parks? Signs with the message: 'Cigarettes contain ammonia. So does dog poop.'"

Boom. There's the outdoor. (Or what some call *wild postings*.)

Then they took the same small sign and turned it into a print ad. The ad featured three dog poop signs, die cut and ready for the reader to deploy. Boom. Print's done.

Then they filmed some truth volunteers at a park sticking these signs in dog poop as curious passersby looked on. Boom. TV's done.

An entire campaign from *one* idea, expressed seamlessly in several media — boom, boom, boom (Figure 6.3). Man, if advertising gets cooler than this, I haven't seen it. A warning here, though, from Saatchi's Tony Granger: "Simply checking the boxes across every possible new media channel is no longer enough to stand out. . . . Each piece of creative should stand on its own as a great expression of the big idea."[5]

This truth campaign did happen to employ some of our usual suspects (TV and print), so let's go back to our self-imposed rule and pretend TV and print don't exist. How could we promote, say, a retail client that needs some buzz for a new store — without TV or print?

IKEA decided to get buzz going for a store opening in Toronto by putting a living room full of their sleek furniture on the public sidewalk of the train

Figure 6.3   The sign in the dog poop reads: "Cigarettes contain ammonia. So does dog poop." An entire multimedia campaign from this one idea.

station. But to make it an event, the creatives at Crispin Porter + Bogusky*
(Mike Lear and Dave Swartz) attached notes to the furniture that read: "Steal
me." The copy went on to ask, "What better way to make a friend than to say,
'Excuse me, want to help me steal this sofa?' The two of you will then be able to
look back at this day and say, 'Hey, remember that time we stole that sofa?' And
you'll laugh. Of course, you and your new friend could always just go to IKEA
and buy a Klippan sofa, seeing as they're only $250."

People didn't believe it at first, but after the first two strangers helped each
other cart off a couch without the cops rolling up, the whole ensemble disap-
peared in an 8-minute scene of helpful, harmonious larceny.

Of course, the creative team was across the street filming the whole thing to
post on the Web. IKEA repeated the exercise for a store opening in another
city, and this time someone dropped a dime to the local news and the event was
covered from a helicopter overhead. Roughly 10 grand to pull off, a quarter mil
of free airtime, serious buzz, and no TV commercials.

With practice, you should be able to start thinking more and more in big
honkin' ideas like this. Of course, not every job that slides cross your desk will
require this type of thinking—just the really fun ones, the big ones, and of
course, new business pitches. However, you may be able to create something big
and cool out of a small print-and-radio assignment just by finding some nugget
of a concept and blowing it up way beyond what's been asked for.

Shoot one idea through the lens of another.

In a screenwriting book I read years ago, I stumbled on this basic Hollywood
trick that seems to apply to what we do here in advertising. To create a story, the
author said, "Create one world and then look at it through the eyes of another."

Long before the term was popular, this author was talking about *mash-ups*.
For instance, *Blade Runner* is basically an old-fashioned gumshoe detective story
seen in the future, right? More recently we had *Cowboys & Aliens*. Since I don't
mean to go all sci-fi geek on you, how about *Brokeback Mountain?* . . . One
could argue it was sort of a *Cowboys and Gay Guys*. One world, seen through
the eyes of another.

My point is this: thinking in terms of mash-ups may be a good mental exercise to add to your regular creative process, a doorknob you'll want to rattle as
you search up and down the hallways of your brain for ideas.

One of my very favorite mash-ups was a piece used to create talk for Mingle2,
a dating site. It was called Zombie Harmony, a dating site for the undead. It's
worth a visit.

---

*Yes, I know, yet another campaign created by Crispin Porter + Bogusky. If I seem to be
favoring these guys a bit in this section, sue me. I use a lot of Volkswagen in this book for
similar reasons: VW is a company that figured out how to do print and outdoor long before
anyone else did. Crispin Porter + Bogusky happens to be one of the leading agencies in
executing integrated campaigns and in the innovative use of media.

*Figure 6.4   Jesus on a Kit Kat. I wish I had been in
that meeting.*

For an Aussie beer named Tooheys, they mixed the worlds of money and beer. In this world, doing a favor like helping a buddy move in to a new place was worth a bottle of Tooheys. Helping him move in with your ex-girlfriend? That would cost him a case.

Another way to start the mash-up engine is with a meme. Take a popular cultural image or saying and shoot it through the world of your client's brand. Kit Kat candy bars started a nationwide buzz by taking the whole silly Shroud-of-Turin, Jesus-on-toast thing and mixing it with the world of candy (Figure 6.4). Voila, you have Jesus on a Kit Kat, a "story" that was planted in Facebook and eventually picked up by the news media (on what I can only hope was a very slow news day).

Memes are in great supply on YouTube, as are mash-ups. With a few edits, *The Shining* + comedy became a trailer for a happy family movie. You can also mash up media. Foursquare is Google Maps + social. And Google Maps + Twitter = Twittervision, a site displaying the location of tweets and tweeters in real time. And TiVO + lots of marijuana = the Domino's/TiVO ordering service that lets stoners order pizza without having to stop watching *The Princess Bride* for the 800th time.

Do anything but an ad.

In an interview on AdCritic.com, Lee Clow said, "Everything is media." As an example, he said the Apple stores now in malls across America are "the best ads Apple's ever done." Similarly, Alex Bogusky said a drink cup at Burger King can have as much reach as a commercial on the Super Bowl.

Stores, cups—it's all media and it's all a canvas an ad person can use to paint a brand story. Clow might agree with my painting metaphor given that he sees TBWA\Chiat\Day is becoming what he calls a "media arts company." Media arts—that's actually a pretty cool way to think about what we do. But the key word here, folks, is *art*. Just because some building has a flat side doesn't mean we should put an ad there. If we do, we need to remember what Howard Gossage reminded us back when we were discussing outdoor in Chapter 3: our work, particularly in outdoor, must delight the people who see it. *Delight* them.

Figure 6.5   This Lego ambient installation recreates the very background it stands in and then adds a bit of Lego creativity.

This is the attitude I encourage you to adopt when you're working in any sort of nontraditional medium, whether you call it ambient or guerrilla advertising. Wikipedia defines this activity as "an unconventional way of performing promotional activities on a very low budget." It's a form increasingly popular with both clients and creatives, the former liking its ability to pinpoint a target segment, the latter its creative possibilities. The marvelous little campaign depicted in Figure 6.5 for Lego recreates a pixelized version of the background of the very location where the ad appears—while adding a bit of whimsy—to show the fun of "imagining" with Legos.

The very environment where the ad appears affects the way people interpret it, and because their ad guard is down, it has an additional element of surprise. But if it's missing that element of art, that element of delight, it's gonna feel like just another corporate hijacking of the environment. In her book *Advertising by Design*, Robin Landa gets to this very point:

> "Guerilla" advertising is effective when it is entertaining. It is offensive when it accosts or seriously intrudes. As advertising creeps more and more into our environment, we must be judicious about its placement and its effect on popular culture and on people. Respecting people is critical.[6]

Don't suck, people, is basically where I'm goin' with this. And don't let people make you suck, particularly in regard to outdoor and guerrilla advertising. This isn't a medium people can switch off.

One last thing: unless you have something really important to tell me, please stay out of my bathroom stalls and off of my urinal pucks. Stuff like that—really *any* "hot new" medium being marketed by a vendor—has probably already lost its element of surprise anyway. The whole bathroom advertising gig reminds me of when my boys were little; they'd bring their fight to the outside of my bathroom door demanding that I immediately render judgment. Through the door I'd say, "Boys, can't this wait?"

Through the door I ask again today, can't the wheels of capitalism wait long enough for me to take care of business here? *Lordy.*

Instead of doing an ad, change the product, or make a new one.

You're never going to be at the agency one day and get a job request saying, "Change the product." But this is precisely what smart agencies are doing more and more, and they're making a bunch of money for their clients in the process.

The reason they do it is either to create a difference worth talking about or to find a new way to bring the brand promise to life, to create a proof point that the brand really *is* what it says it is, really *does* what it says it'll do. Burger King's promise of "Have It Your Way" came to life when Crispin Porter + Bogusky sold the idea of a new product called Chicken Fries—fry-cut chicken in a round cup that fit in car's cup holder. Chicken Fries didn't exist until Crispin Porter + Bogusky made them up, and once they did, Burger King had something new to talk about that paid off the brand promise of "chicken, your way."

What can you do to change the product to *create* a story you can talk about? Start from the bottom up, at the store level or with any direct consumer experience, and then solve the customer's problem by creating or changing the product to bring the overall brand promise to life. Look at every little facet of the company, every contact point with the customer. How can it contribute to the brand story and help prove it? How can you bring it to life through the lens of the big idea you came up with in the first place?

Here's another example, also from Crispin Porter + Bogusky: It started with a video game developer asking Burger King if they wanted to buy some "signage" within one of their games. Crispin Porter + Bogusky and Burger King renegotiated the deal and ended up with much more than just a BK logo in the background of some fight scene: The King actually became a player in the game. Creative Director Bill Wright told me the success of this experiment led to bigger things: "After a year of development, three Xbox 360 games went on sale inside Burger King restaurants. During its short five-week promotional period BK sold 2,478,000 games. Instead of just watching the King, people were playing him."

Not every product change has to be as big as Burger King's Xbox games. Colle McVoy made a simple change to the wrapping of their client's sub sandwiches (Christmas wrapping paper) as a great way to sell gift cards (Figure 6.6). Digital media also allows us to make changes to the product without having to change the product itself. Almost anything can have a digital extension online—perhaps you can turn the product or service into a game or some other brand experience.

Perhaps the most well known new product idea is one we've mentioned already: Nike+. Nike and R/GA knew that runners liked listening to music while

Figure 6.6   Changing the product is often the most visible way to get your message in front of a customer.

they ran. So they introduced a $29 Sport Kit sensor that, when synched with an iPod, tracked a runner's speed, mileage, and calories burned. When finished, a runner could dock the iPod and share the data on NikePlus.com. So in addition to being a cool product in its own right, Nike+ became a social platform where runners share information as well as provide inspiration to Just Do It. It's a perfect example of how creating a product or service—instead of just an ad—can play a big part in the future of the ad business.

Don't do an ad. Create an event. Create an experience.

Getting good public relations (PR) for our clients is one of the very best things we can do. Some of the most fantastic selling concepts I've ever seen weren't ads per se; they were events.

Back in Chapter 3 we said, "You know those ideas that make you laugh but you think, nah, we can't do that?" When it comes to creating events, these are the very ideas you have to do. The stuff you can't do is where the coolest stuff happens.

What if someone said "Naahhh" to this next one?

At an Australian agency, the creatives were working on a new beer campaign, and as they clicked through the background information online they come upon some interesting posts from expats living in London; heartfelt letters from British Aussies who wrote about missing their home brew, Speight's. And they asked, "Hey, what if we took Speight's to them? What if we took a whole Aussie pub to London?" And they did (Figure 6.7). They put a pub on an old tub of a boat and filled its hold with beer. They ran ads in New Zealand newspapers to hire the "crew" (and kick off the PR) and then took the brand experience through the Bahamas to New York and then all the way to London.

Another example that comes to mind is Diesel's insane idea for marketing its Intimate Collection. I would love to have been in the conference room when they presented this idea.

> "Okay, basically, what we're suggesting is we're gonna have two pretty girls— both of whom we'll name 'Heidie'—and these two girls, they're gonna steal a bunch of this new underwear you got, kidnap one of your sales managers, and then lock themselves in a hotel for five days. Consumers will be able to talk to the Heidies by phone and online. And we'll broadcast the whole thing live on the Web."

Man . . . I've been in meetings where suggesting "Let's run *two* newspaper ads" would put the account into review. But in this case Diesel said yes and their servers nearly melted down as customers jammed the lines trying to interact with the Heidies.

> "Can you say my name on the air, Heidie?"

> "Heidie, will you please play my favorite song?"

Figure 6.7   An Australian beer sends an Aussie pub to expats in the U.K.

189

Everybody was in on the joke, and the entire promotion garnered massive PR because of its intelligent parodying of reality TV, Facebook, and the global fever dream of being famous for a Warholian 15 minutes. It was incredible.*

Authors of *Oh My God, What Happened and What Should I Do?* touch on this same point:

> If you want your idea to pick up steam and generate media coverage, you should simply imagine people's response. The best response would be: *"Holy s••t! They really did this!??"* If this is the response you want, there's a simple rule to follow: Do it for real. Burger King really fed people who had never seen a burger in their life with the Whopper. 7-Eleven actually re-built their stores into Kwik-E-Marts. The Swedish agency, ACNE, really did throw a pair of oversized dice down a glacier and had people bet on the outcome. All these campaigns have received intense media coverage. Why? Because it was not fake; they did it for real.[7]

These ideas are fairly unhinged. This is what people pay attention to. As we'll note in a later section, you will never see a newspaper with the headline "Area man mows lawn."

Events can start offline and go digital, or the other way around.

Wikipedia says *viral advertising* is generally "any Internet-driven promotion in the form of video clips, interactive Flash games, or SMS text messages." The really good ones get passed from one person to another and spread like global infection to become viral.

Keep in mind that viral is a result, not a strategy. I continue to see the word *viral* written into client briefs like it's something you can request: "Need one print ad, one radio spot, annnnd . . . oh, a viral video too, please." We decide to go viral about as much as the Beatles decided to go famous. Before anything viral happens, somebody has to do something mind-roastingly cool.

Honda's famous "Cog" commercial (Figure 6.8) was that cool, and not surprisingly, I first saw it through a link someone e-mailed to me, as did millions of others; same with Burger King's "Subservient Chicken." If "Cog" and "Subservient Chicken" were digital events, equally powerful events can be staged in the real world and then pulled back online. Depending on how cool these analog-to-digital events are, promoted properly they can often go nuclear.

Some are best described as events, or hoopla (to borrow the title of Warren Berger's book about Crispin Porter + Bogusky): to do something out in public so interesting or so cool that the press picks it up and people who hear about

---

*Just so you know the conclusion, the siege came to an end when the son of Diesel founder Renzo Rosso cut a deal with the Heidies and freed the salesperson. The deal—which pulled the idea into other media—was to use the Heidies in a Diesel print campaign.

Figure 6.8   When they filmed "Cog," only six hand-built pre-mass-production Accords existed. And they had to completely disassemble one of them for this spot.

Figure 6.9   A cool T-Mobile event. (To see some cool events done for no commercial reason whatsoever, Google "Improv Everywhere.")

it watch it later online. These events we create have to answer to a strategy, of course, just like any other ad. In London, Saatchi & Saatchi beautifully brought to life T-Mobile's credo "Life is for sharing." In London's Liverpool Street Station, 400 "commuters" busted out into a well-rehearsed Michael Jackson–like dance (Figure 6.9). Everyone else in the station scrambled to find their cameras/cell phones to capture the joyous event. Of course, the agency had film crews in place to record images for the commercial that aired the next day, the online videos, as well as the fully integrated campaign that followed.

As you can see, this idea can be expressed as a press release. It was kicked off in reality and went nuclear on the grid (30 million views when I checked the site yesterday). The same reality-to-digital dynamic happens with this next stunt.

In Italy, Heineken leveraged the emotion that soccer fans have for the game by getting hundreds of evil accomplices to convince their spouses to sacrifice watching a championship match and attend instead a (fake) performance of some boring classical music and poetry. Fifteen minutes into the tedium the ruse was revealed, the game appeared on a theater-sized screen and 1,000 extremely happy soccer fans drank free Heinekens. In addition to being a brand experience for these lucky few, when the agency pulled the event online, 12 million people got a similar experience. Again, it's an idea that can be expressed as a press release.

To promote an exhibition of famous press photos at the New Zealand Netherlands Foundation, Clemenger BBDO wrote to 74 world leaders inviting them to actually come view these provocative and politically charged photos. The agency correctly guessed that the leaders would all send letters declining, and when the expected mail arrived, the agency simply posted their letters—the actual letters—on bus shelter boards, underneath headlines like: "We invited Tony Blair to our exhibition. Here's the response" (Figure 6.10). Tellingly, the copy signed off with "See the photos they should be seeing." Follow-up phone calls to their offices were turned into radio spots, and once the campaign broke, the press snapped up the story (how could they not?) and the campaign blew off the museum's doors. It was a press release kind of idea, one that's interesting on *paper*.

Wieden + Kennedy's famous 1-second Super Bowl commercial Miller High Life was a media stunt. Their spokesman (from the campaign discussed in Chapter 3) stood in a warehouse and was filmed saying, "Miller High Life!" It wasn't the 1-second commercial on the big game that got the attention, but the whole idea of the stunt. Which, of course, can be written as a press release.

On the other hand, what attracted the worldwide press to cover JWT's event for the Human Rights Watch was the sheer artistry and graceful metaphor of the idea. At New York's Grand Central Station, commuters found a bank of small backlit images of the 2,100 political prisoners in Burma. The clever placement of black ball-point pens over the images turned them into jail cells; pens that viewers were asked to use to sign the petition calling for their release (Figure 6.11). As the pens were removed, so were the bars. The PR writes itself.

Figure 6.10: Even when the event doesn't happen, it can still be an event.

Figure 6.11   This is advertising at its best. Artistry in service of a good cause.

This whole thing about "idea as press release" is simply a way to ask yourself, "Is my idea good on paper? And can it be summed up quickly?" When the answers are both yes, your idea will be just as interesting as news as it is as advertising.

It's all about ideas that are cool on *paper,* like these ideas: A TV show is purposely advertised on the least-seen billboards on the planet—People are asked to make bets on two half-ton dice that a new casino rolls down a mountainside—A live TV commercial uses 19 skydivers to spell HONDA—Coca-Cola tries to sue itself for Coke Zero's "taste infringement"—Burger King tells customers they no longer sell the Whopper—Someone releases a "smile-activated" vending machine.*

Ideas this interesting can begin and end life entirely online as well. HBO's well-known Voyeur Project is an example, as was the breakout video "I've got a crush on Obama."

For pure stopping power I think Droga5's video for the clothing line Ecko Unltd is hard to beat (Figure 6.12). The brief was to position the brand (started by graffiti artist Mark Ecko) as an urban icon. What Droga5's team did was to create an extremely realistic "home video" of two people climbing over a fence, creeping up to Air Force One, and tagging "Still free" on the President's iconic plane (as in stillfree.com). Dropped anonymously onto 20 websites, within 24 hours the video was the most-talked-about piece of media on the planet.

VW's promotion for its Golf took place entirely online. Taking its cue from an old-fashioned contest seen in the documentary *Hands on a Hard Body,* VW

Figure 6.12   It took a lot of production value to make this video look like it didn't have a lot of production value.

---

*There is a good collection of event-based marketing stunts online at www.taylorherring.com.

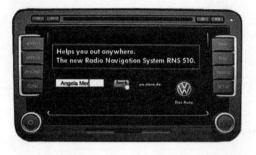

Figure 6.13   Bringing a product experience to life online can be tough.
This one did a good job.

promised to give away a Golf to the person who could longest keep his or her cursor on an image of the car. News organizations followed the story (which lasted 16 days, by the way), and it all tied in nicely with the endurance capabilities of the vehicle.

Online sounds like a tough place to demonstrate the dangers of noodling with a phone while driving, until I heard this idea. People registered to receive an online video. As they were watching the video (a driver's point of view in a moving car), they received a phone call. The call came from the website itself. If they answered their phone, they caused a car crash in the video. I haven't even *seen* this site and here I am telling you about it. Because I heard about it on the news.

All these ideas were cool on paper first and now are cool online. So were these next four ideas: Customers got to write or draw things on a huge map using the GPS in their new BMW motorcycles—472 students uploaded their own images to create and be featured in a mobile phone commercial—Gamers who love the violence of Sega's *Condemned 2* were encouraged to "offset the evil" by playing their new happy-crappy games *Pony Heart Quest, Clown Flower Time,* and *Lollipop Gift Parade*—VW actually bought space on the white "Site Not Found" page to demonstrate its helpful navigation system (Figure 6.13). Again, all cool on paper first.

Mix the right cultural cocktail, serves 300 million.

Then there was Ogilvy Toronto's marvelous "Evolution" commercial for Dove that rode a wave of mass Internet interest all the way to the top prize at Cannes (Figure 6.14). In this simple online video, we see an ordinary-looking woman sit down in

Figure 6.14   This one hit a cultural nerve at the right time.

front of a camera. From the sides come the hands of makeup artists, which begin to touch her up, to groom her. The hairstylist's hands follow; the lighting is similarly fussed over. A minute or so into it, this ordinary-looking woman is approaching cover girl material, and that's when her image is transferred to computer. Here, even more radical makeovers morph her image into the totally fake "10" we see up on a billboard and the video ends. Two supers come quietly onscreen with the message "No wonder our perception of beauty is distorted. Take part in the Dove Real Beauty Workshop for Girls. Visit campaignforrealbeauty.ca."

The whole thing was set to a great piano track and, except for the words at the end, could have passed for a cool music video.

Janet Kestin, creative director at Ogilvy Toronto, assured me they did not "decide" to go viral.

"We really had no idea it was going to do what it did," she told me in an interview. "It started with the art director/writer, Tim Piper, posting it on YouTube and at the same time Dove sent out an e-mail blast. A couple of days was all it took before it was on everything from CNN.com to BBC, even talk shows in Korea. It was starting to get momentum but the posting on YouTube and the PR push were the real catalysts."

It would seem we're back to what Bogusky said earlier: "If you're about to spend advertising dollars on a campaign and you can't imagine that anybody is going to write about it or talk about it, you might want to rethink it. It means you probably missed injecting a truth or social tension into it."

Dove's "Evolution" had both of those. Kestin's partner, Nancy Vonk, added: "As a society, we're so celebrity-obsessed and appearance-obsessed. Dove's Campaign for Real Beauty came at the moment when people were asking themselves, 'Have we gone too far?' It didn't hurt that it was released right when it was Fashion Week in New York City and there were lots of news stories about too-skinny models and all of that. To use Gladwell's phrase, it really did seem like a tipping point."*

"Evolution" indeed had a truth and social tension built into it. It also had pretty much everything else we've been talking about through this entire book. A quick look back at all the things we've talked about so far convinces at least me that Dove's "Evolution" was a big honkin' idea that hit on every cylinder.

Say something believable. Say something relevant. Be simple. Try not to look like an ad. Open strong. Have one theme. Show; don't tell. Actually prove your point while giving your message. Make sure your idea works fast. Reduce your number of moving parts. Find a villain. Tell the truth and run. Be provocative. Use simple language. Entertain throughout the spot. Leave a picture in the listener's mind. End dramatically. Don't suck. And create something so cool you don't have to pay people to see it.

"Evolution" did all of those things and more. What's not in "Evolution" is also important: there's no spokesperson telling you Dove is soft on your skin. Quoted in *Life after the 30-Second Spot,* Chuck Porter seems to agree viral has its own rules.

> So far, the only two ways I can see to get people to even pay attention to you in the interactive world are to offer information or entertainment. And if you really have dreams of viral, entertainment will always win. Imagine two sites. One has really useful information on caring for delicate fabrics. The other has the funniest joke you've heard since high school. Which one are you going to send to all your friends? . . . People are very tuned into the fact that whatever you forward to your e-mail list says something about you. And hardly anyone would ever send a salesman over to a friend's house.[8]

PARTING THOUGHTS.

The days of solving business problems by doing an ad or shooting a spot are over. In an interview, Rob Schwartz of TBWA\Chiat\Day, agreed and encouraged ad students to start seeing assignments on a much larger scale: "It's not just 'I can do one good print ad.' It's 'I can do a holistic, fully integrated, major, big chunky thought that is media infinite.' It can run on TV, it can run in print, it can run in someone's dinner conversation, the public relations people can work with it."[9]

In closing, I give the advice the ever redoubtable Mark Fenske offers: "If you are near a big idea, get out of its way. Lay flat."

---

*Gladwell's best seller, *The Tipping Point,* is good reading.

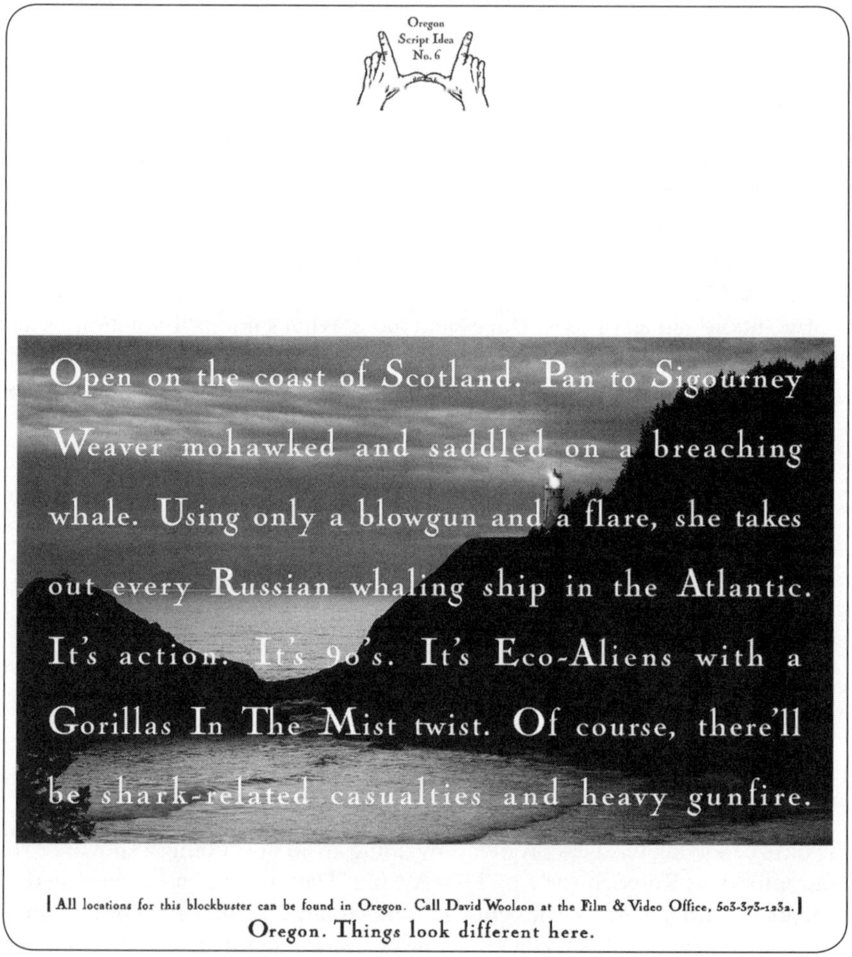

Oregon
Script Idea
No. 6

Open on the coast of Scotland. Pan to Sigourney Weaver mohawked and saddled on a breaching whale. Using only a blowgun and a flare, she takes out every Russian whaling ship in the Atlantic. It's action. It's 90's. It's Eco-Aliens with a Gorillas In The Mist twist. Of course, there'll be shark-related casualties and heavy gunfire.

[All locations for this blockbuster can be found in Oregon. Call David Woolson at the Film & Video Office, 503-373-1232.]
Oregon. Things look different here.

Figure 7.1   If print advertising is the book, television is the movie.

7

In the Future, Everyone Will Be Famous for 30 Seconds

Some advice on telling stories visually

SOMEWHERE IN AMERICA IS THE NATION'S WORST DENTIST; he's out there somewhere. We don't know where he is, but he's out there right now, probably sticking a novocaine needle in somebody's nose or putting a silver filling in his patient's dentures. He is the single worst dentist in the entire country.

And here's the thing: no one knows who he is.

Yep, the worst dentist in all of America and he does his horrible work in anonymity. You don't hear people gathered in the company kitchen goin', "Oh, man, did you see that piece-of-crap bridgework Dr. Hansen did last week? Teeth made outta old paperback books and Bubble Yum? Guy's a complete idiot."

On the other hand, where is the worst commercial in all of America?

It's right there on national TV, playing night after night.

Unlike the anonymity the worst dentist enjoys, here in the ad industry our failures are very public. The worst commercials from the worst agencies (and the worst clients) are all right up there on the big screen in all their digital horror, seen by tens of millions every night. And people *do* talk about them at the office.

Here's my point: you don't wanna suck in this business of advertising, and you *really* don't want to suck at TV. Even your mom's gonna see it. As hot as social media has become these days, television is still a *very* big dog, and if you want a mass audience this is where you play. Yes, YouTube is cool and so is Hulu and all the other online video platforms. But according to the venerable *New York Times*, at this writing, 99 percent of all video consumed in America today happens on the big screen in the living room.[1]

Many of the suggestions from the chapters on general concepting apply to this medium, the virtues of storytelling and simplicity being perhaps the most important. The skills you develop learning to concept and write for TV should also help you create pretty much any kind of video content, whether it's for online videos or sales films. Here are a few other things I've learned from my colleagues along the way.

CREATING THE COMMERCIAL.

Rule #1 in producing a great TV commercial: first, you must write one.

It takes exactly as much work to produce a bad TV spot as a good one. If you have a so-so idea approved, you're going to put in the same hours producing it that they put in making Apple's famous "1984" commercial (Figure 7.2).

Figure 7.2   This is 1/1,440th of TBWA\Chiat\Day's famous "1984" commercial for Apple Computers.

The creative's job on a TV spot doesn't end with coming up with the idea. That's just the beginning of a long process—a process the creative team will play a part in all along the way. Sell a so-so print idea and at least you'll have the thing out of your hair relatively quickly. A so-so TV spot will haunt you for weeks, or months. You'll have the same long casting sessions you would producing a great spot, the same boring hours on the set during prelighting, and the same tepid coffee in the editing suites. But when you're done, you'll have a ho-hum commercial.

Put in the hours now, during the creative process. Make the concept great. Otherwise, you will have a long time to wish you did.

Make sure you know what kind of money is available for your project before you start.

It's no fun to waste time coming up with a great campaign the client can't afford. So ask your account people to provide a real production estimate. Don't let them tell you the client doesn't really know. That's like walking into a Mercedes dealership and telling the salesperson you don't really know how much you have to spend. *("I might have $70,000 . . . I might not. I don't really know.")*

Typically, production estimates are 10 percent of the total TV buy. Getting this figure is sometimes difficult, but somebody *somewhere* at the client has a dollar amount in his head, and it's best you find out what it is now.

Remember, just because you can think it up doesn't mean you can shoot it.

Before you get too excited about selling an idea, make sure your idea can be executed within your budget. Even the simplest effects can be surprisingly expensive, and some are hard to pull off regardless of the money available.

Study the reels.

There's nothing like seeing a great commercial on a screen. They just don't make the transition to the printed page very well. (That's why I've included only a few stills from favorite spots in this chapter.) You need to see the actual work.

Most of the commercials mentioned in this book are viewable online somewhere. With a few prudently chosen search words, you should be able to see all the spots (and the websites) that are covered here.

Solve the problem visually.

TV is a visual medium and it begs for visual solutions. Now me? I happen to prefer visual over verbal approaches in any medium. I'm not the only one. There's a whole school of thought that says, "Don't talk at customers. Tell them a story with pictures. Start with images. Stay with images."

I've also heard the saying: "The eye will remember what the ear will forget." Which kinda makes sense. I mean, remember the last time you tried to tell somebody about a great commercial? Did you recite the script? Or paint a picture?

Still, on the other hand, it must be stated here that words can rock.

Just when you think the sun rises and sets on eye candy and visual storytelling, along comes Wieden + Kennedy with a spot like the one for Chrysler that premiered on Super Bowl XLV and blew everybody away—with words. It was called "Imported from Detroit," and the copy was the coolest part.

(Against a long montage of sometimes beautiful, sometimes blighted Detroit, we hear a male voice-over.)

MALE VO: I got a question for you. What does this city know about luxury? Huh? What does a town that's been to hell and back know about the *finer* things in life? I'll tell ya, . . . more than *most.* You see, it's the hottest fires that make the hardest steel. Add hard work, conviction, and the know-how that runs generations deep in every last one of us. *That's* who we are. *That's* our story. Now it's probably not the one you've been readin' in the papers. The one being written by folks who have never even *been* here 'n' don't know what we're capable of. Because when it comes to luxury, it's as much about where it's *from,* as who it's *for.* Now we're from America, but this isn't New York City. Or the Windy City. Or Sin City. And we're certainly no one's *Emerald* City. [Motown rapper, Eminem, to camera:] This is the Motor City. And this is what we do. [SUPER: The Chrysler 200 has arrived. Imported from Detroit.]

Can you make the picture do all the work?

Let your TV concept be so visually powerful that a viewer would get it with the sound turned off. In the living room where your spot airs, the sound may very well be turned down and since so many TV spots now also run online (where the sound *is* probably turned off), it's not a bad idea to have your idea work visually. This isn't a rule; it doesn't always work. But when it does, it's great. It means you have a simple idea.

My current favorite for an all-visual spot was done for the Sussex Safer Roads Partnership in the U.K. It visually demonstrates why wearing a seat belt is important to both driver and family and does it without showing seat belts or even cars. Shot in gorgeous slow motion, we see a man sitting in his living room pretending to drive as his loving family looks on. When the man's face shows us he's about to be in a bad accident, his wife and daughter rush to wrap their arms around him—one set of arms across his chest like a shoulder belt, the other across his waist. The spot is already great up to this point but then it blows your mind when the quiet living room environment explodes as if it is itself a moving vehicle in an accident (Figure 7.3). The super comes up: "Embrace Life. Always wear your seat belt."

The video exploded online as well with a million views in its first two weeks on YouTube, and by three weeks, it had reached 129 countries. Writer/director Daniel Cox said, "We developed 'Embrace Life' to engage the viewer purely visually and be seen and understood by all, whoever they are and wherever they lived."[2]

Figure 7.3   Go online and look at this spot right now. I'll wait here.

Think in terms of story.

We talked about the importance of storytelling earlier, and nowhere is it more important than here on television.

A good place for beginners to start is the classic three-act structure. The curtain goes up on an interesting scene where some conflict is already evident. Also evident at a glance is a backstory (hints about who these people are or how things got this way). Things get tense or weird or complicated, usually because of some challenge to the characters. Finally, it's all resolved in an unexpected way and the characters are changed because of it.

This is my little working definition just to get you started. But storytelling is a many-splendored thing, and it's the differences between them all that capture and thrill us. Tarantino turned the linear three-act definition on its head in *Pulp Fiction* and won an Oscar for best original screenplay. But for beginners, the three-act paradigm serves nicely.

Find one great image and build a story into or out of it.

Try looking at your TV assignment as a poster. If you had to settle on a single image to convey your point, what would it be? Once you've found that image, try spinning a story into or out of it. It's only a guess, but it *is* possible the Sussex Safer Roads concept discussed previously (Figure 7.3) started life as a print ad sort of image, a wife and daughter's arms forming a seat belt around a man.

If you try this exercise, make sure you move far enough away from that one image to develop some real story, some beginning, middle, and end. If you don't, you may end up with what's often called "a print idea on TV"—a spot with one moving part. Viewers can see it coming, and once they've seen it . . . *meh.*

Print ads on TV often work, but I try to avoid them because they don't take full advantage of the medium. Are there exceptions? Of course. I'm thinking of an incredibly simple GEICO caveman spot. The caveman was on one of those conveyor belts at the airport and sees an "insulting" poster headlined, "So easy even a caveman can do it." The subtlety of his reaction, the slight roll of the eyes. Yes, it's a bit of a moving print ad but it's a stellar one.

Think in campaigns.

Clients love campaigns and I don't blame them. Every time a spot from a campaign runs, it's another deposit in the brand-equity bank. Campaigns allow us to tell a product story on a per-spot basis while building a larger brand story over time. A good campaign can be held together by a concept, story, distinctive art direction, and occasionally by a spokesperson. When it's part of a great campaign, this repeating element sends a quick signal to a viewer that says, "Hey, it's worth leaning in for this one."

A quick side on spokespeople here: be careful with them. A spokesperson's idea can go wrong in all kinds of ways, the worst being flavor-of-the-month celebrities (they almost *always* suck). Perhaps the best campaign I've seen in recent years featuring a spokesperson is actor Dean Winter portraying "Mayhem" for Allstate Insurance (see Figure 7.4b). Creative Director Leo Burnett and creator Britt Nolan told me the original idea for Mr. Mayhem was based on Harvey

Figures 7.4a and 7.4b   Left, the original sketch of Mr. Mayhem. Right, Dean Winter represents mayhem personified; here he's an undependable GPS device. Watch all the spots from this fantastic campaign on YouTube.

Keitel's character, "Mr. Wolff," in the movie *Pulp Fiction*: a strangely menacing, yet charming, man who protects you from things; in this case, the slings and arrows of everyday life (see Figure 7.4a). Once they created Mr. Mayhem's character, Leo Burnett was able to use him to promote all kinds of Allstate products, year-round, adding to the brand-equity bank with every airing.

Be simple.

The advice about staying simple applies to TV just as it does to print. And nowhere does it apply more than in low-budget commercials.

If you've been assigned a cheapo TV spot, congratulations. It's going to force you to pare away the dross and get to the essence of the client's marketing problem. So valuable is this kind of thinking, you should start here even if your client has a large budget. Apple probably had a large budget, but when the long-running "Mac vs. PC" campaign (Figure 7.5) was awarded Campaign of the Decade by the One Club it wasn't for brilliant special effects. Just its simple brilliance.

Even if you do happen to have a decent budget, start with a clean slate. Empty the stage in your mind, not to copy Apple's "Mac vs. PC" mind you, but to strip down your thinking. Minimally dress this mental stage with, say, just a ladder and a chair like Thornton Wilder did in *Our Town*. This intellectual challenge of working with a small budget (or any constraint) is one of the best mental reset buttons there is. It's such a fruitful place to begin that my friend Ernie Schenck wrote an entire book about it. Check out *The Houdini Solution: Put Creativity and Innovation to Work by Thinking Inside the Box.*

One last thing. These days, the Internet is very friendly to what they call "lo-fi" (as opposed to high-fidelity) production values. Viewers are used to

Figure 7.5 Two guys on a seamless saying and doing silly stuff = Campaign of the Decade. Simplicity is good.

shaky-cam clips filmed by backyard directors. Depending on the idea, lo-fi can add a bit of credibility and authenticity. As of this writing, "Charlie bit my finger!" has almost 150 million views, and no one's complained about the film quality so far. Don't worry too much about the production values. Worry about the idea.

It's okay to think big, too.

Big spots are cool. They take forever to produce and you'll be out of town for months, but when they finally air? Oh, man.

Wieden + Kennedy's famous "Write the Future" spot (Figure 7.6) for Nike aired during the European Club final when every soccer fan on the planet was watching. The three-minute film gathered the world's greatest players and greatest teams all vying for the championship. What made the story cool was how the success of a single kick created a series of different alternate futures. Nations rose and fell depending on the outcome of the game. Tying into such a big idea was also fun I'm sure, as they show in Figure 7.6 with this online/outdoor ad done for the Johannesburg market. Like all big spots, this is one you have to see. Look for it on YouTube.

Another Cannes-winning high-production-value spot that comes to mind was done by Amsterdam's Tribal DDB for Philips to introduce its 21:9 LCD television. The 21:9 was the first production TV with proportions matching the cinema screen (Figure 7.7). In a spot called "Carousel," mind-roasting production values brought to life an armored car heist gone wrong with one continuous shot tracking through a long frozen moment of violence and insanity.

Figure 7.6   Nike, often the champion of big-production TV, outdid themselves with their World Cup spot, "Write the Future."

Figure 7.7   A crew of 100, a cast of 60, 7 shots, made over 2 days, stitched into one mind-boggling great online video.

You could *see* the money on the screen and the wow factor was part of the fun as well as its staying power. Yeah, big can be good. But remember, it's the same with commercials as in Hollywood. If you don't have a good story, you don't have a good video.

Write sparely.

Don't carpet your spot with wall-to-wall copy. Leave breathing room. Lots of it. After you've written your script, get out a really big, scary knife. Like the one in *Halloween 4.*

You'll be glad you did, come editing time. You'll find you need space to let those wonderful moments on film just happen by themselves, quietly, without a voice-over jabbering in your ear.

Author Sydney Smith suggested, "In composing, as a general rule, run your pen through every other word you have written; you have no idea what vigor it will give to your style."

For 15-second spots, if you must write at all, write sparely.

A 15-second TV spot is a different animal than a 30-second spot. You have no time for a slow build. With 4 to 5 seconds already set aside for the wrap-up and client logo, you're looking at around 10 to 15 very skinny seconds to unpack your show, put it on, and hit the showers.

So strip your 15-second TV spots down to the bones. And then strip again down to the marrow. Lock off the camera and keep it to one scene if you can. Even two cuts can make a :15 look choppy.

I remember a Toyota :15 that was this simple. The camera is locked down on an empty red Toyota parked on a quiet suburban street. Suddenly a barking dog comes rushing down the driveway of the house behind it and careens into the back of the car. Type comes up to silently explain: "Looks Fast." A pause. Then: "The New Celica Action Package."

Avoid showing what you're saying or saying what you're showing.

This idea, discussed in print advertising, has a counterpart here in broadcast, with a few twists.

You have two tracks of information in a video occurring simultaneously: audio and visual. To some degree, they have to match up. If either track wanders too far afield of the other, viewers will not know which to attend to; they'll lose interest and begin feeling around in the couch for change. On the other hand, you don't want to have the voice-over and video so joined at the hip that viewers hear again what they've already seen on screen.

It's better to have one track complete the other, or play off the other, just as you do in print. That 1 + 1 = 3 thing works to great effect here in television. The words and the visuals can supply slightly different pieces of information, tracks that viewers can integrate in their heads.

Sometimes you can add creative tension between what is seen and what is heard by giving the copy an unexpected tone, perhaps of irony or understatement. For instance, I remember a Reebok spot featuring a popular Dallas Cowboy running back crashing into defensive players. What you heard, though, was the player quietly musing about how football "allows you to meet so many people."

If you can make the first two seconds of your spot visually unusual, do so.

Think about it. Your viewer's watching TV, eyes glued to it. The cop shoots the bad guy. The camera closes in. Oh, no! He shot his partner. Fade to black. You now have two seconds to keep the viewer's eyes on the screen before he heads to the kitchen to eat chili out of a can over the sink.

Competition with the strong tidal pull of kitchens and bathrooms isn't the only reason you should open strong. When you open with something that's inherently interesting or dramatic, you create what George Loewenstein called a curiosity gap. He says we feel curiosity when there's a gap between what we know and what we want to know, and he describes curiosity as an itch. When you set up your spot with something that opens this gap, it creates an itch, and watching the rest of the commercial is the only way to scratch it.

As an example, a well-known spot by Jamie Barrett and Mark Wenneker for Saturn automobiles (Figure 7.8) starts with a very curious image: a man running backward out of his garage. It's hard to see that image and not wonder "What's next?" Eventually we understand that the man's just "backing out" of his garage into a world without cars. They illustrated Saturn's value of "People First" by showing a world of human beings on the road without their cars wrapped around

Figure 7.8   Open strong. You're competing against getting a second bag of Cheetos or going to the bathroom—sometimes both, sadly.

them. (The voice-over explains: "When we design our cars, we don't see sheet metal. We see the people who may one day drive them. Introducing the redesigned L, the VUE, and the all-new ION. It's different in a Saturn.") Here on paper, the spot sounds almost simplistic, but it was elegantly shot, was set to an understated piano score, and was a thing of beauty.

David Ogilvy once said, quite vividly, "When selling fire extinguishers, open with fire."

Solve the last five seconds.

There's an old Hollywood axiom that says "Movies are all about their last twenty minutes." Writer/creative director David Fowler reiterates that advice in *The Creative Companion:*

> The most important part of any television advertisement is its conclusion, the last five seconds. That's the part that resolves, explains, summarizes, or excuses the preceding twenty-five seconds. If you're not clear about the last five seconds, you're not clear about anything, because that's where your premise gets pounded home. Try to write the last five seconds first. If you can't, you don't need to write a spot, you need to develop a premise for a spot.[3]

Another Hollywood axiom seems appropriate here: "Audiences will forgive almost anything in the first half of a movie and almost nothing in the second."

A television commercial should entertain throughout the entire spot.

Avoid a long buildup to an "unexpected" conclusion, or what I call a "waw-waw" ending. (You know, that pair of muted trumpet notes on shows like *Leave It to Beaver*?) Once you know a commercial's unexpected ending, how many times will you really enjoy watching it? A great spot like Nike's "Write the Future" is a joy to watch from beginning to end, over and over. There's something new to look for in each frame.

Please don't take this to mean I'm against surprise in a TV spot—just those gimmicky little switcheroos at the back of a spot. Those suck. Real surprise, the gasp you hear when you move a viewer's whole mind-set from one place to another and in doing so create insight and a fresh new way of seeing—that's pretty cool.

━━━━

THE GIANT DIGITAL HAIRBALL

I hope these few pieces of advice will be enough to help frame your thinking as you begin working in this cool medium. Its high visibility and public forum make it one of the most exciting media we work in—and it's not going anywhere. It's just going to keep changing.

I claim no prescience as to the future of TV. Like most of us, I'm "skating with the puck at my feet" as they say (versus skating to where the puck's gonna be). Are we moving toward Google TV? Apple TV? Facebook TV? A combo platter? Nobody knows, but there are a few changes we can discuss with some reasonable certainty: one's being driven by the networks; the other, by viewers.

The networks are just starting to figure out what Web advertisers have been working on for several years: how to make TV completely measurable in terms of calculating return on investment (ROI), how to pinpoint target and customize their content, and how to become more interactive. Meanwhile, it's that interactive part the viewers are driving and where they're going seems to be the "second screen"—they're using laptops, smartphones, and tablets to augment the viewing experience. They want to interact with the TV, and yet it's not likely going to be *through* the TV. In a *Business Insider* interview, Pascal-Emmanuel Gobry explains: "Consumers . . . love TV and they love the internet. [But] they love TV as TV and they love the internet as the internet. . . . TV is a fundamentally lean-back experience while the internet is fundamentally lean-forward. They may both be bright rectangles but they perform different functions."[4]

Some experts say tablets are best positioned to become the preferred second screen, that tablets will likely offer apps that allow real-time interactive experiences with TV networks while connecting us to social networks. TV is, after all, a social experience *("Come over; we're watchin' the game"),* but soon we'll watch with friends no matter where they are *("Log on, we're watchin' the game").* Already my son Preston watches movies with a distant buddy via

Xbox. In the U.K., a popular TV game show recently hosted an equally popular Facebook version where friends competed against friends; fully 10 percent of its TV audience played the Facebook game, effectively monetizing the second screen. Even non–game show TV will likely see more "gamification," with a probable increase in competition, prizes, checking in, social rewards, and voting in all kinds of genres.

Massive real-time conversations about popular culture all happening simultaneously on several interactive platforms—this is the social and media ecosystem we culture tweakers will be tapping into as the world rolls forward. Whether everything converges one day and comes in as one big-ass dot-com, who knows?

I *can* make one prediction with some certainty. *FOX "News"* will continue to suck, and you can take that to the bank.

Figure 8.1   Just because an ad has to have a coupon in it doesn't mean it has to suck. I think this is an elegant ad, perfect for budget-minded book readers.

8

But Wait, There's More!

Seriously, does direct-response TV have to suck?

THE DARK AGES PRODUCED A THING called the Iron Maiden—a coffin with spikes on the inside that slowly skewered the victim as its lid was closed. Yet even the Dark Ages—that period of superstitious insanity and violence—never came up with a torture as horrifying as Suzanne Somers telling me about all the great benefits of the ThighMaster.

The direct-response TV (DRTV) part of our industry has traditionally produced some of the most horrible blather in the history of television: Richard Simmons and his Deal-A-Meal cards; the old lady in the First Alert spots who said, "I've fallen and I can't get up!"; and most recently, the plague of ab workout machines—the Ab-Ripper, the Ab-inator, the Ab-Whatever. George Orwell must've foreseen the state of modern infomercials when he referred to advertising as "the rattling of a stick inside a swill bucket."

But here's the deal. The guy who did that ThighMaster thing? He's a multimillionaire. So are Richard Simmons and Ron Popeil. (Popeil sold his company in 2005 for $55 million.) And all those commercials you hate? They sell products by the Mall-of-America load.

Given this, it would seem we've come back around to Mr. Whipple and the main question we started with: To be effective, do DRTV spots and infomercials have to suck?

I like selling things. I think it's cool. But when I look at the Home Shopping Network and the geeky way they honk that horn when people call in, well, I throw up in my mouth a little bit. (Is it just me?) Yeah, I know they're makin' money hand over fist and the people who own it could buy and sell me a thousand times. But, again, it comes down to this: for me to actually work in this field of DRTV and infomercials, I need to be able to look my kids in the eyes and say, "Yeah, you should see this thing I worked on today. It's pretty cool."

So, despite evidence to the contrary, I don't believe DRTV spots and infomercials *have* to suck to be effective.

Although we're not in the majority, there are some of us who believe DRTV can do the heavy lifting required of it, and do it without tossing taste, intelligence, and common decency under the treads of capitalism's tanks. Yes, DRTV has some special considerations—rules, if you will—that help yield better results. And results are why your client comes to work every morning. Results are why more and more blue-chip clients are adding DRTV to their marketing mix. Results are why the big agency holding companies are buying up direct-response agencies left and right. But does getting results mean DRTV has to make us feel so urpy?

Well, remember the two overlapping circles in Figure 3.3? Pretend for a minute that one circle represents all the rules the DRTV specialists know about how to make the phone ring and the other circle represents Things That Don't Suck. Isn't it possible the two circles could sometimes overlap?

Perhaps the best way to begin is by exorcising some of the horrible things associated with this industry.

SPRAY-PAINT TOUPEES AND PSYCHIC FRIENDS.

The entire DRTV industry was created by entrepreneurs solely for the purpose of selling widgets on TV. None of these gadgets had a brand—or, at least, not a brand with a purpose beyond making money. Things like the Salad Shooter and the ever-creepy GLH (bald-spot spray paint) were created solely to be promoted on TV. Many of these items weren't even manufactured until after the infomercials ran and the marketers had the customers lined up. There was simply no brand to protect, build, or polish; it was all about getting people to call now and cough up $19.95 to get an Inside-the-Shell Scrambler. Since the marketers weren't looking for any long-term relationship, they had no scruples about trying every carnival trick in the book. *("Now how much would you pay?")* According to an industry magazine,* the top 25 products being sold via DRTV this very month include three male enhancement creams, four weight-loss supplements, two power wheelchairs, and Urine Gone, an odor elimination spray. Not exactly an august lineup of blue-chip clients. God, next they'll be selling lawyers. *(They what? They do already? Never mind.)*

---

*Electronic Retailer magazine, April 2007, page 26, retail rankings for February 2007 of Short-Form Products Sold on TV.

Because of this pedigree, DRTV has remained advertising's mutant stepchild, kept in a box under the basement stairs. Creative people still walk across the street to avoid saying hello. I don't blame them. I ordered copies of the top 20 all-time moneymakers in DRTV, and after some study I can testify that it looks as bad up close as it did from across the street. Most of these infomercials plugged their made-for-TV product into a prefabricated format: the fake talk show format, the fake news show, and fake rallies (where hundreds of supposed brand advocates filled the studio just to cheer on a can of spray-paint hair). I noted an almost complete absence of production values. Every actor was horrible, reading from a transparent sales script, saying things no human being would say. Then there's the wall-to-wall voice-over of the Constantly Talking Man, as well as the nonstop graphics. The overall feeling one gets watching these shows is of being cornered by a salesman in an elevator at a crack convention. They are exhausting. I also note the music, most of which has the cheap synthesized sound that — a friend of a friend tells me — sounds like porn. And finally, DRTV is frequently used to sell products that people are too embarrassed to buy from an actual human being: male enhancement creams, spray-paint hair, psychic friends.

Almost every spot I reviewed was dreadful. So it's not surprising that mainstream creatives and good directors avoid DRTV. Its reputation is deserved. The whole category should be torched and rebuilt. But on our way out, let's grab a few of the good things that seem to work, and then set a lighter to the rest.

IF IMAGE = EMOTION, THEN DRTV = REASON.

Recently, marketers have begun to use DRTV to sell real mainstream products such as computers and brokerage services; it's no longer all about kitchen widgets.

Part of the reason for this surge is that stations charge a lot less to air DRTV. (There are a couple of reasons for this, but suffice it to say that it costs clients a lot less.)

The main reason marketers like DRTV isn't cost anyway, but accountability. Clients can track exactly what they're getting for their money. If brand TV is a shotgun, DRTV is a sniper. My friend Richard Apel is a DRTV expert and explained it to me this way: "To use a bad analogy, God in his infinite beneficence lets the sun shine on the just and the unjust alike, right? Which is kinda like brand advertising. But in DRTV, we're not as benevolent. We want the sun to shine only on the just — you know, those exact people most likely to respond to our spot. The unjust?" he concluded with a smile, "They can go to hell."

The ability to pinpoint a client's message to just the right audience and then to track that data in nearly real time has incredible marketing power. Today, customer data is easier, cheaper, and faster than ever to obtain and analyze. My buddy Richard says, "Once clients have had the taste of raw, segmented, or analyzed response data, I swear, it becomes like an addiction."

Because of this power, DRTV has started to move from late night into the more respectable hours of daytime and prime-time TV. Along the way, the discipline has attracted lots of blue-chip companies, including Apple and Nokia. These are companies that want a revenue-building vehicle like DRTV in their portfolio but aren't willing to cheapen the brand just to make a sale. These brands continue their regular image advertising, which helps give customers a certain feeling about their brand, and then use DRTV to make them act on those feelings. Brand provides the air cover; the troops of retail and direct response do the rest.

DRTV takes several forms. Any ad with a consumer response that can be specifically tracked is technically DRTV, but for our purposes we're talking about long form and short form. Long form is any commercial longer than two minutes (the infamous infomercial), and the short form, anything two minutes or under.

My friend Jim Warren is a specialist in DRTV, and he sees DRTV existing along a spectrum (Figure 8.2). On one side there's pure brand advertising; on the other is hard-core DRTV. But, he continues,

> ROI and accountability pressures are requiring agencies to move away from both extremes and instead find sweet spots along the spectrum that satisfy *both* of the objectives most important to their clients: (1) building a brand that people love, and (2) selling the products to those people. In other words, all advertisements should have at least some of both components, and there's only limited reason for ads on the extreme ends of the brand-demand spectrum.[1]

Here's another way to think of the brand-to-direct spectrum. (It's creepy, but bear with me.) If image advertising is kinda like a first date, DRTV is the second.

On a second date, you're done trying to get someone's attention, right? You have it, obviously. The other person seems to like you and now just wants to know more about you. Your relationship with the customer has moved from catching his or her eye from across the room to having a nice, long conversation. It's moved from a chemistry check to looking for rational reasons to buy. (And get married.)

Okay, enough with the creepy metaphor. The point is, DRTV is all about providing information, and lots of it. This is your opportunity to remove any objection that could keep a customer from buying your product. It means answering all the questions customers might ask if they were standing in front of you. "The more you tell, the more you sell," says my friend Jim, and if he tells me one more time, I'm gonna barf.

Brand   "25/05"   Transactional

*Figure 8.2   On the left, pure image advertising. In the middle, a little of both.
And on the right, pure transaction.*

But the guy's right. Let's go back to that brand-demand spectrum again. On the left side, it's pure brand image stuff. Cool, we've covered that in Chapter 5. On the right is DRTV, purely expository and full of facts. (And way over on the right is the hard-sell "Call right now!" kind of spot—the kind this book will not touch, even with Ronco's new Ten-Foot Pole. *["The new Ten-Foot Pole® lets you touch all kinds of skeevy stuff with no muss, no fuss!!"]*)

But in between those two extremes, there's a variety of hybrids that allow an advertiser to dial up or down the amount of information and the call to action.

With creatives on the general advertising side, the most popular is the lead generation format, which is usually in the shape of a "25/5." It's more on the brand side of the spectrum because here you have 25 seconds of what amounts to brand image advertising followed up with a five-second call to action. The brilliant GEICO campaign is a perfect example. In the first 25 seconds, GEICO says that it's so easy to lower the cost of your car insurance "even a caveman could do it." (At which point we see modern, well-dressed Neanderthals taking offense at the insult.) The spots all end with a simple call to action: with the phone number up on the screen, the voice-over says, "Fifteen minutes could save you 15 percent or more on car insurance."

Lead generation spots like this don't need to answer all of a customer's questions, only enough to get them to call. And in GEICO's case, the calls came in. According to Mike Hughes at the Martin Agency, the long-running caveman series was one of GEICO's biggest successes.

Now, as we push farther to the right on the spectrum, we dial up the amount of information. Typically, as the amount of information goes up, you move from buying 30-second spots to 60s, and even two-minute spots. It's here where the challenge lies. The more you tell may well mean the more you sell, but it could also mean the more you suck—*if* you don't find a graceful and intelligent way of telling your story.

SHORT- AND LONG-FORM DRTV.

Short-form DRTV works best for products that sell themselves quickly because they can be explained in two minutes or less. GEICO's lead generation is a good example of a quick get. But let's say you have a bit more of a story to tell.

Well, here's where DRTV differs somewhat from brand image work. You've got a lot of information to impart. You need to present it in a way that makes sense and doesn't bore people. You need a structure. In a great article on DRTV, OgilvyOne's Bruce Lee put it this way:

> Structure comes down to how you want to organize your information, and since most DRTV spots carry a lot of information (the better to convince you to act), the easier you can present that information, the easier the viewer can absorb it. And I've never met an organizing method more viewer-friendly than linear storytelling.[2]

To make his point, Lee cites a 60-second DRTV commercial, one I like every bit as much as any brand image commercial. It tells a marvelous story, has two great characters, and is fun to watch from beginning to end.

Here's the entire script of the Ameritrade DRTV commercial:

(We open on a staid office setting, where we see a goofy-lookin' twentysome-thing lying on the copier, photocopying his face. A much older man brusquely motions the kid into his office.)

MR. P.: Stuart, can I see you in my office, please?

OLDER WOMAN STANDING NEARBY: That kid is sick. Very sick.

MR. P.: Stuart, get in here.

STUART: Sure thing, Mr. P.

(Stuart enters, closes door. The smile on Mr. P's face tells us quickly that Stuart's not in trouble. Something else is going on.)

MR. P.: Stuart, I just opened my Ameritrade account.

STUART: (Conspiratorially.) Let's light this candle. Let's go to Ameritrade-dot-com. It's easier than fallin' in love. What do you feel like buying today, Mr. P?

MR. P.: Kmart.

(Phone number comes up and stays up in lower left-hand corner.)

STUART: So research it. All this stuff is provided for you free of charge.

(As Mr. P. types, the camera shows us the easy-to-navigate Web page.)

MR. P.: No charge?

STUART: Yeah, that's synonymous with free.

MR. P.: Looks like a good stock.

STUART: Let's buy!

MR. P.: Let's buy a hundred shares.

STUART: All right, click it in there! How about five hundred?

MR. P.: One hundred, Stuart.

(Stuart imitates the sound of a chicken squawking.)

STUART: You feel the excitement? You're about to buy a stock online.

(Stuart writhes in a victory dance while Mr. P. makes his buy.)

MR. P.: Fabulous! I'm thrilled! What did it cost me?

STUART: Eight dollars, my man.

MR. P.: Eight? My broker charges me two hundred dollars.

STUART: You're riding the wave of the future, my man. I've got to get a soda, Mr. P. Hey, I'm having a party on Saturday night. (He hands Mr. P. an invitation.) If you really want to go . . .

MR. P.: I'm gonna try to get there.

STUART: Happy trading.

(Mr. P. sees Stuart to his office door.)

MR. P.: Thank you.

STUART: Rock on.

MR. P.: All right, Stuart.

(Graphics with phone number, URL, and logo.)

ANNOUNCER VOICE-OVER: Call toll-free, 800-573-9914, or visit Ameritrade-dot-com. Ameritrade. The way to trade. Period.

Wow. In that 60 seconds I learned Ameritrade is an online brokerage where I can do it myself. I learned it costs $8, or $192 less than what a broker charges. I learned that I can research a buy before I make it and that the information is free. I learned that it's fast and that the site is easy to navigate. I learned this is not only a new product but a whole new category. I learned where to go to get this cool new thing. And not for 1 second was I bored.

This script observes the one ironclad rule for any form of advertising—do something interesting—but it also observes several important DRTV guidelines.

Have a crystal clear call to action.

Along with imparting a lot of information, the other big difference about DRTV is the call to action (the CTA). DRTV isn't embarrassed about asking for the sale. The advertiser has to move a viewer from "Hey, that's pretty cool" to "I have to get that right now." Talk about pressure to perform. Just slapping a phone number on the back of a brand image spot probably won't do it. The CTA is a big deal, and in DRTV it's generally the first thing you create.

In the very first part of the CTA it's a good idea to quickly revisit all the main highlights of your product, probably in both voice-over and a super. (But please don't blink or spin the words at me, okay?) It's also a good idea to have your voice-over say the phone number, URL, or mailing address a couple of times. Number and address supers should stay up about twice the time it takes to actually read them.

Don't shortchange the time on any of this. This isn't brand image TV. If you cut the CTA too short, it'll mean fewer calls and that means a higher cost per response or cost per sale, which are the main metrics used to measure the effectiveness of

DRTV. On the other hand, if you try to pack too much stuff in your CTA, it'll sound rushed and your credibility will suffer. Instead, try to include all the information you can while maintaining an unhurried, assured voice.

Find a structure that allows you to impart a lot of information in an entertaining way.

In the case of Ameritrade, the story is two unlikely characters—the older boss and the office knucklehead—buying stocks online. That's it. The entire structure is a conversation—the vessel into which all the other information is poured.

But other structures can work equally well, including some of the ones that work in brand image TV, the basic problem-solution architecture, for example. All I'm asking here is *please* don't use the structures so common in this industry now: the fake game show, the fake call-in show, the fake news show, the fake pep rally. Yes, folks, I know we're in advertising. But as Bill Bernbach showed us, we can sell things and have our dignity, too.

Logically map out the main reasons your product or service rocks.

If you organize your information in a logical flow and pace it well, you'll be surprised how many benefits you can impart in a one- or two-minute format. Yes, this is different from the advice everywhere else in this book (say one thing, stay focused, etc.). But this is different—it's DRTV. It's advertising to people who are nearing the end of the purchase process and are about to buy. They might be at home watching TV, but they may as well be in the dealer showroom kickin' tires. Does this give us license to wear a plaid coat and bark at them? No, not if we want them to like our brand. But we can point out to them some cool features they probably didn't know about. We *can* give them that one last push.

Bruce Lee put it this way:

> While information is critical to breaking down a prospect's barriers and getting him to act, you cannot tell everything. A DRTV commercial is not a brochure. It is a movie. It has to move. So you must be selective and pick your . . . strongest points. You are trying to persuade and persuasion takes time. So take your time. Unfold your selling proposition lovingly. But don't forget to hurry.[3]

Be passionate.

This advice isn't about pushing the talk button in the recording studio and telling your voice-over to be passionate. It's about how you pace the entire spot. Passion can come through in your cut.

I like how Lee says, "Unfold your selling proposition lovingly." DRTV is not afraid to brag on its products a bit. Be front and center with what's cool about your product. Look at the Ameritrade TV spot. They're using the product and talking about it for almost the entire length of the spot. Remember, you're not asking someone to think about buying something. You're not asking the person to form an opinion. You're asking the person to buy it right now. That means tooting your own horn a bit. Just don't lean on the horn, okay? Most of the DRTV literature out there will tell you to not only lean on the horn, but spot weld the horn in an on position and park it on top of the customer's head. Almost every author on the subject has a chapter on how important it is to use "magic" words like *free* and *new* and *announcing* and *revolutionary*. I'm not an expert, but I have two thoughts here. The first is that you can yell at customers only so long before they start to hate you. We're trying to sell our brand's products here without throwing the brand under the bus. And second, my guess is that for many of these marketers of male enhancement creams and psychic friends, magic words are all they have—they don't have a bona fide product because it's all tommyrot and flimflam. (I love sayin' "tommyrot" and "flimflam.") They have no steak to sell, only sizzle. (*"Are you tired of steak?! Announcing revolutionary new SIZZLE!"*)

That said, let's not throw out the baby with the bathwater, either. If you have a free offer, great, say so. Unfold your selling proposition passionately. If you can say it twice, do so. It will increase sales. But do you have to scream it? Probably not.

Be clear.

Nowhere in advertising is it more important to make perfect sense than in DRTV. There's no room for ambiguity here. Yes, you need to be interesting, but it cannot be at the expense of being crystal clear about what your product or service does. You need to point out as many benefits as is prudent while you move the viewer along a logic trail from Reason A to Reasons B and C and D, and then end on "Call this number." Remember, we're working the rational side of the room now, removing barriers to purchase. We're giving people logical support for what is an emotional decision.

Say the product's name.

I read somewhere that you're supposed to say the product's name three times every minute. I assume they suggest this so that people tuning in late will know what's going on. Although there's no evidence that constantly repeating a client's name will increase sales, DRTV probably isn't the place to be coy.

Get a good director, fer cry-eye.

Over the years, the DRTV category has developed its own list of go-to directors and production houses. Meanwhile, all the good directors have stayed away from DRTV because of its reputation for male enhancement creams and psychic friends. The DRTV marketers didn't seem to care, either, given the higher costs charged by the fraternity of mainstream directors and production houses. But now that DRTV is coming in from the cold and we care as much about the brand as about the sale, it's time to get a decent director.

LONG-FORM DRTV: "NOW THAT'S BASS!"

Long-form TV has been so bad for so long that the infomercial has become one of the most parodied communication forms on the planet. *Saturday Night Live*'s Bass-O-Matic fish blender was a memorable skewering. More recently, Crispin Porter + Bogusky parodied the long form by manufacturing and selling silly made-for-TV accessories for the MINI Cooper. Interestingly, they made the MINI infomercials so delightfully dreadful, there was no loss of points to the brand. Viewers *knew*.

Okay, so what if you have to create an infomercial and you can't suck, even on purpose? Here are a few things I've learned from some of the smart DRTV folks I've come to know.

Before you get to the concept, write the CTA.

Again, writing the CTA comes first. It's the most important part of the info-mercial. All the same CTA advice from short form applies here. How long it is depends on the product or service, but boiling your offer down is a good exer-cise in clarity. You'll be forced to think through the most logical and compelling way to express it.

Have a unique TV offer in your CTA.

When what's being sold on TV is also available in stores, DRTV specialists know that fewer phone orders will come in. (Customers say, *"Feh! We'll buy it at the store."*) Therefore, it pays to make your TV offer unique. It builds in urgency and makes the proposition of calling more logical. Anything else you can do to add to the uniqueness of the offer and its urgency, do so. If it's a limited-time offer, say so. Anything that overcomes couch inertia is good.

Add an incentive on top of the offer.

First you lay out the basic offer. Then when you get to the CTA, you sweeten the deal with an incentive of some kind. (Yes, this is the genesis of that tired old line: *"But wait! There's more."*) Yet it's here where the real science of DRTV comes in. Experienced direct-response marketers have found that by rotating different incentives and measuring the difference in sales they can, as James Twitchell says, "readjust the pitch until they find the point of harmonic conver-gence." Since 75 to 95 percent of all phone calls are made within 30 minutes of broadcast, the marketer can tell exactly which offers and incentives are working best; then they readjust. They fiddle with the media buy, the offer, the incentive, and the edit, always comparing the new results against a control.

Bring in the phone number at just the right time.

If you put your client's phone number up on screen in the first two seconds and then leave it up till the end, you may end up actually losing your client money. Think it through. If you put up the phone number before you've fully explained what it is that you're selling, you're likely to get thousands of phone calls from people who ultimately reject the offer because they haven't heard the whole offer or they don't know the details. Let the show be its own self-selecting mechanism. Let your story play out. Putting up an 800 number after the offer is spelled out will net a higher rate of sales even though the number of calls will be lower. (Plus you won't tie up your client's call center with people who happen to have a cool new cell phone, but all their friends are asleep.)

You've got 30 minutes of time. Find a big stage to play on.

The infomercial writer's primary goal is to motivate an immediate response. The secondary goal, and nearly as important, is to keep viewers watching as long as possible.

Once you've boiled down your offer in your call to action, it's time to draw a concept out of it. And now, for a little while, you can think the same way you do when you concept for brand print or TV. You're searching for the *story* and the emotion in the product. You might find it in the product, or it may come out of what you know about the customer. You may find it in problem-solution architecture or in simple storytelling. And long form is a great place to tell a story. Think of Ken Burns's *Civil War*—just a voice-over and black-and-white photographs, yet it was riveting.

In the 30-second brand image world, we try to reward our viewers for staying with us by entertaining them. DRTV is no different. Long form can reward viewers with interesting content above and beyond the sell copy. As an example, I refer to a long-form show done by Mark Fenske for a brand of golf club, a putter called Never Compromise (Figure 8.3). The show had an interesting story at its core: a famous golfer named Jean Van de Velde used a putter to play the entire course at a famous Scottish golf course, a course where he'd failed the previous summer in a World Cup sort of game. I'm not even a golfer, and I found it fascinating. They'd cut between scenes of the golf pro whacking long fairway shots with a putter and then cut to detailed product information segments where the voice-over explained the special way the putter was made. Viewers who stayed with it got to watch a famous golf pro talk about a difficult game he played on a famous course in Scotland, all while playing 18 holes with a putter.

Build your idea out in segments.

The average unit of TV time that American couch potatoes eat in one sitting is 8 to 10 minutes. With network programming, that's what they're used to anyway—8 to 10 minutes of sitcom, then a pod of commercials. So it may make sense to build your infomercial the same way, perhaps in three self-contained segments.

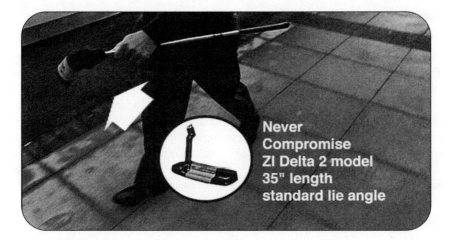

Figure 8.3   Jean Van de Velde walks through the March cold of Scotland's Carnoustie golf course in Fenske's fascinating long-form spot for Never Compromise putters.

8 to 10 minutes of selling

Call to action #1

8 to 10 minutes of selling

Call to action #2

Final 8- to 10-minute segment

Final call to action #3

Network viewing habits aren't the only reason this format seems to work. Marketers have found that half of an infomercial's viewers watch for 20 minutes or more and the other half watch for 20 minutes or less. By completing a selling cycle in 10 minutes, you're ensuring that most people who watch will have an opportunity to place an order.

Do not suck.

We what? We covered this? Never mind.

Move back and forth between rational and emotional.

Don't stay too long in either place. After you've rolled out two or three rational benefits, swing over to the emotional side and remind the viewer of the higher emotional state the product appeals to. Is it joy or security? Safety or vanity? Whatever that higher-level emotion is, connect to it; connect what you're selling to that stuff that really drives us as people. Then go back to laying out rational support for buying now. You'll find that going back and forth recharges each side.

Testimonials can work.

When done correctly, seeing and hearing a real person talk about a product or service can be compelling. Doing it correctly means you have to interview hundreds of customers to find those few, that handful of people who are both comfortable on camera and come across as real people. There's nothing like a true believer to extol the virtues of a brand.

Currently, most infomercials shoot fakey testimonials in fake sets that feel like the fake lobby of a fake hotel. Shooting on site seems more credible. The U.S. Navy's recruiting DRTV did this particularly well, showing real people talking about their service on the aircraft carriers, submarines, and other really cool locations. Bose speakers also went on location for their show, and instead of testimonials, they used third-party experts. To tout the value of their sound quality for home entertainment systems, they did long interviews with sound engineers in Hollywood, audio experts who talked at length about how much work they put into creating sound effects for movies. It was interesting content and, to audiophiles, relevant.

CAN WE TAKE THE EXCLAMATION POINT OUT OF DIRECT RESPONSE?

I'm not an expert in DRTV. Far from it. In fact, I'm so far from being an expert that you'd have to use some of your airline miles to get from DRTV expertise to my house. Also, I don't have the sales figures on the DRTV ideas I've included in this chapter. For all I know, they had miserable cost-per-sale figures.

Still, I stand by what I said.

I don't think DRTV has to suck in order to sell.

My friend Jim Warren *is* an expert, and he thinks only 1 in 100 infomercials or DRTV spots breaks even. Given those numbers, it seems fair to posit that many of the tried-and-true ham-fisted formulas espoused by traditional DRTV marketers may simply not be valid and that DRTV may ultimately be subject to some of the same things that make or break brand image TV. Perhaps simply being interesting and doing something really cool is the answer.

If you decide the direct-response side is for you, good. DRTV is a growing field. And even if you're on the brand advertising side of the business, it's likely that fortune may bring you a client who doesn't have a direct agency and needs a commercial that has to make the phone ring. If so, good for you, too. Make something cool happen.

My friends in Canada, Nancy Vonk and Janet Kestin, seem to feel the same way. In *Pick Me,* they wrote:

> At the top direct marketing agencies, many of the writers are refugees from general agencies. And the work they do is clever, idea-driven, surprising, exciting, and every bit as good as the work they did in their previous agencies. The lines are blurring everywhere. Today's best strategy may be to learn to write for a broader number of media channels.[4]

Figure 9.1   Everybody wants to go on the TV shoot. Everybody wants to do the big website. And then there's radio.

9

Radio Is Hell.
But It's a Dry Heat

*Some advice on working
in a tough medium*

IF YOU HAVE A CHILD AGE FIVE OR YOUNGER, you already understand the basic problem facing the radio writer.

"Put that down. No, do NOT draw on the dog. Do NOT draw on the dog! Didn't you hear me? I said do not stick that crayon in the dog's . . . NO! Put that down!"

Both the parent and the radio writer are talking to someone who is not listening.

In the end, parents have a slight edge. They can send their children to their room, but the poor radio writer is left to figure out a way to get customers to listen.

If you think about it, the whole radio medium is used very differently than is print, online, or TV. In print, you have readers actively holding the magazine or newspaper up to their faces; they're engaged, as is the TV watcher or the Web surfer. But radio is typically just sort of on in the background while people stay busy doing other things. It's just sorta there. People tune into and out of it depending on how interesting the material being broadcast is.

And so we're back to our old problem. We must be interesting.

First rule: do not suck.

It is one of the great mysteries of advertising. Most radio is . . . well, it's not very good.

Over the years, I've judged many awards shows. In every show I can remember, the judges loved poring over the print. Looking at the TV was fun. But when the time came to sit down and listen to several hours of radio commercials, the room thinned out. Nobody wanted to judge it because most of it sucked. It wasn't interesting.

Senior writers at agencies often turn radio jobs over to the juniors. Great. Here's your chance. Knock it out of the park. It pays to learn to write radio; not many people know how. The thing is, as fast as digital technology is changing everything, radio's going to keep chugging along. In fact, as long as there are carpenters, lifeguards, and cars, there's gonna be radio. Even if the day comes when the Internet gets wired directly into our brains, anyone who can write a great radio spot will probably have a job somewhere in this business. I'm not the only one who thinks this way. In *Breaking In,* creative director Rosann Calisi from Eleven said, "I think one of the most difficult things to find is a copywriter who can do radio. If I find a radio writer, to me that's like gold because that's writing in its most pure form." [1]

───────

WRITING THE COMMERCIAL.

Radio is visual.

It's a tired old cliché, but there's truth in it. Radio has been called "theater of the mind." The good commercials out there capitalize on this perception. In radio you can do things you can't in any other medium.

You can make listeners see the impossible image of a cactus man in a werewolf mask pour through the keyhole and eat your cat. (Actually, I did see this once in college, but I . . . never mind.)

The point is, in radio the canvas is large, stretching off in every direction. Radio lets you do impossible things—things way too expensive to make into TV commercials. *"Hey! Let's have the entire Third U.S. Armored Division crash through the atrium at the mall to go buy our client's burgers."* In radio, you can.

Lewis Carroll wrote, "Sometimes I've believed as many as six impossible things before breakfast." So should you.

Cover the wall with scripts.

When you're working in radio, come up with a lot of ideas, just like you do when you write for print. You don't have to write the whole script; for now, just scribble down the general concept on a Post-it Note.

Come up with radio platforms you can describe in a sentence.

The most awarded radio campaign of all time can be summed up simply. With a stirring musical score, Bud Light raises its glass and extols the virtues of "unsung" American heroes. As in, "Here's to you, Mr. Giant Foam Finger Maker." (The spot closes with: "So crack open an ice-cold Bud Light and know we speak for sports fans everywhere when we say . . . you're number one.")

And for Dos Equis beer, the whole idea is a fanciful description of the "most interesting man in the world" and the beer he happens to drink (when he drinks beer). This is one of the scripts. The campaign won the big $100k prize at the Mercury Radio Awards and you can hear it there along with some other great radio.

> SUBDUED ANNOUNCER: The police often question him just because they find him interesting. His beard alone has experienced more than a lesser man's entire body. He is the only man to ever ace a Rorschach Test. When it is raining, it is because he is thinking about something sad. He is . . . the Most Interesting Man in the World.
>
> THE MAN: I don't always drink beer, but when I do, I prefer Dos Equis. Stay thirsty, my friends.

These two concepts can be summed up in a sentence. They're funny just as ideas. Imagine what happens when you can take your funny idea, expand it to a 60, and then produce it. Things get very cool. (There are many places online you can hear these and other award-winning spots. Either Google the brand name or go to the One Show online or the Radio Mercury Awards.)

Singles vs. campaigns.

Radio is one of the few media where I don't feel bound by any particular campaign structure. Plenty of great radio campaigns out there have a campaign architecture (I'm thinking Bud or Motel 6). And if you've stumbled upon a format or a platform that's yielding great spots one after another, by all means, stick with it. But if such a platform eludes you, there is no dishonor to you nor loss to your client if you end up creating simply a string of great stinkin' radio spots—as long as the spots report to the same strategy and as long as they're great spots.

See, I think radio is different than other media. A radio spot exists only as long as it's playing. (Okay, so does TV. Pipe down; I'm on a roll here.) And unlike TV or print, there's no visual graphic standards to worry about. So whenever I sit down to do radio, I allow myself at least the *option* of attacking the brief one spot at a time. I happen to hit on a single spot that has a repeatable format, that has legs, of *course* I'll go with a very campaign-y campaign. But if I don't, there's nothing wrong with simply coming up with the funniest or coolest or scariest spots I can. The thing is, if you're diligently writing to one strategy, to one brief, your spots will likely all add up to one brand anyway. No matter how different the structures of the spots or the sound of their voice-overs, if the commercials are written to one thought, the listener will take away *one* thought.

It's likely what you just read is a minority opinion. All I can tell you is this: in all my 33 years as a working writer in the agency business, my all-time favorite work was a radio campaign I did for Dunwoody Technical Institute, a small client in Minneapolis. It was a series of wildly dissimilar spots all based on one brief that holds together quite well . . . in this writer's opinion. I have them posted at HeyWhipple.com so you can decide for yourself.

Figure out the right tone for your commercial.

I can assure you that humor is the first fork in the road taken by every copywriter in the nation on every radio job they get. I don't blame them. It's fun to laugh, and the medium of radio just seems to beg for it.

But before you rush to the keyboard to start being funny, figure out what you want your listeners to feel. What do you want them to do? This is a decision you should make early in the process and it should be based partly on your product, partly on what the competition is doing, and partly on what you know about the customer. Once you get a feeling for the general tone your finished commercials should have, avenues will open up to you.

I can hear some of you saying, "Oh come on! This isn't Shakespeare. I've got a car client and they need a spot for their spring sale. It's gonna be humor!" I agree. Humor sounds perfect for that. All I'm saying is, think it through. There may be approaches other than humor that are not only more effective but cooler as well.

Here's an example. It's a very straightforward, very sober-minded radio spot for a bank, written by my friends Phil Hanft and Pat Burnham when they were at Fallon McElligott. I doubt this spot (or any of the following commercials) will come off as well on paper as they do on the radio. Broadcast advertising rarely makes the translation to print very gracefully. On this page you can't hear the nostalgic instrumental rendition of "Stand By Me" playing quietly underneath this 90-second script. And you can't hear the simplicity and honesty in the actor's voice.

> MAN: I guess you could say I'm kinda slow to do the big things in life. I mean, there's some stuff I think we'd all agree you just shouldn't rush into. Like buying a house. Took me a long time to do that. Some might say too long. Now when I tell friends who are younger about the benefits of buying a house, I can see that familiar doubt. That look behind the eyes that says "Yeah, I hear you and yeah I know you're right and that's true and I agree, but you know I can't tell you this because I know you won't understand, but it's a big deal and I'm just not sure it's going to go the same way for me as it did for you because

I haven't done it." I guess somebody could say that's fear, but I don't think so. That's fear, like, like jumping off a building is courage. Forget that. All I can say now is what everybody said to me back then. It's the best thing to do. I did it. You should do it. I would also add . . . I know how you feel right now. And it's okay.

ANNOUNCER VOICE-OVER: A reminder from First Tennessee that whatever stage of life you're in, it's far less difficult when you have money in the bank. First Tennessee. Member FDIC.

Maybe it's one of those you-had-be-there things, but this radio spot stands out in my mind as one of the best I've ever heard. Partly because of its incredible production values. And partly because it isn't another Yuk-Fest, Laff-A-Minit radio script cranked out by a frustrated stand-up comedian doing time in an ad agency until his agent calls. It was real.

Two more reasons not to be funny.

Hey, what if *you* aren't funny? It's possible to be a really good writer and still not be particularly adept at comedic dialog. I'm just sayin'. Here's another reason. What if your product or service doesn't call for a funny treatment?

Don't get me wrong. I am not against comedy. But I am against assuming all radio spots should be funny. They don't. They need to be *interesting*.

Okay. Okay. If you are gonna be funny, at least avoid these comedic clichés.

My friend Clay Hudson is a terrific writer and particularly good at radio. He came back from judging the radio for the One Show and wrote me this e-mail: "Everything I heard was pretty good. But as I listened to all of it what kept going through my head was, 'Heard it, heard it, heard it.' There were so many tired, overused formats in radio I found myself waiting for something really different."

Clay concluded his e-mail with a list of tired clichés to avoid, which I pass on to you, word for word.

Anything that sounds like Don Pardo

Spots that start with, "I'm here at . . ."

Just about anything that starts with "(Client name) presents . . ."

Fake game shows

Fake call-in shows

Fake newscasts

Bleeping out the dirty words to show how *edgy* you are

Using the NFL Films voice-over guy

Way over-the-top, abrasive, cartoon voices

Spots that start off all warm and fuzzy and then turn out to be for something—gasp!—totally *edgy*!!!

Spots where there's no idea but they rip off Dennis Miller's style and throw in 15-word hyphenated phrases full of equestrian-jock-itch-monkey-pimples to show us they can write weird crap even if they don't have an idea

Voices that age or get younger during the spot

Neanderthal spots that border on misogyny because they're for "guys"

Soap opera parodies (organ music and bad actors playing bad actors)

Morphing several voices together during the spot

Jingle parodies

Movie ad parodies ("In a world where . . .")

And did I mention parodies?

Funny isn't enough. You must have an idea.

Should you do something humorous, don't mistake a good joke for a good idea. Funny is fine. But set out to be interesting first. You must have an idea.

Here's an example of an interesting premise, written by my friend, the late Craig Weise.

> ANNOUNCER: Recently, Jim Paul of Valley Olds-Pontiac-GMC was driving to work when . . . (Man: "Gee, look at that.") . . . he noticed a large inflatable gorilla floating above another dealership. He'd noticed several of these inflatable devices floating above car dealerships lately and he asked himself some questions. Did anybody ever go into that dealership and say, "Great gorilla. Makes me feel like buying a car." Why don't other businesses use gorillas? Would people be more likely to buy, say, a new home with a gorilla tethered to the chimney? "Three bedrooms, two-and-a-half baths, sun porch . . . gorilla." Would people have more confidence in the doctors if a medical clinic featured a gorilla on the roof? Without car dealers, would there even be an inflatable gorilla business? Right then, Jim Paul made an important, courageous decision on behalf of his fine dealership. (Man: "I don't think I'll get a gorilla.") Just 8 miles south of the Met Center on Cedar Avenue, Jim Paul's Valley Olds-Pontiac-GMC. A car dealership for the times.

Over lunch one day, Craig pointed out that there are no gags in this spot, no goofy-sounding voice-over. Just a guy reading about 160 words. And although radio is often described as a visual medium, Craig called this an example of radio as print. I think he's right. This commercial is simply an essay. Yet I think it's an incredibly funny spot. So did a lot of listeners. This commercial made a bunch of money for Mr. Paul.

Make sure your radio spot is important or scary or funny or interesting within the first five seconds.

Your spot just interrupted your listener's music. It's like interrupting people having sex. If you're going to lean in the bedroom door to say something, make it good: "Hey, your car's on fire."

If your spot's not interrupting music, it's probably following on the heels of a bad commercial. Your listener is already bored. There's no reason for him to believe your commercial's going to be any better. Not a good time to bet on a slow build.

Also, awards show judges, like consumers, are very harsh. They'll grumble "fast-forward" in about five seconds if your spot isn't striking their fancy.

The following spot has an interesting opening line. (I include it for more reasons than just the setup: it's a simple premise, 130 words long, with no sound effects, and it entertains the whole way through.) It's a British spot, and it may help to hear it read with a droll English accent.

MALE VOICE-OVER: My life. By an ordinary HP grade battery.

Monday. Bought by the Snoads of Jackson Road, Balham. Placed in their flashlight. At last. A *career.*

Tuesday. How can I describe the cupboard under the stairs? After much thought, I've come up with . . . "dark."

Wednesday. The Snoad's hamster goes walkabout. After nearly five hours of continuous blazing torchlight, we track it down on Clapham Common.

Thursday. Oh *dear.* I'm dead. They swapped me for Duracell. It can power a torch nonstop for 39 hours. Which is nearly a full eight hamsters.

Friday. How can I describe the garbage can? After much thought, I've come up with . . . "rank." Still, I've led an interesting life. It's just been a bit . . . short.

ANNOUNCER 2: Duracell. No ordinary battery looks like it. Or lasts like it.

Find a way to quickly set up your scene.

You want your listener to immediately get what's going on, and your first five seconds is the place to make sure this happens. If your idea is a vignette of, say, a restaurant patron talkin' to a waitress, use that first five seconds to give your listener the cues needed in order to see this restaurant in his or her head. Maybe the waitress says, "I'm sorry, our restaurant is just about to close." Or maybe you use the sound effects of a short order diner. *I* don't know; I want you to figure it out. Otherwise your *listener* is left to figure it out, and in my experience, the listener is more apt to tune you out than figure you out.

Find your voice.

Imagine how a novelist's fingers must start to fly over the keys once she discovers her character. Finding your voice in radio can be just as liberating.

Think about who your character is. What's his take on your client's product or on the category? Is he thoughtful or sarcastic? Cynical or wry? Once you find this voice, you will see the material unfold before you, see all the possibilities for future executions, and your pen will start to move. Some of the best radio out there is just one voice reading 10 sentences. But it's that attitude the voice has, its take on the material, that makes it so compelling.

Write radio sparely.

Unless your concept demands a lot of words and fast action, write sparely. This allows your voice talent to read your script slowly. . . . Quietly. One word at a time.

You'll be surprised at how this kind of bare-bones execution leaps out of the radio. There is a remarkable power in silence. It is to radio what white space is to print. Silence enlarges the idea it surrounds.

But even if your idea isn't a bare-bones kind of idea, write sparely. There's nothing worse than showing up at the studio with a fat script. You'll be forced to edit under pressure and without client approval.

Another safeguard you can use against overwriting is to get the mandatories done and timed out first. For instance, if your bank commercial has to end with a bunch of legal mumbo jumbo, write it as sparely as you can and then time it. What you have left over is where your commercial has to fit.

Overwriting is the most common mistake people make in radio. Be a genius. Underwrite.

If a 60-second spot is a house, a 30 is a tent.

A :30 is a different animal. If you think you're writing sparely for a 60-second commercial, for a :30 we're talking maybe 60 words. Thirties call for a different brand of thinking. It's a lot like writing a 10-second TV spot. If your :30 is to be a funny spot, the comedy has to be fast. A quick pie in the face.

Here's an example of a very simple premise that rolls itself out very quickly.

ANNOUNCER: We're here on the street getting consumer reaction to the leading brand of dog food.

VARIOUS VOICES ON THE STREET: Yelllllchh! Aaaarrrrrgh! Gross! This tastes awful!

ANNOUNCER: If you're presently a buyer of this brand, may we suggest Tuffy's dry dog food. Tuffy's is nutritionally complete and balanced and it has a taste your dog will love. And at a dollar less per bag, it comes with a price you can swallow.

Various voices on the street: Yellllch! Aaaarrrrrgh!

Announcer: Tuffy's dry dog food.

One other thing to keep in mind: most radio spots are promotional in nature, and many clients will have different promotional tags they'll want to add on at the end. This, too, cuts into your total time. So remember, write sparely.

Another way commercials can be tagged is in the middle of the spot, in a place called a donut. As you can see, the metaphor describes a hole in the middle, and it's for this reason that I urge you to avoid putting promotional material in a *donut*—it creates a hole in the middle of your spot and hurts continuity and flow. In my opinion, it's generally better to add promotional stuff at the very end.

Get a stopwatch and time it.

Read it slowly while you do. Sometimes I'll find myself cheating the clock in order to convince myself there's time to include a favorite bit. I'll read it fast but pretend I'm reading it slowly. I know, it's pathetic, but it happens. Read your script s-l-o-w-l-y.

If you're doing a dialog, do it extremely well.

Write it exactly as people actually speak. This can be tough.

One of the problems you face with dialog is weaving a sales message into the natural flow of conversation. "Can I have another one of those Flavor-rific® brownies, now with one-third larger chocolate bits, Mom?" Always hard. Better to let a straight voice-over do the heavy lifting. Remember also that real people often speak in sentence fragments. Little bits of talk. That start, but go nowhere. Then restart. Also note that two people will often step on each other's lines or complete each other's thoughts.

Remember, just as the eye isn't fooled by cheap special effects, the ear picks up even slight divergences from real speech. Be careful with dialog. Encouraging your voice-over talent to ad-lib where it feels natural may be a good way to help get to an authentic sound.

This next spot is a good example of dialog and a personal favorite. It's written by London's Tim Delaney, and if it's a bit politically incorrect, well, that's partly because it was written in the 1980s . . . and partly because it was written by the talented Tim Delaney. (Again, if you can read this copy with an English accent, all the better. Or listen to it on HeyWhipple.com.)

SFX: Shop door with bell, opening and closing.

Customer (*clearly an idiot*): Morning, squire.

Clerk (*patient and wise*): Morning, sire.

Customer: I'd like a videocaster, please.

CLERK: A video recorder. Any one in particular?

CUSTOMER: Well, I'd like to have some specifications . . .

CLERK: Yes?

CUSTOMER: . . . and functions. I must have some functions.

CLERK: I see. Did you have any model in mind?

CUSTOMER: Well, a friend mentioned the Airee-Keeri-Kabuki-uh-Kasumi-uh whatchamacallit. You know, the Japanese one, the 2000. 'Cause I'm very technically minded, you see.

CLERK: I can see that.

CUSTOMER: So I want mine with all the little bits on it. All the Japanese bits. You know, the 2000

CLERK: What system?

CUSTOMER: Uh, uh, well, electrical, I think, because I'd like to be able to plug it into the television. You see, I've got a Japanese television.

CLERK: Have you?

CUSTOMER: Yeah, I thought you'd be impressed. Yeah, the 2000, the Oki-Koki 2000.

CLERK: Well, sir, there is this model.

CUSTOMER: Yeah, looks smart, yeah.

CLERK: Eight hours per cassette, all the functions that the others have, and I know this will be of interest. A lot of scientific research has gone into making it easy to operate . . .

CUSTOMER: Good, yeah.

CLERK: . . . even by a complete idiot like you.

CUSTOMER: Pardon?

CLERK: It's a Phillips.

CUSTOMER: Doesn't sound very Japanese.

CLERK: No, a Phirrips. I mean, a Phirrips. It's a Phirrips.

CUSTOMER: Yeah, it's a 2000, is it?

CLERK: Oh, in fact it's the 2022.

CUSTOMER: Hmmmm . . . no. Hasn't got enough knobs on it. Nope. What's that one over there?

CLERK: That's a washing machine.

CUSTOMER: Yeah? What? It's a Japanese? (Fade out.)

ANNOUNCER VOICE-OVER: The VR 2022. Video you can understand. From Phirrips.

It's obvious from the get-go in the "Phirrips" spot that the advertiser is being funny. It's very broad humor at that. Here's another bit of great dialog, a spot called "Shower" by Aaron Allen of Black Rocket—very funny, but much more tongue-in-cheek. Picture it over a soundtrack of a running shower. (Note: Some of the spots discussed in this chapter can be heard at www.radiomercuryawards .com/audiolibrary.cfm. If they're not right on the home page, scroll down and fill in the title in the search bar.)

SFX: Shower.

MAN: (*from the living room*) Hey, honey?

WOMAN: (*Speaking a little loud, over the running water of her shower*) Hi, sweetie.

MAN: Were you doing something to the lawn?

WOMAN: Yeah, I put in a sprinkler system.

(*Pause.*)

MAN: What?

WOMAN: I put in a sprinkler system.

MAN: When did you do that?

WOMAN: Today.

MAN: But how di . . . *really*?

WOMAN: Yep.

MAN: I would've done that.

WOMAN: Oh, that's okay. It was kind of fun.

MAN: Does it work?

WOMAN: What?

MAN: Nothing. (*Pause.*) You know those trenches have to be at least ten inches deep or the pipes will freeze.

WOMAN: Yeah, I know. They're seventeen.

(*Long pause.*)

MAN: Don't use my conditioner, okay?

WOMAN: I'm not.

ANNOUNCER: Tools. Materials. Advice. Sanity. OurHouse-dot-com. We're here to help. Partnered with Ace.

Read your radio out loud.

You'll hear things to improve that you won't pick up just by scanning the script. The written and spoken word are different. Make sure your writing sounds like everyday speech. Read it aloud.

Avoid the formula of "shtick—serious sales part— shtick reprise."

You've heard them. The spots begin with some comic situation tangen- tially related to the product benefit. Then, about 40 seconds into the spot, an announcer comes in to "get serious" and sell you something. After which there's a happy little visit back to the joke.

One of the problems with this structure is that ungraceful moment when the salesperson pops out of the closet, donning the infamous plaid coat. This shtick- sales-shtick structure can work, but make sure you don't hurt your listener's neck when you yank the wheel to the left to switch over to sales mode.

Personally, I think it's better to construct a comic situation that you don't have to leave in order to come around to the sale. Remember our earlier meta- phor of the dog and the pill? How it's best to wrap the baloney all around the pill? Well, same thing here. Here's "No Kenny G," a great example of the prod- uct being completely embedded into the premise.

ANNOUNCER VO: Your attention please. Kenny G will not be appearing at this year's Kansas City Blues and Jazz Festival . . . even though Kenny G was never *scheduled* to appear at this year's Kansas City Blues and Jazz Festival we want to make it absolutely clear that Kenny G would not be appearing at the Kansas City Blues and Jazz Festival even if Kenny G *underwrote* the entire cost of the event (although he is certainly welcome to do that). Frankly, if every blues and/or jazz musician on the face of the earth were to mysteri- ously vanish . . . Kenny G would *still* not be appearing at this year's Kansas City Blues and Jazz Festival. But, you ask, what if Kenny G were to somehow seize control of the military? Under this scenario, Kenny G would still not appear with Ramsey Lewis, Arturo Sandaval and nearly 50 other authentic blues and jazz greats at this year's Kansas City Blues and Jazz Festival. Finally, on a personal note, if you are Kenny G, under no circumstance will you be appearing at the 11th Annual Kansas City Blues and Jazz Festival July 20th through the 22nd at Penn Valley Park. For tickets, call 1-800-xxx-xxxx.

Here's another example of what I mean when I say bake your sales idea right into the concept.

(This spot was recorded in environment, all one continuous single take — breaths, ambient noise, warts, and all. The read begins at a natural pace and builds.)

KID: Tobacco companies make a product that's responsible for one death every eight seconds. Which means another person will probably die in the time it takes me to tell you that tobacco companies make a product that's responsible for about one death every eight seconds. And that means another person probably just died while I was telling you that another person will probably die in the time it takes me to tell you that tobacco companies make a product that's responsible for about one death every eight seconds. And that would also mean that about two people probably just died in the time it took me to tell you that another person probably died while I was telling you that another person probably died in the time takes me to tell you that tobacco companies make a product that's responsible for about one death every eight seconds. And you know what? Another two people probably just died in the time it took me to tell you that about two people probably died in the time it took me to tell you that another person probably died while I was telling you that another person will probably die in the time it takes me to tell you that tobacco companies make a product that's responsible for about one death every eight seconds. And that means that during this commercial somewhere in the world, tobacco companies' products killed about eight people. This message brought to you by truth.

Make your spot entertaining all the way to the end, particularly when you get to the sell.

I've heard many radio spots that start out great, but when they get to the selling message, they sputter out and fail. You can't just write the sell off as "the announcer stuff." It is part and parcel of the spot. It's the hardest part to make palatable but also the most important.

A humorous radio spot is like a good stand-up comedy routine. You need to open funny and end funny. And in the middle, you need to pulse the funny bits, to keep 'em coming. Do a funny line and then allow some breathing room, another funny bit, then more mortar, then another brick, more mortar, brick, mortar. Actually, such a structure can serve a commercial of any tone — just keep reeling out something interesting every couple of feet.

This commercial from BBDO West sells all the way through. But the way it's written, you are entertained all the way along. It's just one guy, a very straight-laced voice-over reading 189 words without a trace of irony.

ANNOUNCER: Fire ants are not lovable. People do not want fire-ant plush toys. They aren't cuddly. They don't do little tricks. They just bite you and leave red, stinging welts that make you want to cry. That's why they have to die. And they have to die right now. You don't want them to have a long, lingering illness. You want death. A quick, excruciating, see-you-in-hell kind of death. You don't want to lug a bag of chemicals and a garden hose around the yard.

It takes too long. And baits can take up to a week. No, my friend, what you want is Ant-Stop Orthene Fire Ant Killer from Ortho. You put two teaspoons of Ant-Stop around the mound and you're done. You don't even water it in. The scout ants bring it back into the mound. And this is the really good part. Everybody dies. Even the queen. It's that fast. And that's good. Because killing fire ants shouldn't be a full-time job. Even if it is pretty fun. Ant-Stop Orthene Fire-Ant Killer from Ortho. Kick fire-ant butt.*

Once you get an idea you like, write the entire spot before you decide it doesn't work.

Tell your internal editor to put a sock in it. Just get that raw material on paper. You may find that in the writing, you fix what was bothering you about the commercial.

Avoid the temptation to use any sort of brand name or other copyrighted material.

As an example, I once wrote a script where I referred to the Beatles. They weren't the focus of the spot; their name was used in an offhand sort of aside. The spot was approved, but one week before we recorded the script, the lawyers landed on it like a ton of hair spray and cell phones. When I tried to rewrite it, days after the original heat of the creative moment had cooled, I found myself unable to replace the line without repair marks showing.

Lesson: Don't even touch copyrighted stuff. Famous people, brand names, even dead guys who've been taking a dirt nap for 50 years—their lawyers are all still alive and slithering about, full of grim reptilian vigor. Stay generic.

Don't do jingles.

Do I have to say this? Jingles are a boring, corny, horrible, and sad thing left over from Eisenhower's 1950s—a time, actually, when everything was boring, corny, horrible, and sad. Avoid jingles as you would a poisonous toad. They are death.

━━━━

THE JOY OF SFX.

A sound effect can lead to a concept.

It's an interesting place to start. Find a sound that has something to do with your product or category and play with it.

Here's an example of a sound effect, set inside a good comic premise and used to great effect.

---

*Used by permission of © Monsanto Company.

SFX: Telephone ring.

MAN: Hello.

CALLER: Oh. I'm sorry. I was looking for another number.

MAN: 976-EDEN?

CALLER: Well . . . yeah.

MAN: You got it.

CALLER: The flyer said to ask for Eve.

MAN: Yeah, well she's not here. I can help you.

CALLER: Oh . . . no. That's okay, I'll just . . .

MAN: Hold on, hold on. Let me get the apple.

CALLER: The apple?

MAN: You ready? Here goes . . .

SFX: Big juicy crunch of an apple.

CALLER: That's . . . you're eating an apple. That's the "little bit of paradise" you advertised?

MAN: Well, that's a "little bite of paradise." The printer made a mistake.

CALLER: I'm supposed to sit here and listen to you eat an apple?

MAN: Well, it is a Washington apple.

SFX: Crunch.

CALLER: Look, I'm not going to pay three dollars a minute just to sit here while you . . .

MAN: Nice, big, Red Delicious Washington apple.

SFX: Crunch.

CALLER: . . . eat an apple. . . . It does sound good.

MAN: It's nice and crisp, you know.

CALLER: Sounds good.

MAN: Kinda sweet.

CALLER: Uh-huh.

MAN: Fresh.

CALLER: I shouldn't . . . this is silly . . .

SFX: Crunch.

CALLER: What are you wearing?

MAN: Well, a flannel shirt and a paisley ascot.

CALLER: Oh. Describe the apple again.

MAN: Mmmmm-hmmmm.

ANNOUNCER: Washington apple.

SFX: Crunch.

ANNOUNCER: They're as good as you've heard.

You can also base a spot on a sound effect that doesn't even exist. To arrive at this spot for the technical school I mentioned earlier—Dunwoody—I started by thinking about what sound effect communicated a feeling of being all alone. I settled on the classic sound effect of a cricket, which I thought ably represented the loneliness of a person living in their parents' basement, a liberal arts graduate waiting by the phone for a job offer that may never come. Once I completed the script, the fun part was messing around at the controls with the engineer, Andre, trying to morph the sound of a cricket into the sound of a ringing phone and then into a hallucination. It was fun.

MALE VOICE-OVER: After graduation, as you sit in your parents' basement waiting for the phone to ring with job offers that will never come, you'll begin to hear them. The crickets.

SFX: Crickets.

VOICE-OVER: That lonely sound. The theme song of the disenfranchised. Sometimes you think you hear the phone ringing, with a job offer.

SFX: Telephone ring, which then becomes crickets again.

VOICE-OVER: But it's just them—the crickets. Soon you start to hear what they're really saying.

SFX: Cricket sound morphs into a teasing, high-pitched, vibrating voice that says, "Looooser. Looooser."

VOICE-OVER: Now's probably not a good time to hear about the graduates of Dunwoody Institute.

SFX: A few regular cricket chirps, then a few saying "Loooooser."

VOICE-OVER: How there's an average of four job offers waiting for every Dunwoody graduate. No, you're going to hold out. For a call that will never come.

SFX: Actual real phone, ringing loud. Phone is picked up.

Guy: Hello????

SFX: Cricket, heard through phone speaker, says, "Looooser." Laughs and hangs up. . . . One last little cricket chirp.

Voice-over: Call Dunwoody Institute and get training in one of sixteen interesting careers. Call 374-5800. 374-5800.

Radio is where you can think of six impossible things before breakfast and then actually do them.

Don't overdo sound effects.

Sound effects can be great tools for radio. They can help tell a story. They can be the story. But don't overuse them or expect them to do things they can't.

Since 90 percent of radio listening is done in the car (to and from work, during what media buyers call drive time), *minute subtleties are going to be lost*. The buttoning of a shirt does indeed make a sound, but it probably isn't enough to communicate somebody getting dressed.

My friend Mike Lescarbeau says that any day now he expects a client to ask him to open a radio spot with "the sound effect of somebody getting a great value."

Don't waste time explaining things.

Screenwriter William Goldman advised, "Cut into a scene as late as you possibly can." Good advice. Crisp self-editing like this keeps your story moving along with a minimum of moving parts. His advice has a classical precedent. In Greek plays, this technique was called *in media res* — to begin the story "in the middle of things."

Cut right to the important part of a scene. For instance, in your radio spot, we hear the sound effect of a knock at the door. Does the next line really have to be "Hey, someone's at the door"? Probably not. Let the sound effects tell your story for you. People are smart. They'll fill in the blanks if you provide the structure.

Avoid cacophony.

You might as well learn now that you can't put sirens in a radio spot. At least not in my market. I can see why. It confuses drivers. They hear a siren sound effect on their radio and pull over to let an ice cream truck pass by.

While we're on the subject of irritating noises, keep any kind of cacophony out of your spot. That includes yelling — even "comedic" yelling. It grates on the listener. Especially on the third and fourth airing.

I've always thought of radio as the best medium to target carpenters. These guys have their radios on all day. They're not just going to hear your spot; they're going to hear the entire radio buy. One carpenter told me he actually changes stations to avoid hearing an irritating spot played over and over again.

Keep carpenters in mind when you write. Remember, these guys have hammers. (And power saws.) (And nail guns.) (And chisels.) (And wire cutters.)

CASTING: BORING, TEDIOUS, ESSENTIAL.

Cast and cast and cast.

Casting is everything. In radio, the voice-over you choose is the star, the wardrobe, the set design, everything all rolled into one. It's the most important decision you make during production.

Start casting as soon as possible. Send your script to as many casting houses in as many major cities as you can. I strongly suggest that two of those cities be Los Angeles and New York. Along with the scripts, send your casting specs: some description of the quality of voice you have in mind.

About a week later, the auditions will turn up, usually via a link on the Internet. Listen to all of them (at the agencies I worked at, 60 to 100 auditions for one voice was normal). Make your selections and then make a short list of the best voices back-to-back so that you can zero in on those nuances that make a real difference. Your final short list should be your top three. You'll also have a second and third choice to return to if your client has a problem with the one you recommend. (Also, you can pick one voice from New York, another from Los Angeles. It doesn't matter; you digitally patch them into your local recording studio.)

One last note: Consider using the voice of just "some guy"—a friend, the babysitter, or somebody in the media department. A modicum of talent is necessary, but it can work and sound fresh and different.

Cast people who have some edge to them.

Spielberg is alleged to have responded to the question, "What is the key to making great movies?" with "Eccentric casting."

This is good advice. Most of the auditions you'll be listening to during casting are going to be vanilla. That's because you're hearing a lot of highly skilled voice people doing reads they think will keep them on the short list. They'll be taking their edges off, moving toward the middle, and going white-bread on you.

Listen for authenticity. Listen for grist. Don't listen for a great voice talent who will read your fake script for money. Listen for real.

As you listen to the casting, keep an open mind about the voice you're looking for.

You may discover someone who brings a whole new approach to your script. Sometimes it comes from an ad-lib or from an actor who doesn't understand the soul of the spot. These fresh approaches to your material may open up new possibilities for how you might produce the final commercial.

Rewrite based on what you learn from the casting.

You'll have one last chance to make your radio spot better. When you're listening to the actors read your lines, keep an ear cocked for those sentences where the actors stumble.

If more than one actor has a problem with a line, it's likely it's the line that's the problem, not the actors.

I usually discover that if I have a dialog, one or two of the lines I have given the actors are too long. The dialog is flowing along and suddenly it's a monolog. So as you listen to the casting tapes, listen for the general flow. Is it entertaining in the first 10 seconds? In the second 10? The last? Are you saying the same thing twice? Are you saying the same thing twice? If you can take something out, do it now. It's your last chance to make a change and have the client sign off before you go into the studio.

Sometimes the best way to present a spot is to do a demo.

Ask your producer if there's a couple hundred in the budget you could use for this purpose. If your spot depends on the unique presentation of a particular actor's voice, this may be the way to go.

PRODUCING A RADIO COMMERCIAL.

Production is where 90 percent of all radio spots fail.

For some reason I don't quite get, radio is an all-or-nothing medium. It works or it doesn't. There is no in between. I urge you to learn how and learn well all the elements of production.

Copywriter Tom Monahan on radio:

> In radio, there's simply no place to hide anything. No place for the mistakes, the poor judgment, the weaknesses. Everything is right there in front for all 30 or 60 seconds. Everything must be good for the spot to be good. The concept, copy, casting, acting, production—everything. One of them goes wrong, sorry, but it's tune-out time.[2]

So, start with a good idea. Craft it into a great script. Congratulations, you are 10 percent of the way there.

Sit down with your producer. Let him in on your idea.

It'll pay to take a moment to go over the soul of your radio ideas with your producer. Your producer needs to get a good feeling for the kind of read you're looking for, for the kind of voice, for the whole tone of the spot. He can't bring his best game until you let him in on all the nuance. And when you do, the whole production can go up several levels.

Develop a good working relationship
with a local audio engineer.

My friend, copywriter Phil Hanft, reminded me of the importance of finding a good recording engineer in your town—a technician with a great ear who will add to the process. One who understands timing and the importance of the right sound effects and the right music. Not someone who wants to get you in and out as fast as possible or someone who agrees with every idea you have. As William Wrigley Jr. said, "When two people in business always agree, one of them is unnecessary."

Keep the studio entourage to a minimum.

Try to produce your spot alone. Well, just you and the engineer, I mean. No clients. No account executives. Not that they're bad people and you, you *alone*, are a Radio God. It's just that large crowds bring tension into those small rooms. Your spot will have more focus if it isn't produced by a committee of six.

Provide your talent with scripts that are easy to read.

Unless your actor really needs to see the cues of sound effects (or the lines of another actor), cut out everything except what he or she has to read. Set the type in something like 14 point and double-space it so that there's room for the talent to scribble in any coaching advice or last-minute changes.

Don't worry about proper punctuation. Write for the flow of speech. And underline or italicize words you know you want the voice-over to hit. But don't OVERdo it <u>or</u> *your final* read IS <u>going</u> to SUCK.

Also, come to the session prepared to cut certain lines, in the event your script runs long. Know in advance what to cut, or you'll find yourself rewriting under pressure at the studio. Not good.

When you're in the recording studio, tell the voice-over
to read it straight.

Most of them have been trained by years of copywriters telling them to "put a smile in your voice" or hit the word *tomorrow* in the line "So come on in tomorrow." People don't talk like that. Have your voice-over talk like you talk. I find a flat read is almost always best. (Those last seven words are probably the most important ones in this chapter.) A flat read is almost always best.

When directing talent, be precise in your choice of words.

My engineer friend Andre Bergeron says he often sees writers directing with flabby, inarticulate language that leaves the talent confused and uncomfortable. "Can you make that read more . . . um . . . more green?"

What I'm asking is to try not to be so . . . so . . . what's the word? . . . *irritating.*

My advice: For the first few takes, let the talent read it the way she wants. Some of them are very experienced. If your script is great, she may pick up on what you want right at the outset. If she doesn't, fine; you've involved the talent up front and now you both have a baseline from which to work.

Also, don't wear out your talent by making her start from the top for every take. If you've got a good opening on tape, do what's called a *pickup* and start the read further into the script. Then do a quick edit to see if it cuts together. It usually does.

Don't let the talent steamroll you.

If you're a young writer on your first studio session, let your engineer in on this fact, but not the talent. The engineer, if he's a good soul, will show you the ropes and teach what you need to know. But if the voice-over catches a whiff of "junior meat" in the studio, she'll take over the session, particularly if you're working with some of the higher-priced Hollywood or New York talent. Don't let it happen.

TV shoots are controlled by the director. Radio, by the writer. Stay in charge of the room. Give-and-take is fine, but ultimately you're the one who has to show up back at the agency with a spot. If you're new to the business, ask a senior writer if you can observe a few recording sessions before you tackle one alone. Your producer can give you some good advice as well.

Don't be afraid to stray from the script.

It's just the architecture. Get the client-approved script in the can, but if something else seems to be working, explore it. Record those other ideas and come back to experiment with them later.

Spread your production over a couple of days.

Record voices on the first day, review all the takes, and make your selections of the best tracks. Maybe get a rough cut done. But save the music, sound effects, and final mix for the next day. That second day gives you a chance to react to your spot more objectively.

Don't overproduce.

I've seen it happen a million times. You get into that tiny room with all the knobs and buttons. You drink too much coffee. You start messing with the "s" on the end of the word *prices,* borrowing the "s" from take 17 and putting it on *price* from 22. You start taking a breath out here and adding it there. By the time you're done, you have a slick, surgically perfect piece of rubbish that sounds as natural as Michael Jackson.

When painting a picture, never put your nose closer than two inches to the canvas.

If your client can afford it, always produce one more radio spot than you need.

It's the darnedest thing. But the script you thought was the hilarious one turns out to be the least funny. It happens every time I go into the studio. One or two spots are simply going to be better than the others. The more you have to choose from, the better.

One way to get a few more spots out of the session is to record your alternate scripts at what they call *demo* rates and then upgrade the talent (pay the full rate) if the client approves the commercials.

SOME RADIO SPOTS THAT WERE FUNNY *BEFORE* THEY WERE RECORDED.

"Ba-Donk-a-Donk" for Subway Restaurants

GIRL CASHIER: (*Heard through tinny speaker*) Welcome to Burger Bonanza, may I take your order?

GUY: Yeah, I'd like an extra large pot belly.

CASHIER: You want just the Pot Belly, or the combo?

GUY: I'lllll . . . go with the combo.

CASHIER: And what would you like for your side?

GUY: Ummmmm . . . do you have Love Handles?

CASHIER: Yep, two to an order.

GUY: Yeah, I'll have two of those and, oh, a Double Chin as well. (Laughs) I *love* those things. Honey? What do you want?

WOMAN: Can I get a Badonkadonk Butt?

CASHIER: You want the Badonkadonk Butt or the Ba-*DONK*-adonk Butt?

WOMAN: Umm, just the Badonkadonk.

CASHIER: Okay, but you can get Extra Flabby for only 49¢ more.

WOMAN: Um, sure. Oh, and what kind of thighs do you have?

CASHIER: We have Thunder Thighs and Cottage Cheese Thighs.

WOMAN: How about the Thunder Thighs?

CASHIER: Sure. So that's one Extra Large Pot Belly Combo with a side of Love Handles, a Double Chin and an Extra Flabby Badonkadonk Butt with Thunder Thighs on the side.

ANNCR: What are you really getting with your combo meal? Try Subway restaurant's new California Fit menu options, with raisins, apple slices and low-fat milk. A tasty nutritious alternative to burgers and fries. Subway. Eat Fresh.

"He Was at a Ball Game" for Bud Light

MUSIC: Quiet Inspirational Music Under Throughout.

ANNOUNCER VO: (*Anncr is, or sounds like, Charlton Heston and delivers this "tale of woe" as if it's a story of great struggle.*) Today I'd like to talk to you on a very serious note. Because this is the story of a man overcoming monumental physical pain and suffering to make it a Bud Light. There's nothing funny about what you're about to hear.

YOUNG GUY: Well, *actually*, it is kinda funny.

ANNCR: Work with me, son.

GUY: Oookay. I was at a ball game.

ANNCR: HE WAS AT A BALL GAME!

GUY: (*Taken aback a bit, a pause*) . . .Yep . . . and so when I like saw the Bud Light vendor . . . I went to raise my arm so he'd see me . . .

ANNCR: HIS ARM AROSE!

GUY: Exactly. But I hit my funny bone on the seat next to me.

ANNCR: (*As if feeling the kid's pain*) OHH, NO! NO!!!

GUY: Yeah, so I just raised my other arm instead and, you know, got his attention and the Bud Light.

ANNCR: HE GOT THE BUD LIGHT! (*Pause, and now ANNCR'S voice is back down to conversational level.*) Young man, do you ever look back and wonder what would've happened if you'd just . . . given up? If you *hadn't* followed your dream of making it a Bud Light?

GUY: Uhhh, not really.

ANNCR: Probably a wise idea. . . . So for the great taste that won't fill you up and never lets you down, make it a Bud Light. From Anheuser-Busch, St. Louis, Missouri.

"Monkey juice" for VW Jetta GLI

SFX: *(Ring of phone, picked up.)*

GUY: *(We hear his voice through the phone. He seems distracted and distant throughout spot)* Yeah.

WOMAN: Hey baby.

GUY: Hey.

WOMAN: So, how's your day going?

GUY: *(Clearly the guy is in the zone and is not really hearing anything the woman is saying.)* Um, Good.

WOMAN: How did that meeting go?

GUY: Hah, yeah, . . . wow.

WOMAN: You're driving your Jetta right now, aren't you?

GUY: That's great.

WOMAN: Ya know, monkey juice is delicious if you're wearing comfortable pants.

GUY: Yeah, I totally agree.

WOMAN: I'm having an affair with the plumber. He's here right now. You want to talk to him?

GUY: Oh well, what're you gonna do?

WOMAN: Um, can I borrow your Jetta tomorrow?

GUY: *(Suddenly very alert and very attentive)* Wh-What do you *need* it for???

ANNCR: The 200 hp VR6 engine, a six speed manual transmission and 17-inch alloy wheels, Volkswagen Jetta GLI owners take driving seriously. A little too seriously. Make sure to test drive the 200 hp Jetta GLI today.

"Directions to the mall" for VW Beetle Convertible

SFX: (Office ambience in the background throughout.)

GUY: Got a pen? Alright, write this down. First, you'll go through this, like, canopy of trees. And when you look up, you'll notice that moon goes away . . . and like reappears and goes away again . . . okay? At that point, right overhead you'll see a streetlight right overhead with a blinking bulb in it. As soon as you see that, take a left. Then you go straight, straight, straight, you'll pass this area that smells like Korean food, you'll pass this bar that always has, like, live music coming from it? 'Kay? Then hang a right when you see . . . I guess it's like a gargoyle head on top of a hotel and . . . from there you should remember it. You pass under that footbridge with the aluminum bottom . . . annnnd my apartment is up on the left. Didja get all that? See ya in a bit.

SFX: (Phone is hung up.)

Music: (Comes up and under ANNCR.)

Woman anncr: With the new Beetle Convertible, you get the road, the sky and everything in between. Experience it for yourself at your local Volkswagen dealer.

Figure 10.1   An author of a book on creativity wrote: "An idea is nothing more or less than a new combination of old elements." Which doesn't quite explain this ad for Sony's Playstation.

10

"Toto, I Have a Feeling We're Not in McMann & Tate Anymore"

Working out past the edge

PICASSO PROBABLY LEARNED TO DRAW a realistic head before he began putting both eyes on the same side of the nose.

Getting the eyes in the right place has been the subject of the first chapters of this book. Once you learn how, it's time to go further out. So take everything I've said so far and just chuck it. Every rule, every guideline, just give 'em the old heave-ho.

Let's assume you know how to sell a vacuum cleaner in a small-space ad with a well-crafted headline. Let's assume you know how to put a great visual idea on paper and how to come up with the sort of idea that makes colleagues who see it go, "Hey, that is cool."

Doyle Dane art director Helmut Krone had this to say on the subject:

If people tell you, "That's up to your usual great standard," then you know you haven't done it. "New" is when you've never seen before what you've just put on a piece of paper. You haven't seen it before and nobody else in the world has ever seen it. . . . It's not related to anything that you've seen before in your

253

life. And it's very hard to judge the value of it. You distrust it, and everybody distrusts it. And very often, it's somebody else who has to tell you that the thing has merit, because you have no frame of reference.[1]

There's going to come a point in your job when the compasses don't work. When you're so far out there that up ceases to be up, west isn't west, and "Hey, great ad" is replaced with "What the hell is this?" Perhaps this is how the lay of

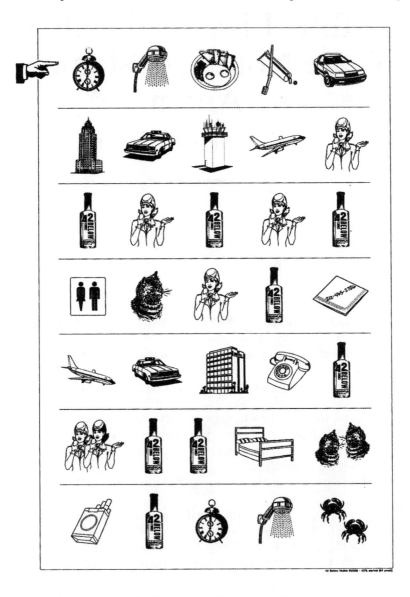

Figure 10.2   More proof of Hegarty's observation that "Creativity is not a process." What process lead to this?

the land looked when Brian Ahern and Philip Bonnery at Saatchi & Saatchi, New York, came up with the ad for 42 Below Vodka shown in Figure 10.2.

What rules, what advice in this book could possibly have led a creative team to come up with this? None that I can think of. There is no bridge across some chasms. Only leaps of imagination can make it across. We're not talking about small increments of experimental thinking anymore, or reformulations or permutations, but entire new languages. New ways of looking at things.

Once you've learned to draw a realistic head, this creative outland is where you're going to need to go. This point is important enough that I've devoted this whole, albeit short, chapter to it. The last rule is this: once you've learned the rules, throw them out.

Any further advice I give at this point is counterproductive to the creative process. It's as if I'm looking over the artist Jackson Pollock's shoulder saying, "I think you need another splat of blue over there."

But even out in deep space, there is one rule you are obliged to obey. You must be relevant.

You're never going to get so far out there that you can dare not to be relevant to your audience. No matter how creative you think an idea is, if it has no meaning to your audience, you don't have an ad. You may have art. But you don't have an ad.

"LOVE, HONOR, AND OBEY YOUR HUNCHES."

— Leo Burnett

Bernbach said, "Execution becomes content in a work of genius."

It is never more true than out here, where concepts can sometimes be all execution without the traditional sales message. To have such an execution succeed, you're going to need to know your customers better than the competition. You're going to need to know what they like, how they think, and how they move through their world. If your idea reflects these inner realities, you'll succeed, because your viewer's going to get a feeling that "This company knows me."

Here's a good example of how keen awareness of the customer, an intuition, and incredible production values colluded to make advertising history.

Consider the following TV script. There is no music.

BANKER: "There's a lot of paperwork here. There's always paperwork when you buy a house. First one says that you lose the house if you don't make your payments. You probably don't want to think about that but . . . you do have to sign it. Next says the property is insured for the amount of the note. And you sign that in the lower left corner. This pretty much says that nobody's got a gun to your head . . . that you're entering the agreement freely. Next is the house is free of termites. Last one says that the house will be your primary residence and that you won't be relying on rental income to make the payments. I hope you brought your checkbook. This is the fun part. I say that all the time, though most people don't think so. (Chuckle.)"

This was one of the TV spots for John Hancock Financial Services that swept every awards show at the time. Accompanying this voice-over were images of a young married couple buying their first house as they sat in front of a loan officer's desk. The scenes were cut with quick shots of type listing different investment services offered by John Hancock.

I'm sure that, on paper, the board looked a little flat. In fact, it probably still looks flat here. But this is precisely my point. In the hands of a director other than Pytka or a less seasoned creative team, this little vignette could have been flat.

But what made this storyboard work was the gut feeling the creatives had for the cotton-mouthed, shallow-breathing tension some people have upon buying a first home. They successfully brought the full force of this emotion alive and kicking onto the TV screen.

There were no special effects, no comic exaggerations, no visual puns, or any other device I may have touched on in this book. Just an intuition two guys had, successfully captured on film. Check it out. It may be hard to find online, but it's worth a viewing.

While you're in the archives, look also for a spot called "Interview" for United Airlines, done by Bob Barrie and Stuart D'Rozario (Figure 10.3). Nothing "clever" happens in this spot, either. It just shows a guy shave, put on a suit, and fly to some faraway city for a job interview. There's no dialog, and if there's any

Figure 10.3   Set to Gershwin's classic Rhapsody in Blue, *the United campaign was all in the execution. This frame's from a spot called "Rose."*

drama to the spot, it's when he realizes he put on mismatching shoes. But the interview goes well, and he gets a call that makes him do a small jump for joy in the street. As we see him sleep on the plane on his way home, the voice-over says, "Where you go in life is up to you. There's one airline that can take you there. United. It's time to fly."

If none of this exactly blows your socks off, again, that's the point. What makes this spot so different and so good is the understated illustration style used in place of film. Go online somewhere, find the spot, and watch it. Like Bernbach said, "Execution can become content." How you say something can become much more important than what you say.

Mark Fenske told me, "You cannot logic your way to an audience's heart." People are not rational. We like to think we are, but we're not. If you look unflinchingly at your own behavior, you may agree that few of the things you do, you do for purely rational reasons. Consumers, being people, are no different. Few purchases are made for purely logical reasons. Most people buy things for emotional reasons and then, after the fact, figure out a logical explanation for their purchase decision.

So that's the other piece of advice: trust your intuitions; trust your feelings. As you try to figure out what would sell your product to somebody else, consider what would make you buy it. Dig inside. If you have to, write the damn strategy after you do the ad. Forget about the stinkin' focus groups and explore the feelings you have about the product.

If an idea based on these feelings makes sense to you, it'll probably make sense to others. So sort out the feelings you have about the product and then articulate them in the most memorable way you can. Someone once told me, "The things about yourself you fear are the most personal are also the most universal." Trust your instincts. They are valid.

BUILD A SMALL, COZY FIRE WITH THE RULE BOOKS. START WITH THIS ONE.

It's been said there are no new ideas, only rearrangements. Picasso himself said, "All art is theft." Historian Will Durant wrote, "Nothing is new except arrangement."

I've used logic like this to defend ads I've written that were sound and good but weren't new ideas. I think I was wrong. Instead, I think it's better to believe there really are whole new ways of communicating, ways that nobody has discovered yet. I urge you to look for them.

In 1759, Dr. Samuel Johnson wrote, "The trade of advertising is now so near to perfection that it is not easy to propose any improvement."[2] That was written in 1759, folks; probably with a quill pen. I don't want to make the same mistake with this book. So I repeat: Learn the rules in this book. Then break them. Break them all. Find something new. It's out there.

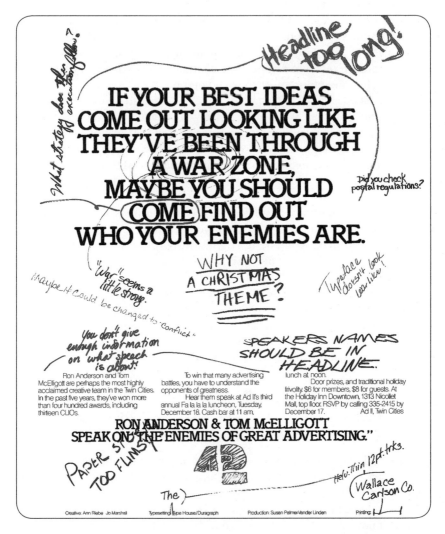

Figure 11.1 As it turns out, there are actually quite a few things "more powerful than an idea whose time has come." There's the marketing manager, the product manager, the research department, the CEO, and that loud, opinionated guy who shows up at every focus group.

11

Only the Good Die Young

The enemies of advertising

IN A PERFECT WORLD, IT WORKS LIKE THIS. You come up with a great ad. You take it over to the client, who agrees it solves the problem and approves it for production.

In all my years in the business, this has happened a total of three times. What usually happens is your ad dies. I don't know why it is this way, but it is. Get ready for it. It doesn't matter how good your ad is; it can die. I once watched a client kill a campaign between sips of coffee. Two months in the making, and he killed it all—every TV spot, every magazine ad, and every newspaper ad—with one chirpy line.

"Good first effort."

The thing to remember is, clients are perfectly within their rights to do this. We are in a service business. And our service isn't over when we present something we like. It's over when we present something they like. The trick is to do both, the first time.

There are good clients out there. Bless them. When you have one, serve them well. Work nights for them. Work weekends. You will produce the best work of your career on their behalf.

And then there's the other kind: the really tough clients. I'm not talking about the ones who hold your feet to the fire and push for greatness. This is about the ones who misbehave. Fortunately, good clients outnumber them. But the bad ones are out there, and you need to be able to spot them. Here are some of the kinds

I've run into in my career. Let me rephrase. Here are some of the kinds that have run over me in my career.

There isn't a lot you can do about them. They're like mines buried in the field of advertising. Try not to step on any.

THE SISYPHUS ACCOUNT.

Those familiar with Greek mythology know Sisyphus, the king of Corinth. The gods sentenced him to an eternity in hell, pushing a large rock up a hill. He'd get it to the top, only to watch it roll to the bottom, where his job awaited him again.

So how do you spot an account like Sisyphus Corp.? By the smell of foamcore—that stiff board that agencies use to mount ads for presentations. You'll notice the smell the minute you get off the agency elevator. They won't tell you what it is during the interview, but you'll find out soon enough.

The creative director comes in and says, "I'm putting you on Sisy Corp. You're perfect for them." You'd be excited about it, were it not for the pallid look of the passing secretary who overhears your assignment.

Pretty soon you start to catch on. One day you're walking down the hall and you notice you've never seen an ad for Sisyphus displayed up on the wall. Not one. Then you see the delivery guys from the local art supplies company; they're in the lobby again with another cart full of foamcore. *("Weren't they just here yesterday?")*

Then one day you're looking for markers in the storeroom and you find 200 dead storyboards for Sisyphus, all of them great ideas, all dead as doornails and hidden in the corner like Henry VIII's closet of heads.

When they hired you, they told you Sisyphus Corp. was the next VW. The next Nike. "We're turning it around." But now you're starting to understand: Corporations like Sisyphus don't want to actually *run* advertising. They want to look at it. They want to talk about it. They want to have meetings about it. But they won't run an ad. Not this year anyway.

"If we were to run advertising—we're not, but if we *were* to run an ad—could you show us what it might look like?"

You've just been handed a shovel and told to feed the Foamcore Furnace. You will work as hard as somebody whose ads are actually being published. You'll spend the same late nights and long weekends and order in the same pizza. But when the year is over, you'll have nothing to show for it but some ads mounted on foamcore and a pizza gut.

This kind of account, although it can drive you crazy, isn't the worst. (More on them in a minute.) They're like blind giants, a Cyclops with something under his contact lens. They're big. They have money. And if they lumber about and head in the wrong direction, it hardly matters. As long as they make their numbers, they don't care. They've lost the entrepreneurial spirit. Winning isn't important. Not losing is.

There isn't much you can do about this kind of account. There's an old saying: "The only way out is through." Sometimes it's best simply to feed the beast its daily minimum requirement of concepts and then sneak out to a movie when the Foamcore Gods aren't hungry. Call it paying your dues. After you've put in a few months papering the walls of your client's meeting rooms, appeal to your creative director. Show him your battle scars. If he's any good, he'll occasionally put a fresh team in front of Sisyphus's rock.

Sisyphus isn't the worst kind of account. Not by a long shot. There's another enemy of good advertising. Fear.

━━━━━

THE MEAT PUPPET.

A very talented woman named Lois Korey, an ad star from the 1960s, described this kind of account:

> Clients seem to get the advertising they deserve. The good ones, they're risk takers. They're willing to risk failures for extraordinary success. . . . The bad clients? Fear dribbles down from the top. No one says so, in so many words, but you know no risks will be tolerated, no rules will be broken, that mediocrity is the measure by which your work will be weighed.[1]

Fear dribbles down from the top, says Ms. Korey. The Chinese have a more colorful phrase: "A fish stinks from the head."

You can actually smell it on the vice presidents, the fear. No amount of roll-on is gonna cover up their terror of the boss. It may be their boss, or their boss's boss—it doesn't matter.

But the boss has done a terrible thing to these vice presidents. He has put them in charge of something they're not in charge of. The nameplates outside their cubicles may sport words such as "Assistant Director of Marketing," but they are not directing marketing or anything else, for that matter. They are, in effect, meat puppets.

Invisible strings, thin but powerful, dangle down from management and are attached to every part of their bodies. Everything these guys do, everything they think, every memo they write, every decision they don't put off, will be second-guessed.

When you're a meat puppet, what you do is say "No." An ad lands on your desk, and that invisible string connected to your hand makes you reach for the big NO stamp, pulls it back over the ad, and wham!

"NO!"

I have seen fear completely unravel a meat puppet.

She was the director of marketing for a large corporation whose name you'd recognize. She needed a TV spot, just one 30-second spot, for a new product being introduced the following spring. It was a great product. It deserved a big, wonderful introductory spot. We worked hard and presented an idea we believed was very good.

We flew in. Shook hands. Found a room with an easel, did our setup, and unveiled. She looked at the storyboard, looked at her notebook, then wrote something down. (When clients do this, I always assume it's: "Begin new agency search immediately.") She looked up and said, "I just don't like it."

The strategy wasn't the problem. How we were saying it wasn't the problem. "I just don't like it."

Good clients are allowed this. If they're buying good work most of the time, well, they deserve to have those simple human reservations we all feel now and then. We decide to let her play the "Just don't like it" card. Fine. We go back. Time is running out, so we bring three storyboards to the next meeting. Luckily we're on a streak and all three are good. We'd have been happy to go with any one.

"I just don't like it."

"All three?"

"I just don't like it."

"What is it you don't like?"

"I can't say." And then she said the one thing all the really bad clients say sooner or later. "I'll know it when I see it."

Copywriter and author Dick Wasserman said this phrase is tantamount to a general telling his armies, "March off in all directions, and when I see where one of you is headed, I'll have a better fix on where I'd like the rest of you to go."

And so we marched off in all directions. Meeting after meeting was adjourned with, "I just don't like it." The boards piled up. After a while, we didn't bother to fly in for meetings and started e-mailing scripts, always getting the same answer.

Some 25 boards passed before her. And 25 died. I assure you, we didn't give up. It was a good product. A fallow field lay before us. We presented good work right up to the end.

"I just don't like it."

Time began to run out. Directors' January schedules were filling up. The media was bought, and the client was panicking. Client panic sometimes works in the agency's favor. Not this time. She asked for more. In the final phone meeting, the agency simply refused to provide any more boards.

And the client unraveled. I mean, she completely fell apart.

I remember listening to her voice on the speakerphone, hearing it begin to waver. She began to cry and then, God help me, beg like a junkie for more work.

She had become addicted to indecision.

"Come on! It doesn't even have to be a 30. Gimme a stinkin' 15. I'll take a 15! You got to have some 15s! Oh baby, baby, come to momma with another board." (Okay, she didn't say exactly that, but . . . she said exactly that.) I'd never seen anything like it. It got worse, too.

Somehow, around board number 29, she bought something. The agency wasn't proud of the piece. We were just holding our noses, hoping to simply produce the thing and pray we would prevail on the next assignment. A second-tier director was chosen. A location in Miami was scouted and approved. There was a listless prepro meeting. Sets were built. The team assembled in Florida the night before the cameras rolled. And the phone rang.

In the 11th hour, in the 59th minute, and at the tail end of the 59th second, the client's antiperspirant failed again. "I just don't like it."

The agency was forced to come up with a new concept and do it under the constraints of an existing set and a locked-off budget. Which is a lot like being told to build a plane, and here's a coffee can, a crayon, and an old copy of *Sports Illustrated*. It was insane. It was like that famous line from journalist Bill Mellor: "We are sorry. But the editor's indecision is final."

These incredible dervish-like turnarounds are known as doing a 360°. It's like doing a 180°, but twice. It could be argued that this client did a 540° or even a 720°. (Apparently, a 900° once happened in New York but nobody could tell really; after a while it got hard to count.)

The agency had to go back to the drawing board yet again. This time, getting the idea took just 10 minutes. The tired writer and the dispirited art director walked to the end of a nearby pier and just sat there looking out at the ocean.

Idea number 30 limped into the writer's mind like a sick dog with its ribs showing, and the writer said, "Okay, what if we did this?"

The art director looked at the dog. The dog looked up at the art director. "Fine."

They took their sick little animal of an idea and walked it back down the dock toward the nearest phone.

The client loved it.

It should come as no surprise that the final spot sucked. It was so bad we were trying to change channels on it during the final editing session. "See what else is on," someone would say. What is surprising is how the client later decided they didn't like it and blamed the agency. "Why aren't our commercials as good as the work you do for your other clients?"

The spot never aired. I swear this happened.

There is a list I've seen posted on bulletin boards in many agencies. One of those jokes that get photocopied and passed around until the type decays. This was the list:

THE SIX PHASES OF AN ADVERTISING PROJECT

1. Enthusiasm
2. Disillusionment
3. Panic
4. Search for the guilty
5. Punishment of the innocent
6. Praise and honors for the nonparticipants

What was once a joke tacked to a bulletin board had become grim reality. What began with enthusiasm ended as a new agency search.

Funny thing, though. The account did in fact leave the agency, but a month later we heard the woman was fired.

And, wouldn't you know it, in her absence the client's advertising improved. Which is always a little hard to take. I mean, the mature thing to do is wash the blood off your hands, wave good-bye to an account, and wish the client the best. But you secretly wish your old girlfriend, after she dumps you, ends up dealing crack from a culvert or pushing a mop at the Bun 'N' Burger. Currently, the on-the-job life expectancy of the average chief marketing officer is a scant 23 months[2] before being fired and replaced by the next one (who always has his own ideas, if not his own agency). This often means the only steady hand on the rudder of a brand is the ad agency's junior account person.

I had another client who was a meat puppet, working in a company run by fear. He was about as far down the corporate food chain as you could get—cubicle plankton. He even looked the part: that pale-white kind of guy who always gets killed in the first five minutes of a movie. Yet, to get an ad approved, you had to run it by this guy. And a bullet from his ratty little Saturday night special was as deadly as any other.

He was perhaps the tensest person I ever met. One morning, he was seen standing in front of the company coffee machine holding an empty cup, growling through clenched teeth, "Brew, goddammit." He had such high blood pressure, we worried that if he sustained even a paper cut, arterial spray would redden the ceiling.

But as scared as he was, he had a little power game he ran. It was brilliant. Whenever you presented ads to him for his approval, he wouldn't look at you. Or the ads. Wouldn't look at all. He'd just stare down at his legal pad in front of him.

There you were, having taken a 2-hour plane ride, lugging your portfolio in and out of cabs to arrive in his conference room. You did your setup and then presented the ads, ta-da! . . . to the top of his head. And if it was a visual concept, it drove you crazy. Because you found yourself having to use words to explain an image that you came up with to avoid using words in the first place.

He, too, was a meat puppet. Unable to make any decision without imagined repercussions from above, he chose to make none and, instead, passed his decision on to the next guy up the food chain.

There is nothing you can do about a meat puppet. Your boss is going to have to go above him, to whoever's yanking his strings. Such a decision is not yours to make, and you'll need one of your higher-ups to talk with one of theirs. Sometimes it works. You may discover the client culture isn't, in fact, fear-based and that your contact person is living in a backwater of fear he created on his own.

PABLUM PARK.

It's a 10 o'clock meeting on Monday morning at Martini, Yesman & Longlunch. Coats come off, and hands are shaken. Coffee poured and ties flattened. Everybody's excited because the client, the big regional power company, wants a new campaign.

"Okay," asks the agency, "about what?"

"Well, just about us. You know. *Us.*"

"Okay, but what about . . . *us?*"

"We care."

"You care?"

"We care."

"You care about what?"

"We just . . . care."

"Okay, I get the caring. I get it. But what is it you care about?"

"Why do we have to care about anything in particular? Just a general sort of caring, I think, would be fine. In fact, Dick here was just saying on the way to the agency how that would be a workable theme-slogan sort of thing—'We *Care.*'"

Dick nods, sagely.

Uh-oh. It's a client with absolutely nothing to say. You are now entering Pablum Park. Abandon all relevance, ye who enter here.

A power company is a good example of this kind of client. There's nothing they can say without ticking customers off. Why they advertise at all is beyond me. Where else are you going to "shop" for electricity? *("Oh, I think I'll use that plug over there.")* Many hospitals and health care plans have the same problem. They can't say, "Our doctors are better than their doctors." They can't say. "We cost less." They can, however, say, "We care."

So the Pablum Machine is turned on, and everything begins to run together in a saccharine slurry of Caring and Sharing and People Helping People. In fact, Pablum Park is populated entirely by "People People®."

"We're not just a giant corporation. We're People People® Helping People."

In Pablum Park, the police are "People Protecting People from People." Morticians are "Living People Helping Dead People." And lawyers are "People, Trying to *Be* People, Trying People."

If you watch even an hour of television, you'll see many commercials spouting drivel. Peel away the bluster and bombast, the jingles and clichés, and you'll find drivel. Nothing of substance. Words that sort of sound like you should be paying attention to them but are ultimately empty.

The best drivel I've ever read was in a wonderful parody called *Patriotic Spot—60 Seconds,* by Ellis Weiner. I reprint it here in abbreviated form.

You're waking up, America. It's morning—and you're waking up to live life like you've never lived it before. Say hello to a whole new way of being awake, America. Say hello to us. . . .We're watching you, America. We're watching you when you work—because, America, you work hard. And we know that afterward you've got a mighty big thirst. Not just a thirst for the best beer you can find. But a thirst for living. A thirst for years of experience. America, you're thirsty. . . . America, say hello to something new. Say hello to quality. Quality you can see. Quality you can feel. Quality you can say hello to. (How do you spell "quality," America? Real quality—quality you can trust? The same way we've been spelling it for over a hundred and fifty years.) . . . We're

Number One. You're Number One. You're a winner, America. And we know what you're thinking. We know how you feel. How do we know? Because we take the time to tell you. We take the time to care. And it pays off. We're here, America. And the next time you're here—the next time we can tell you who we are and what we do—we'll be doing what we do best.[3]

You're not completely without hope with this kind of client. But it'll take some work on your part. Every client has a story. Even the big, ugly ones with

How to write with style

By Kurt Vonnegut

International Paper asked Kurt Vonnegut, author of such novels as "Slaughterhouse-Five," "Jailbird" and "Cat's Cradle," to tell you how to put your style and personality into everything you write.

Newspaper reporters and technical writers are trained to reveal almost nothing about themselves in their writings. This makes them freaks in the world of writers, since almost all of the other ink-stained wretches in that world reveal a lot about themselves to readers. We call these revelations, accidental and intentional, elements of style.

These revelations tell us as readers what sort of person it is with whom we are spending time. Does the writer sound ignorant or informed, stupid or bright, crooked or honest, humorless or playful – ? And on and on.

Why should you examine your writing style with the idea of improving it? Do so as a mark of respect for your readers, whatever you're writing. If you scribble your thoughts any which way, your readers will surely feel that you care nothing about them. They will mark you down as an egomaniac or a chowderhead – or, worse, they will stop reading you.

The most damning revelation you can make about yourself is that you do not know what is interesting and what is not. Don't you yourself like or dislike writers mainly for what they choose to show you or make you think about? Did you ever admire an empty-headed writer for his or her mastery of the language? No.

So your own winning style must begin with ideas in your head.

1. Find a subject you care about

Find a subject you care about and which you in your heart feel others should care about. It is this genuine caring, and not your games with language, which will be the most compelling and seductive element in your style.

I am not urging you to write a novel, by the way – although I would not be sorry if you wrote one, provided you genuinely cared about something. A petition to the mayor about a pothole in front of your house or a love letter to the girl next door will do.

2. Do not ramble, though

I won't ramble on about that.

3. Keep it simple

As for your use of language: Remember that two great masters of language, William Shakespeare and James Joyce, wrote sentences which were almost childlike when their subjects were most profound. "To be or not to be?" asks Shakespeare's Hamlet. The longest word is three letters long. Joyce, when he was frisky, could put together a sentence as intricate and as glittering as a necklace for Cleopatra, but my favorite sentence in his short story "Eveline" is this one: "She was tired." At that point in the story, no other words could break the heart of a reader as those three words do.

Simplicity of language is not only reputable, but perhaps even sacred. The *Bible* opens with a sentence well within the writing skills of a lively fourteen-year-old: "In the beginning God created the heaven and the earth."

4. Have the guts to cut

It may be that you, too, are capable of making necklaces for Cleopatra, so to speak. But your eloquence should be the servant of the ideas in your head. Your rule might be this: If a sentence, no matter how excellent, does not illuminate your subject in some new and useful way, scratch it out.

5. Sound like yourself

The writing style which is most natural for you is bound to echo the speech you heard when a child. English was the novelist Joseph Conrad's third language, and much that seems piquant in his use of English was no doubt colored by his first language, which was Polish. And lucky indeed is the writer who has grown up in Ireland, for the English spoken there is so amusing and musical. I myself grew up in Indianapolis, where common speech sounds like a band saw cutting galvanized tin,

Should I act upon the urgings that I feel, or remain passive and thus cease to exist?

To be or not to be?

"Keep it simple. Shakespeare did, with Hamlet's famous soliloquy."

Figure 11.2a   Long-copy ads can be great. Even if a customer doesn't read every word, they make it look like the company has a lot to offer.

names like Syntheti-Corp have a story that can be made relevant and meaningful to the average reader.

International Paper's trade campaign by Ogilvy & Mather back in the 1980s is a good example. International was a faceless corporation that made a product not famous for brand loyalty—paper.

Yet their campaign of award-winning ads was exquisitely readable (Figure 11.2). Above a spread filled with long, well-written copy were headlines like "How to improve your vocabulary" or "How to enjoy poetry." Each ad was

"Be merciless on yourself. If a sentence does not illuminate your subject in some new and useful way, scratch it out."

and employs a vocabulary as unornamental as a monkey wrench.

In some of the more remote hollows of Appalachia, children still grow up hearing songs and locutions of Elizabethan times. Yes, and many Americans grow up hearing a language other than English, or an English dialect a majority of Americans cannot understand.

All these varieties of speech are beautiful, just as the varieties of butterflies are beautiful. No matter what your first language, you should treasure it all your life. If it happens not to be standard English, and if it shows itself when you write standard English, the result is usually delightful, like a very pretty girl with one eye that is green and one that is blue.

I myself find that I trust my own writing most, and others seem to trust it most, too, when I sound most like a person from Indianapolis, which is what I am. What alternatives do I have? The one most vehemently recommended by teachers has no doubt been pressed on you, as well: to write like cultivated Englishmen of a century or more ago.

6. Say what you mean to say

I used to be exasperated by such teachers, but am no more. I understand now that all those antique essays and stories with which I was to compare my own work were not magnificent for their datedness or foreignness, but for saying precisely what their authors meant them to say. My teachers wished me to write accurately, always selecting the most effective words, and relating the words to one another unambiguously, rigidly, like parts of a machine. The teachers did not want to turn me into an Englishman after all. They hoped that I would become understandable – and therefore understood. And there went my dream of doing with words what Pablo Picasso did with paint or what any number of jazz idols did with music. If I broke all the rules of punctuation, had words mean whatever I wanted them to mean, and strung them together higgledy-piggledy, I would simply not be understood. So you, too, had better avoid Picasso-style or jazz-style writing, if you have something worth saying and wish to be understood.

Readers want our pages to look very much like pages they have seen before. Why? This is because they themselves have a tough job to do, and they need all the help they can get from us.

7. Pity the readers

They have to identify thousands of little marks on paper, and make sense of them immediately. They have to *read*, an art so difficult that most people don't really master it even after having studied it all through grade school and high school – twelve long years.

So this discussion must finally acknowledge that our stylistic options as writers are neither numerous nor glamorous, since our readers are bound to be such imperfect artists. Our audience requires us to be sympathetic and patient teachers, ever willing to simplify and clarify – whereas we would rather soar high above the crowd, singing like nightingales.

That is the bad news. The good news is that we Americans are governed under a unique Constitution, which allows us to write whatever we please without fear of punishment. So the most meaningful aspect of our styles, which is what we choose to write about, is utterly unlimited.

8. For really detailed advice

For a discussion of literary style in a narrower sense, in a more technical sense, I commend to your attention *The Elements of Style*, by William Strunk, Jr., and E.B. White (Macmillan, 1979). E.B. White is, of course, one of the most admirable literary stylists this country has so far produced. You should realize, too, that no one would care how well or badly Mr. White expressed himself, if he did not have perfectly enchanting things to say.

SOAP

"Pick a subject you care so deeply about that you'd speak on a soapbox about it."

Today, the printed word is more vital than ever. Now there is more need than ever for all of us to *read* better, *write* better, and *communicate* better.

International Paper offers this series in the hope that, even in a small way, we can help.

If you'd like to share this article with others—students, friends, employees, family—we'll gladly send you reprints. So far we've sent out over 15,000,000 in response to requests from people everywhere.

Please write: "Power of the Printed Word," International Paper Company, Dept. 5X, P.O. Box 954, Madison Square Station, New York, NY 10010. ©1985 INTERNATIONAL PAPER COMPANY

INTERNATIONAL PAPER COMPANY
We believe in the power of the printed word.

Figure 11.2b (continued)

authored by a marquee name like James Dickey or Kurt Vonnegut. And at the end of the ads, the copy seamlessly brought you around to International's take on the deal: "We believe in the power of the printed word."

THE KONCEPT KRUSHER 2000®.

This actually happened.

After several weeks of work, we finished a campaign for a large account and presented it to the client. The client approved it, "pending research."

The account guys sent the boards to an advertising research firm retained by the client. A week later, the results came back. We'd scored okay with the traditional focus group tests. But we'd failed the "Andrea" test and had to start all over.

"What is the 'Andrea' test?" I asked the client.

With a straight face, she said, "Well, the thing is, we give your story boards to a guy there at the research place. And he and another guy, they take it into a room and they close the door and then come out about, oh, three hours later with the results. And we know if your spot works. Yours didn't. I'm sorry."

"But what did they do in there?"

"The research firm tells us that's proprietary."

"Pro . . . can I *talk* to this 'Andrea'?"

"'Andrea' is just the name for the test. There is no Andrea, and the methodology is proprietary, as I've said. They don't have to tell us what they do in there. The results they come out with always seem to be right on the money."

I stood there, blinking. The client, I'm sure, thought I was trying to think of some counterargument. But what I was thinking about was social work. ("I like people. I could help someone, maybe a little kid. It would be nice to get away. Peru or something. Maybe a little shack. Wouldn't be so bad.")

I came to in the cab on the way to the airport, holding a fat spiral notebook full of all the things wrong with my ads, courtesy of "Andrea."

Clients who rely on test results to approve work will always be with us. There's no escaping it. That's the good news. The bad news is, with some clients, research will kill all of your work all the time.

A few large corporations have whole floors devoted to advertising-slash-research, and they have it down to a system. They feed your storyboards into one end of a process that's very much like a machine, with a name like, I don't know, "Koncept Krusher 2000®." As your campaign goes through the device, you hear all kinds of nasty things happening . . . ("It's negative!" Muffled sounds. "We can't say that." Unidentified thwacking noise. "Why can't they all be happy?") . . . and what comes out the other end you wouldn't want to air on a clothesline, much less network television.

The really bad news is that there isn't a thing you can do about it. Once these huge research machines are in place, they're usually there to stay. Somebody somewhere is making a *lot* of money off this research (and it isn't the client). No good idea will ever get out alive. Generally, it's the older, larger clients who've been advertising for years that have an overheated K/K 2000 down in the basement, running day and night.

I worked for several clients like this, where I think I did some of the best work of my career. But you've never seen it. On one particularly baneful project I remember, the Krusher must've been set on "high" because it went through hundreds, literally hundreds, of storyboards.

After I burned out on the project, the agency threw other people at the snapping jaws of the research machine. And then another team. And another. A full year later, the Krusher spit out this tepid little storyboard that both research and the client had approved.

There on the conveyer belt lay the TV spot—a trembling, pathetic thing that did not like being looked at directly. A sort of marketing Frankenstein—chunks of different departmental agendas and mandates, all sewn together by focus groups and researchers into something that looked like a TV spot but was, in fact, an abomination. We should have hammered a spike through its heart right there.

Koncept Krushers can be bigger machines than just a client's research department. The whole company may, in fact, be structured to blowtorch new ideas. This sounds cynical, I know, but I've seen it. I've stood right next to these furnaces myself and felt the licking of the flames.

Try this on.

The client in question was one of those Sisyphus accounts I described earlier. A big Fortune 500 company. Huge. The kind that asks for tons of stuff that's always due the next morning, and you find out later it's for a product they're thinking about introducing 10 years from now.

So, anyway, this poor art director is stuck on a Sisy Corp type of account. She doesn't know this, so the day she gets a job for a big TV commercial, she's excited, right?

Well, she and her partner begin working on it. After a vast amount of work, they have a couple cool ideas. I mean some really smart things that also happen to be potential award winners (or "podium wobblers," as they're called in Britain).

Cut to next scene, meeting number one with the client—all of their ideas are dead. The reason? Doesn't matter. (You'll see.)

So they get to work on another series of ideas to present in meeting number two. Days later, there's excitement in the creative department, rejuvenation. "We've done it again!"

Time wipe: It's meeting number three. The client opens the meeting by announcing they've changed the strategy.

Okay, here's where we cut to that movie cliché—the clock hands spinning 'round and 'round, the calendar pages flying off the wall. The changes keep coming in. The client doesn't like the idea. Or they cut the budget. Or they change the product, or they change the strategy. One time it's the client *himself* who's changed—fired, actually—and now there's a new client who wants something totally different. Whatever it is, it's always something.

It gets worse.

During meetings number 4 through number 63, the campaign is watered down, softened, and diluted so much that the final commercial is precisely as interesting as a bag of hair. The last interesting thing in the commercial is successfully removed in meeting number 63. An optimist might say that things should have gone smoothly from here on out. *("For cryin' out loud. It's a bag of hair! What's left to complain about?")* But there are no optimists in advertising.

It's Friday. The scheduled day of meeting number 64.

Meeting number 64 isn't even a very important meeting, given that the CEO signed off back around meeting number 50 or so. But there needed to be a few dozen more "For Your Information" sort of presentations, and if any of them went badly, the agency would have to start over.

The meeting begins. The art director goes through the old moves, trying to remember the fun of presenting it the first time. But there's no spark left. She just . . . presents it.

The client sits there. Says nothing at first.

The client then reaches down into her purse and pulls out a small Kermit the Frog doll. (This really happened.) It's one of those flexible dolls, and she begins bending the frog's arms around so that its hands are covering its ears. Then the client says: "Mr. Froggy doesn't like some of the things he's hearing."

This really happened.

The client actually said, "Mr. Froggy doesn't like some of the things he's hearing" (Figure 11.3).

Let me put it this way. There are two kinds of hell. There's "Original" and then there's "Extra Crispy." This was Extra Crispy.

Well, Ms. Froggy-Lady, as she came to be known, wasn't able to kill the commercial, only make it a little worse—a feat in itself. And so, finally, in meeting number 68, the whole company had signed off on this one storyboard.

All in all, it took 68 presentations to hundreds of MBAs in dozens of sweaty presentation rooms. In fact, there were some sarcastic agency memos to the media department suggesting that since the commercial had been shown to thousands of people already, there may not be a need to air it at all.

The creative team went back to the agency, opened two beers, and sat looking at the sunset through the windows of their offices on the 30th floor. There, over the body of the original storyboard that lay on the floor, they performed an advertising postmortem, discussing the more shocking moments of its horrifying death.

Eavesdropping, a casual listener might have thought the two had just come out of the theater and were talking about a horror movie. *("Yeah! And remember when that one guy came in and ripped all its guts out? Man, I did not see that coming at all.")*

That's when they noticed something out their window—something disturbing.

Outside their window was a 40-story building.

tomlichtenheld.com

Figure 11.3   I'm not kidding. This really happened.

The thing is, the 40-story building wasn't *there* the day they began working on the commercial.

With horror, the creative team realized that a building had been raised, built from a 30-foot-deep hole in the ground and 40 stories into the sky, faster than their little 12-frame storyboard had been destroyed and approved.

Why do I tell you this? To chase you away from the business?

No, to steel you for it.

This stuff happens all the time. And keep in mind, none of these clients were stupid people. (Well, we can discuss Froggy-Lady later.) They were all pretty sharp businesspeople, trying as hard as they could to solve a problem for their brands. But as smart and nice as they all were individually, a calcified approval process had crept into the company's structure, and it became completely impossible to get a decent idea out the door.

This happens all the time. Be ready.

THE LIZ ACCOUNT.

Then there's Liz. Liz is a glamorous and famous brand. Everyone knows Liz.

Over the years, the Liz account moves its tired old derriere from agency to agency to agency to agency. Every shop along the way thinks, wow, what a catch, and a year later every one of them has that hangdog look of desperation.

The thing is, many Liz companies make products that are incredibly great. But you couldn't tell it by their ads, which are always terrible, no matter which agency they're currently shacking with. Good products, though, and that's the shame of it.

About once every two years, you'll see this client's name pop up in the trades: the honeymoon's over, old agency is out, new agency in. Photos are taken of big smiles shaking hands in front of banners with corny lines like "Partners in Progress" or "Thanks for the Biz, Liz."

"Compton & Curry Walk Away with $65M Liz Co," reads *Adweek*. Six months later, Compton is in rehab and Curry's on the phone to *Adweek* with something about "creative differences." Liz is back at the altar and agencies are lining up, lured by the siren song of that blue-chip logo still looking "okay" after all these years.

I have a friend who just started working for a Liz client.

One day the client phones my friend and says, "Okay, I want you guys to start thinking about our next TV campaign. And don't worry. I already have the elephant."

She was serious. She actually said, "Don't worry. I already have the elephant."

She had, in fact, already booked an elephant through an animal trainer. She didn't have the idea all worked out but felt certain that the marketing answer was somewhere in the whole pachyderm thing. All that was left for the agency to do was coax the idea out of its pen at the zoo and onto prime-time TV.

See, Liz's problem is that she thinks she knows advertising; she already has her own executions in mind. She knows enough to recognize somebody else's good work when she sees it, which is why she's always flirting with the good agencies. But she doesn't know enough to let them solve the problem. She thinks she knows better.

Once they're in bed with her, the mask comes off and Liz says, "All right, scribblers, here's the idea I want executed," and she proceeds to bend them around like red licorice.

One morning, long after the excitement of that famous logo is gone, you'll roll over in bed and see Liz without makeup. Not a pretty sight.

But Liz, as certain as she is of her own ideas, is nice about it. Worse than a Liz client is one who bullies you. Mistreats you. There aren't many, but they're out there.

THE BULLY.

There is another kind of bad account. The account run by the Bully client. Bullies anywhere are bad. But Bullies with real power are enough, as Anne Lamott says, to make Jesus drink himself to sleep.

Bullies aren't born that way. They develop over many years, like wine gone sour in a forgotten cellar. They come out of the cellar with a vast amount of knowledge, all of it wrong, down to the syllable. The one I'm thinking of had been in the business some 20 years when I was put on his account.

He had spent most of his career on a second-rate brand of beer and was personally responsible for one of the worst campaigns ever to foul a TV set. And he was so proud of that beer campaign. Women with big breasts. Wild beach parties with lots of what he'd call "jiggle." And always ending with that tired old shot, a bartender holding two frosty bottles in each hand, offering them to the camera. "Product ID!" he'd say.

He would brag about this awful campaign, measuring our work by it one day, smacking our hands with it the next. When it was just us guys in the room, he'd say, "You wanna know why that campaign worked? I tell ya why that campaign worked. We had girls with them big ol' titties and trucks and everything."

I'm not kidding. He said that. It was like every nightmare Gloria Steinem ever had about the way some men behave behind closed corporate doors. He was a pig.

Even his boss knew his beer campaign stank and would occasionally interrupt him in midbrag to tell him so. The Bully would good-naturedly chuck his boss's shoulder and remind him of the slight upward drift of his beer's sales curve. He projected his own inadequacies onto the market and made the mistake of thinking that the customer is none too bright. And it was reflected in the advertising he forced all of his agencies to do. Pile-driving, "no-nonsense" nonsense.

During your career in advertising, you will meet this man. He will know nothing about advertising but will wield great power. "All hat and no cattle," I've heard him described. No argument will be eloquent enough to sway him from his sledgehammer approach to advertising. There is no poetry in the man. No subtlety. He is a paper tiger. A tin-pot despot lording over his little product fiefdom, spouting rules from advertising's Bronze Age, and pointing to modest sales increases whenever his excesses and crudities are exposed.

And the day all intelligence in American advertising dies, he should be brought in for questioning.

HALLWAY BEAST #1: THE HACK.

Yes, clients can misbehave. Thank God, most of them don't. And to account for all that awful work you see on TV every night, those bad clients must have a few friends on the agency side of the business. They do.

Like everything else in life, America's list of agencies makes up a big bell curve. There are a few truly great agencies, then a whole bunch of agencies that are just okay, and then a few bad ones.

To get off to the right start in this business, you're going to need to know how to spot those bad agencies. And it's not as easy as you think. Just because an agency has a commercial in the latest awards annual doesn't mean you want to work there.

What you've got to do is, during your interviews, look for the Hack. (Let's call him Hallway Beast #1. There are others in the menagerie.)

The first warning sign that you're in the presence of a Hack is that he'll somehow bring up his One Good Ad from Way Back. He won't call it that. In fact, he'll show it to you and say something like, "This is the kind of work we do here." That's when you notice the ad is on brittle, yellowing paper from a magazine like *Collier's*.

All Hacks have one of these ads. They made their name on it. They've been riding its tired old back for decades and look about as silly doing it as Adam West would now look in his old Batman suit.

It can be a great ad. Doesn't matter. Ask yourself, what else has the agency done? Talented people with a gift for advertising keep doing great work, time and again, for a variety of clients.

Another warning sign that should send your Hack-O-Meter into the red is how the person talks. And oh how this kind does talk. In fact, talk is all a Hack can do, being incapable as he is of producing an ad that a fly won't lay eggs on. He'll know the buzzwords. And worse, he'll have a few of his own. "At this agency, we believe in advertising with Clutter-Busting® Power." If you hear something like this, just drop your portfolio and run. You can put together another book. Just run. Don't risk the elevator. Go for the stairs.

Agencies are the way they are for a reason. It's no accident they're doing awful work. They have clients on one side asking for awful work, Hacks on the other side giving it to them, and a guy in the middle counting all the money. Talk is cheap. Especially talk about how "we're going to turn this place around." If you hear this phrase, you should turn around. Again, go for the stairs.

The quintessential giveaway, however, is the creative director who denigrates creativity in general and awards shows in particular. This was the kid in the playground who didn't have a big red ball, so he told the other kids, "Big red balls are stupid." He can't do it. So, of course, he's going to denigrate it.

Some of these guys kill ideas simply because they're unable to generate ideas of their own. In fact, to kill what you've come up with actually seems like an idea to them. They'll go: "Hey wait! Shhhhh! . . . I have an idea! Let's . . . *not* do your idea!" Their ideas are like antimatter. They don't really exist until yours does, and when they meet, they're both gone in an instant.

In an interview, this guy will look you straight in the eye and say, "Creativity is overrated. Client sales are what we're all about." He'll get out a case history. Show you some commercials he'll call "hardworking" and then tap his finger on a number at the bottom of the results page. "This, my little friend, is what we do."

Someday I'd like to try an experiment. It will cost $40 million. I'll give a fifth grader a brand name and tell him to shoot a commercial. Whatever he comes up with, I'll spend the rest of the $39-some million airing on prime time. In a couple of months, I'll bet Little Jimmy can take off his baseball glove and tap his finger on a similar sales increase. The point is, with a 2-ton sledgehammer even a fifth grader can ring the bell at the top. (I suspect Mr. Whipple's war chest of several trillion had something to do with his high recall scores.)

On the other hand, you have what's called *creative leverage*—beating out the competition's advertising by doing something that is more interesting. Years ago, writer Ed McCabe said, "Disciplined creativity is often the last remaining legal means you have to gain an unfair advantage over the competition."

Compare that quotation from McCabe with this next one. I can't print this man's name, but to a national trade magazine he said blithely and without shame, "Sheer repetition can build awareness and equity for a client even if an ad is not considered creatively brilliant. A dumb dollar beats a smart dime any day."

Sheer repetition? If I were this guy's client, I'd take my dumb dollar over to an agency that can give me 10 times the wallop with a dime's worth of sheer brilliance.

Hacks get easier to spot as they feed and prosper. In their mature years, they sprout long titles, some growing up to 10 inches in length. Recently, I saw a picture of a Hack in *Adweek*, and below it, this title: "Executive Vice President/ Vice Chairman/Chief Creative Director North America/General Manager/ Worldwide Coordinator." I'm not kidding—word for word.

Agencies may keep them on, sort of as expensive hood ornaments. They'll trot them out at big pitches, but during the rest of the year they'll give them what I call a Nerf account—something they can bat around without hurting themselves or anybody else. They are well known, as one wag put it, chiefly for being well known.

A closing thought on Hacks. One of the great things about this business is that you'll be surrounded by vibrant, interesting, and genuinely nice people. I don't know why the industry attracts them; it just does.

And Hacks are no exception. Most of the ones I've known are people just as nice as you could want to meet. After office hours, they're great fishing buddies, loving mothers, and intelligent bridge partners.

But I warn you against joining their team during working hours. As a junior, you'll learn bad habits from them, habits that will be hard to break, even when you come under the tutelage of more talented teachers. We improve by surrounding ourselves with people whose work we admire.

THE GOLDEN HANDCUFFS.

If you take a job at a big, dull agency, you might, without your seeing it happen, slip into a pair of "golden handcuffs." That big agency may be willing to pay you a lot of money to crank out the dull ads. You get used to the money. A couple of years go by, and as your bank account fills with money, your book fills with bad ads—ads you can't show without embarrassment or explanation.

Agencies will do all kinds of silly things to keep you happy at your desk cranking out bad stuff. I remember one agency that started handing out vice presidencies like candy from a Pez dispenser. Anybody who complained or was seen putting his portfolio together was suddenly a vice president.

After a while, though, it seemed almost everybody in the creative department was a VP, and the distinction began to lose its luster. That didn't stop them. They just started handing out secret vice presidencies.

The boss would motion you into his office. He'd say, "We love your work. You're gonna be a superstar. So we're making you a vice president, but . . . uh, we don't want you to tell anyone. Some people, well, they aren't as good as you and aren't being promoted." By the time I left, the entire creative department was full of "superstars" who were vice presidents, half on the up-and-up and half "secret" vice presidents.

Most of the time, these assistant-vice presidencies and other titles don't add up to much anyway. I had a friend who worked for a large, stuffy old agency. The morning after he was promoted, he was standing outside his cubicle chatting with a coworker. The kid from the mail room shows up with a hammer and says, "Your name Buchner?" My friend nods yes. The kid proceeds to wedge one corner of the cubicle open, hammers in a modular two-foot extension piece, says "Congratulations," and walks away.

HALLWAY BEAST #2: THE PRIMA DONNA.

This is the writer or art director who thinks he is God's gift to advertising. And they are all over this business.

The one I'm thinking of right now had that one dead giveaway, something all Prima Donnas share—the swagger. That walk people get when they think their DNA is better than everybody else's. There he goes now, down the hallway. And in his hand, a paper bearing his latest brilliant headline. *("Oh, how I wish he'd let me see what it is now and not make me wait till next year's awards annuals come out.")*

Why they develop the swagger, I don't know. I mean, if that paper was a blueprint for world peace instead of a coupon ad for Jell-O, okay, sashay a little bit. But the Prima Donna seems to have forgotten what he does for a living. He's a word-slinging schmuck like the rest of us. But you'll never convince a Prima Donna he's the same species as we.

Wherever the Prima Donna is swaggering, when he gets there, you can bet he'll have something nasty to say about either how excruciatingly dumb account executives are or what blind bastards every single one of his clients is.

But you, you're okay—that is, if the Prima Donna is standing within 10 feet of you. Prima Donnas obey what I call the 10-Foot Pinhead Rule. Anyone farther than 10 feet from the Prima Donna is a pinhead. He'll walk into your office and say, "Oh, you wouldn't believe the pinhead I was just talking to." Of course, the rule applies when he leaves your office. Eleven feet down the hallway, he'll be telling whomever he's with, "God, I'm glad we left that pinhead's office."

Prima Donnas would have made great Nazis, because they cultivate an air of entitlement and genetic superiority. Each one believes he is the center gear in capitalism's great machine. What the pen of Herr Donna writes today will tomorrow be on the lips of all the haggard supermarket moms he makes fun of in his off-hours.

You see, Prima Donnas have so much to teach us. If we would only listen. But as the years go by and he casts more of his pearls before swine, his poison ferments and his talons curl. Prima Donnas just get mean.

It's like this: When I look out my tall office building, I think all the people look like ants. He thinks that when he's on the street.

There was this one Prima Donna I remember. His first day at work he called the office manager in and calmly directed that his desk be raised 3 inches. Three inches—I'm not kidding. Apparently, his keyboard had to be a certain distance from his chin to invoke the visions. When he could bully the producers into it, he'd fly only first class. And any suggestions from coworkers on how to improve an idea were laughed off or explained away. It got so bad finally that no art director would work with him. He was about to be fired when he quit and took a job somewhere else.

The hurt and anger he left behind in the agency lingered for some time. Secretaries came out of hiding and admitted to farting in his office when he was gone. After a while, we tried to be philosophical about his character. The best we could say about him was: "If you cut him open, you'd find a heart of gold. And if you didn't, hey, you've cut him open."

HALLWAY BEAST #3: MR. IMPORTANT PANTS.

If this were a movie we'd introduce the brutal creative director by opening on an agency meeting. It would be a Sunday, naturally; maybe even during the Holidays. We see the nervous creative team tacking ideas up on the wall. But where is Mr. Important Pants?

Ahh, here he comes.

His untroubled gait belies the fact that he's fully 35 minutes late for a meeting he called. After setting down his soy mocha-decaf latte he begins to look grimly at the ideas on the wall. He brushes his ponytail off of his shoulder. He sneers, rips an idea off the wall, crumples it, and drops it to the floor.

He then dispenses what he calls creative direction. To his little clutch of "scribblers" he gives this helpful and articulate redirection.

"It's crap."

Now he's working his way down the bulletin board and the campaigns begin to die one after another, in waves. Accompanying the death of each idea comes similarly helpful creative advice:

"Crap."

"Bitch, pleeease."

"Like *I'd* do that."

And finally the wall is bare. No ideas are good enough for his majesty. As he takes leave, over his shoulder he quips, "I'll know it when I see it, people." No discussion about what was right about the work, what was wrong. And though his title is creative director, there is no direction given to creative.

As Stephen King said, it's just a *shame* the things you see when you don't have a revolver handy.

Okay, this latte-ponytail guy, he's just one kind of brutal creative director but these douche-bags come in different flavors. The worst ones actually berate and browbeat creatives, bludgeoning them with words that serve to improve neither the work nor the morale.

And when their words do, in fact, improve the creative, these guys will defend their behavior by describing it as "brutally honest." Unfortunately, all that the employees remember is the brutality, not the honesty.

Imagine how stupid this kind of brutality would look if we could see it in some other venue.

CUT TO McDONALD'S MANAGER DRESSING DOWN A NEW EMPLOYEE.

"Hey, I didn't get to wear this red paper *manager's* hat by makin' milkshakes as crappy as this!"

Why advertising creates so many of these angry little dictators is a mystery. What, pray tell, warrants any kind of arrogance at all? Dude, this is advertising. You're not pullin' babies out of burning buildings. You're not curing cancer or making peace. You make commercials for cry-eye. Websites. *End-aisle displays.*

If I could get one of these guys alone, my speech might go like this. *"Dude, sit down. And toss that latte. Listen, I don't care. . . . I said* zip it, Ponytail. *. . . I don't care that you were once on a 'big Volvo shoot' with Robert Goulet. I don't care you won an award that one time. I don't care that you wear sunglasses when you're indoors. The thing is, none of that crap gives you the permission to treat people poorly. Somewhere along the line, dude, you seem to have gotten the idea that establishing a high bar means you can whack people with it."*

In a recent post about good creative directors on the *Denver Egoist,* I read this:

You don't get people to want to work harder for you by shouting, . . . abusing and humiliating. Motivation comes from a place of respect and trust. Good creative directors will want you to do well for you, not for them. They instill in you the kind of passion and drive that makes an eight-hour day become a 13-hour day. If your CD's idea of motivation is to threaten you with pay cuts, demotions, crappy accounts or losing your job, you don't want to work for that CD any more. . . . Sure, you'll work for the d-bag for as long as it takes you to find another job, but word will soon spread that the CD is in fact a d-bag, and the agency will find it more and more difficult to hire genuinely good creative talent.[4]

My advice?

If you find yourself working for one of these people, drop a dime on him or her and let human resources know. If you can get another job, do it and do it fast. And on your way out, spread the word. This isn't gossip. You're providing a valuable service to your creative brethren by putting up a warning sign: "Steer Clear. Toxic Douche-Bag Ahead."

HALLWAY BEAST #4: THE WHINER.

Lord knows, I've been one of these. And in my early years, I wasted a lot of time doing it. (Does this chapter count as whining? . . . Wait. Don't answer.)

It has been said that whining is simply anger coming through a very small hole. If so, then the Whiner is a very angry little man.

What he whines about most is his job. And he whines all the time. All of his clients suck. All account executives suck. The sad part is, if he could just convert half the energy he spends whining in the hallways to working in his office, he'd be doing better work. Yes, that work might die because sometimes a client may, in fact, suck. But those are the breaks of the business. Get over it.

The Whiner can have a job at the best agency in the world and he'll still find something to bitch about. And it's such a *disconnect* to listen to a Whiner strum his blues as he reclines amid the opulence of a large ad agency.

You'll find him whining in the employee kitchen while guzzling his 80th free Coke and eating a free lunch. *("My book is, like, so at the headhunter's.")*

You'll find him in a first-class seat of a jet on the way to a commercial shoot in sunny California, bitching about how they made him mention the client's product in a commercial about the client's product. *("That is, like, so expected.")*

You'll find him working in a comfortable conference room, grousing about having to work on smaller jobs like a brochure or direct mail. *("My old partner is on a TV shoot right now, and I'm here doing this crap.")*

Whiners can be poison to other people in the agency. It's hard enough to keep your spirits high in this business, and it doesn't help to have a Whiner draped over the chair in your office, going through the agency phone list rating employees. *("Loser, Hack, Mule, Mule, Hack, Loser . . .")*

When the Whiner moves on to that agency he thinks is so much better, it's the old truism: "Wherever you go in life, there you are." To his horror, he discovers ad agencies are pretty much the same everywhere. There are hard clients, misguided research, and unreasonable deadlines everywhere, and because that's all he focuses on, these Harpies will follow him throughout all of his sad days.

I'm not saying you can't whine. It's good to let off some steam now and then. True Whining, however, has a vituperative edge to it. It's toxic. Pestilential. There's no hope in it. After a while, you wonder why Whiners don't just leave the business altogether.

Cut to the next scene, the Whiner's new job at the shoe store: "I should get a job over at Foot Locker. Those guys are so good. This place sucks."

HALLWAY BEASTS #5 AND #6: WACK JOBS AND SLASH WEASELS.

If this book were politically correct, our next hallway beast might be described as a person who "does things differently." But this is not that kind of book. I'm talking about people who are as crazy as six-toed cats on crack in a Chinese whorehouse; people who are total Wack Jobs.

What makes Wack Jobs such interesting specimens is that they look crazy even in the loosey-goosey atmosphere of an ad agency. I'm remembering this one guy who could write only if he was wearing a full-face knit ski mask. Or this other one who could write only on days that were approved by his astrologist.

Also legendary was the Wack Job who had so little life outside the agency that he slept there. When you worked late at the agency, you grew used to the sight of him in his underwear walking through the hallways to the bathroom for a midnight pee. Which reminds me of this other guy who stood at the urinal in the company men's room with his pants and underwear dropped all the way down around his ankles. When you came into the bathroom, he would give you a look that just dared you to say anything.

Wack Jobs usually have very screwed-up personal lives that they vaguely allude to in the few meetings they turn up for.

"Sorry, I'm late. I was in court."

"Oh, jury duty?" someone asks.

"No."

"Ooooooookay, well, let's start our meeting, shall we?"

Wack Jobs move from giving you no information about themselves *("I'm from . . . out West.")* to giving way too much *(in the middle of a meeting, they'll lean over and whisper something like, "Years ago my mother was killed by clowns, and I feel sad today.").*

Sometimes that excess information is medical. We had this one Wack Job call in sick and leave a long voice mail with grisly details about the viscosity of his mucus and the water content of his phlegm. The voice mail was played publicly at maximum volume the entire week.

The most damaging kind of Wack Job is the crazy creative director. One of the early warning signs of possible wackage in a creative director is a proliferation of props in his office—like those giant six-foot pencils. A giant wristwatch on the wall. A giant anything, really. Or a dentist's chair. *("See, it's an actual dentist's chair!")* Jukeboxes and pinball machines are popular; mannequins, too.

Wack Job creative directors think their office props say, "I'm creative! Who knows what I'll say or do next?" What they say or do next, however, is drive everyone insane because they change their minds about the work up to the last stinking minute.

I have a friend who worked for a Wack Job. Crazy-ass boss comes into my friend's office 1 hour before a client meeting with huge changes to the campaign. When my friend groans, the Wack Job whips out a small vial of pills and says, "Sure you don't want to split a Xanax?"

Creative directors can stay crazy even on vacation. I remember getting a phone call from a creative director's assistant: "Jim called from Barbados to kill that campaign he approved. Fax new ideas to his boat tonight, okay?"

Wack Jobs are, of course, relatively easy to spot in the agency hallways. More insidious is the Slash Weasel.

First thing you need to understand is the word *slash*. In ad parlance, it means "shared credit." When an ad is accepted into a national awards show, the credits are listed below the ad. And when two people contribute to an ad's art direction or its writing, their names are listed together, separated by a slash (/).

But those names in the award books? That's credit. And credit is what the Slash Weasel craves. So he'll creep around the creative department trying to get "slashed" into the credit lines of other people's work. They're basically the goal hangers of advertising. To ride your coattails, a Weez thinks all he has to do is make a suggestion about your ad. Upon seeing your work, he'll rattle off a couple of "Did you try . . ." statements and walk away. Later, he'll insist he "helped" with your work and will include your ad in his portfolio. This really happens.

Remember that saying, "There is no 'I' in 'team'"?

Well, there *is* a "we" in "weasel," which is why they throw the word "we" around a lot, regardless of whether they're part of your team or any other. They'll just stand in your office when the boss comes by and go, "Man, we really like these ads a lot." Another stunt is to pop into the creative director's office right before you present and say something like, "You're really gonna like what you're about to see."

There's not much you can do about a Weez except steer clear. What's sad about them is that Slash Weasels sometimes actually have talent. The problem is, they're in the business for the wrong reason—they don't care as much about their clients' brands as they do their own.

HALLWAY BEAST #7: THE HOUR GOBBLER.

Hallway Beast #7 isn't a person. It's a thing. The Meeting. If you see one, run.

Run, little pony, run, and *never* look back.

If the wheels of capitalism ever grind to a halt, the agenda of a meeting will be found caught in the gears. And in the advertising business, meetings thrive like mutant weeds, making actual work impossible.

There are meetings with doughnuts and meetings without doughnuts. Meetings to talk about ads you're going to do and meetings to talk about the ads you just did. All these meetings will be held in small, windowless rooms heated to forehead-dampening temperatures by overhead projector bulbs and all held during that torpid postlunch lull around 2:30.

As a junior, you probably should just shrug and show up for any meeting you get memo'ed on. But as your radar develops, you'll start to be able to detect which meetings are important—where big plans are made and things get done—and which aren't.

The ones I'm talking about are those meetings that are called because somebody needed something to do. "Background" meetings. Or "touching base" meetings. These aren't called because decisions need to be made. They're just called. And oh, how they go on. I was in one of these Hour Gobblers once, and I swear time actually stopped. I'm not kidding. Swear to God, as plain as day, the second hand on the wall clock just *stopped*. No more ticktock. Just . . . tick . . . and that was it.

It was a particularly useless meeting and 3 hours long. Just when we thought we were going to get out, someone raised his hand and asked a question—the kind of tired, lifeless query I call a meeting extender. A meeting extender is a question like: "Well, Bill, how do those figures compare with the results from *Chicago?*" That's when the clock stopped and began to sag like a Dali painting.

Speakerphone meetings are the worst. And the worst of the worst is the three-way speakerphone, client-on-a-car-phone conference call meeting. There you are, eight nervous people all huddled around a little black box, listening to an art director in L.A. describe a picture nobody can see, to a client nobody can hear.

Ending a meeting is an art it pays to develop. When the business at hand seems at an end even though the meeting is not, start stacking your papers together, evening up the edges, the way news anchors do at the end of their broadcast. It's body language that says, "Well, nothing interesting is going to happen anymore in *this* room."

I hate it when I get sucked into an Hour Gobbler and have no work I can sneak into the meeting. I usually start writing jokes to myself to pass the time. In one meeting, I remember trying to make my buddy Bob Barrie laugh and instead blew my own cover. I started writing a joke: "Bob's List of Things to Do." I thought I'd just slip it under his nose. Try to crack him up. So I started scribbling:

BOB'S LIST OF THINGS TO DO:

1. Ointment on rash?
2. Rotate bricks under car in front yard.
3. Apologize to that kid's parents.
4. Wash blood out of clown suit.
5. Peek under scab.

When I wrote "Peek under scab," I did one of those bursting laugh-out-loud kind of explosions, and the whole room stopped thinking about Chicago and glared at me for an explanation. I simply had to fess up: "Hey, I'm sorry, I just thought of something funny, completely unrelated to these proceedings. I'm very sorry. Please continue."

But the image of Bob Barrie peeking under a knee scab finally did me in. I just collapsed, boneless, and had to excuse myself from the room.

But it got me out of the meeting.

Yet as much as I try to avoid meetings, all the really important stuff in this business ultimately happens in one meeting—the client presentation.

This is where all the hard work you've done lives or dies. And where the future audience of an idea is decided. Will it be billions of people seeing your TV commercial on the Super Bowl? Or the janitor who glances at the sad crumpled pieces of paper before cramming them into the garbage can?

It's an important meeting. Be prepared.

Figure 12.1 *In focus groups, bad things happen to your storyboards. Very bad things.*

12

Pecked to Death by Ducks

Presenting and protecting your work

ABOUT 20 PERCENT OF YOUR TIME IN the advertising business will be spent thinking up ads. Eighty percent will be spent protecting them. And 30 percent doing them over.

A screenwriter was looking out onto the parking lot in front of Universal Studios one day. It occurred to him, said this article, that every one of those cars was parked there by somebody who came to stop him from doing his movie.

The similarity to advertising is chilling. The elevator cables in your client's building will fairly groan hauling up all the people intent on killing your best stuff.

When word gets around the client offices that the agency is here to present, vice presidents and assistant vice presidents will appear out of the walls and storm the conference room like zombies in *Night of the Living Dead,* pounding on the door, hungry arms reaching in for the layouts, pleading, "Must kill. Must kill."

I have been in meetings where, after the last ad was presented, an eager young hatchet man raised his hand and asked his boss, "Can I be the first to say why I don't like it?"

I have been in meetings surrounded by so many vice presidents, I actually heard Custer whisper to me from the grave, "Man, I thought I had it bad. You guys are, like, *so* dead."

You will see ads killed in ways you didn't know things could be killed. You will see them eviscerated by blowhards bearing charts. You will see them garotted by quiet little men bearing agendas. A comment from a passing janitor will pick off ads like cans from a fence post and casual remarks by the chairman's wife will mow down whole campaigns like the first charge at Gallipoli.

Then there's the "friendly fire" to worry about. A stray memo from your agency's research department can send your campaign up in flaming foamcore. Your campaign can also be fragged by the ill-timed hallway remark of an angry coworker.

War widows received their telegrams from ashen-faced military chaplains. You, however, will look up from your desk to see an account executive, smiling.

"The client has some issues and concerns about your ideas."

This is how account executives announce the death of your labors: "issues and concerns."

To understand the portent of this phrase, picture the men lying on the floor of that Chicago garage on St. Valentine's Day. Al Capone had issues and concerns with these men.

I've had account executives beat around the bush for 15 minutes before they could tell me the bad news. "Well, we had a good meeting."

"Yes," you say, "but are the ads dead?"

"We learned a lot."

"But are they dead?"

"Well, . . . your campaign, it's . . . it's with Jesus now."

When you next see your ideas, they will be lying in state in the account executive's office. Maybe on the desk. Maybe down between the desk and the wall. (So thoughtless.) Maybe they'll bear crease wounds where they were crudely folded during the pitch team's hasty MedEvac under fire.

But you'll remember them the way they were. *("They look so . . . so natural.")* Say your good-byes. Try to think about the good times. Then walk away and start preparing for the next attack. I hear the drums.

What follows are some quixotic arguments that may help protect your loved ones in future battles. If you find any of them useful, I recommend you commit them to memory. Go into meetings armed and with the safety off. It's my experience that what a client decides in a meeting stays decided.

━━━━━━━

PRESENTING THE WORK

Learn the client's corporate culture.

Spend some serious time with the client. Talk to the quiet guy from R&D. Tell jokes with the product managers. The more they know you, the more they're going to trust you. The more they trust you, the more likely they are to buy these strange and disgusting things you call ideas.

But you're going to learn something about them, too. You're going to get a feel for the tone of this company. How far the executives will go. What they think is funny. You'll save yourself a lot of grief once you understand this. Remember, they see you as their brand ambassador. They're trusting you to accurately translate their corporate culture to the customer.

This doesn't mean doing the safe thing. It means if your client is a church, you probably shouldn't open your TV spot with that scene from *The Exorcist* where Linda Blair blow-chucks pea soup on the priest.

Present your own work.

Nobody knows it better than you. Nobody has more invested in it than you. And if you screw up, you have nobody to blame but you.

Two addenda: (1) If you are a truly awful presenter, don't. At least not the big campaigns. Better to have a skilled account person or creative director sell them. (2) Learn to present. It's a skill, and like any other skill, the more you do it the better you'll get. Start small. Sell a small-space newspaper campaign. Present to the account folks. Just do it. Creatives who can brilliantly present work go a lot further and make more money in this business than those who cannot. Not being able to present your own work (or the work of other people) will handicap you throughout your entire career. Pilots can't be afraid of heights. It just doesn't work.

Practice selling your campaign before you go in to present.

Don't just wing it. I used to think winging it was cool. But that was just bravado. As if my ideas were so good they didn't need no stinkin' presentation. Wrong. Practice it.

Don't memorize a speech for your presentation.

Trying to memorize written material will make you nervous. You'll worry you're going to forget something. Write out a speech if it helps you organize your thoughts, but toss it when you're done. All you need to do is establish what marks you have to hit along the way and then make sure you hit them. *("I need to make Points A, B, and C.")* Once you see the light go on in a client's eyes regarding A, move on to B.

Don't be slick. Clients hate slick.

You know all those unfair stereotyped images we sometimes have about clients? Uptight, overly rational, number-crunching politicians. They've got a similar set of incorrect images about us. Slick, unctuous, glad-handing, promise-them-anything sycophants. Is it fair? No. But that's the thing about stereotypes. You're a little behind before you even start. So don't be slick.

But if you're not slick, what should you be?

Be yourself. Be smart. Be crisp, be to the point, be agreeable. Don't be something you aren't. It never works. You will appear disingenuous, and so will your ideas.

Keep your "pre-ramble" to an absolute minimum. Start fast.

That doesn't mean start cold. It's likely you'll have to do some amount of setup. But make it crisp, to the point, and fast.

In a book on the art of good presentations called *I Can See You Naked,* author Ron Hoff said the first 90 seconds of any presentation are crucial. "Plunge into your subject. Let there be *no* doubt that the subject has been engaged."[1]

In those first 90 seconds, the client is unconsciously sizing you up, making initial impressions, and probably deciding prematurely whether or not they're going to like what you have to say. So don't wade into the water. Dive.

Don't hand out materials before you present.

Stay in command of the room. The minute you hand a piece of paper to a client, you're competing with that piece of paper. Clients are human and will want to read whatever it is you've just handed them. Don't hand out anything till the meeting is over. Remain in control of the room's attention.

Don't present your campaign as "risk-taking work." Clients hate that.

In the agency hallways, it's fine to talk about work being risk taking. But it's just about the worst thing you can say to product managers. They don't want risk. They want certainty. Whether certainty is possible in this business remains in doubt, but clients definitely do not need to hear the R word.

Find other ways to describe your campaign. For instance, "It goes against the grain," or "It's interesting; it's memorable." *Anything* is more palatable than risk to a client with his job on the line, a mortgage to pay, and two kids to put through reform school.

Okay, before we go on to the next paragraph, I just want to say that it is really good. I worked on it a long time and it may in fact be the best paragraph of this whole book. I think you're going to love it.

Before you unveil your stuff, don't assure the client that they're "going to love this."

This is known as leading with your chin. Somebody's gonna take a swipe at it just to keep you humble.

As they say in law school, don't ask a question you don't know the answer to.

Same thing in presentations. Anticipate every objection you can and have a persuasive answer in the chamber, locked and loaded.

If you're presenting print work, why not paste the ads into one of the magazines in which they'll be appearing?

If you've done it right and the ads avoid the visual clichés of your category, they should be head and shoulders above the clutter. You don't have to say, "Trust us." You can hand the magazine over to the client and say, "See for yourself."

Never show a client work you don't want them to buy.

I guarantee you, second-rate work is what clients will gravitate to.

The reasoning I have used to allow myself to present so-so ads goes like this: "Well, we gotta sell something to get this campaign going, and time is running out. So we'll present these five ideas, but we'll make sure they buy only these three great ones. The two so-so ones we'll include just to, you know, help us put on a good presentation. They'll be filler."

But what happens is, the client will approve the work they feel safer with, less scared by, and that is almost always the second-rate work.

Conversely, don't leave your best work on the floor at the agency.

"Oh, the client will never buy this." How do you know? The client may surprise you. Maybe not. But don't do the work for him. McElligott once told me, "Go as far as you can. Let the client bring you back."

At the presentation, don't just sit there.

No matter how right your campaign may feel to you, it's not going to magically fly through the client approval process. Even if the client appears to buy it out-right, sooner or later someone will start taking potshots. "Little changes" here and there, here and there.

You need to learn to be an articulate defender of your own work. Don't count on your account executive to do it. Don't leave it to your partner. Pay attention in the meeting. Try to understand exactly what might be bothering your client. And then take the initiative to either fix the problem to your satisfaction or come back with the most articulate defense you can.

As you form a defense, your first instincts may be to build a bridge from where you are to where your client is. *("If only I could get them to see how great these ads are.")* Instead, get over to where your client is and build a bridge back to your position. With such an attitude, your argument will be more empathetic and more persuasive. Because you are seeing the problem from your client's perspective.

Base your defense on strategy.

Your client is not sitting at his office right now twiddling his thumbs, waiting for you to bring in your campaign. A director of marketing for a consumer products company may spend as little as 5 percent of her time on advertising issues—the balance on manufacturing, distribution, financing, and product development. In fact, the managerial strengths that got her to the job position in the first place likely had nothing to do with her ability to judge advertising.

Keep this in mind when you go in to present: it isn't a client's job to know great work when they see it. They're generally numbers people.

Copywriter Dick Wasserman put it this way: "Corporate managers are inclined towards understatement. They value calm and quiet, abhor emotional displays, and do everything possible to make decisions in a dispassionate and objective manner. Advertising rubs them the wrong way. It is simply too much like show business for their taste."[2] I liken it to "Selling Invisible Poetry Machines to Scientists." They can't see the machines, they *sound* expensive, it all feels so magical and weird, and they're pretty sure they don't like poetry anyway.

To prevail with an audience like this, Alastair Crompton says, "Think like a creative person, but talk like an accountant."[3] Don't defend the work on emotional grounds or on the creativity of the execution. *("This visual is, I'm tellin' you; it's monstrous. It kills.")* Instead say, "This visual, as the focus groups bear out, communicates durability." Base your defense on strategy.

You must be able to strategically track, step by step, how you arrived at your campaign. That means having all the relevant product/market/consumer facts at your fingertips. There's no such thing as bulletproof, but your ads might be able to dodge a few rounds if you can keep the conversation on strategy alone. After all, that's something the client had a hand in authoring. It's a scary thing to do, but let the work's creativity speak for itself.

Buying creative work is hard. Cut your client some slack.

Before you get angry at a client for not immediately signing off on your brilliant idea, put yourself in his shoes. It's hard buying creative work.

In a subjective business where there are 30 "right" answers for every problem, deciding which ad to go with is, at best, a mix of business acumen, gut instinct, second-guessing, and a scarecrow in a cornfield pointing down two different yellow-brick roads.

Buying creative work is hard. Remember this the next time your work is on the table. Help your client by offering rational reasons to support what is essentially an emotional decision.

"They may be right."

According to ad legend, Bill Bernbach always carried a little note in his jacket pocket. A note he referred to whenever he was having a disagreement with a client. In small words, one sentence read, "They may be right."

Here's my advice, and it starts a few rungs further down the humility ladder: always enter into any discussion (with clients, account executives, anybody) with the belief that there is a 50 percent chance that you are wrong. I mean, really believe in your heart that you could be wrong.

I think that such a belief adds a strong underpinning of persuasiveness to your argument. To listeners, it doesn't feel like you're forcing your opinion on them.

I often think it's analogous the two kinds of ministers I've seen. The quiet and anonymous minister at a small church who invites me to explore his faith. And the noisy kind I see on TV, sweaty and red-faced, telling me the skin's going to bubble off my soul in hell if I don't repent now.

Which one is more persuasive to you?

Listening doesn't mean saying "yes."

Listen, even when you don't want to. It doesn't cost you anything to listen. It's polite. And even if you think you disagree, by listening you may gather information you can later use to put together a more persuasive argument. (As they say: "Diplomacy is the art of saying 'nice doggie' long enough to find a big rock.")

I think our culture portrays passive postures (such as listening) as losing postures. But I think listening can help you kick butt. Relax. Breathe from your stomach. Listen.

You do not have to solve the problem in the meeting.

When a client asks you to make a change, you aren't required to either fix it or refute it right there in the meeting. Be like that repair guy you see in the movies. Blow your nose, scratch yourself, and say, "Well, looks like I gotta take 'er back to the shop."

Seriously. It's tempting to want to alleviate client concerns by fixing something on the fly right there in the presentation. If it's an easy and obvious one, well, go ahead. But resist the temptation to do any major work there in the room.

Listen. Note their concerns. Play the concerns back to them so you know you have it right and they know you heard them. And then say, "Let us come back again and show you how this can work."

In *The Creative Companion,* David Fowler put it this way:

> [For] now, listen to the input you've received and solve the problem on the terms you've been given. Your anger is beside the point right now. Once you've proven you're a trooper by returning with thinking that follows the input, you can bring up your original idea again. It may get a better hearing the second time. Then again, it may have been a monkey [of an idea] all along. Or, most likely, you'll have forgotten all about it, because you're onto something better.[4]

Choose your battles carefully.

No matter how carefully you prepare your work, no matter how impeccable you are about covering every base, crossing every "t," dotting every "i," the red pencil's gonna come out. Clients are going to mess with your visual and change your copy.

H. G. Wells wrote, "No passion in the world is equal to the passion to alter someone's draft."

We need to pause here for a minute so I can make this point as clear to you as I am able. It's an important one.

Millions of years of evolution have wired a network of biological certainties into the human organism. There is the need to eat. There is the need to sleep. And then, right before the need to procreate, is the client need to change every ad his agency shows him. This need is spinal. Nothing you can do or say, no facts you lay down, no prayers you send up, will stop a client from diddling with your concept. It's something you need to accept as reality as early in your career as you can.

It didn't start with you, and it'll still be going on the day some Detroit agency presents its campaign for the new antigravity cars. The fact is, we're in a subjective industry—partly business and partly art. Everybody is going to have an opinion. It's just that the clients have paid for the right to have their opinion. Advertising, ultimately, is a service industry.

Consider the drawing reprinted in Figure 12.2 of a client making changes to an ad as a frustrated copywriter looks on. I found it in a book called *Confessions of a Copywriter* (published in 1930 by the Dartnell Corporation). That date again—1930.

They were doing it then, and I suspect they've been doing it since earliest recorded history. I have this image of a client in Egypt, 3,000 years before Christ, looking at some hieroglyphs on the walls of the pyramids, saying, "I think instead of "𐤀𐤀𐤀𐤀𐤀𐤀" we should say, "𐤀𐤀𐤀𐤀𐤀𐤀.""

Get used to it. Even some of the writing on this page about rewriting was rewritten by my publisher's editor. Nothing is safe.

I say, if they want to mess around with your body copy, let them. If they want to change the colors from red to green, let them. Any hieroglyphs they want to change, let 'em. Protect the *pyramid*. If you get out of there with the big idea intact, consider yourself a genius.

Tom Monahan says, "[Squabbling over body copy and other details is] not where the advertising battles are won. Ideas—big, differentiating, selling ideas—are what win. And anything that takes away even an ounce of energy from the creating or selling of those ideas is misdirected effort."[5]

The moral: Don't win every battle and lose the war.

RESEARCH: BE AFRAID. BE VERY AFRAID.

Research isn't science.

Here's how advertising works: You toil for weeks to come up with a perfect solution to your client's problem. Then your campaign is taken to an anonymous building on the outskirts of town and shown to a focus group—people who've been stopped on the street the previous week, identified as target customers, and paid a small amount of money for their opinion.

After a long day working at their jobs, these tired pedestrians arrive at the research facility and are led into a small room without windows or hope. In this

*Figure 12.2 Except for the clothes, this 1930 engraving of a client changing
a writer's copy looks like it could have happened yesterday.*

© Reprinted with permission of Dartnell Corporation.

barren, forlorn little box, they are shown your work in its embryonic, half-formed state while you and the client watch through a two-way mirror.

Here's the amazing part. These people all turn out to be advertising experts with piercing insights on why every ad shown them should be force-fed into the nearest shredder fast enough to choke the chopping blades.

Yet, who can blame them? They've been watching TV since they were kids and have been bored by a hundred thousand hours of very, very bad commercials. Now it's payback time, Mr. Madison Avenue Goatee Man. And because they're seeing mere storyboards they think, wow, we get to kill the beast *and* crush its eggs.

Meanwhile, in the room behind the mirror, the client turns to you and says, "Looks like you're workin' the weekend, idea boy."

Welcome to advertising.

A committee, it has been said, is a cul-de-sac down which ideas are lured and quietly strangled. The same can be said for the committee's cousin, the focus group. But this research process, however wildly capricious and unscientific, is here to stay.

Clients are used to testing. They test their products. They test locations for their stores. They test the new flavor, the packaging, and the name on the top. And much of this testing pays off. So don't think they're going to spend a couple of million dollars airing a commercial based solely on your sage advice: "Hey, business dudes, I think this spot rocks."

Used correctly, research is great. What better way is there to get inside the customer's head and find out what people like and don't like, to understand how they live? The thing is, the good research isn't done in those beige suburban buildings, but right downtown in the bars, asking drinkers about their favorite booze, asking shoppers how they choose a product, eavesdropping on real people as they talk about a category or a brand.

Of course, there's another place you can hear all this conversation. This marvelous place with reams of up-to-the-minute real-time research and customer verbatims is all free. In Pete Barry's *The Advertising Concept Book,* Mike Troiano of Holland Mark Digital, reveals a secret: "Introduce your clients to better, faster, cheaper and more reliable feedback about their category, brand and competition. Let them know they can ask questions and get instant answers. Or listen in on ongoing conversations. Eventually you may have to tell them it's called Twitter and Facebook, but what's the rush?"

The thing is, the best people in the business use research to generate ideas, not to judge them. They use it at the beginning of the whole advertising process to find out what to say. When it's used to determine how to say it, great ideas suffer horribly. Should your work suffer at the hands of a focus group, and it will, there isn't much you can do except appeal to the better angels of your client's nature.

What follows are some arguments against the reading of sheep entrails. Or the subjective "science" of copy testing.

Testing storyboards doesn't work.

Testing, by its very nature, looks for what is wrong with a commercial, not what is right. Look hard enough for something wrong and you'll sure enough find it. (I could stare at a picture of Miss November and in a half hour I'd start to notice, is that some broccoli in her teeth? Look, right there between the lateral incisor and left canine, see?)

Testing assumes that people react intellectually to commercials, that people watching TV in their living rooms dissect and analyze these interruptions of their sitcoms. *("Honey, come in here. I think these TV people are forwarding an argument that doesn't track logically. Bring a pen and paper.")* In reality, both you and I know their reactions are visceral and instantaneous.

Testing is inaccurate because storyboards don't have the magic of finished commercials. Would a focus group approve this copy had it just been read to them? "Chestnuts roasting on an open fire. Jack Frost nipping at your nose." Probably not. I can just see a focus group member putting down his doughnut to protest: *"I hate those chestnut things. And also, who wants to sing about wind chill? Can't the song be about something happy?"* But despite the lyrics, generations of people love this song.

Testing is inaccurate because customers simply do not know what they'll like until they see it out in the world. It's like what William Goldman said about movies and Hollywood: "Nobody knows what works." If we did, every movie would be a blockbuster.

Testing rewards commercials that are vague and fuzzy because vague and fuzzy doesn't challenge the viewer.

Testing rewards commercials that are derivative because commercials that have a familiar feel score better than commercials that are unique, strange, odd, or new. The very qualities that can lift a finished commercial above the television clutter.

If tone is important to a client, testing is inaccurate because 12 colored pictures pasted to a board will never communicate tone like actual film footage, voice-over, and music.

Testing, no matter how well disguised, asks consumers to be advertising experts. And invariably they feel obligated to prove it.

Finally, testing assumes we really know what makes a commercial work and that it can be quantifiably analyzed. You can't. Not in my opinion. It's impossible to measure a live snake.

Bill Bernbach said, "We are so busy measuring public opinion, we forget we can mold it. We are so busy listening to statistics that we forget we can create them." This simple truth about advertising is lost the minute a focus group sits down to do its business. In those small rooms, the power of advertising to affect behavior is not only subverted, it's reversed. The dynamic of a commercial coming out of the television to consumers is replaced with consumers telling the commercial what to say.

I say, big deal if a group says your storyboard doesn't reflect their opinions. With a good director and a couple of airings on the right programs, their opinions may reflect your commercial's.

These arguments, for what they are worth, might come in handy someday, especially if you have a client who likes the commercial you propose, but has to defend poor test scores to a management committee.*

---

*For more information about the pitfalls of testing concepts, I refer you to Jon Steel's excellent book on planning, *Truth, Lies, and Advertising: The Art of Account Planning* (New York: John Wiley & Sons, 1998). In particular I direct you to Chapter 6, "Ten Housewives in Des Moines—The Perils of Researching Rough Creative Ideas."

Extensive research has proved that extensive research is often wrong.

From a book called *Radio Advertising* by Bob Schulberg, I bring this research study to your attention:

> J. Walter Thompson did recall studies on commercials that ran during a heavily-viewed mini-series, "The Winds of War." The survey showed that 19 percent of the respondents recalled Volkswagen commercials; 32 percent, Kodak; 32 percent, Prudential; 28 percent American Express; and 16 percent Mobil Oil. The catch is that none of these companies advertised on "The Winds of War."[6]

In the mid-1980s, research told management of the Coca-Cola Company that younger people preferred a sweeter, more Pepsi-like taste. Overlooking fierce customer loyalty to this century-old battleship of a brand, they reformulated Coca-Cola into New Coke, and in the process packed about $1 billion down a rat hole.

"We forget we can mold it."

Research people told writer Hal Riney that entering the wine cooler category was a big mistake. Seagram's and California Cooler had it locked up. Then Riney began running his Bartles & Jaymes commercials, and a year later his client had the number one wine cooler in America.

"We forget we can mold it."

Research people told writer Cliff Freeman when he was working on Wendy's hamburgers, "Under absolutely no circumstances run 'Where's the Beef?'" After it ran, sales shot up 25 percent for the year and Wendy's moved from fifth to third place in fast-food sales. The 20,000 newspaper articles lauding the commercial didn't hurt, either.

"We forget we can mold it."

And what some call the greatest campaign of the 20th century, Volkswagen—none of it was subjected to pretesting. The man who helped produce that Volkswagen campaign had a saying: "We are so busy measuring public opinion, we forget we can mold it."

Because focus groups can prove anything, do they prove anything?

British ad star Tim Delaney, in a famous article on the value of intuition, wrote:

> Have you noticed what happens when five agencies are competing for an account? They all come up with completely different strategies and ideas—and

yet, miraculously, each of them is able to prove, through objective research, that their solution is the right one. If nothing else does, this alone should devalue the currency of focus groups. . . . Researchers think that if you spend a lot of time analyzing a problem beforehand, it will bring you closer to the advertising solution. But the truth is, you only really begin to crack advertising problems as you get deeper and deeper into the writing. You just have to sit down and start writing on some kind of pretext—and that initiates the flow of ideas that eventually brings a solution. In [my] agency, we start writing as early as possible, before the researchers have done their analysis. And we usually find that the researchers are always trailing behind us, telling us things we've already thought of.[7]

The writing itself is the solution to the problem. It's in the writing itself that the answers appear, when you're in there getting your hands dirty mucking about in the mud of the client's marketing reality. The answers are right there in that place where there's direct contact between the patient and the doctor. And if the doctor has a question about how to proceed, whom would you want him to ask for advice? A focus group of grocers, lawyers, and cab drivers? Personally, I'd want it to be another *doctor*.

I have a friend who walks around the agency trying to find out if a concept he's done is any good. He keeps going around until the "It's cool" votes outnumber the "It sucks." Sometimes he doesn't get the answer he wants and keeps working.

You know what? In my opinion, it's the only pretesting that works. The agency hallway.

Science cannot breathe life into something. Dr. Frankenstein has already tried this.

David Ogilvy once said that research is often used the way a drunk uses a lamp-post: for support rather than illumination. It's research used to protect preconceived ideas, not to explore new ones.

Another way that research can be used poorly is what I call Permission Research. Permission Research happens when agencies show advertising concepts to customers and ask if they like them or not. *("Man, it would be really great if you guys all say you like this, 'cause then we can put it on TV. C'mon, whattaya say?")*

What's unfortunate about Permission Research is that it's often used by clients and agencies to validate terrible advertising. Yes, it all looks and sounds like science, but as prudent as such market inquiries appear on the surface, the argument is specious—because the very process of Permission Research and all its attendant consensus and compromise will grind the work into either vanilla or nonsense.

As an example of what the process of Permission Research can do, I cite an interesting and very funny study done in 1997 by a pair of Russian cultural anthropologists—Vitaly Komar and Alexander Melamid.[8] With tongue firmly planted in cheek, these two researchers set out to ask the public, "What makes for a perfect painting? What does a painting need to have in order for you to want to hang it in your home?"

They did massive amounts of research, hosting hundreds of focus groups all over the world. Their findings, meticulously prepared and double-checked with customers, were as follows: 88 percent of customers told them, "We like paintings that feature outdoor scenes." The color blue was preferred by 44 percent of respondents. "Having a famous person" in the painting got the thumbs-up from a full 50 percent. Fall was the preferred season. And animals! You gotta have some animals.

All this research was compiled, and an actual painting was commissioned. The final "art" that came out of the lab (to nobody's surprise) was very bad, as you can see in Figure 12.3.

The point? Research is best used to help craft a strategy, not an execution. As journalist William F. Buckley once observed, "You cannot paint the *Mona Lisa* by assigning one dab each to a thousand painters."

To end on a positive note? These research companies make money by selling fear to clients. But as advertising campaigns evolve out of traditional media and into forms that can't be presented to focus groups, this may change. They won't be able to "measure a live snake" and they'll begin to hold less sway over clients. Knock on wood.

Figure 12.3   Here's what happens when you ask customers to art-direct a painting. And yes, that's George Washington standing to the left of a modern-day family.

PROTECTING YOUR WORK.

Well, so much for research. If your concept manages to limp out of the focus groups alive, congratulations.

But even if your idea fares well in tests, if it's new and unusual the client is still likely to squirm. As the scientist W. I. Beveridge noted, the "human mind likes a strange idea as little as the body likes a strange protein and resists it with a similar energy."

Even if they like your idea, they'll begin suggesting "minor changes." The Chinese call this "the death of a thousand cuts." Minor changes kill great ads, very slowly and with incredible pain. By the time they've inflicted their thousandth minor change, both you and your ad will be begging for a swift bullet to the head.

Sometimes you're going to need to deliver that bullet yourself. If client changes have hurt your original idea, pull the trigger. You think it's hard to look at your "fixed" ad on a layout pad? Wait till you see it as a spread in *Time* magazine.

Over the years, I've heard clients bring up the same minor changes time and again. Here are a few of them.

Your client asks that you feature more than one product or benefit.

Clients often ask for an ad to tout their full line of fine products. Who can blame them? The page they're buying seems roomy enough to throw in five or six more things besides your snappy little idea, doesn't it? But full-line ads are effective only as magazine thickener, nothing else.

The reason is simple. Customers never go shopping for full lines of products. I don't. Do you? *("Honey, start the car. We're going to the mall to buy everything.")* Customers have specific needs. It stands to reason that ads addressing specific needs are more effective. There's that old saying, "The hunter who chases two rabbits catches neither."

Smart companies know this. Coca-Cola owns nearly 80 brands of soft drinks, but they've never run an ad for all of them with some catchall claim like, "Bubbly, sugar-based liquids in a variety of vastly different tastes for all your thirst needs."

So if your client says he has three important things to say, tell the account person that the client needs three ads.

If that doesn't work, perhaps you'll just have to convince your client that there's a certain part of the audience that he's just not going to reach. Filling his ad with extraneous claims or peripheral products may attract some of this fringe audience, but the dilution will be at the cost of the main audience he needs most.

It's this simple: you can't pound in a nail that's lying on its side.

Somebody says, "Negative approaches are wrong."

Well, you can start by pointing out that what he just said was negative but communicated his position quite respectably. But there are some other rebuttals you can try.

Take a look at the photograph reprinted in Figure 12.4. It's a very positive image, isn't it? There's happiness and cheerful camaraderie all around, and everybody's enjoying the client's fine product. It's also so boring I want to saw off my right foot just so I can feel something, feel anything.

It's boring because there is no tension in the picture. No question left unanswered. No story. No drama. And consequently, no interest.

Perhaps you could begin by explaining to your client that one of the basic tenets of drama (and we are indeed in the business of dramatizing the benefits of our clients' products) is conflict. The bad guy (competition) moseys into town, kicks open the saloon door, and Cowboy Bob (your client) looks up from his card game.

Conflict + drama = interest. Without it, you have no story to tell. No friction between the tire and the road. No beginning, middle, or end. And consequently, no interest.

"Humorists have always made trouble pay," said E. B. White.

"Humor is also a way of saying something serious," said T. S. Eliot.

The brutal truth is that people don't slow down to look at the highway; they slow down to look at the highway accident. Maybe we're ashamed to admit that, but trouble and conflict are always riveting.

Figure 12.4   Q: "Why can't you do something positive?" A: This is why.

The thing to remember about trouble and conflict in a commercial is this: as long as your client's product is ultimately portrayed in a positive light or is seen to solve a customer problem, the net takeaway is positive.

As Tom Monahan pointed out, "The true communication isn't what you say. It's what the receiver takes away."[9]

Here are some other arguments you might try on an intransigent client.

Remind your client that one of the biggest success stories in marketing textbooks is Federal Express, a tiny outfit in Memphis that became an international commodity. This company owes its success almost entirely to a series of television commercials featuring terrible conflict — things going wrong, packages arriving late, nitwits getting fired.

Tell your client about a small classified ad that ran in 1900. (This is another story stolen from Neil French.) The ad read: "Men wanted for Hazardous Journey. Small wages, bitter cold, long months of complete darkness, constant danger, safe return doubtful. Honor and recognition in case of success — Ernest Shackleton."

When the famous explorer placed this ad looking for fellow adventurers to trek with him in search of the South Pole, he received many responses. Should it instead have read, "Happy snow bunnies needed for Popsicle Party"? Probably not. It worked because readers were piqued by the honesty of the ad and the challenge of the imminent journey.

If that doesn't convince your client, try this one from copywriter Jim Durfee: "Would you call the following statement positive or negative: 'Don't step back or you'll fall off the cliff.'"

Negatives have power. Try writing the Ten Commandments positively. If you did, I bet it wouldn't all fit on two stone tablets. Negatives are a linguistic construction we're all familiar with, one we've been hearing since we were caught dangling the cat over the baby. They're neither good nor bad; they are merely an executional detail.

So try to keep your client from focusing on the details. It isn't the details customers remember anyway. If you look at most day-after testing results, you'll find that customers may not remember a single word of a commercial. Just the main idea and what's good about the product — which is all that matters.

Somebody says, "Our competitors could run that same ad!"

They'll usually go on to say, "If you cover up our logo, this could be the other guys' ad."

"We said it first" is the simple answer. "Their logo isn't down there. Yours is."

Sometimes clients need to be reminded that their product isn't substantially different from the competition's. All that may distinguish the two is the advertising you propose. Nothing else.

Your client needs to see that although there's no explicit claim in the ad different from what his competitor might be able to say, the ad and its execution have many implicit messages the client can call his own. Whether it's the strategy, the concept, the tone, or the look of the campaign—together, they are giving the client a personality like no other.

Don't force your hand, though. If you can get the client to find in his product a unique selling proposition, all the better. Agree to start over if any significant difference can be found.

If not, you need to get your client to see that execution can be content and that personality can be proprietary. They're called *preemptive claims*—claims any competitor could've made had they moved fast enough. Your client may see that it's simply a matter of which company's going to get first dibs on the ground staked out by your concept.

It comes down to "We were here first." Reebok could've said "Just Do It." Nike got there first.

They ask you to print the phone number in big, bold type.

Ask if they'd also like to have their number shouted in radio spots. Will people be more likely to call the number if we scream it at them? No? Then why do it in print?

If readers want your phone number after seeing the ad, they'll get it. From the ad, from the phone book, or from 411—somehow they'll get it.

Picture this: A woman (man) at a bar slides a folded matchbook across the mahogany and under your napkin. You open it and see a phone number. Are you more likely to call if the number is written in inch-thick numerals with a fat red crayon? Of course not.

Yes, the phone number should be in there, probably in the last sentence or maybe by the logo. But advise the client that transmogrifying the type so that you can needlessly shriek a phone number not only is desperate and without class but adds yet another element to a crowded space and can only hurt the effectiveness of an ad.

Somebody asks, "Why are you wasting 25 seconds of my TV spot entertaining people?"

Other ways clients ask this is, "Can we mention the product sooner?" Or "Can't we just get to the point?"

This is a client who mistakenly believes that people watch television to see his commercial. *("Honey, get in here! The commercial's almost on!")*

There is no entitlement to the customer's attention. It is earned.

And make no mistake, we're not starting from zero with customers. Thanks to Whipple, Snuggles, and Digger the dermatophyte nail fungus, we're starting at less than zero. There is a high wall around every customer. And every day another brick is added.

You need to get your client to see that those 25 seconds of "wasted" time in the commercial are his ticket through the gate. You're not welcome until customers like you. And they won't like you until they listen to you. And they won't listen to you if you open your pitch with bulleted copy points of your product's superiority.

To visit the door-to-door salesman analogy again, you can't just dispense with knocking on the door. Clients who say, "Let's lose all that entertainment stuff" are really saying, "Forget the introducing ourselves at the door. Forget that doorbell crap, too. In fact, let's just jimmy the lock with a brochure and barge into the kitchen with a fistful of facts. We'll *make* 'em listen."

You can't. You're not welcome until they like you.

Your client takes your concept literally.

This is a hard one.

Let's use one of Cliff Freeman's hilarious Little Caesars pizza spots as an example (Figure 12.5)—the ones featuring the famous "stretchy cheese." In these spots, goofy-looking customers pull slices of pizza out of the box and attempt to carry them away to their dining table. The cheese, connecting the slice with the pizza still in the box, stretches like a rubber band, snaps them back, usually causing some sort of cartoon injury along the way.

"Well, I don't know," says the client. "Our cheese doesn't really stretch that far. And if it never breaks, doesn't that mean it's kind of rubbery?"

Figure 12.5   Out in TV-Land, nobody ever wondered, "Gosh, if Little Caesars cheese stretches that much, doesn't that mean it's kind of rubbery? Let's go to Domino's instead."

The client is taking the storyboard literally. It would be pleasant if simply pointing that out would make the client say, "Oh, my mistake. By all means, produce the spots." This is known as a hallucination.

What the client needs is someone to shift his paradigm so that he can see the commercials as a TV viewer does and not as the product manager of a large corporation.

But first, back him up.

Is it agreed that the job of advertising is to *dramatize* the benefit of the product? (In this case, the extra helpings of cheese.) Not to show the benefit, but to dramatize the benefit? If showing the benefit is the goal, we need only picture someone holding a slice of pizza and saying, "Look at all this extra cheese. Now that's value." We could also throw our money down the middle hole of an outhouse and achieve the same effect, since no one will watch or remember Smiley Pizza Man.

So it's agreed that dramatizing the benefit is our goal?

"Yes, but the cheese never breaks," says the client. "Maybe the stretching part is funny, but rubbery cheese is no good. I'm telling you, I've been in food services for 15 years, and I've watched focus groups and heard customers say those very words."

Here's where the client needs to take a leap of faith. Take his hand. Lean out over the precipice and tell him this: "In TV-Land, the rules are different."

And jump.

The rules of acceptable logic are different in TV-Land. Not only do viewers know the rules are different, they expect them to be. If the rules aren't different, they might as well be watching the news. TV-Land is not reality. It is entertainment. Television is watched by tired people needing escape from reality.

In reality, cops don't catch the bad guy. In TV-Land, they do. In reality, coyotes kill roadrunners. In TV-Land, coyotes end up under the big Acme-brand anvil.

And while rubbery cheese isn't appetizing in reality, in TV-Land the comic device of stretchy cheese that's both rubbery and delicious is perfectly acceptable logic. The device, one the viewer tacitly knows is created for entertainment, transcends all reality-based concerns about edibility, leapfrogs all taste issues of rubbery/nonrubbery cheese, and lands with a big, welcome splash in the mind of the customer with its intended message—this pizza has lots of yummy cheese.

The rules are different in TV, but they're still rules. You must obey them as long as you wish to retain the attention of your audience. Stretchy cheese, rubber logic, and other dramatic devices are the accepted currency in TV-Land. They are the only way to communicate what is often a bland corporate message.

In fact, that rubbery cartoon cheese is a bland corporate message *("Our pizza has more cheese.")*, but one that's seen through the fun house prisms of TV-Land. At a certain level, all corporate messages that show up in TV-Land are bland because they weren't invited. In order to come to the table, the ante is entertainment.

But the chasm between the cool fluorescent lights of America's corporate meeting rooms and the play school colors of TV entertainment is deep and wide.

It takes a client who's either imaginative or brave to make the leap. Clearly, Little Caesars was both.

In a wonderful book for clients called *That's Our New Ad Campaign?* Dick Wasserman takes on this sticky issue:

> When [clients] evaluate advertising executions, they do not understand that consumers react to ads in a generalized, unanalytical, emotional way. . . . Consumers are much more imaginative than many advertisers are willing to give them credit for. Readers and viewers do not have to be led by the hand to understand what a client's advertising is getting at. All they need is a couple of key verbal and visual guideposts, and they are quite capable of filling in the blanks.[10]

Your client will be uncomfortable in TV-Land. Once you get back to the safety of the conference room, you need to convince him that the literal approach is actually riskier than obeying the wacky rules of TV. A literal approach, where you simply tell the client's story is, as Wasserman says, a speech; what viewers want is a play.

Your client may be agreeing with you at this point, but he's not going to like it. He's going to be like that one guy in every disaster movie, up to his knees in mud but still checking his hair in the mirror. He is out of his element.

Remind him his discomfort is natural. This isn't Wall Street. But it isn't Sesame Street either. It's the intersection — that place where the odd bedfellows of business and advertising meet. The corner of Art and Commerce.

Bill Bernbach was perhaps talking to this same kind of client when he said: "Is creativity some obscure, esoteric art form? Not on your life. It's the most practical thing a business[person] can employ."[11]

Your client says (as federal law requires), "Can you make the logo bigger?"

Clients are about their logos like guys are about their . . . you know.

They love talking about them. They love to look at them. They want you to look at them. They think the bigger they are, the more effective they are. And they try to sneak looks at other guys' logos when they can.

But as any woman will tell you, nobody cares.

Just the same, when you swagger into a client's boardroom with a full-page newspaper ad punctuated by a logo you could cover with a dime, fur's gonna fly.

I remember we had one client who called the agency, very angry. He had just seen an outdoor board our agency had done for his company, and he couldn't see the logo very well.

"Uh-oh," said the account executive who fielded the call. "Where did you see this billboard?"

From a plane.

The client was angry because he couldn't see his logo from a *plane* as it circled LaGuardia airport.

But let's back up a little. If it's agreed the ad successfully stops readers and engages them with an offer that intrigues, what do you suppose the readers will look for next? It's doubtful they'll look at the logo of some *other* ad. It's doubtful they'll take their attention off the leash and let it wander into the park like a stray dog. There's a dynamic involved here. The readers have just seen something they want. Where can they get it? The logo. Unless you're using a watermark, readers will almost certainly find it, no matter what its size.

"But why can't you just make it a little bigger? What does it hurt?"

It's a matter of taste. The Latin saying is *De gustibus non est disputandum.* "Taste cannot be disputed." But, forget Cicero; let's dispute.

In every ad there are explicit and implicit messages, both equally important. The explicit message is what the headline and visual are saying. But implicitly, the layout of the ad is sending many messages about the quality of the product, about the class, the demeanor, the personality of your client. They are all subtle. And although explicit messages can sometimes be adjusted with a wrench, implicit messages need an expert's touch.

Your client needs to know that the art director's decision to make the logo the size it is was arrived at after careful consideration of these implicit messages. Too much logo and the ad becomes a used-car salesman. Increase the size of the logo a little more and the lapels on his suit become wider; increase it again and the plaid of his coat becomes louder.

The biggest logo I've ever seen towered 20 stories over Times Square: a giant Prudential logo, easily 30 yards square. No sales message, no headline, just yards and yards of blue logo. When people look up and see this giant logo, what are they to do with the information? Would it be more relevant or more persuasive if it were 50 yards square? Ooooh, what if we made it *100* yards square?

Where is it written that large logos increase sales? When introducing yourself, do you say your name in a booming voice? "Hi, my name is

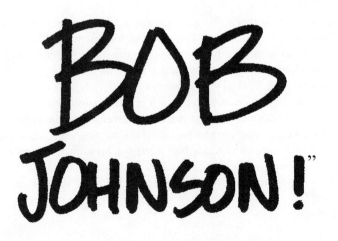

Do the large bottles of Coke with bigger logos sell faster than the cans? Are your business cards the size of welcome mats? If cattlemen heated immense brands and seared the entire sides of cows, would fewer be rustled?

Ads without any logos at all are often the most powerful. I know, clients aren't likely to buy this argument, but it's valid nevertheless. A logo says, "I'm an ad!" and an ad says, "Turn the page!" But an intriguing message without any logo to defuse it can be a riveting interruption to a magazine. It doesn't say, "This message brought to you by . . ." It says, "This message." Some of the most effective ads I've ever seen worked without the benefit of a logo. Three of them are in this book.

The reason they worked is that customers don't buy company logos. They buy benefits. If an ad successfully communicates benefit, logo size is relevant only in terms of quality of design, something best left to the art director's well-trained eye—his intuition.

Find a way to give the client a gentle reminder that this intangible thing, this intuition, is our business. Ask him if he would presume to tell his doctor what the diagnosis should be and what prescription to write. Or if he would instruct his lawyer in the nuances of contract law. I know I wouldn't.

I won't even tell the trashman not to lift the garbage can with his back. I figure he knows what he's doing.

Your client gets a few letters from "offended" customers and pulls the campaign.

Many clients worry that their ad may offend somebody, somewhere. And they begin yanking commercials off the air after they receive one or two phone calls about the commercial. Or they begin telling their ad agencies to write everything in such a way that not one soul in a country of 250 million will find a scintilla of impropriety.

This is advertising by fascism, pure and simple. The marketing plan to the many, overruled by the pious sensibilities of the few. It is a form of political correctness, which is itself a politically correct word for fascism. It may be Fascism Lite, but it's still book burning—only we're burning them one adjective, one headline, and one script at a time.

Don't give in. Tell the truth and run.

In the next ad you craft, say what you think is the right thing. Remember, your job is to sell the client's wares to as many people as you can. To appeal to the masses, not the minority. Tell the truth and run. And let the chronically offended pen their lugubrious letters. Let them whine.

The trick will be to get your client to see what a quark-size minority these Kleenex-dabbing, career whiners are. The way I put it: "The letter flooded in." Dude, it's a *letter,* not Omaha Beach.

I say: B-F-D. The letter flooded in. Fine. Even if it's a hundred letters, big deal. Smart clients know they'll get angry letters just for hanging out their shingle.

You build a factory; you get a letter. Sell a product; get a letter. I'll wager you could publish the cure for AIDS in tomorrow's paper and by Friday you'll get a missive scribbled in crayon on the back of a Burger King place mat from someone sniveling, "Why didn't you cure cancer *first?*"

Advise your client to run the ad. The world, amazingly, will not stop. In fact, 99.99 percent of the people who see the ad will somehow manage to get on with their lives. The other 0.01 percent will turn down the volume of whatever wrestling show they're watching and reach for the nearest number 10 envelope. Fine. Let them mewl.

To soften the ad in advance or pull the ad once it's run is to surrender your company's marketing to a consumer group you could fit in a phone booth—an angry clutch of stamp-licking busybodies with nothing better to do than go through magazines looking for imagined slights to their piety. Ask your client, "Do you want your company being run out of a church basement? Do you want to give every pursed-lipped, pen-wielding, moral policeman with a roll of stamps free rein to sit on your board of directors and dictate marketing plans?"

Tell your client these people are the minority. That's the fraction with the "1" above the line and the really *big* number on the bottom. And this is America. Where the Constitution says in so many big, fancy words, "What the majority says, goes."

Outlast the objections.

I hope that having one or two of these counterarguments tucked away in your quiver helps you save an ad one day. But the reality of this business is that sometimes nothing you can do or say is going to pull an ad out of the fire. If a client doesn't like it, it's going to die.

The reasons clients have for not liking an ad often defy analysis. I once saw a client kill an ad because it pictured a blue flyswatter. Why the client killed it, he wouldn't say. "Just consider it dead." When pressed for an explanation months later, he implied that he'd had a "bad experience" with a blue flyswatter as a child. The room grew quiet, and we changed the subject.

So get ready for it. It's gonna happen, and I wish I could tell you why. In a world full of all kinds of phobias (fear of germs, fear of spiders), there is no phobia of mediocrity.

All is not lost, though. You have one last weapon in your arsenal: persistence. I once read that the definition of success is simply getting up one more time than you fall.

To that end, I urge you to simply outlast the client. I don't mean digging in your heels, but rolling past his resistance like a stream around a rock. I once did 13 campaigns on one assignment for a very difficult client. Thirteen different campaigns over the period of a year, and each one was killed for increasingly irrational reasons. But each campaign we came back with was good.

They kept killing them, but they killed the campaign only 13 times. The thing is, we presented 14.

Remember who the enemy is.

Lest these last few pages give the impression I think the clients are the enemy, they're not. Remember, the enemy is your client's competition—the other guys across town with the crappy overpriced products. But like any marriage, there are going to be arguments with your client. Unlike marriage, in advertising you can actually win some.

PICKING UP THE PIECES.

There's always another ad.

Instead of fighting, here's another idea. After you come up with an idea, do what Mark Fenske told me. "Pat it on the rear and say 'Good luck, little buddy' and send it on its way." Mark believes you shouldn't make a career of protecting work. Alex Bogusky has said the same thing. He says the agency is an idea factory. "You don't like this one? Fine. We'll make more." Maybe they're right. In the end, perhaps the best way to work is this: come up with an idea and then walk away. There's going to be another opportunity to do a great ad tomorrow.

Don't lose vigilance when work is approved.

I find that when I have sold an ad I didn't think I'd ever sell, I become so happy I lose my critical faculties and blithely allow the ad to go off into production unescorted. I forget to keep sweating the details.

Moral: Don't fumble in the end zone.

Don't get depressed when work is killed.

The ads you come back with are usually better. And when you're feeling down in the dumps, remember that nothing gets you back on your feet faster than a great campaign.

Sometimes the playing field changes when a campaign is killed. For one thing, you know more now about what the client wants. Also, you'll probably be left with a shorter deadline. A curse, but a blessing, too. A time crunch may force a client to buy your next campaign. If the media's been bought, the client may *have* to buy your idea. So make it great.

A short deadline also has remarkable motivating properties. Someone once told me that the best amphetamine is a ticking clock.

If the client doesn't buy number two or three or four, hang in there. The highs in the business are very high and the lows very low. Learn not to take either one too seriously.

James Michener once observed, "Character consists of what you do on the third and fourth tries."

After you've totaled a car, you can still salvage stuff out of the trunk.

Okay, so the client killed everything. (I actually had an account executive come back from a meeting and say, "They approved the size of the ads!" Yaaaay.) But you know what? You can still get something out of the deal.

If you're part of the presentation, you can at least improve your relationship with the client. I don't think there's any client who actually enjoys killing work. Ask any creative director; it's easier to say yes and avoid the confrontation. The client knows you've worked hard on it. But remember, he's not completely without insight into what sells his product.

If you can take the loss like a professional and still sit there and be your same funny self and ask, "Okay, so what the hell do you want?" you can build rapport. The client's going to like you for it. And he's going to trust you more the second time around.

Even if your work is killed, produce it.

This is another piece of advice from Mark Fenske. If you're working at an agency where most of your stuff is fed to the Foamcore Furnace, you need to begin worrying now what you're going to show at your next interview. (*"Well, see, the client really sucked and made me do this one. . . . And this one, too. . . . Yeah, but I had this other idea, no really, you shoulda seen it, . . . Hey, why are we walking to the elevators?"*) If you can somehow get to tight layouts, even on the dead ads, at least you'll have something to show a prospective creative director what you're capable of.

If you're not producing agency work, do freelance.

This is dicey advice. Some agencies don't like it. They figured they invited you to the dance, so you should dance with them.

But you do have to watch out for yourself. You need to keep adding to your portfolio. So if you find yourself in an agency that's producing only meeting fodder, foamcore, and rewrites, maybe it's fair to flirt with a small client who needs a few ads. Just don't pin it up in the company break room.

Not only will doing the occasional freelance campaign keep your book fresh, it can keep your hopes alive and keep you excited about the possibilities of this business.

Keep a file of great dead ideas.

I've referred back to mine many times and have reanimated lots of old ideas, sometimes for the same client who originally killed them. I know many creative people who do all their writing in big, fat blank books that they put on the shelf when the books are full. Nothing gets thrown away. Except by clients.

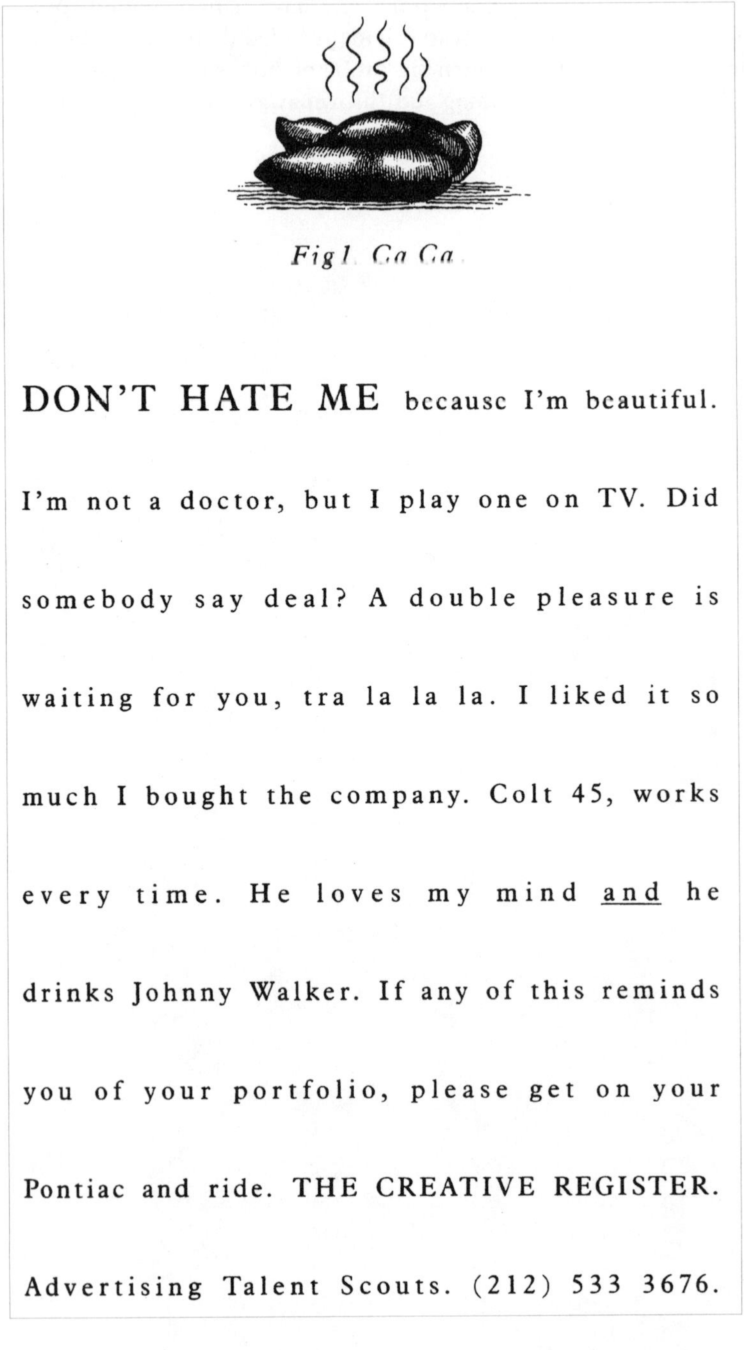

Fig 1. Ca Ca.

DON'T HATE ME because I'm beautiful.

I'm not a doctor, but I play one on TV. Did

somebody say deal? A double pleasure is

waiting for you, tra la la la. I liked it so

much I bought the company. Colt 45, works

every time. He loves my mind <u>and</u> he

drinks Johnny Walker. If any of this reminds

you of your portfolio, please get on your

Pontiac and ride. **THE CREATIVE REGISTER.**

Advertising Talent Scouts. (212) 533 3676.

Figure 13.1   A good portfolio should attract job offers, not flies.

13

A Good Book or a Crowbar

Some thoughts on getting into the business

GONE ARE THE DAYS WHEN JUNIORS were hired off the street because of a few promising scribbles on notebook paper and the fire in their eyes. The ad schools are pouring kids out onto the street, many of them with highly polished portfolios. Question is, should you go to one?

If you can afford tuition to an ad school, go.

When I got into the business, there were only a few such schools in the country. Now they're popping up all over. There's a list of some first-rate schools I include here, but the list will likely change by the time this book reaches your hands and will keep changing.

That said, as of this writing, the top-rated professional schools on my list are the Art Center College of Design in Pasadena, the Creative Circus in Atlanta, Miami Ad School (they've got campuses in a bunch of cool cities), NYC's School of Visual Arts, the University of Texas in Austin, Virginia Commonwealth University's Brandcenter in Richmond, and the Savannah School of Art & Design. (Full disclosure: Yours truly works at this latter fine institution.)

Up in Canada, my friends Nancy Vonk and Janet Kestin say they've seen good students come out of Ontario College of Art and Design. And in the

U.K., most people seem to like the Watford Course at West Herts College. Also well-respected there is University College Falmouth and Central St. Martins College of Art and Design. In Australia, check out the AWARD School as well as RMIT University; for New Zealanders, there are Axis/Media Design School, and Auckland University of Tech's communications course.

If you're more of the tech type, it's hard to beat Hyper Island (nestled in the Swedish town of Karlskrona). Here in the United States, our version of Hyper Island is Boulder Digital Works. I'm sure new digital schools will appear before this book goes to print. (Which is the main problem with all "papyrus-based" media; it takes time to print and to distribute it.)

Don't beat yourself up trying to decide which of these schools is the very best. They all offer various degrees, and they all rock. Find one where you like the vibe.

If you simply haven't got the money and can't attend a school, don't give up. You will have a much steeper hill to climb, undoubtedly, because you'll be competing with students who've set aside a year or two of their lives to fully concentrate on putting together a terrific portfolio. In the end, however, it all comes down to the work you can put together—your book.

To get a job in the creative side of this business, you will need a portfolio, or a book, as it's called—some eight to nine speculative campaigns you've put up online to show how you think. If you can put together that many great campaigns, the top graduate of the best school has nothing on you. On the other hand, if you're still pounding the pavement after a year with your homemade book, maybe it'll be time to think about enrolling in one of the creative schools. This is particularly true if you want to be an art director. Unlike copywriting, even junior art directors have to have certain graphic, production, and computer skills to get in the door.

Before you start, be ready for the possibility that you suck.

Writing and art direction, storytelling and information architecture, things like these? They're skills; they're crafts, something you can get good at with practice. As Mark Fenske told one of his classes: "This isn't brain surgery, people. Brain surgery can be learned."

I think he's right. When it comes to being truly creative, either you are or you aren't. I don't subscribe to the rah-rah cheers of corporate retreat leaders who insist, "We're *all* creative!!" No, we're not. Some of us suck at this stuff. The creative schools are aware of this fact, and after a few unproductive semesters, students who aren't cut out for the creative path will often be redirected by the schools. Many students figure this out for themselves along the way and, undeterred from agency life, go on to find fulfillment as agency strategists, media planners, and account people. Until you know for sure, keep all the doors open.

Once you decide to go for a creative career, give your portfolio everything. Your book will be the single most important piece you work on in your career. It is your foot in the door, your resume, your agent, your spokesperson, and a giant fork in the road to your eventual career. And like a good chess opening, the better it is, the more advantages you will discover through the rest of the game.

PUTTING TOGETHER A BOOK

Art director? Copywriter? Creative technologist? User-experience specialist? If you're not sure what you wanna be yet, that's okay.

You don't *have* to know right now. Many people enter the advertising field knowing only that they dig it. They like the creative vibe, the huge range of challenges and opportunities they see there. As you enter college or an ad school, it's okay to keep your options open for a while.

You may find yourself leaning toward art direction; or maybe it'll be digital design. Or you may become one of those hybrids we discussed in Chapter 5, what some call creative alchemists, others T-shaped people. That vertical line of the T? That's the one area where you'll bring some deep knowledge to the team, some polished skills. There's no room any more for "idea guys"—you know, those guys who gesture with finger guns while saying, "I just come up with the *ideas,* babe." Whatever area you choose, you will ultimately need to be able to *make* stuff. So get really good at something.

If you want to be a writer, team up with a promising art director.

And if you're an art director, find a writer you get along with. You need each other's skills, and together you will add up to more than the sum of your parts. More than anything, look for someone with energy, with drive. Someone who's hungry. It's a long, uphill battle putting a great book together, so you'll need all the firepower you can muster.

An art director can help the ads look great, and given the rise of the advertising schools out there, the way your work looks is getting more and more important—even if you aspire to be a copywriter. Books with good ideas that are poorly art-directed will simply not get the same attention from agencies. (And when you think about it, it's not any different from high school. The good-looking kids got all the attention with all their *cool* clothes and their *daddy's* car and . . . excuse me, I digress.) Bottom line: The competition is fierce. Look your best.

If you're a writer working alone, you can still pull it off . . . with a lot of work.

To see what you're up against without an art director (and to learn what you should at least shoot for), ask an agency recruiter or a helpful person at one of the professional ad schools to e-mail you some samples of their best student portfolios.

What you'll see will probably be daunting, but you have to remember that creative directors will *also* be looking for the quality of your ideas.

Here's the big piece of advice, and I don't care if you're on your own or at a top ad school. Technology is making it easier to put a nice finish on things; true.

*Figure 13.2   To make my point, I have redrawn this famous Nike ad
with my left hand, although I'm right-handed. A highly polished
layout of a so-so concept won't hold a candle to a great idea,
even one produced like this.*

But right now *you* need to spend most of your time making the concept great. Concept comes first; *then* work on execution.

Here's an example of a concept that's so good, even a bad drawing doesn't get in the way. I am right-handed. With my left hand, I have rendered a famous Nike ad from a British agency (Figure 13.2). The concept is still extraordinary.

Come up with monstrous ideas, not just monstrous ads.

My friend Mike Lear (teacher, friend, ACD at the Martin Agency) gives students this advice: "A book full of cool ads doesn't guarantee you a great job. A book full of brilliant thinking does."

The point is, when you sit down to work don't just "do an ad."

Do something big and marvelous and wonderful. Position a shoe company as environmentalists (as they did for Timberland). Reinvent the whole idea of driving (as they did for BMW's MINI). Improve the product (like they did by bringing iPod and running together in Nike+). Brilliant thinking has less to do with what's in some campaign than what's behind it—the thinking you do strategically, the brass-tacks business ideas you come up with that can move a brand forward.

It was brilliant business thinking that moved Vegas's tourism away from a me-too Disney strategy to the naughty idea that reversed their declining visitor counts—"What happens in Vegas, stays in Vegas." R&R Partners' simple and refreshingly honest idea was the engine for years of incredible advertising, one sample of which is the fabulous ad shown in Figure 13.3. A lint roller covered

Figure 13.3   The best advertising is true to the core of the product.
Few campaigns did this better than the advertising for Las Vegas.
"What happens in Vegas, stays in Vegas."

with naughty detritus like spangles, sequins, and false eyelashes brings to life the strong business idea underneath all of the Vegas work. The brilliant thinking came first. The brilliant ads, later.

Famous copywriter Ed McCabe once described the size of the ideas we're talking about here: "I'm not interested in day-after recall of ads. I'm interested in 10-year recall."

Come up with stuff that is *interesting*.

I remember interviewing this one kid for his first job. He'd just graduated from a good ad school, and as we clicked through his book he said, "I'm sorry there's not much advertising in there but . . ." and I interrupted him. "Dude, you had me at 'Sorry.'" There was, in fact, not a lot of advertising in his book. But it was filled with fascinating things, interesting content, and yes, pretty much everything except traditional advertising. And I loved it.

What a book needs isn't necessarily cool advertising. Just cool creative stuff. Yes, ultimately your work needs to have some sort of commercial aspect to it, has to report to some sort of purpose, some strategy . . . but the main thing is to show something cool, something interesting.

Think of it this way: there's no difference between a consumer going through all the ads in a magazine and a creative director looking at a whole bunch of books. They're both distracted, both a little tired, and to get this person's attention you've got to do something extraordinary.

Nobody expects your first portfolio to have TV or radio.

If you're new to the business, don't try to tackle TV or radio. Concentrate on everything else: online platforms, print campaigns, outdoor advertising, posters, point-of-purchase, mobile. That said, if you happen to have a mind-roastingly great TV idea, fine, put it in. Overall, though, it's better to address TV by including it as part of an integrated campaign; describe the spots in a sentence or two and throw in a key frame if the idea needs it.

Same with radio. You probably should avoid it but if you happen to have some monstrous idea (I mean, *monstrous*), include it.

If there's ever a time to study the awards annuals, this is it.

Study them. Read, learn, memorize. Don't just concentrate on the most recent issues, either. Dig up old annuals. Go online. Go to the ad blogs. Design fads come and go, but the classic advertising structures endure. See what makes the ads work. Take them apart. Put them back together. Some of the ads are humorous and work. Some are straight and work. Why? What's the difference?

One way to start is simply to redo some existing ads.

Page through *Time* magazine and look for a bad ad. You probably won't have to go past page three. Find the idea buried in the body copy, where it almost always is. Pull it back out and turn it into an ad.

Choose a website you like and do a campaign for it. Pick a state and do its tourism work.

Round out your portfolio with a variety of goods and services.

If you're just starting out, don't try to add to the latest, award-winning Nike campaign. It's tempting to do so, but you set yourself up for a harsh comparison to work that's extremely good.

Just pick some products you like. Start a file on them. Fill it with great ads from the awards annuals and bad ideas from the magazines or online. Start jotting down every little thing that feels like an idea. Don't edit. Just start. You like mountain biking? Maybe do a campaign that pitches the sport to joggers. Now find two other things you like and do two campaigns there.

Then it's time to choose some boring products—products without any differences that distinguish them (besides the ads you're about to do). Insurance. Banking. You figure it out. But find a way to make them interesting.

You might try writing ads for a product you've never used and likely never will. If you're a guy, write subscription ads for *Brides* magazine. The fresh mind you bring to the category may help your concepts ring new.

And, finally, take a shot at a campaign for a packaged good. Like lipstick, soup, or bouillon cubes. But don't touch Hot Wheels toy cars or Tabasco sauce. Everybody in the space-time continuum is doing ads on these. Also, I implore you, please, no pee-pee jokes, potty humor, and for the love of God, no condoms. All of these things have been done to death. You won't just be beating a dead horse. You'll be beating the dust from the crumbling rocks of the fossilized bones of an extinct species of pre-horse crushed between two glaciers in the Precambrian Age.

To get you started on the kind of products that might make for a good student book, I provide the following list. It's by no means definitive, just stuff I've seen over the years.

Nicorette	A bookstore
The local newspaper	Tiffany & Co.
Lasik Eye Centers	Sealy mattresses
Prudential Insurance	Scope
BlackBerry	24 Hour Fitness

A wine	A deodorant
Tupperware	Silent Air purifier
A major airline	Marshall's
Trash bags	La-Z-Boy recliners
Domino Sugar	Sherwin-Williams
Fidelity Investments	Snapple
AARP	NASDAQ
Brawny towels	A laundry detergent
Polaris snowmobiles	Hampton Inns
Frye boots	Home Depot
Samsonite	Church's Chicken

When you're done, your book should show the ability to think creatively and strategically on goods and services, both hard and soft. It should show conceptual muscle, tech savvy, a unique point of view, and some range.

One last thing. Avoid public service campaigns. They're too easy. *("Hey, look at these fish I caught. Sorry the holes in their heads are so big, but they were at the bottom of a barrel when I shot them.")*

Now is not the time to play it safe.

As you put your book together, err on the side of recklessness. It's the one time in your career you get to pick the client and write the strategy. If you're not pushing it to the edge now, when are you going to start? A junior book should be the most fun thing a recruiter gets to look at all day, just for the reasons listed. It's not real, so live a little. It's better to have stuff that's fresh and strategically naive than a nice, sensible portfolio of ads so dull you laminate them mostly to cut down on the smell.

Nor is this the time to be clueless and naive.

Don't fill your book with outrageous ads that have no chance of ever running.

Swearwords in the headlines, pee-pee jokes, stuff like that is all fine and dandy when you're working with your partner, telling jokes, and messing around. But when you actually include stuff like this in your book, what it says about you isn't flattering. *("Hello, I'm a clueless young creative. My work is 'edgy' and 'provocative,' and I think putting a sanitary-pad belt on the real Statue of Liberty would be a cool outdoor idea for Tampax.")*

Do stuff that actually has a chance of running.

Fill your portfolio with campaigns, not one-shots.

Almost anybody can write a decent headline if they work at it long enough. Skilled ad people think in campaigns. Don't send your book out until it has eight or nine great campaigns in it. And remember, the best campaigns aren't three one-shots strung together by a common typeface, but one big idea executed across a whole bunch of different media. The Skittles, truth®, and BMW MINI campaigns are good examples.

If you have a couple of great one-shots, go ahead, throw 'em in. But they should be icing. Not the cake.

Don't fill your portfolio with cute campaigns for microscopic clients.

A book full of ads for the local bakery, your brother's auto shop, and the dry cleaner will not be impressive. You need to do ads for checking accounts, newspaper subscriptions, a brand of clothing, a cologne. Real stuff.

These are the tough day-to-day projects you'll actually be working on most of the time in this business. Ads on products like these are a better measure of your abilities than dashing off a zippy headline for portable toilets or an acupuncture parlor.

Jamie, my agency recruiter friend, told me: "My favorite books are the good ones that come from shops with crappy clients. If a person can make something good from some of the godawful products I see . . . that, my friend, is someone with brains and drive."

My friend Bob Barrie concurs: "Do great ads for boring products."

If you're looking to land a copywriter's position, show some writing, for pete's sake.

Visual solutions are all the rage. Fine, do some. But as a junior copywriter in an agency, your first 500 assignments are all likely to be writing headlines for some airline's 500 destinations or a telco's 500 calling plans. So show me you can write. Show me some muscular, intelligent headlines. In *Breaking In,* creative director Pat McKay says, "It's good to have . . . a headline campaign. I want to see if [you] can spit out great headlines, crystallized clever distillations of the main idea."[1] For a reminder of what crystallized clever distillations look like, revisit the *Economist* work in Chapter 4.

Short bursts of brilliance in headlines is good, but show me you can write something longer. A long-copy ad, some digital content, or a brand manifesto—it doesn't matter, as long as it's substantial, intelligent, and well put together.

Remember that Land Rover ad in Chapter 3 (Figure 3.18)? That's a great example of a long-copy ad. Will your prospective employers read every word? Probably not. But have it in there.

In addition to having a variety of clients, make sure you show a variety of styles in your book.

Not all ads, not all websites, not all headlines, not all visuals, but a good mix of everything you're capable of. This advice applies particularly to aspiring art directors. Show ads that demonstrate your ability to handle type and ads that are all visual, ads that are all headline, ads with a lot of stuff in them that require a good sense of design. Flex a lot of muscles. The same advice applies to writers. Show a range of voice. I've seen books written entirely in one wiseass voice, and the only brand that comes through is the writer's.

Let me repeat: flex a lot of muscles.

In the past couple of years, 90 percent of the student portfolios that I've seen are made up almost entirely of visual solutions. A visual solution is fine; I've been harping about them in this book, yes. But they're not the only solution out there. I see so many of these ads now that it's getting to feel a little formulaic. (This trend, I'm guessing, is driven by the predominance of visual solutions currently filling the awards annuals.)

A book full of visual solutions will not show your prospective employer how good a designer you are. How could it? The typical visual-solution ad is a photograph with a teeny copy line down next to the logo.

So, show off. Do a long-copy ad. Do one that's all type. Dazzle us with your art direction. Show us you know how to handle headlines and body copy. Show us you know how to bend those 26 letters to your will and make them hop through any hoop you hold, no matter how high. Show us you know how to assemble a page that is blazing with the craft of design.

The ad shown in Figure 13.4 for North Carolina's tourism commission from Loeffler Ketchum Mountjoy is an example of excellent craft. (The reprint here doesn't do it justice. You can see a nice printed version in *Communication Arts* #38, page 46, and other North Carolina Tourism ads online.)

Remember, as an art director your job isn't over when you come up with the concept; it begins all over again. And it's at this phase that you have a chance to move a great concept into the orbit of perfection with a booster push of amazing design and execution. You probably won't get into this orbit with a book full of picture ads with teeny lines down by the logo.

Don't show just ads. Show cool, big-ass ideas executed in a lot of different media.

This is where the big brands play. It's the stage on which big ideas can best show their stuff. It's what clients are asking for. And it's pretty much *all* that creative

Figure 13.4   There is attention to detail, graceful design, and craftsmanship evident in this marvelous ad for North Carolina. As an art director, you should have work like this in your portfolio.

directors are looking for in student books these days. It's all that stuff we talked about in Chapter 6, the big honkin' ideas.

So, as you begin to build your first workable portfolio, you're gonna need to create an impressive lineup of media-infinite ideas and put them through their paces.

Keep in mind that the same idea sized to fit newspaper, then outdoor, then online, is not a campaign. In fact, that's where the word *brochure-ware* comes from, trying to drag a print-based idea kicking and screaming into the digital space — by the time it gets there, it's dead anyway. Nope. You need to show us how muscular and flexible your core idea is with different executions across a *variety* of media, with the executions in each medium that surprise and delight by leveraging that medium's core strengths. Could your print campaign extend to the side of a coffee cup? Could it be an environmental installation and website combination? Can your mobile app be activated by your outdoor concepts? Could you write something on a Post-it Note that, applied to a lamppost, becomes a cool idea? How would your idea work as a handout at a trade show? As a place mat? A receipt?

Remember, this isn't a nice-to-have. It's a must-have.

Put a short three-sentence setup in front of each campaign.

It helps the person assessing your book to know what he is looking at, to have some context. So set up each campaign with a dedicated page that quickly spells out the business challenge and describes your main idea. Don't just bang this copy out. This is writing. It needs to be done carefully. Smartly.

Think about the order in which you want your work to appear in the book.

My advice: Start strong; end strong. Put your very best campaign first. Right on page 1. How you open can affect how the person reading it sees the rest of your work. Put your next-strongest campaign at the end. And in between, vary the styles and the emotions. Funny, serious, sexy, funny, serious . . . just keep the flow moving along.

Just before you put the final book together, get out a big knife and cut everything that isn't great.

Novelist Elmore Leonard had this great line that went, "I try to leave out the parts people skip." That's good advice about writing as well as for assembling your final book. But it's hard advice to follow. All of those creations are your babies, I know, but some of your babies might be ugly. Thin the herd. If you have doubts about something, cut it, because leaving even one bad piece in your book makes a creative director doubt your judgment. It's weird, but people often judge you based on the weakest work in your book, not the strongest.

There's another reason to pare the book a bit. If a pared-down book you've sent an agency lands you an interview, you'll have something new to show once you're face-to-face. Perhaps the best candidates to leave out are any one-shots you have or perhaps a campaign from the middle of the book.

One more note on the phrase "final book"—it will never be final. The day you get your first job you begin working to replace all your student work. Then you work to replace all good campaigns with award-winning campaigns. And so on and so on. Because good enough isn't.

Real work that's actually been produced is not a good enough reason to put something in your book.

It also has to be great. Yes, it's good that you've had some real-world experience. It's good that you've tackled some real-world problems. Mention this experience in your interview, but if the work isn't great, don't put it in.

Make your own website.

This is a no-brainer and a must-have.

When you use one of the online portfolio showcases, it's easy to do, easy to update, and amazingly cheap. There are some free services; some cost money. If you create your own site, all the better. Just make sure it's easy to navigate and that the load times are minimal or nonexistent. There's nothing wrong either with just putting all your work up on one long scroll with the option to download it as one big-ass PDF.

Say up front whether you're a writer or art director or whatever. And please, don't forget to put your phone number and e-mail address all over the place. There are kids I have wanted to hire, *tried* to hire, but couldn't get ahold of them because of this oversight.

And as for the design, the same rules apply to your website as to all the work you're putting in it. Don't get hung up in the presentation. Just showcase your ideas and get out of the way. The work is everything.

If you're going to make mini-books, make sure that reading them doesn't require tweezers.

A mini-book is a portable portfolio, and having a bunch of them around during your job search is a good idea. Typically, the work is sized down to an 8½-by-11-inch format to make it inexpensive and something you can pop in the mail. Their main purpose in life is usually as leave-behinds for interviews, but they've also been known to save the day when your computer fails.

Oh, and be careful not to make the work too small, in both your book and your site. The rule is, don't make me work to see your awesomeness.

Don't do "clever" mailers.

It's tempting to demonstrate your creativity this way. But don't. I've seen the weirdest things sent to the agency. A foot from a department store dummy in a box topped with the expected line: "I'd love to get my foot in the door of your agency." I saw about 20 of those. One guy tiptoed into the mail room and sat inside a Federal Express box. And in the creepy category, I note an Igloo cooler that arrived with a label stating "creative brain inside." I also remember getting an envelope stuffed with "bloody" bandages with some message about how "I'd kill to work at your agency."

Don't do a clever mailer. I've never seen anything as clever as a good portfolio.

Don't do a cute resume.

Your portfolio is where you should showcase your creativity. Your resume should say who you are. Keep it to one page and get right to the point. This is my name. I'm a writer, or I'm an art director. This is the job I want. Here's my experience, my address, and my phone number. Thank you and good night.

E-mailing, or dropping your book off at the agency, isn't enough.

This is a people business.

Although there may be a small sense of accomplishment in securing a name and sending your book off to one of your target agencies, don't check that agency off your list, lean back at the pool, and wait for the phone call. You need to get in there. You need to follow up with phone calls, letters, e-mails. You need an interview. It's rare that a dropped-off book results in a phone call.

This is a people business. Although the ante to the game is a great book, the winning hand is a great interview where you impress the person who actually has the job opening.

If you're just beginning, don't count on a headhunter to find you a job.

Typically, headhunters work with midlevel to senior positions that have higher salary potential. (They make their money on a percentage of the salary.) In addition, most agencies don't want to pay recruiters' fees to fill entry-level jobs when they're getting all the applicants they can handle walking in off the street.

Just the same, you may decide you want to use a creative recruiter to supplement your search. Fine. They're great people to get to know in this business, and, who knows, if they can't place you now, they could be of great help down the road. Keep in touch with them. It's called networking.

"Networking."

I swore I'd never use the word as a verb, but nothing else seems to fit here. If you don't have relatives working in the business, networking's precisely the thing you'll have to do. You'll have to send out feelers far and wide. Obviously, the social Web is where you'll do much of this work. Use all the platforms and don't be shy. LinkedIn, Facebook, Twitter—they all have their strengths; leverage them all.

Tell every living person you know you're trying to land a job at an ad agency. You may find that the friend of a friend has a name. And a name is all you need to start building your contacts.

So you ask around and get a name. Maybe this person doesn't even work in the creative department. It doesn't matter—you call. Even if the company is not hiring, you ask for an "information interview" or for a little advice on your book.

When you meet this person, be your usual charming self. Listen more than you talk, and before you leave, ask if he knows of job openings anywhere. Or simply get the name of another contact. Ask if you can use your interviewer's name to land another interview somewhere. Keep this up and over time you'll slowly build a list of names, numbers, and contacts. One day the phone will ring.

Establish a phone or mail relationship with a working writer or art director.

There are plenty of friendly and helpful people in the business who will be willing to coach you along. The trick is finding one.

Take a risk. Write a letter to somebody whose work you admire. Or call 'im. (Call before 9 AM or after 6 PM. It's less crazy then.) Tell him you really like the stuff his company does. No brownnosing. Just matter-of-factly. Tell him you're trying to get into the business and ask if he could take a look at your work and give you advice on how to improve it.

Once you get a dialog going, there are two important things to do. One, take the advice you get. And two, don't stalk the person. Keep a respectful distance. Don't call more than once or twice. If somebody doesn't return your call after three tries, take the hint—stop calling, at least for six months or so. And get back to the person only when you've significantly improved your book.

Get a cell phone.

And when you go on the road for interviews, bring something to read.

————————

THE INTERVIEW.

Before each interview, study the agency.

It's probably smart to begin your search by looking closely at the agencies that are doing work compatible with your style.

Get online and familiarize yourself with their best work. Memorize the names of their top clients. Google the people who created their best work and check to make sure they still work there. Of course, none of this is for the purposes of brownnosing. *("Gee, Mr. Alexander, I thought your work for Spray 'N' Wipe was so meaningful.")* It'll simply help you be able to ask smart and relevant questions. It'll also show you're a student of the business and that you're serious enough about getting into it that you've done your homework.

Avoid the rush at the front door. Try the side door, or even a window.

Many agencies now employ creative recruiters. These people are generally not writers or art directors, just folks with a decent sense of what makes for a good portfolio. As good as some of them are, try to get your book into the agency somewhere over their head. If you can do so, you stand a better chance because you're removing a layer of approval. Yes, it's good to get to know the names of the recruiters in your target agencies. Keep their names in your address book, but don't limit your calls only to them.

If you can't get in to see the general, talk to a lieutenant.

You don't have to get an interview with the creative director to get your foot in the door at an agency. If you have a great book, see if you can get 15 minutes of time with a senior creative person. This person will know when the agency is hiring, even if he's not the one doing it. If he likes you, it's relatively easy for him to slide your name under the creative director's nose at the right moment.

If you come on board and do great work, it reflects well on him. I've helped several juniors get on board and have watched with some measure of undeserved pride when a kid "I discovered" does well.

It may happen for you this way. If it does, someday maybe you can return the favor to a kid who comes into your office with a bad hair and a great book. Take the time to help. We're all in this together.

In the interview, don't just sit there.

I don't care how good your book is, you can't just throw it on a creative director's desk, park yourself on his sofa, and wait to discuss company health plans and vacation time. You must make it clear you have a pulse. Advertising is a business that requires a lot of people skills, and it will help if the creative director sees you have them—that you're personable, that you can handle a business meeting with verve and confidence, and that generally you aren't a stick-in-the-mud.

One famous creative director I know is more interested in your hobbies than anything else. "They tell me a lot about you." And Andy Berlin once confided to a recruiter that hiring sometimes comes down to chemistry. "A lot of people could probably do this job," he said, "but what it's really about is . . . who would we wanna go have a beer with?"

Also, it's probably not a bad idea to bring a notebook along. It says you're there to listen.

Have an opinion.

This is another version of "Trust your instincts."

If the interviewer asks you what kind of advertising you like or what campaigns you wish you had done (and many do), don't be afraid to have an opinion. Say what current or classic campaigns you like and describe why. It's a subjective business, and unless you pick Mr. Whipple as your dream campaign, you'll probably do fine.

What's bad is having no opinion at all. "Oh, I like . . . well, I like whatever's good is what I like."

Don't explain your book.

When you are finally in the creative director's office and watching her page through your book, resist the temptation to explain anything (unless, of course, you've actually been asked a question). I know it's tempting to explain. You'll want to set up what a certain assignment was or how you had this "way better" idea that was killed.

Don't.

The fact of the matter is this: you won't get a chance to explain your ad to a person who sees it in *Time* magazine at the airport. *("Excuse me, I see you're reading that ad for the new Toyota Camry. If you'll allow me to explain, basically those blur lines right there, they really don't need to be behind, the car but we felt it was the only way to indicate the vehicle was in motion . . . which you need to make the concept work, which it does, right?")*

If you ever feel the slightest urge to explain something in your book, cut the piece. That urge means the piece isn't working. As someone once said, "If your work speaks for itself, don't interrupt."

If you are asked about some work, be ready with an articulate explanation of how you came up with it.

"So, I like this campaign," says the creative director. "How'd you come up with it?"

"We just thought it up, man. Just sorta . . . poof! And I went like, whoa, dude, this rocks."

You are being considered for employment at a firm that sells the intangible. (Remember the "invisible poetry machines" we talked about?) Agencies sell ideas. So your ability to precisely articulate how you created an idea and to persuasively pitch it to a neutral (and sometimes hostile) audience is a very important skill.

Have your answers ready.

Trust your instincts.

Go to 10 different interviews and you're going to get 10 different opinions on your work. It will be confusing. *("The guy with the goatee liked this campaign, but the guy with the ponytail said it sucked.")*

If the majority say the same thing, take the hint. But you don't have to agree with everybody. If you do, you'll water down your book. Trust your instincts. Keep what you believe in. Change what you don't. Keep reworking your book until the weak parts are out and the good parts are great.

One way to get a good read on what needs improving is to ask each person you meet in an interview what he thinks is the weakest campaign in your book.

If more than a couple point to the same campaign, take it around the back of the barn. You know what to do.

Relax. Ask some questions.

Keep in mind as you interview that you can learn as much about the agency during this meeting as they can about you. Remember that even though you're young and on the street, you have options. You don't have to take this job, even if it's offered. You have choices.

With that in mind, relax a little bit. Your interviewer is not there to pin you to the felt like a butterfly. If you've been invited to come in, the agency already likes your book. The person is trying to see if he likes *you*. So be yourself. Have an opinion.

After the interview don't forget to follow up with a friendly "Thanks very much" e-mail and/or letter. And don't ask to friend them on Facebook; that borders on the creepy. But asking for a connection from your LinkedIn page, that's okay. Go for it.

Offer to do the grunt work.

My very first assignment in the business was to write some 50 "live" radio scripts for a hotel corporation. Live radio is simply a script read by the local DJ in between the farming updates and wrestling reports. I suspect if that awful live radio job hadn't come through the agency door, I might not have, either. But I was more than happy to do it.

I recommend you take the same attitude. Express your willingness to take on any assignment thrown at you. Many young people come in wanting to work on an agency's national TV accounts. My advice is, offer your shoulder to any wheel, your nose to any grindstone. I overheard a junior creative wisely coach a student by saying, "Trust me, you don't want to be on a TV shoot. You can't imagine how clueless you are right now."

Although it's possible you could land some TV relatively early on in your career, it's more likely you'll have to first pay your dues. Get ready to do some live radio, or what we cynics call "the brochures of the airwaves."

Sell your ability to think strategically.

Your work should speak for itself. You should speak for you.

Don't make the mistake of explaining everything in your book. If you must talk, discuss the strategic thinking behind the ads you're presenting. Creative directors don't hear much of this kind of talk during interviews, and your strategic abilities and overall business acumen are just as important in estimating your worth as your creative abilities.

Let them know if you are willing to freelance.

Agencies often have more work than their staffs can handle, and even if they don't need another full-timer, they may need temporary help. Ask if this is the case at your target agencies. Let them know you're willing to freelance. It gives the creative director a chance to work with you, to see if you should keep "dating" before you get married.

If you can't get into the creative department, get into the agency.

I can name quite a few good creative people who started their agency careers in the mail room, or as coordinators, assistants, even account executives. Ed McCabe, for example—mail room boy. Jamie Barrett—junior account guy.

The thing is, once you're in, you can learn more. You'll be able to watch it happen firsthand. You'll also start making friends with people who can hire you or help move you into the creative department. Unlike companies such as IBM, ad agencies are loosely structured places that often fill job openings with any knucklehead who proves he can do the work. They don't care what you majored in.

So get in there, do the job, keep your ears open and your book fresh, and when a creative position opens up, whom do you think they'll hire? A stranger off the street or the smart young kid in the mail room who has paid his dues and is still chomping at the bit?

How to talk about money.

I had a long discussion about money matters with Dany Lennon, one of the best creative recruiters in the ad business. (The ad that opens this chapter, for "The Creative Register," that's her.) She gave me this advice, and I pass it on to you.

"Do your homework," Dany told me. "Before you go into an interview you should know what the starting salary levels for that city, and that area, are. Talk to headhunters, talk to the agency recruiters, make phone calls, but find out. Then, when you and the creative director begin to talk about money, you won't be left in the position of saying, 'Okay, so what do you think I'm worth?' An agency might be tempted to low-ball you.*

"Instead you say, 'Well, this is what I understand to be the starting salary at comparable agencies in this area.' Drop the name of an agency if you like. But take the responsibility of knowing about money. Don't leave it up to the agency.

---

*The Internet may also be a good source for assessing average salaries. Currently the sites talentzoo.com and salary.com seem to be fairly accurate. Whether they're still operating by the time this book reaches your hands is another matter. Still, the best place to get salary information is from a recruiter.

If you do it forthrightly, your CD is going to see an intelligent person who's done their homework and money won't be a federal case. Just one of fairness. It's not so much the money you get that matters anyway, but the way in which you conduct yourself during the negotiation. A mature, intelligent, and fair negotiation says a lot about your character, also very important in an interview."

"Once you've negotiated your salary," Dany went on, "you may want to tell your CD you would appreciate a review in six months. Not a raise, but a review. This says to him, 'I'm going to work my tail off for this place and I'm confident in six months you'll see you've made a great hire.' And six months is all it usually takes for a CD to get a good read on you: on how hard you work, your attitude, your overall value to his company."

More than anything, Dany warned me, don't cop an attitude and start pitting one agency's offer against another. According to Ms. Lennon, there is, unfortunately, a burgeoning "brat pack" movement within the industry. Standard starting salaries, which were once etched in stone, are a thing of the past, and negotiations are more common. Not a bad thing in itself, but it has created a situation where talented newcomers are swaggering into agencies with good portfolios and bad attitudes.

I heard this story from the president of one of the country's top ad schools. He happens to be visiting a New York agency, chatting in the office of the creative director. Phone rings, and it's a young graduate of another ad school. (The agency had previously agreed to fly this kid up to New York for a better look at him and his book—translation: a real interview and a likely job offer.)

But on the phone, the kid cops a 'tude and tells the agency creative director he isn't coming unless he makes such-and-such kind of money (a salary way outside of what juniors usually make). Before slam-welding the phone receiver to its cradle, the creative director shrieked into it a string of invectives so toxic that common decency prevents their retelling here.

A man named Frederick Collins once said, "There are two types of people in the world. Those who come into a room and say, 'Well, here I am!' and those who come in and say, 'Ah, there you are.'"

Be that second type of person.

Don't choose an agency based on the salary offered.

If you're lucky enough to get a couple of offers, you may find that the better salary is offered by the worse agency. It has always been thus. And Lord knows, it will be tempting to take that extra 10 grand when it's held out to you. Don't.

One of Bill Bernbach's best lines was, "It isn't a principal until it costs you money." In this case, the principal in question is the value you place on doing great work. I urge you to go with the agency that's producing good advertising. You may work for less, but it's more likely you'll produce better ads. And in the long run, nothing is better for a great salary than a great book.

More than once I've seen a talented kid go for the bigger check at a bad agency and a year later take a cut in pay just to get the hell out of there. The bad part was that even after a year in the belly of the beast, he hadn't added so much as a bro-chure to his original student portfolio.

If you get a fair offer from a good agency, take it. Take in four roommates if you have to, live in your parents' basement, but get on board—that's the trick. I read somewhere not to set your sights on money anyway. Just do what you do well and the money will come. McElligott once told me, "You'll be underpaid the first half of your career and overpaid the second."

Take a job wherever you can and work hard.

All you need to do to get on a roll is produce a couple of great campaigns and have them run. And it's possible to do great work at almost any agency in America. (Note judicious use of the word *possible.*) Once you do a great cam-paign, creative directors will remember it. And you can make the next move up.

Don't be crestfallen if you can't get into one of the "hot" shops. The agency offering you your first job will be a launching pad, a stepping stone. (However, it's probably not a good idea to tell them this as you're shaking hands: *"Thank you, sir. I guess this job will just have to do until something opens up at Wieden + Kennedy. In fact, I think I'll just leave my coat on if you don't mind."*)

Here's the other thing: starting at an elite shop right out of school may be a little too intimidating for some. Also, if an A-agency is your first job in the industry, you won't be able to appreciate how good you have it. Mike Hughes of the Martin Agency notes: "People who start in [great places like] Goodby and leave are forever disappointed in their other agencies. And when they were at Goodby, they didn't think it was that good."

Remember, wherever you land a job, there'll be plenty to learn from the peo-ple you'll meet. Think of that first job as continuing your education. In *Breaking In,* BBH creative director Todd Riddle agrees, stating, "That first job is a criti-cal part of your career. Even more critical than the college or education you got. Because everyone will forget where you went to college after two or three years—whatever school you went to, nobody's going to care. All they'll want to know is what have you done in the past two or three years. And if you've been surrounded by really great, smart, bright creative people, and it's rubbed off on you, . . . that's all you'll have to have."[2]

Just get on board and work like hell. Early in your career's the time to do it, too, when you don't have children calling you from home asking how to get the top off the gasoline can in the garage.

It may seem that you can't outthink those senior creatives right now, but you can definitely outwork them. Make hard work your secret weapon.

"Interns? Cleanup in aisle three, please."

The answer on whether to intern or not depends on the agency. Look for a paid internship, and expect to work hard. It's not likely you'll be creating Super Bowl spots. Doing image searches for an art director or making copies for a pitch is more like it. But that's life in an agency, and an internship can be a great place to learn what it's really like. Offer to do anything for anyone. If you see a senior team working late, lean into their office and offer to help. They may take you up on it. That's the break you need.

A word of advice: Don't stay in an internship too long; a couple of months is enough. And whatever else happens, make sure you're not taken advantage of, either financially or personally. Sadly, it's been known to happen.

SOME FINAL THOUGHTS.

Once you land a job, stick with it awhile.

There are going to be rough spots no matter where you work. There are no perfect agencies. I like to think I have worked at a couple of the best, and there were plenty of times I thought just about everything that could be wrong was wrong.

Hang in there for a while. Things can change. An account that's miserable one year can suddenly become the one everybody wants to work on. There's also value in learning to stick with something long enough to see it through. Plus, it doesn't look good to bail on a place inside of a year. Show some patience.

If you've heard that the best way to increase your salary is to change jobs, it's true. But I advise against job-hopping solely for that reason. If you're at a good agency making a fair wage, stay there. Every six months or so, take a long, hard look at your portfolio. If it's getting better, stay. Move on only when you've learned as much as you possibly can. You don't want a resume that's a long list of brief stints at agency after agency.

Don't let advertising mess up your life.

On the same page that I say work hard, I also warn against working to the exclusion of all else. We all seem to take this silly advertising stuff so seriously. And at some shops, the work ethic isn't even ethical. People are implicitly expected to work till midnight pretty much full-time.

When this happens, we end up working way too hard and ignoring our spouses, our partners, our friends, and our lives. Remember, ultimately, it's just advertising. Compared with the important things in life, even a commercial that runs on the Super Bowl is still just an overblown coupon ad for Jell-O. Love, happiness, stability, sanity—those are the important things. Don't forget it.

Don't underestimate yourself.

Don't think, "I shouldn't bother sending my book to that agency. They're too good."

All people are subject to low self-esteem, and I think creative people are particularly prone to it. I can think of several people in our creative department who didn't think they were good enough but sent their book on a lark, and we took them up on it.

Don't overestimate yourself.

For some reason, a lot of people in this business develop huge egos. Yet none of us is saving lives. We are glorified sign painters and nothing more.

Stay humble.

Figure 14.1   *Although Joe Paprocki and I did this ad, we didn't think up the*
visual for it. We just borrowed it from some other ad. Then we went to lunch.
What a great business.

14

Making Shoes versus Making Shoe Commercials

Is this a great business, or what?

THIS IS A GREAT BUSINESS.

What makes it great are all the knuckleheads. All the people just slightly left of center. This business seems to attract them. People who don't find fulfillment anywhere else in the business world somehow end up on advertising's doorstep, their personal problems clanking behind them like cans in back of a just-married car. They come for very personal reasons, with their own agendas. They bring to the business creativity, energy, and chaos, and from the business they get discipline, perspective, and maturity.

All in all, they make for an interesting day at the office, these oddballs, artists, misfits, cartoonists, poets, beatniks, creepy quiet guys, and knuckleheads. And every one of them seems to have a great sense of humor.

David Ogilvy once wrote, "People do not buy from clowns." He was suggesting there is no place for humor in effective advertising. Forgetting for a moment whether Mr. Ogilvy was right, wrong, or extremely wrong, the thing is this: people do buy from clowns. Every day, millions of Americans use something sold by a clown, because the ad industry employs clowns by the tiny-circus-car-load.

Don't get me wrong; most of the people in the stories that follow are smart businesspeople. You'd want them on your team. But they're world-class knuckleheads as well. Agencies are full of 'em.

It's just one clown after another all the way down the hallway. Knuckleheads in the mail room, knuckleheads answering the phones, knuckleheads in the CEO's office . . . they're everywhere.

Why this should be so eludes me. I know only that most of every working day I spend laughing—at cynical hallway remarks, tasteless elevator bon mots, and bulletin board musings remarkable for their political incorrectness.

Submitted for your approval: this collage of images, incidents, and idiocy culled from agency hallways and stairwells around the nation. All true. And all stupid.

A finicky agency president has his own executive bathroom. No one else is allowed to use it, much less step in there. One day when the president is out to lunch, creatives are seen going into the bathroom carrying two muddy cowboy boots and a cigar.

Cut to boss coming back from lunch. He goes into his private restroom and immediately comes back out, really pissed off. "Who in God's name is the dumb cowboy sittin' in my stall smokin' a stogie?" His assistant has no clue.

The boss waits outside for the cowboy to emerge. Ten minutes pass, and the boss peeks back in only to see the same creepy tableau—muddy boots below the stall door, blue smoke curling above it.

Cigars can smolder for about half an hour. Bosses, even longer.

A creative director at a big agency decides to build a "communal area where creatives can relax." The problem is, he builds it right outside his office. Any creatives with enough time to hang out there are usually spotted by the creative director and handed one of those awful last-minute assignments nobody wants. ("Hey, can you write this live promotional tag?")

Creatives dub the area "The Meadow," inspired by the movie *Bambi*—a dangerous wide-open area where hunters can put you in the crosshairs. The name catches on. Everybody starts referring to the area as The Meadow. So does the creative director, although he never understands the reference and wonders why his happy new area is constantly deserted.

Left behind in an empty conference room, a piece of paper with this idea for Penn tennis balls, using a spokesman (well, a spokesperson): "I got rid of my old balls and now I use Penn."

                                                                —Renee Richards

---

A senior account guy decides to hose the "new meat." Sends an e-mail to all the junior account people in their modular offices, informing them that the building management has hired "burlap rakers" to come in and spruce up the walls of the cubicles. "Please remove all materials tacked, stapled, or taped to your walls until you receive further notice from the burlap rakers."

The young account executives obey but never receive further notice. A week later, the receptionist's left eyebrow goes way up when a young account guy asks him, "Hey, do the burlap rakers come in at night or on the weekends?"

━━━━━━

Retrieved from the wastebasket in a writer's office, this headline for a new dog shampoo: "Gee Your Ass Smells Terrific!"

━━━━━━

A big New York agency lands the Revlon account. The client says that only females understand the market and wants only women to work on the account. But a staffing crunch forces the traffic manager to assign a male writer—a guy named Mike. Mike is assigned a new name—Cindy. The client never meets Cindy, but receives e-mail from Cindy and reviews and approves great work from Cindy. "Cindy understands women."

━━━━━━

Two copywriters working on national accounts at a big agency play a word game under the noses of the account people and client. They agree on a random word or phrase and the first guy to use it in a produced ad, wins. Weeks later, no one in America notices the winning phrase in the copy of an ad for a giant tire manufacturer: "fancy pants."

━━━━━━

Quotes from actual creative work sessions:

"Which is funnier? ADHD or narcolepsy?"

"Obviously, it needs more vomiting references."

"I'm serious, man. I just don't think Julie Andrews would ever *do* that."

━━━━━━

A writer, notorious for rummaging through people's desks to steal food, purloins some specially made brownies containing four bars of Ex-Lax. Writer is seen half an hour later in the hallway, looking pale, and is not seen again till the following Monday.

━━━━━━

Another account guy and a creative are having a heated discussion about the creative person's vision for the agency.

"So," asks the account guy, finally getting testy. "What kind of work do you want to see the agency doing?"

Creative says: "I wanna do the kind of work that's in CA."
Account guy goes: "Then move back to California!"

━━━━━━━

Junior account person writes this note next to every single paragraph of a rough ad layout with greeked-in text: "Please translate."

━━━━━━━

Favorite brave comeback to a client who said to make the logo bigger: "Put your face closer to the ad."

━━━━━━━

Left over from the technical equipment purchased for a TV commercial is a curious piece of acoustic equipment, one that shoots a targeted laser-like beam of sound toward a single person with such precision that no one on either side of the target can hear a thing. The device has been hidden behind the ceiling tiles in an agency meeting room, and we cut now to the scene happening there: The creative director is sitting in the target chair and listening to some creatives present work. Suddenly his face turns pale. The creative director whips around, looks to his left, his right. "Who said that??" The creatives go, "Who said *what?*" The creative director says, "Nothing. Never mind." Everybody shrugs and the presentation continues . . . as do the evil words the creative director hears being whispered directly into his skull: "*Kill them. . . . Kill them all.*"

━━━━━━━

Okay, that last story, a prank, it happened to me. So did this next one.

I'm on a morning flight to a client meeting in St. Louis. It's just me and my old boss, the president of a large advertising agency.

It's not a full flight, so I stake a claim to an empty row, set up shop, and get a little work done. My boss settles down a row behind me. After a while, I doze off. When I wake up 20 minutes later, my tray table is down, and on it, wide open to the centerfold, is a *Penthouse* magazine.

Behind me I can hear my boss, snickering.

God only knows how many stewardesses have walked by, seen me slumped there, my mouth gaping open. Twitching, probably.

━━━━━━━

The "I quit" and the "You're fired" stories are usually pretty good in this business; more florid and dramatic than what you'll find in, say, the banking business. From my "Pathetic" file, here's my favorite "You're fired" story.

Okay, so they have to fire this art director—lay him off is more accurate, because the agency had lost some business. They need to lay him off that very week, but the problem is, the guy's suddenly in the hospital—some infection or something, but no big deal.

Still, the gears of capitalism must grind on, even if they're in reverse, and so the guy's boss shows up at the hospital asking to see him. The boss is told he's not allowed in the infectious wing of the ward, so the poor schmuck is summoned from his hospital bed out to the lounge area, where he is fired and handed his severance check.

The boss returns to the agency with a sad story that ends with the image of this poor guy limping back down the hospital hallway, one hand wheeling his IV apparatus, one hand holding his walking papers, and no hand left to hold his hospital gown shut. His freshly fired ass is last seen peeking out of his thin hospital gown as he walks back down the infectious hallway.

The "You're hired" stories aren't bad, either.

Realizing that hotshot creative directors have been known to Google their excellent selves from time to time, one smart kid *buys their names* as search terms. And when the creative directors logged on for some digital mirror-gazing, boom, up pops a little one-line ad with a link to this kid's site. No one was surprised when he was hired within the week. Cost to the kid: six bucks.

Another aspiring ad student cut a picture of an agency's creative director out of a trade magazine, mounted it on a fake driver's license and then laminated it. He tucked the fake ID into an old, tattered wallet along with small copies of his best student work in the photo holders.

Here's the cool part. He visits the agency, asks to use the bathroom, and then abandons the wallet on the sink counter. The wallet's "returned" to the desk of the creative director, and the kid's hired.*

C'mon, admit it, this is a great business. Can you imagine breaking into the *banking* business with stunts like these? *("Jenkins, people are still talkin' about how you scribbled your investment portfolio on the mirror in the executive washroom. Another round for my man Jenkins here!")*

"ADVERTISING: THE MOST FUN YOU CAN HAVE WITH YOUR CLOTHES ON."

—Jerry Della Femina

This is a great business.

Look at what you're doing. You're an image merchant. You're weaving words and pictures together and imbuing inanimate objects with meaning and value.

Mark Fenske said advertising is the world's most powerful art form. Is he right? Well, Picasso was great, but I've never looked at one of his paintings and then walked off and did something Pablo wanted me to do. I know that sounds

---

*Yes, in Chapter 13, I wrote "Don't do clever mailers." But in Chapter 1, Ed McCabe said, "I have no use for rules. They only rule out the brilliant exception."

silly, but advertising is like no other form of creative communication, because it has the power to affect what people do. It works.

In the 1920s, Claude Hopkins sat down in his office at Lord & Thomas and wrote, "Drink an orange." A nation began drinking fruit juice.

Steve Hayden sat down in his office at TBWA\Chiat\Day and wrote "Why 1984 won't be like 1984" for Apple computers. A nation began thinking maybe computers belong in living rooms, not just in corporations.

Dan Wieden sat down, wrote "Just Do It," and changed the world. In 1978, there weren't many joggers on the side of the road. (Even the word didn't exist — *jogging*. What the hell is *jogging?*) Now you can't throw a stick out the window without hitting five of 'em.

"Nike killed the three-martini lunch," says Fenske. Nike told us to get off our collective butt and just do it, and suddenly it wasn't okay anymore to lie around on the couch wallpapering our arteries with lard. We started taking the stairs. At the wheel of this national change of heart: an advertiser, a great agency, and the world's most powerful art form — advertising. Whether you agree with Fenske that "Nike and Coke brought down the Berlin Wall," the power of advertising to globalize icons and change the behavior of whole continents is undeniable.

We in the communications field — in radio, in television, in magazines, in newspapers, in posters — have developed unprecedented skills in mass persuasion. You and I can no longer isolate our lives. It just won't work. What happens to society is going to affect us with ever-increasing rapidity. The world has progressed to the point where its most powerful public force is public opinion. And I believe that in this new, complex, dynamic world it is not the great work or epic play, as once was the case, that will shape that opinion, but those who understand mass media and the tools of public persuasion. The metabolism of the world has changed. New vehicles must carry ideas to it. We must ally ourselves with great ideas and carry them to the public. We must practice our skills on behalf of society. We must not just believe in what we sell. We must sell what we believe in.[1]

This quotation comes from Bill Bernbach, prescient as usual with his prediction that "new vehicles must carry ideas to it." In 2008, a young state senator harnessed the power of social media to carry his message of change and solidly connected with his constituents. Barack Obama went on to win the presidency with one of the largest voter turnouts in election history.

In *Adcult USA,* James Twitchell wrote: "[Advertising] has collapsed . . . cultures into a monolithic, worldwide order immediately recognized by the House of Windsor and the tribe of Zulu. . . . If ever there is to be a global village, it will be because the town crier works in advertising."[2]

This is indeed a great business.

Look at what you're getting paid for: putting your feet up and thinking. This is what people with real jobs do when they get time off — put their feet up and daydream, drift, and think of goofy stuff. You, you're getting a paycheck for it.

I remember we had this new secretary in the creative department. He kept walking into the offices of art directors and writers, interrupting their work, just to chat. Somebody finally said to him, "Listen, we'd love to talk another time, but we have to get this done. So if you could . . ."

He backed out of the room, apologizing, "Geez, I'm sorry. You had your feet up. You were talking, laughing. It didn't look like you were working."

From *Breaking In,* I quote my old friend Mike Lear as he talked about his job: "I got paid today for looking at different takes of a guy on the toilet. That was my job today. 'Eh, I don't know, does it look like he's constipated or something? This needs to be funnier. Maybe this one where he's on the phone and being coy. . . that might be funnier.' And then? The check shows up in my bank account. That's just awesome."[3]

Yeah, this is a great business.

This fact was recently brought home to me during a train ride from downtown Chicago to O'Hare airport.

I'd just left a very bad meeting where a client had killed a whole bunch of my work. I fumed for the first couple of miles. (*"That was a really good campaign! They can't kill it!"*)

As I sat there feeling sorry for myself, the gray factories passed by the train windows. Miles of factories. On the loading docks, I could see hundreds of hardworking people. Laborers forklifting crates of Bic pens onto trucks, hauling boxes of canned peaches onto freight cars. They'd been there since six o'clock in the morning, maybe five o'clock. These were hardworking people. With real jobs.

And then there was me, feeling sorry for myself as I whipped by in an airconditioned train on the way to my happy little seat on the plane with its free peanuts. Peanuts roasted and packed by some worker in another gray factory as he looked up at the clock on the high brick wall, waiting for the minute hand to hit that magic 10:30 mark so he could get out of the noise for 15 minutes, drink a Coke, smoke a Winston, and then it's back to packing my stinkin' peanuts.

I must remember this.

There are research firms out there that will tell me the sky isn't blue. Clients who will kill an ad because it has a blue flyswatter in it. And agencies that will make bloody fortunes on ideas like Mr. Whipple. Yet tomorrow I'll be back in the hallways telling jokes with the funniest people in corporate America, putting my dirty sneakers on marble tabletops, and getting paid to think. Nothing more. Just to think. And to talk about movies.

You should remember this, too.

You'll be paid a lot of money in this business. You'll never have to do any heavy lifting. Never have dirt under your fingernails or an aching back when you come home from work. You're lucky to be talented. Lucky to get into the business.

Stay humble.

Feel free to give me your feedback on this text and how I might improve subsequent editions. Go to the *Hey, Whipple, Squeeze This* page on Amazon.com and leave a message in reader comments. Or visit HeyWhipple.com. Oh, and feel free to follow @heywhipple on Twitter. I try not to bore.

SUGGESTED READING

WHICH DOCTOR WOULD YOU WANT to have perform your next surgery? The doctor who has one introductory biology textbook from college collecting dust on the shelf behind his desk? Or the doctor whose office is a library of the latest medical texts and whose desk is buried under the past four years worth of the *New England Journal of Medicine?*

I'm serious. Which doctor do you want standing over you with a scalpel? Well, in terms of expertise, is what we do here in advertising any different? If we propose to sell ourselves as experts to our clients, we actually have to *be* experts.

I encourage you to read. And learn. And learn a lot. There is no shortcut to being the best. No easy way around it. You have to know your stuff and know it cold.

The short list of books and online resources I've included here is only the beginning. They happen to be my favorites in the creative area. But there are many other disciplines you should be studying—marketing, branding, interactive—all of which will be relevant to your craft.

There is no shortcut. This is how we learn it. Bit by bit.

Remember: "Chance favors the prepared mind."

Read every old *One Show* and *Communication Arts* you can get your hands on. Read every *British Design & Art Direction* annual you can find.

Become a student of advertising history. On the subject of history, I'll list these titles: *When Advertising Tried Harder,* by Larry Dubrow; *Remember Those Great Volkswagen Ads?* by David Abbott; *From Those Wonderful Folks Who Brought You Pearl Harbor,* by Jerry Della Femina; *Inside Collett Dickenson Pearce,* by Ritchie and Salmon; *A Book about the Classic Avis Advertising Campaign of the 60s,* by Ericksson and Holmgren; *Helmut Krone. The Book,* by Clive Challis; and also *Advertising Today,* by Warren Berger.

Then there's Warren Berger's other book, *Hoopla: A Book about Crispin Porter + Bogusky*. Expensive, but a good look inside that agency.

Advertising: Concept and Copy, by George Felton, is a wonderful textbook on the craft. Excellent, detailed advice on how to think, how to write. Good stuff.

The Advertising Concept Book, by Pete Barry. To hammer home the point that idea comes before execution, every piece of advertising in Barry's book is a pencil sketch.

The On-Demand Brand: 10 Rules for Digital Marketing Success in an Anytime, Everywhere World, by Rick Mathieson. This is probably the best book out there right now on understanding the new digital marketing space.

Engage! by Brian Solis. I met him at SXSW Interactive, where I discovered both author and book. Solis does a great job of explaining social media, with good examples and best practices.

Cutting Edge Advertising, by Jim Aitchison, is one of the better books out there on how to write a decent print ad.

Ernie Schenck is the author of *The Houdini Solution: Put Creativity and Innovation to Work by Thinking Inside the Box.* The smaller your budgets, the more you probably need this book.

Creative Advertising: Ideas and Techniques from the World's Best Campaigns, by Mario Pricken. This hard-to-find and kind of expensive book is very good. Great ideas on getting great ideas. Lots of cool ads in it, too.

Don't Make Me Think: *A Common Sense Approach to Web Usability,* 2nd edition. A great primer on user experience. Written in English, not geek, the wonderful book helps you understand the ideas behind information architecture and user experience design.

e, by Matt Beaumont, is a novel of life inside an agency told entirely in e-mails. It is hilarious.

Truth, Lies, and Advertising: The Art of Account Planning, by Jon Steel, is the single best book on how smart brand planning adds value to the whole creative process. Steel is also the author of *Perfect Pitch: The Art of Selling Ideas and Winning New Business.* He's a joy to read and so smart.

Eating the Big Fish: How Challenger Brands Can Compete against Brand Leaders, by Adam Morgan. Such a brilliant read. The title pretty much explains what this book is about: how to outsmart the competition when you can't outspend them.

The Cluetrain Manifesto: The End of Business as Usual, by Christopher Locke and company, who wrote the book on social media long before social media even existed.

Strunk & White's The Elements of Style is required reading for anyone who holds a pencil anywhere near paper.

For the sheer joy of writing, I recommend Natalie Goldberg's *Writing Down the Bones* and Anne Lamott's *Bird by Bird.*

If you're just trying to break into the business, I recommend Vonk and Kestin's *Pick Me: Breaking into Advertising and Staying There.* Then there's *Breaking In: Over 100 Advertising Insiders Reveal How to Build a Portfolio That Will Get You*

Noticed, by William Burks Spencer. It features interviews of creative directors and what they look for in a book. A little older, but still very helpful, is Maxine Paetro's *How to Put Your Book Together and Get a Job in Advertising.* (Yes, *that* Maxine Paetro, the mega-best-seller lady.)

And, if you can get them to, have your client read Dick Wasserman's wonderful *That's Our New Ad Campaign?* It's out of print, but if you find one, get it. It's great.

Also, next time you're in Czestochowa or Gdansk, pick up a copy of the excellent *Jak Robic Switene Reklamy.* And for you readers in Constantinople, I highly recommend the delightful *Satan Reklam Yaratmak.* (Okay, I'm kiddin'. They're just translations of this book.)

BIBLIOGRAPHY

Abraham, Leif, and Behrendt, Christian. *Oh My God, What Happened and What Should I Do?* New York: Books on Demand, 2010.

Adams, James, L. *Conceptual Blockbusting.* Reading, MA: Addison-Wesley, 1974.

Aitchison, Jim. *Cutting Edge Advertising: How to Create the World's Best Print for Brands in the 21st Century.* New York: Prentice-Hall, 1999.

Barry, Pete. *The Advertising Concept Book.* London: Thames & Hudson, 2008.

Berger, Warren. *Hoopla: A Book about Crispin Porter + Bogusky.* Brooklyn, NY: Powerhouse Books, 2006.

Bernbach, Bill. *Bill Bernbach said . . .* New York: DDB Needham, 1995.

Blewett, Bob. *Paste-Up: Or How to Get into Advertising in the Worst Way.* Minneapolis: self-published, 1994.

Bogusky, Alex, and Winsor, John. *Baked In: Creating Products and Businesses That Market Themselves.* Evanston, IL: Agate B2, 2009.

Burton, Phillip Ward, and Scott C. Purvis. *Which Ad Pulled Best: 50 Case Histories on How to Write and Design Ads That Work.* Lincolnwood, IL: NTC Business Books, 1996.

Clark, Eric. *The Want Makers.* New York: Viking, 1988.

Cook, Marshall. *Freeing Your Creativity: A Writer's Guide.* Cincinnati: Writer's Digest Books, 1992.

Corporate Report magazine, Minneapolis: 1982.

D&AD Mastercraft Series. *The Art Director Book.* Switzerland: Rotovision, 1997.

D&AD Mastercraft Series. *The Copy Book.* Switzerland: Rotovision, 1995.

Dru, Jean-Marie. *Disruption: Overturning Conventions and Shaking Up the Marketplace.* Hoboken, NJ: John Wiley & Sons, 1998.

Felton, George. *Advertising: Concept and Copy.* Englewood Cliffs, New Jersey: Prentice-Hall, 1994.

Foster, Jack. *How to Get Ideas.* San Francisco: Berret-Koehler Publishers, 1996.

Fowler, David. *The Creative Companion.* New York: Ogilvy, 2003.

Goodrum, Charles, and Helen Dalrymple. *Advertising in America: The First 200 Years.* New York: Harry N. Abrams, Inc., 1990.

Gossage, Howard Luck. *The Book of Gossage.* Chicago: The Copy Workshop, 1995.

Hegarty, John. *Hegarty on Advertising: Turning Intelligence into Magic.* New York: Thomas & Hudson, 2011.

Higgins, Denis. *The Art of Writing Advertising.* Lincolnwood, IL: NTC Business Books, 1965.

Hoff, Ron. *I Can See You Naked.* Kansas City, MO: Andrews & McMeel, 1992.

Iezzi, Teressa. *The Idea Writers: Copywriting in a New Media and Marketing Era.* New York: Palgrave Macmillan, 2010.

Ind, Nicholas. *Great Advertising Campaigns.* Lincolnwood, IL: NTC Business Books, 1993.

Jaffe, Joseph. *Life after the 30-Second Spot: Energize Your Brand with a Bold Mix of Alternatives to Traditional Advertising.* Hoboken, NJ: John Wiley & Sons, 2004.

Kawasaki, Guy. *Enchantment: The Art of Changing Hearts, Minds, and Actions.* New York: Portfolio Hardcover, 2011.

Lamott, Anne. *Bird by Bird.* New York: Doubleday, 1994.

Landa, Robin. *Advertising by Design.* Hoboken, NJ: John Wiley & Sons, 2004.

Lee, Bruce. *Acting on TV: Direct Response Television and How It Works.* From the Ogilvy website, www.ogilvy.com/viewpoint/index.php?vptype5TOC&iMaga Id54, retrieved June 28, 2007.

Levenson, Bob. *Bill Bernbach's Book.* New York: Villard, 1987.

Levine, Rick, et al. *The Cluetrain Manifesto.* New York: Perseus Books, 2000.

Li, Charlene, and Bernoff, Josh. *Groundswell: Winning in a World Transformed by Social Technologies.* New York: Harvard Business School Press, 2008.

Lyons, John. *Guts: Advertising from the Inside Out.* New York: Amacom, 1987.

Mathieson, Rick. *The On-Demand Brand: 10 Rules for Digital Marketing Success in an Anytime, Everywhere World.* New York: Amacom, 2010.

Matthews, John E. *The Copywriter.* Glen Ellyn, IL: self-published, 1964.

Mayer, Martin. *Whatever Happened to Madison Avenue?* Boston: Little, Brown & Company, 1991.

McAlhone, Beryl, and David Stuart. *A Smile in the Mind: Witty Thinking in Graphic Design.* London: Phaidon Press Ltd., 1996.

Minsky, Laurence. *How to Succeed in Advertising When All You Have Is Talent.* Chicago: The Copy Workshop, 2007.

Monahan, Tom. From *Communication Arts* magazine, Palo Alto, CA.

———. *The Do-It-Yourself Lobotomy.* Hoboken, NJ: John Wiley & Sons, 2002.

Mumaw, Stefan. *Chasing the Monster Idea: The Marketer's Almanac for Predicting Idea Epicness.* Hoboken, NJ: John Wiley & Sons, 2011.

Myerson, Mitch. *Success Secrets from Social Media Superstars.* Newburgh, NY: Entrepreneur Press, 2010.

Ogilvy, David. *Confessions of an Advertising Man.* New York: Atheneum, 1963.

One Club, The. *Pencil Pointers* newsletter. New York: 1995.

Othmer, James P. *Adland: Searching for the Meaning of Life on a Branded Planet.* New York: Anchor Books, 2010.

Paetro, Maxine. *How to Put Your Book Together and Get a Job in Advertising.* Chicago: The Copy Workshop, 1990.

Pricken, Mario. *Creative Advertising: Ideas and Techniques from the World's Best Campaigns.* London: Thames & Hudson, 2002.

Ries, Al, and Jack Trout. *Marketing Warfare.* New York: McGraw-Hill, 1986.

————. *Positioning: The Battle for Your Mind.* New York: McGraw-Hill, 1981.

Rock, Dr. David. "How to Have More Insights: Neuroscience shows us how to have more insights." *Psychology Today* magazine, September 5, 2010.

Roman, Kenneth, and Jane Maas. *The New How to Advertise.* New York: St. Martin's Press, 1992.

Rose, Frank. *The Art of Immersion, How the Digital Generation Is Remaking Hollywood, Madison Avenue, and the Way We Tell Stories.* New York: W.W. Norton & Company, 2011.

Schenck, Ernie. *The Houdini Solution: Put Creativity and Innovation to Work by Thinking Inside the Box.* New York: McGraw-Hill, 2006.

Schulberg, Bob. *Radio Advertising: The Authoritative Handbook.* Lincolnwood, IL: NTC Business Books, 1994.

Solis, Brian. *Engage! The Complete Guide for Brands and Businesses to Build, Cultivate, and Measure Success in the New Web.* Hoboken, NJ: John Wiley & Sons, 2011.

Spencer, William Burks. *Breaking In: Over 100 Advertising Insiders Reveal How to Build a Portfolio That Will Get You Hired.* London: Tuk Tuk Press, 2011.

Steel, Jon. *Truth, Lies, and Advertising: The Art of Account Planning.* Hoboken, NJ: John Wiley & Sons, 1998.

Twitchell, James. B. *Adcult USA: The Triumph of Advertising in American Culture.* New York: Columbia University, 1996.

————. *Twenty Ads That Shook the World.* New York: Crown Publishers, 2000.

Vonk, Nancy, and Janet Kestin. *Pick Me: Breaking into Advertising and Staying There.* Hoboken, NJ: John Wiley & Sons, 2005.

Wakeman, Frederick. *The Hucksters.* Scranton, PA: Rinehart & Company, 1946.

Wallace, Dave. *Break Out!* Grand Rapids, MI: Ainsco Incorporated, 1994.

Wall Street Journal, Creative Leaders Series. New York: Dow Jones & Company, 1993.

Warren, Jim, and Sheena Paul, *Smart Advertising.* Austin: unpublished paper, 2007.

Wasserman, Dick. *That's Our New Ad Campaign?* New York: The New Lexington Press, 1988.

Weiner, Ellis. *Decade of the Year.* New York: Dutton, 1982.

Williams, Eliza. *This Is Advertising.* London: Laurence King Publishing, 2010.

Wypijewski, JoAnn, ed. *Paint by Numbers: Komar and Melamid's Scientific Guide to Art.* New York: Farrar, Straus & Giroux, 1997.

Young, James Webb. *Technique for Producing Ideas.* Chicago: Advertising Publications, Inc., 1944.

ONLINE RESOURCES

ONE OF THE BEST WAYS TO LEARN about the world of advertising is to bookmark the good websites that are out there. Some are blogs, some are rants, and some are just cool places to look at new work.

I surveyed my ad friends, asking them what their favorite online resources are. They were all nice enough to return e-mails positively glowing with underlined links in blue type ready to whisk me into the ether. I went down the rabbit hole and must have studied 200 or 300 of them by the time I realized that trying to publish a list of the best sites (on paper, in a book, at least) would suck. The online world *constantly* changes, and any working Web address I list here today may return a "Can't find server" message tomorrow. You'll also find that a single address is enough to get you started, because most of the sites (the blogs, anyway) include a list of favorite links; one attaches to another like coat hangers at the bottom of your closet. Grab one and you get the rest.

I have my favorites posted on my blog roll at heywhipple.com. They're as good a place to start as any.

NOTES

CHAPTER I

1. Martin Mayer, *Whatever Happened to Madison Avenue?* (Boston: Little, Brown & Company, 1991), 46.
2. Kenneth Roman and Jane Maas, *The New How to Advertise* (New York: St. Martin's Press, 1992), 38.
3. John Lyons, *Guts: Advertising from the Inside Out* (New York: Amacom, 1987), 115.
4. Frederick Wakeman, *The Hucksters* (Scranton, PA: Rinehart & Company, 1946), 22.
5. Ibid., 45.
6. *Wall Street Journal, Creative Leaders Series* (New York: Dow Jones & Company), 12.
7. Phillip Ward Burton and Scott C. Purvis, *Which Ad Pulled Best: 50 Case Histories on How to Write and Design Ads That Work* (Lincolnwood, IL: NTC Business Books, 1996), 24.
8. Bill Bernbach, *Bill Bernbach Said . . .* (New York: DDB Needham, 1995).
9. William Souder, "Hot Shop," *Corporate Report* (September 1982).
10. Al Ries and Jack Trout, *Positioning: The Battle for Your Mind* (New York: McGraw-Hill, 1981), 24.
11. Ted Morgan, *A Close-Up Look at a Successful Agency,* p. 300.
12. Bill Bernbach, *Bill Bernbach Said . . .* (New York: DDB Needham, 1995).
13. John Ward, "Four Facets of Advertising Performance Measurement," in *The Longer and Broader Effects of Advertising,* ed. Chris Baker (London: Institute of Practitioners in Advertising, 1990), 44.

14. Sandra Karl, "Creative Man Helmut Krone Talks about the Making of an Ad," *Advertising Age* (October 14, 1968).
15. Bill Bernbach, *Bill Bernbach Said . . .* (New York: DDB Needham, 1995).

CHAPTER 2

1. James Charlton, ed., *The Writer's Quotation Book: A Literary Companion* (New York: Viking-Penguin, 1980), 55.
2. *Wall Street Journal, Creative Leaders Series* (New York: Dow Jones & Company), 5.
3. Eric Clark, *The Want Makers* (New York: Viking, 1988), 24.
4. Pete Barry, *The Advertising Concept Book* (London: Thames & Hudson, 2008), 225.
5. James Webb Young, *Technique for Producing Ideas* (Chicago: Advertising Publications, Inc., 1944).
6. John Hegarty, *Hegarty on Advertising* (New York: Thomas & Hudson 2011), 28.
7. D&AD Mastercraft Series, *The Copy Book* (Switzerland: Rotovision, 1995), 68.
8. *Wall Street Journal, Creative Leaders Series*, 41.
9. Rick Mathieson, *The On-Demand Brand: 10 Rules for Digital Marketing Success in an Anytime, Everywhere World* (New York: AMACOM, 2010), 159.
10. Rick Levine, *The Cluetrain Manifesto* (New York: Perseus, 2000); online at www.cluetrain.com/book/95-theses.html.
11. John Hegarty, *Hegarty on Advertising,* 39.
12. Bernbach, *Bill Bernbach Said . . .* (New York: DDB Needham, 1995).
13. *Wall Street Journal, Creative Leaders Series*, 12.
14. Jean-Marie Dru, *Disruption: Overturning Conventions and Shaking Up the Marketplace* (New York: John Wiley & Sons, 1998), 151.
15. John Hegarty, *Hegarty on Advertising,* 81.

CHAPTER 3

1. Pete Barry, *The Advertising Concept Book* (London: Thames & Hudson, 2008), 56.
2. George Felton, *Advertising: Concept and Copy* (New Jersey: Prentice Hall, 1994), 85.
3. Warren Berger, *Hoopla: A Book about Crispin Porter + Bogusky* (Brooklyn, NY: Powerhouse Books, 2006), 160.
4. Rick Mathieson, *The On-Demand Brand: 10 Rules for Digital Marketing Success in an Anytime, Everywhere World* (New York: Amacom, 2010), 54.

5. Frank Rose, *The Art of Immersion: How the Digital Generation Is Remaking Hollywood, Madison Avenue, and the Way We Tell Stories* (New York: W.W. Norton & Company, 2011), 315.
6. Ibid., 240.
7. Warren Berger, *Hoopla,* 160.
8. Al Ries and Jack Trout, *Marketing Warfare* (New York: McGraw-Hill, 1986), 70.
9. Tom Monahan, *The Do-It-Yourself Lobotomy* (New York: John Wiley & Sons, 2002), 84.
10. Eric Clark, *The Want Makers* (New York: Viking, 1988), 54.
11. Pete Barry, *The Advertising Concept Book,* 153.
12. Jean-Marie Dru, *Disruption: Overturning Conventions and Shaking Up the Marketplace* (New York: John Wiley & Sons, 1998), 157.
13. Matthew Weiner and Robin Veith, "The Wheel," *Mad Men,* season 1, episode 13.
14. Marshall Cook, *Freeing Your Creativity: A Writer's Guide* (Cincinnati: Writer's Digest Books, 1992), 7.
15. David Fowler, *The Creative Companion* (New York: Ogilvy, 2003), 7.
16. Anne Lamott, *Bird by Bird* (New York: Doubleday, 1994), 23.
17. Mario Pricken, *Creative Advertising: Ideas and Techniques from the World's Best Campaigns* (London: Thames & Hudson, 2002), 22.
18. Dr. David Rocks, "How to Have More Insights," *Psychology Today,* http://www.psychologytoday.com/blog/your-brain-work/201009/how-have-more-insights, retrieved August 12, 2011.
19. Warren Berger, *Hoopla*, 406.
20. Jim Aitchison, *Cutting Edge Advertising.* (Singapore: Pearson Prentice Hall, 2004), 186.
21. D&AD Mastercraft Series, *The Art Director Book* (Switzerland: Rotovision, 1997), 44.
22. Alex Bogusky and John Winsor, *Baked In: Creating Products and Businesses That Market Themselves* (Boulder: Agate B2, 2009), 122.
23. Bill Bernbach, *Bill Bernbach Said . . .* (New York: DDB Needham, 1995).
24. Teressa Iezzi, *The Idea Writers: Copywriting in a New Media and Marketing Era* Palgrave (Macmillan, New York, 2010), 268 in iBook version.
25. James L. Adams, *Conceptual Blockbusting* (Reading, MA: Addison-Wesley, 1974), 66.
26. Beryl McAlhone and David Stuart, *A Smile in the Mind: Witty Thinking in Graphic Design* (London: Phaedon Press, 1996), 19.
27. John Hegarty, *Hegarty on Advertising* (New York: Thomas & Hudson 2011), 174.
28. Howard Luck Gossage, *The Book of Gossage* (Chicago: The Copy Workshop, 1995), 114, 115.

29. Mitch Meyerson, *Success Secrets from Social Media Superstars* (Newburgh, NY: Entrepreneur Press, 2010), 161.

CHAPTER 4

1. Bob Blewett, *Paste-Up* (Minneapolis: self-published), 34.

2. Dave Wallace, *Break Out* (Grand Rapids, MI: Ainsco, 1994).

3. William Burks Spencer, *Breaking In: Over 100 Advertising Insiders Reveal How to Build a Portfolio That Will Get You Hired* (London, Tuk Tuk Press, 2011), 164.

4. Ibid., 193.

5. Tom Monahan, *The Do-It-Yourself Lobotomy* (New York: John Wiley & Sons, 2002), 90.

6. Rick Levine, Christopher Locke, Doc Searles, and David Weinberger, *The Cluetrain Manifesto* (New York: Perseus Books, 2000); www.cluetrain.com/book/95-theses.html

7. Phillip Ward Burton and Scott C. Purvis, *Which Ad Pulled Best: 50 Case Histories on How to Write and Design Ads That Work* (Lincolnwood, IL: NTC Business Books, 1996), 26.

8. Sandra Karl, "Creative Man Helmut Krone Talks about the Making of an Ad," *Advertising Age* (October 14, 1968).

9. John Hegarty, *Hegarty on Advertising* (New York: Thomas & Hudson 2011), 26.

10. David Fowler, *The Creative Companion* (New York: Ogilvy, 2003), 19.

11. Nancy Vonk and Janet Kestin, *Pick Me: Breaking into Advertising and Staying There* (New York: John Wiley & Sons, 2005), 83.

12. Stefan Mumaw, *Chasing the Monster Idea, The Marketer's Almanac for Predicting Idea Epicness* (Hoboken, NJ: John Wiley & Sons, 2011), 208.

13. George Kneller, *The Art and Science of Creativity* (New York: Holt, Rinehart & Winston, 1965), 55.

14. *Wall Street Journal, Creative Leaders Series* (New York: Dow Jones & Company), 20.

CHAPTER 5

1. Frank Rose, *The Art of Immersion: How the Digital Generation Is Remaking Hollywood, Madison Avenue, and the Way We Tell Stories* (New York: W.W. Norton & Company, 2011), 191.

2. Rick Mathieson, *The On-Demand Brand: 10 Rules for Digital Marketing Success in an Anytime, Everywhere World* (New York: Amacom, 2010), xv.

3. Brian Solis, *Engage! The Complete Guide for Brands and Businesses to Build, Cultivate, and Measure Success in the New Web* (Hoboken, NJ: John Wiley & Sons, 2011), 112.

4. Number of hours of video uploaded, source: www.hypebot.com/hypebot/ 2010/11/guess-how-many-hours-of-video-are-uploaded-to-youtube-every-minute.html.

5. David Gillespie speech on SlideShare: "Digital Strangelove (or How I Learned to Stop Worrying and Love the Internet)," http://www.slideshare .net/DavidGillespie/digital-strangelove-or-how-i-learned-to-stop-worrying-and-love-the-internet, retrieved August 15, 2011.

6. Leif Abraham and Christian Behrendt, *Oh My God, What Happened and What Should I Do?* (New York: Books on Demand, 2010), 66.

7. The original phrase is from author Dan Gillmor in his book *We, The Media;* http://archive.pressthink.org/2006/06/27/ppl_frmr.html, retrieved August 15, 2011.

8. John Hegarty, *Hegarty on Advertising* (New York: Thomas & Hudson 2011), 109.

9. William Burks Spencer, *Breaking In: Over 100 Advertising Insiders Reveal How to Build a Portfolio That Will Get You Hired* (London, Tuk Tuk Press, 2011), 51.

10. Eliza Williams, *This Is Advertising* (London: Laurence King Publishing, 2010), 30–31.

11. William Burks Spencer, *Breaking In*, 246.

12. Rick Mathieson, *The On-Demand Brand,* 46.

13. Ibid., 153

14. Rick Levine, Christopher Locke, Doc Searles, and David Weinberger, *The Cluetrain Manifesto* (New York, Perseus Books, 2000), 151.

15. Frank Rose, *The Art of Immersion,* 253, iBook version.

16. Edward Boches, "Creativity Unbound," http://edwardboches.com/a-brand-isn't-what-a-brand-says-a-brand-is-what-a-brand-does-2, retrieved July 20, 2011.

17. Edward Boches, Creativity Unbound http://edwardboches.com/10-predictions-advertising-in-2010, retrieved August 15, 2011.

18. Alex Bogusky and John Winsor, *Baked In: Creating Products and Businesses That Market Themselves* (Boulder, CO: Agate B2, 2009), 112–113.

19. Frank Rose, *The Art of Immersion,* prologue 24.

20. Teressa Iezzi, *The Idea Writers: Copywriting in a New Media and Marketing Era* Palgrave (Macmillan, New York, 2010), 146.

21. Stefan Mumaw, *Chasing the Monster Idea, The Marketer's Almanac for Predicting Idea Epicness* (Hoboken, NJ: John Wiley & Sons, 2011), 161.

22. Edward Boches, "Creativity Unbound," http://edwardboches.com/five-social-media-recommendations-for-startups, retrieved August 15, 2011.

23. Rick Mathieson, *The On-Demand Brand*, 66.

24. Edward Boches, "Creativity Unbound," http://edwardboches.com/its-time-for-advertising-and-social-media-to-work-together, retrieved August 15, 2011.

25. Edward Boches, "Creativity Unbound," http://edwardboches.com/five-things-that-work-in-social-media#ixzz1SOom5J5a%20, retrieved August 15, 2011.

26. Eric Harr, "Social Media Today," http://socialmediatoday.com/eric-harr-resonate-social-media/317029/bringing-old-school-new-media, retrieved July 20, 2011.

27. Edward Boches, "Creativity Unbound," http://edwardboches.com/we-need-a-facebook-page-and-we-need-it-right-away, retrieved August 15, 2011.

28. Rick Mathieson, *The On-Demand Brand*, 124.

29. http://mashable.com/2011/07/01/zynga-stats-infographic.

30. Rick Levine, *The Cluetrain Manifesto* (New York: Perseus, 2000); online at www.cluetrain.com/book/95-theses.html.

31. http://sellorelse.ogilvy.com/tag/twelpforce, retrieved August 15, 2011.

32. OgilvyOne website, Sell or Else, http://socialmediatoday.com/eric-harr-resonate-social-media/313754/realistic-risks-rewards-social-media-15-things-you-stand-gain, retrieved August 15, 2011.

33. Brian Solis, *Engage!*, 225.

34. *Fast Company*, July/August 2011, 12.

35. Rick Mathieson, *The On-Demand Brand*, 184.

36. Eliza Williams, *This Is Advertising*, 94.

CHAPTER 6

1. "New media," Wikipedia, http://en.wikipedia.org/wiki/Newmedia, retrieved July 7, 2007.

2. John King, *Building a Generous Brand*, http://adage.com/article/goodworks/building-a-generous-brand/136446/, retrieved August 15, 2011.

3. Warren Berger, *Hoopla: A Book about Crispin Porter + Bogusky* (Brooklyn, NY: Powerhouse Books, 2006), 406.

4. Laurence Minsky, *How to Succeed in Advertising When All You Have Is Talent* (Chicago: The Copy Workshop, 2007), 313.

5. Quotation from Tony Granger, *Creativity* (June 2007), 10.

6. Robin Landa, *Advertising by Design* (Hoboken, NJ: John Wiley & Sons, 2004), 236.

7. Leif Abraham and Christian Behrendt, *Oh My God, What Happened and What Should I Do?* (New York: Books on Demand, 2010), 106.

8. Joseph Jaffee, *Life after the 30-Second Spot: Energize Your Brand with a Bold Mix of Alternatives to Traditional Advertising* (Hoboken, NJ: John Wiley & Sons, 2004), 219.
9. Rob Schwartz, *Shoot* (June 7, 2002), 24.

CHAPTER 7

1. Rick Mathieson, *The On-Demand Brand: 10 Rules for Digital Marketing Success in an Anytime, Everywhere World* (New York: Amacom, 2010), 15.
2. Daniel Cox, http://theinspirationroom.com/daily/2010/embrace-life/, retrieved August 12, 2011.
3. David Fowler, *The Creative Companion* (New York: Ogilvy, 2003), 31.
4. Pascal-Emmanuel Gobry, *Business Insider*, http://www.businessinsider.com/facebook-tv-2011–1#ixzz1Uis7rzWP, retrieved August 11, 2011.

CHAPTER 8

1. Jim Warren and Sheena Paul, *Smart Advertising* (unpublished paper).
2. Bruce Lee, *Acting on TV: Direct Response Television and How It Works,* from the Ogilvy website, www.ogilvy.com/viewpoint/index.php?vptype5TOC&iMagaId54, retricved June 28, 2007.
3. Ibid.
4. Nancy Vonk and Janet Kestin, *Pick Me: Breaking into Advertising and Staying There* (New York: John Wiley & Sons, 2005), 112.

CHAPTER 9

1. William Burks Spencer, *Breaking In: Over 100 Advertising Insiders Reveal How to Build a Portfolio That Will Get You Hired* (London, Tuk Tuk Press, 2011), 213.
2. Tom Monahan, *Communication Arts* (July 1994), 198.

CHAPTER 10

1. Sandra Karl, "Creative Man Helmut Krone Talks about the Making of an Ad," *Advertising Age* (October 14, 1968).
2. Daniel Pope, *The Making of Modern Advertising* (New York: Basic Books, 1983), 4.

CHAPTER 11

1. *Wall Street Journal, Creative Leaders Series* (New York: Dow Jones & Company), 44.
2. "The average length of a CMO's tenure across corporate America has been dropping in recent years—down from 23.6 months in 2003 to 23.2 months in 2006, according to a Spencer Stuart study," *Adweek* (June 4, 2007).
3. Ellis Weiner, *Decade of the Year* (New York: Dutton, 1982).
4. "Felix," The Denver Egoist, "The Rant: What Makes a Good Creative Director? Part 1 of 2," www.thedenveregotist.com/editorial/2009/march/5/rant-what-makes-good-creative-director-part-1–2.

CHAPTER 12

1. Ron Hoff, *I Can See You Naked* (Kansas City, MO: Andrews & McMeel, 1992), 30.
2. Dick Wasserman, *That's Our New Ad Campaign?* (New York: New Lexington Press, 1988), 3.
3. Alastair Crompton, *The Craft of Copywriting: How to Write Great Copy That Sells* (Englewood Cliffs, NJ: Prentice-Hall, 1979), 166.
4. David Fowler, *The Creative Companion* (New York: Ogilvy, 2003), 3.
5. Tom Monahan, *Communication Arts* (May/June 1994), 29.
6. Bob Schulberg, *Radio Advertising: The Authoritative Handbook* (Lincolnwood, IL: NTC Business Books, 1994), 234.
7. Tim Delaney, "Basic Instincts," *One to One: Newsletter of One Club for Art & Copy* (November/December 1994), 1.
8. Alexander Melamid and Vitaly Komar, *Paint by Numbers: Komar and Melamid's Scientific Guide to Art,* ed. JoAnn Wypijewski (New York: Farrar, Straus & Giroux, 1997).
9. Tom Monahan, *Communication Arts* (September/October 1994), 67.
10. Dick Wasserman, *That's Our New Ad Campaign?* 37–38.
11. Bill Bernbach, *Bill Bernbach Said . . .* (New York: DDB Needham, 1995).

CHAPTER 13

1. William Burks Spencer, *Breaking In: Over 100 Advertising Insiders Reveal How to Build a Portfolio That Will Get You Hired* (London: Tuk Tuk Press, 2011), 193.
2. Ibid., 120.

CHAPTER 14

1. Bill Bernbach, *Bill Bernbach's Book* (New York: Villard Books, 1987), dedication, x.
2. James B. Twitchell, *Adcult USA: The Triumph of Advertising in American Culture* (New York: Columbia University, 1996), 43.
3. William Burks Spencer, *Breaking In: Over 100 Advertising Insiders Reveal How to Build a Portfolio That Will Get You Hired* (London, Tuk Tuk Press, 2011), 140.

ACKNOWLEDGMENTS

Cover design by Keli Linehan.

I would like to thank the following people for help in writing this book: My wife, Curlin Reed Sullivan; Dan Ahearn; Richard Apel; Mark Avnet; Kim Baffi; Betsy Barnum; Jamie Barrett; Bob Barrie; David Bell; Sam Bennett; Andre Bergeron; Kevin Berigan; Andy Berlin; Bob Blewett; Alex Bogusky; Laurie Brown; Rob Buchner; Pat Burnham; Cathy Carlisi; Tim Cole; Scott Cooley; Coz Cotzias; Peter Coughter; David Crawford; Markham Cronin; Russell Curtis; Gina Dante; Clay Davies; Craig Denham; Arlene Distel; Denese Duncan; James Embry; Mark Fenske; Kevin Flatt; Ashley Fortune; Anne Fredrickson; Betty Gamadge; Yosune George; Tom Gibson; Wayne Gibson; Glenn Gill; Kevin Griffith; Tiffany Groglio at Wiley; Stephen Hall; Al Hampel; Phil Hanft; Cabell Harris; Sam Harrison; David Jelly Helm; Carol Henderson; Joel Hermann; Bill Hillsman; Adrian Hilton; Sally Hogshead; Blue Hopkins; Clay Hudson; Paul Huggett; Mike Hughes; Gary Johns; Pruie Jingle James Jones Johnson; KatMo; Kathy Jydstrup; Claire Kerby; Lori Kraft; Jim Lacey; Greg Lane; Mike, Kelley, Henry, and Owen Lear; Dany Lennon; Andy Lerner; Mike Lescarbeau; Tom Lichtenheld; Jennifer Macha; John Mahoney; Tom McElligott; Tom McEnery; Doug Melroe; Karen Melvin; Lucy Meredith; Ruth Mills; Larry Minsky; Andrea and Natalie Minze; Mister Mister; Tom Monahan; Marina Monsante; Ty Montague; Ken Musto; Richard Narramore (my kind editor at Wiley); Ted Nelson; Tom Nelson; Diane O'Hara; Cathy Orman; Johnathan Ozer; Hal Pickle; Judy Popky; Lance Porter; Gene Powers; Scott Prindle; Kevin Proudfoot; Margot Reed; Col. William Preston Reed; Joey Reiman; Mike Renfro; Hank Richardson; Tania Rochelle; Isvel Rodriguez; Tom Rosen; Nancy Rubenstein; Daniel Russ; Cecily Sapp; Sentient Bean Coffee Shop; Elizabeth Stickley Scott; Ron Seichrist; Fred, Marty, and Jennifer Senn; Mal Sharpe; Joan Shealy; Montrew Smith; Pete Smith; Roy Spence; Thad Spencer; Myra Longstreet Sullivan; Kevin Swanepoel; good ol' Joe Sweet; Kirsten Taklo; Mark Taylor; Diane Cook Tench; Mary Tetlow; Tom Thomas; Rob Thompson; Jerry Torchia; Judy Trabulsi; Eric Valentine; Rob Vann; Carol Vick; Christa von Staaveren; Tiffany Warin; Mary Warlick; Jim Warren; Mike Weed; Craig Weise; Jean Weisman; Howard Willenzik; Judy Wittenburg; Steve and Charlie Wolff; and Bill Wright.

ALSO BY LUKE SULLIVAN

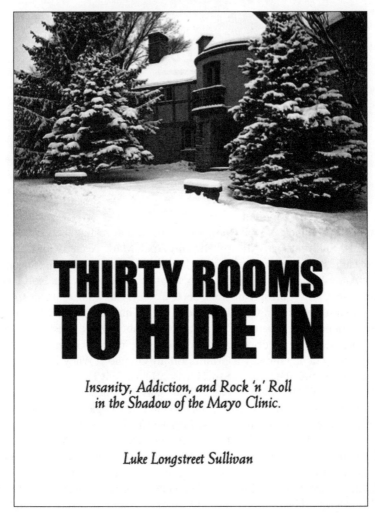

THIRTY ROOMS
TO HIDE IN

*Insanity, Addiction, and Rock 'n' Roll
in the Shadow of the Mayo Clinic.*

Luke Longstreet Sullivan

"*The Shining* . . . but funnier."

That's about the best way I can describe *Thirty Rooms to Hide In*. It's the story of growing up with my five brothers in a big dark house in Minnesota back in the 1950s and 1960s. With winters raging outside and our father raging within, it was our mother's protection that allowed us to have a wildly fun, thoroughly dysfunctional time growing up. With dark humor as the coin of our realm, and the Beatles as true north on our compass of Cool, we made movies, started a rock 'n' roll band, and wise-cracked our way though a grim landscape of Eisenhower's Cold War, fallout shelters, JFK's assassination, and our father's insanity. It's available at Amazon.com. Check out the website at ThirtyRoomsToHideIn.com.

INDEX